Globalization Theory

Globalization Theory

Approaches and Controversies

Edited by

David Held and Anthony McGrew

polity

First published in 2007 by Polity Press

Polity Press
65 Bridge Street
Cambridge CB2 1UR, UK

Polity Press
350 Main Street
Malden, MA 02148, USA

ISBN-10: 0-7456-3210-6
ISBN-13: 978-07456-3210-0
ISBN-10: 0-7456-3211-4 (pb)
ISBN-13: 978-07456-3211-7 (pb)

A catalogue record for this book is available from the British Library.

Typeset in 10 on 12.5 pt Times
by Servis Filmsetting Ltd, Manchester
Printed and bound in Great Britain by MPG Books Ltd, Bodmin, Cornwall.

The publisher has used its best endeavours to ensure that the URLs for external websites referred to in this book are correct and active at the time of going to press. However, the publisher has no responsibility for the websites and can make no guarantee that a site will remain live or that the content is or will remain appropriate.

For further information on Polity, visit our website: www.polity.co.uk

Contents

Notes on the Contributors

Chris Brown is a Professor in the International Relations Department at the London School of Economics and Political Science. He has written widely on International Political Theory/International Ethics; ethics and warfare; justice and international relations; ethics, morality and foreign policy; and human rights. His recent publications include *Understanding International Relations* (2005), co-authored with Kirsten Ainley, *The House that Chuck Built: Twenty-five Years of Reading Charles Beitz* (2005), *Reflections on the 'War on Terror' Two Years On* (2004), and *The 'English School' and World Society* (2004).

Alex Callinicos is Professor of European Studies at King's College, London, and sits on the editorial board of *International Socialism*. His research focuses on social and political theory (especially Marxism); philosophy; and political economy (especially of the advanced industrial countries and southern Africa). He is the author of *The Resources of Critique* (2005), *An Anti-Capitalist Manifesto* (2003), and *Against the Third Way* (2001).

Michael Doyle is Harold Brown Professor of US Foreign and Security Policy and Professor of Law and Political Science in the School of International & Public Affairs at Columbia University. He has served as Assistant Secretary-General and Special Adviser to United Nations Secretary-General Kofi Annan from 2001 to 2003, and is currently the chair of the Academic Council of the United Nations Community. His principal areas of publishing and teaching are international relations theory, international security, and international organizations. His recent publications include *The Globalization of Human Rights*, which he edited with Jean-Marc Coicaud and Anne-Marie Gardner (2003) and *International Law and Organization: Closing the Compliance Gap*, which he edited with Edward Luck (2004).

David Held is Graham Wallas Professor of Political Science at the London School of Economics and Political Science (LSE). Among his books are: *Democracy and the Global Order* (1995), *Global Covenant* (2004) and *Models of Democracy* (3rd edition 2006). He is the co-author of *Global Transformations* (1999) and *Globalization/Anti-globalization* (2002); and editor or co-editor of *Prospects for Democracy* (1993), *Cosmopolitan Democracy* (1995) and *Re-Imagining Political Community* (1998).

G. John Ikenberry is the Albert G. Milbank Professor of Politics and International Affairs at Princeton University in the Department of Politics and the Woodrow Wilson School of Public and International Affairs. Among his numerous books, Ikenberry is the author of *After Victory: Institutions, Strategic Restraint, and the Rebuilding of Order after Major Wars* (2001), which won the 2002 Schroeder-Jervis Award for the best book in international history and politics. He serves on the editorial committee of *World Politics* and he is co-editor of *International Relations of the Asia Pacific*.

Andrew Kuper is a managing director at Ashoka, which supports social entrepreneurs in over 60 countries. His most recent books are *Democracy Beyond Borders* (2004) and *Global Responsibilities: Who Must Deliver on Human Rights?* (2005). He has also been associate producer of 16 movies in the Social Entrepreneurship series, capturing the stories and strategies of the best global innovators. He serves as an independent adviser and lecturer to corporations, government institutions, media and citizen organizations. Prior to joining Ashoka he directed democracy promotion efforts for the Carnegie Council in New York, and was a Fellow or Visiting Scholar at Cambridge, Columbia and Harvard universities. Born and raised in South Africa, he now lives in Washington, DC.

Anthony McGrew is Professor of International Relations and Head of the School of Social Sciences at the University of Southampton. He has published widely on globalization, global governance and global political economy including: *Global Transformations: Politics, Economics and Culture* (1999), *Globalization/AntiGlobalization* (2002), *The Global Transformations Reader* (2003) and *Governing Globalization* (2002), all with David Held. His latest publication is an edited volume, *Globalization, Development and Human Security* (2006).

Layna Mosley is Assistant Professor in the Department of Political Science at the University of North Carolina. Her current research projects include the effects of international capital mobility on government policy choices, the role of private sector actors in global financial regulation, and the relationship between labor rights and foreign direct investment. She is the author of *Global Capital and National Governments* (2003), which was short-listed for the European Consortium for Political Research's XII Stein Rokkan Prize in Comparative Social Science Research, October 2004.

Thomas W. Pogge is Professor in the Political Science Department at Columbia University. He has written extensively on political philosophy and issues of global justice, including his forthcoming edited volume of essays *Freedom from Poverty as a Human Right: Who Owes What to the Very Poor?* and *World Poverty and Human Rights: Cosmopolitan Responsibilities and Reforms* (2002).

Thomas Risse is Director of the Center for Transatlantic Foreign and Security Policy at the Department of Political and Social Sciences of the Freie Universität Berlin. He is the author of *Cooperation among Democracies: The European Influence on U.S. Foreign Policy* (1995) and has co-edited a number of books: with Stephen C. Ropp and Kathryn Sikkink, *The Power of Human Rights: International Norms and Domestic Change* (1999); with Maria Green Cowles and James Caporaso, *Transforming Europe: Europeanization and Domestic Change* (2001); and with Walter Carlsnaes and Beth Simmons, *The Handbook of International Relations* (2002).

Saskia Sassen is the Ralph Lewis Professor of Sociology at the University of Chicago, and Centennial Visiting Professor at the London School of Economics. Her books, which have been translated into thirteen languages, include *Denationalization: Territory, Authority and Rights* (2005), *Digital Formations: Information Technologies and New Architectures in the Global Realm*, with Robert Latham (2005); and *Global Networks/Linked Cities* (2002). Her current research foci include the sociology of transnational processes, and a study of Chicago as a global city.

John Tomlinson is Professor of Cultural Sociology and Director designate of the Nottingham Institute of Cultural Analysis (NICA) at Nottingham Trent University. His books include *Cultural Imperialism* (1991) and *Globalization and Culture* (1999), which together have been translated into eight languages. He has published on issues of globalization, cosmopolitanism, modernity, media and culture across a range of disciplines from sociology, communications and cultural studies to geography, urban studies and development studies.

Preface

This is the fourth volume in the Global Transformations series. It attests to our almost institutionalized intellectual collaboration which for both of us continues to remain as instructive as it did two decades ago. The success of an edited volume depends upon the commitment of the contributors to delivering manuscripts to tight deadlines and to responding generously to the comments of the editors. In this case our contributors, without exception, proved excellent colleagues to work alongside. We are grateful to them. In addition, we would like to thank particularly our extremely patient editor at Polity, Emma Hutchinson, who provided considerable support at various stages and never despaired at a lengthening timetable – or at least did not communicate it to us! Momoh Banya and Andrew Harmer (Tony's research students) provided vital research assistance and ensured the manuscript conformed to the publisher's requirements. Finally the copy editor made exceptionally valuable refinements to the text, while easing the book through the production process. We are indebted to her.

David Held
Tony McGrew

Abbreviations

ASEAN	Association of South East Asian Nations
CSO	civil society organization
ECSC	European Coal and Steel Community
EEC	European Economic Community
EU	European Union
FDI	foreign direct investment
FRG	Federal Republic of Germany
GATT	General Agreement on Tariffs and Trade
GDP	gross domestic product
ICC	International Criminal Court
ICJ	International Court of Justice
IGO	intergovernmental organization
IISS	International Institute for Strategic Studies
IMF	International Monetary Fund
INGOs	international non-governmental organizations
ISO	International Standards Organization
LDC	less-developed country
M&As	mergers and acquisitions
MNC	multinational corporations
NAFTA	North American Free Trade Agreement
NATO	North Atlantic Treaty Organization
NGOs	non-governmental organizations
ODA	official development assistance
OECD	Organization for Economic Cooperation and Development
RTB	race to the bottom
TNCs	transnational corporations
UNCTAD	United Nations Conference on Trade and Development
WTO	World Trade Organization

Introduction: Globalization at Risk?

David Held and Anthony McGrew

Epitaphs for globalization appear with increasing frequency. Among others, the historian Ferguson has written recently of 'sinking globalization', Gray that 'the era of globalization is over', Saul on 'the end of globalism' and Rosenberg that 'the age of globalization is unexpectedly over' (Ferguson, 2005; Gray quoted in Naimi, 2002; Saul, 2005; Rosenberg, 2005). This 'post-globalist' turn connects with a more widespread belief that the catastrophic events of 9/11 were a turning point in modern world history (Kennedy-Pipe and Rengger, 2006). For some, the events represent the beginnings of a peculiar return to 'normality' in global politics as geopolitics, violence and imperialism, following the dashed hopes for a new internationalism in the 1990s, reassert themselves with a vengeance.

Since 9/11 there has been much talk of the end of globalization and the collapse of the liberal world order (Naimi, 2002). Certainly, measured solely in terms of flows within the circuits of the world economy, globalization, or to be more precise economic globalization, temporarily stalled. Among those who wrote sceptically about globalization, the global war on terror is interpreted as a world of heightened nationalism, the reassertion of geopolitics, US military hegemony, the strong state and the closing of borders. For others, such as Hoffmann, the very events of 9/11 and the subsequent responses to it are evidence of an enduring and pervasive 'clash of globalizations' rather than the demise of globalism *per se* (Hoffmann, 2002). Despite the war on terror, patterns of global interconnectedness appear to have proven extremely resilient; global economic flows, in fact, soon picked up and intensified.

What sense should we make of the current conjuncture of geopolitical, economic and cultural trends? What are its implications for our theorizing about the contemporary condition? How are contemporary globalization and its consequences to be conceptualized and understood? Is it meaningful to talk of globalization theory or alternatively theories of globalization? Do such theories transcend, or demand the recovery of, classical social and international relations theory? What are the implications of globalization for our ethical and normative theorizing concerning the contemporary global condition? These are among the central questions addressed by the contributions to this volume.

This book brings together specially commissioned essays, written by leading scholars, which seek to explicate and interrogate the principal contemporary theories and narratives – both explanatory and normative – of globalization. It seeks to transcend the rather stale strictures of much of the current globalization debate. Instead, it focuses upon the theoretical controversies which are inflected in that debate: the varied disciplinary, conceptual, epistemological and historical interpretations of globalization from across the social sciences. In taking globalization seriously the chapters build a powerful riposte to those many misguided and premature obituaries to globalization.

The Demise of Globalism? Globalization in Hard Times

Today borders and boundaries, nationalism and protectionism, localism and ethnicity appear to define an epoch of radical de-globalization: the disintegration and demise of globalism. Ferguson suggests that the current epoch has many similarities with the 'sinking' of the 'last age of globalization' which ended in the destruction of the First World War and the subsequent world depression (Ferguson, 2005). Saul, in similar vein, argues that the ideology or discourse of globalism, upon which globalization as a 'social fact' or social ontology depends, is rapidly receding in the face of the resurgence of nationalism, ethnicity, religious fundamentalism and geopolitics (Saul, 2005). And Rosenberg contends that the current conjuncture demonstrates the follies of so much globalization theory (Rosenberg, 2005). These authors hold that, in the wake of 9/11, the rapidity of the return to 'normality' and a significantly de-globalized world demonstrate the intellectual bankruptcy of 'globalization' as a description, explanation and ideology of world order. Rosenberg wryly suggests that, given this conceptual bankruptcy, the only valid conclusion must surely be that ' "globalization" did not even exist' (Rosenberg, 2005, p. 65).

These obituaries for globalization appear to validate Stiglitz's quip that 'globalization today has been oversold' (Stigltiz, 2005, p. 229). Critics argue that it has been oversold in at least three senses: as a description of social reality, as an explanation of social change, and as an ideology of social progress (a political project). In all these respects, most particularly in the wake of 9/11, globalist rhetoric appears rather hollow. These contemporary critiques of globalization have inherited a theoretically informed and empirically rich scepticism from the work of, among others, Hirst and Thompson, Hay, Rugman and Gilpin (Hirst and Thompson, 1999; Hay, 2004; Gilpin, 2002; Rugman, 2000). Though their analyses differ in significant ways, their studies concur that contemporary globalization is far from historically unprecedented, that the dominant economic trends are towards internationalization or regionalization, and that the discourse of globalization has greater significance than does the concept's descriptive or explanatory value. In effect, they argue that globalization scholarship exaggerates its historical and theoretical significance since the world remains principally one of discrete and competitive national states.

Furthermore, it is contended, many accounts of globalization confuse cause and effect, that is, whether it is the phenomenon doing the work of explanation (the explanans) or alternatively that which is the object of explanation (the explanandum) (Rosenberg, 2005). Eliding the two, such that the social phenomenon to which globalization refers become effectively its causes, is clearly problematic. However, for critics it is not so much this inversion of explanans and explanandum which undermines the intellectual coherence of much globalist scholarship but rather a failure to recognize that globalization is essentially *epiphenomenal*. If, as historical materialists argue, globalization is principally the consequence of an inherent expansionary logic of capitalist societies, then it has no independent causal powers, that is, it is clearly epiphenomenal (cf. Callinicos, chapter 3). Some therefore reject the hasty dismissal of classical social theory and consider the 'globalization turn' as simply the folly of so much contemporary liberal and radical social science in which advocacy has displaced scepticism or 'balanced social scientific reflection' (Rosenberg, 2005, p. 66). What is principally at stake here is the explanatory purchase of the very concept of globalization itself. This strikes at the very *raison d'être* of globalization studies since, as Rosenberg argues, if the concept provides no convincing 'guide to the interpretation of empirical events' it must in any meaningful sense be analytically redundant (Rosenberg, 2005, p. 1; Hay, 2004). In short, globalization is both bad empirics and bad theory.

Qualifying such scepticism, Hay argues that there is one sense in which globalization remains absolutely central to any account of the current human condition: as an idea or discourse which provides social meaning by framing, as well as legitimating, social and political change (Hay, 2004). As an idea or discourse, globalization finds expression almost everywhere in the rhetoric of politicians and social movements as a rationale for social and political action (see, for example, Wolf, 2004). Within an interpretative tradition, globalization, as the discursive construction of the social world, may be essential to understanding the contemporary epoch. But even this is becoming increasingly problematic as vociferous opposition to the project of globalism has become both more widespread and socially entrenched.

Globalization, so the critics suggest, has encountered hard times. It is no longer, if it ever was, a useful description of social reality, nor does it provide a cogent explanation of the social forces shaping our world. Furthermore, globalism as a political and economic project has been replaced by a new imperialism as humanity adjusts to the realities of the unipolar moment and the clash of cultures and religions. Thus, the world is witnessing the demise of globalization as social ontology, explanans and social imaginary.

Embedded Globalism: *Restitutio in Integrum?*

Since 9/11, the limits to globalization have become apparent while the political conditions which facilitated it appeared to be rapidly dissipating. For the first time in almost a decade the simultaneous growth of trade, capital flows and foreign investment turned significantly negative: by 2002 world trade had fallen by a huge 4 per cent; capital flows by 19 per cent (2001) and a further 67 per cent (2002); and foreign direct investment collapsed by 41 per cent in 2001 and a further 21 per cent in 2002 (BIS, 2005, 2006; WTO, 2002; UNCTAD, 2003). This reversal of economic flows also endured for much longer than previous global economic downturns. Furthermore, this slowing of economic globalization was accompanied by dramatic changes in the global political context evidenced in shifts from multilateralism to unilateralism, stability to insecurity, and soft power to hard power. For critics these shifts represented a rejection of the liberal world order, which underwrote the second golden age of economic globalization, heralding a new period of de-globalization. For others this was simply evidence of a slowing of the unprecedented intensity of economic globalization witnessed over the last two decades.

Yet, recent trends suggest that economic globalization *per se* has proven far more resilient than many presumed. Despite record falls, it remains on almost all measures more intensive and extensive than a decade earlier (Kearney, 2003, 2005). In terms of trade, 2004 witnessed the strongest growth in a decade and it reached historic levels of world GDP; foreign direct investment (FDI) flows also rebounded to levels of the early 1990s while flows to less-developed countries (LDCs) accelerated much faster than to OECD economies; in addition, financial flows increased and foreign exchange transactions reached a historic $1.9 trillion per day (WTO, 2005; UNCTAD, 2005; BIS, 2005, 2006). Measured in terms of migration, communication, or even the arms trade there is little evidence of a rush to autarky or de-globalization (Kearney, 2005). Given the scale of the 2001 global economic downturn, the endemic political instability, and global insecurity, a much greater and more sustained contraction might have been expected. Overall the empirical evidence is indicative of the recovery from a cyclical downturn, which began well before 11 September 2001, and as world growth prospects have improved so have the prospects for economic globalization. Beyond the economic domain, most especially in the military and security domains, there has been little diminution, but rather an acceleration, of the militarization of globalism (see McGrew, chapter 1 below).

Rather than the demise of globalization, in its multiple forms, the empirical evidence suggests, to the contrary, that it has proven much more resilient or socially embedded than critics believed or many desired. There is little evidence to suggest that those domestic and transnational social forces upon which the advance of economic globalization is contingent have lost their ardour for it. Furthermore, as the worldwide economic and distributional impacts of slowing globalization became increasingly apparent, those social forces which are its main beneficiaries strongly reasserted their domestic and transnational influence, especially in the wake of the failed World Trade Organization (WTO) Summit at Cancún, to advance the globalization project, albeit in a slightly modified form. As Harold James explains in his analysis of the collapse of a previous era of globalization, the *belle époque* (approximately 1880–1914), 'the pendulum is so slow in swinging back from globality' today because of both its global institutional and social embeddness and the absence of any viable political alternative to an open world economy (James, 2001, p. 224). Globalization, in its multiple forms, remains far more socially and institutionally entrenched than its critics have recognized.

Underpinning the nature and pace of contemporary globalization are, moreover, a number of 'deep drivers' which are likely to be operative for the foreseeable future, irrespective of the exact institutional form globalization takes. Among these drivers are: the changing infrastructure of global communications linked to the IT revolution; the development of global markets in goods and services, connected to the worldwide distribution of information; the new global division of labour driven by multinational corporations; the end of the Cold War and the diffusion of democratic and consumer values across many of the world's regions (alongside some marked reactions to this); and the growth of migration and the movement of peoples, linked to shifts in patterns of economic demand, demography and environmental degradation (see Held, chapter 12 below). These deeply structured processes generate dense patterns of global interconnectedness, real and virtual. As a result, political communities can no longer be considered (if they ever could with any validity) as simply 'discrete worlds'; they are enmeshed in complex structures of overlapping forces, relations and networks. Clearly, these are structured by inequality and hierarchy. However, even the most powerful among them – including the most powerful states – do not remain unaffected by the changing conditions and processes of the many different forms of regional and global entrenchment.

In the inaugural edition of the journal *Globalizations*, Petersen argued that 'we cannot make sense of globalizations through conventional analytical and disciplinary frameworks' (Petersen, 2004, p. 50). Rosenau, also in the same edition, observed that 'social scientists, like the people they study, are prone to habitual modes of behaviour, and thus are more likely to cast their inquiries into habitual frameworks that are taken for granted than to treat their organizing principles as problematic' (Rosenau, 2004, p. 12). Shaw too called for 'the global transformation of the social sciences' (Shaw, 2002, p. 35). For these authors, globalization brings into question the core organizing principles of modern social science – namely the state, society, political community, the economy – and the classical inheritance of modern social theory which takes these for granted as the metrics or focus of social explanation – sometimes referred to as methodological nationalism (Beck, 1999; Agnew, 2005; Scholte, 2005). Recursive patterns of worldwide interconnectedness challenge the very principle of the bounded society and the presumption that its dynamics and development can be comprehended principally by reference to endogenous social forces. By eroding the distinctions between the domestic and the international, endogenous and exogenous, internal and external, the idea of globalization directly challenges the 'methodological nationalism' which finds its most acute expression in classical social theory. It implies, as Scholte and others conclude, the need for 'a paradigm shift in social analysis' in order that the emerging condition of globality – the growing awareness of the world as a shared social space – can be explained and understood in all its complexity (Scholte, 1999, p. 18).

As Holton, among others, has suggested, globalization scholarship has come in three overlapping but distinctive waves: the hyper-globalist, the sceptical, and the post-sceptical (Holton, 2005, p. 5; Bruff, 2005; cf. Held, McGrew et al., 1999). The wave analogy is useful in so far as it alludes to the successive diffusion and churning over of distinct research programmes in which core research problématiques come to be reappropriated and redefined by new research agendas. Significantly, too, it does not imply a simple notion of cumulative knowledge or linear progress. Building upon Holton's schema, while modifying it in a number of respects, four successive waves of globalization scholarship can be identified and roughly labelled as the theoretical, the historical, the institutional, and the deconstructive. As with all such schema, it is neither definitive nor exhaustive but, rather, should be understood as a heuristic for organizing a highly complex field of study.

As manifest in the works of Giddens, Robertson, Rosenau, Albrow, Ohmae, Harvey and Lawrence, among others, the initial theoretical wave was generally concerned with debates about the conceptualization of globalization, its principal dynamics and its systemic and structural consequences as a secular process of worldwide social change (Albrow, 1996; Giddens, 1990; Harvey, 1989; Lawrence, 1996; Ohmae, 1995; Robertson, 1992; Rosenau, 1990). By contrast the historical wave, drawing upon the historical sociology of global development, was principally concerned with exploring in what ways, if any, contemporary globalization could be considered novel or unique – whether it defined a new epoch, or transformation, in the socio-economic and political organization of human affairs – and, if so, what the implications were for the realization of progressive values and projects of human emancipation (see among others, Held, McGrew et al., 1999; Hirst and Thompson, 1999; Frank, 1998; Castells, 2000; Bordo et al., 2003; Dicken, 1998; Baldwin and Martin,

1999; Gilpin, 2002; Gill, 2003; Mann, 1986, 2001; Hopkins, 2002; Sassen, 1996; Hardt and Negri, 2000; Hoogvelt, 1997; O'Rourke and Williamson, 2000; Boyer and Drache, 1996; Appadurai, 1998; Amin, 1997; Taylor, 1995; and Tomlinson, chapter 7 below).

Sceptical of these arguments about structural transformation, the third (institutional) wave sought to assess claims about global convergence (and divergence) by concentrating upon questions of institutional change and resilience, whether in national models of capitalism, state restructuring, or cultural life (see among others here Garrett, 1998, 2000; Swank, 2002; Held, 2004; Keohane and Nye, 2003; Campbell, 2004; Mosley, 2003; Cowen, 2004; Hay and Watson, 2000; Pogge, 2001). Finally, the fourth and most recent wave reflects the influence of post-structuralist and constructivist thinking across the social sciences, from Open Marxism to postmodernism. As a consequence, there is an emphasis upon the importance of ideas, agency, communication, contingency and normative change to any convincing analysis of the making, unmaking and remaking of globalization understood both as a historical process and as a hegemonic discourse. Central to this literature is a debate about whether the current historical conjuncture is best understood as an epoch of competing and alternative globalizations (in the plural), what Hoffman has referred to as the 'clash of globalizatons' (Hoffman, 2002; Rosenberg, 2005; Hay, 2004; Urry, 2003; Bello, 2002; Held and McGrew, 2002; Callinicos, 2003; Keohane and Nye, 2003; Rosamond, 2004; Wolf, 2004; Saul, 2005; Eschele, 2005; Harvey, 2003).

These four broad approaches frame contemporary globalization scholarship. They share in common a recognition that it has systemic or emergent properties which make it causally significant, rather than simply epiphenomenal: in effect it has intrinsic causal powers which are not simply reducible to particular economic, political or social forces whether capitalism, neoliberalism or militarism. Historical materialism conceives imperialism both as a product of capitalist logics but also nevertheless causally significant in its own right. Similarly much globalization scholarship recognizes that, in different narrative contexts, it is both the phenomenon which requires explanation but also one which can do the explanatory work.

If one critical source of academic contention over globalization stems from competing assessments of its descriptive and explanatory value, a second, but no less important, source issues from differing normative and ethical positions. These are inextricably bound together with matters of empirics and theory in so far as analyses of globalization are necessarily imbued with ethical judgements about its tendencies and consequences. Whether globalization is good for the poor, to take an obvious example, involves not just empirical assessments but judgements about whether or why it matters, if it is or is not good for the poor, not to mention how the good might be defined (see Held and Kaya, 2006). Deliberations about globalization, whether in the academy or beyond, are inescapably inflected – whether explicitly or implicitly – with normative reasoning. Every day, to paraphrase Sandel, we live out many of the concepts of normative theory (Sandel, 1996). Whether globalization is considered benign, malign or both is a judgement conditioned by normative reasoning and ethical assessments of its consequences for the human condition. But there is no simple correspondence between particular normative positions – such as left or right – and attitudes towards globalization. Rather, as Tormey has suggested, the more significant distinction is between what might be broadly defined as ideological and post-ideological reasoning, between those who judge globalization in relation to how far it advances or constrains progress towards a particular ideal of the 'good life' – a social or political project – and those who judge it in relation to how far it facilitates or hinders different and multiple 'ways of life', or what Haber refers to as 'radical pluralism' (Tormey, 2004, p. 75; Haber in Noonan, 2003, p. 92). In simply reading globalization, as do many critics, as neoliberalism or Westernization, it is not surprising that resistance to it is interpreted as the demise of globalism as a singular hegemonic political project. However, this overlooks the multiple forms of globalization or the clash of globalizations which define the current conjuncture: from liberal cosmopolitanism to combat fundamentalism. Irrespective of the fact that the neoliberal project is increasingly on the defensive, much of the normative and ethical controversy about globalization concerns its making and remaking – whether different or better worlds are either imaginable or possible – rather than simply its undoing.

Globalization Theory: Approaches and Controversies

This volume brings together a series of specially commissioned original essays which seek to advance critical understanding of the principal theories and narratives of globalization. Their common concern is taking globalization seriously by surveying, elucidating, advocating and reflecting critically upon the primary theories of globalization from across the social sciences. They are concerned, in short, with accounts of the making and remaking of globalization: explanatory and normative theory respectively.

Part I explores the making of globalization through a consideration of its multiple dimensions: from the coercive to the cultural. It commences with an essay by Anthony McGrew which examines the role of organized violence in the development of globalization, from early empires to global terrorism. The discussion raises significant questions about the adequacy of contemporary theories of globalization which tend either to a reductionist economism or cultural determinism. Chapter 2 develops this critique in so far as G. John Ikenberry considers the question of whether globalization can be explained or understood primarily as an extension of American hegemony or American empire. This theme of empire is developed further by Alex Callinicos who, taking a historical materialist approach, argues that globalization is in key respects a synonym for contemporary imperialism, or rather a new form of imperialism without colonies. In chapter 4, Saskia Sassen considers how the very idea of globalization requires a similar rethinking of existing spatial categories within the social sciences. In particular she argues that empirically and methodologically the embeddedness of the global within the local challenges a key assumption of much social theory that the local is synonymous with the national.

If globalization challenges existing theorizations of territoriality and spatiality it also raises questions about global economic convergence and the institutional capacity of states to manage economic openness. In chapter 5 Layna Mosley presents a rich and sophisticated critique of much current theorizing of the political economy of globalization which neither discounts state power nor the power of global markets. Similarly rejecting the convergence thesis rooted in much contemporary theory, Thomas Risse's chapter admirably demonstrates why a constructivist perspective is essential to understanding contemporary globalization. He emphasizes the limits of purely materialist accounts of globalism in revealing how constructivism necessarily reinforces the centrality of politics, rather than economism, to the making of globalization and its possibilities. This emphasis upon contingency, rather than determinism, in relation to global forces is developed further in chapter 7, the final contribution to Part I. John Tomlinson argues for a phenomenological approach to globalization that transcends the stale categories of cultural imperialism, homogenization and difference.

Part II reflects upon contemporary normative theories of globalism: how and why globalization can or should be remade. It commences with an essay by Chris Brown which addresses the central question as to whether international society – the society of states – requires reimagining in the context of the post 9/11 world. Brown concludes that in many respects it does not, since the tension between solidarism and pluralism remains a powerful reality in the contemporary world order. In chapter 9, Michael Doyle emphasizes the limits to the liberal peace in the context of globalization arguing that the latter in key respects undermines the former. Moreover, while the demand for global norms has become more critical the absence of legitimate and accountable global deliberative mechanisms makes their realization more difficult. This theme is taken up in Thomas Pogge's chapter, which makes the case that the demands of global redistributive justice require a fundamental reframing of the coercive institutional order which imposes so much misery on the majority of humankind. In the final two chapters Andrew Kuper and David Held present a case for why such an institutional reframing might both be more politically feasible than is often presumed and how it could be made to accord with cosmopolitan principles. In chapter 11 Kuper identifies eight institutional innovations which would create the basis for more just, democratic and legitimate global governance. Adopting a more radical position in chapter 12, David Held advocates global social democracy as the only convincing path to saving globalization from itself: to making globalization safe for humanity rather than, as is currently often the case, making the world safe for globalization.

References

Agnew, J. (2005). *Hegemony: The New Shape of Global Power*. Philadephia: Temple Press.

Albrow, M. (1996). *The Global Age*. Cambridge: Polity.

Amin, S. (1997). *Capitalism in the Age of Globalization*. London: Zed Press.

Appadurai, A. (1998). *Modernity at Large*. Minneapolis: Minnesota University Press.

Ayres, J. (2004). 'Framing Collective Action against Neoliberalism', *Journal of World Systems Theory*, 10(1): pp. 11–34.

Baldwin, R. E. and P. Martin (January 1999). Two Waves of Globalisation: Superficial Similarities, Fundamental Differences. Retrieved November 2003 from www.nber.og/papers/w6904.

Barber, B. (1996). *Jihad versus McWorld*. New York: Ballantyne Books.

Beck, U. (1999). *What is Globalization?* Cambridge: Polity.

Bello, W. (2002). *Deglobalization*. London: Zed Press.

BIS (Bank for International Settlements). (2005–6). *BIS Quarterly Review*. Geneva: BIS.

Bordo, M., A. M. Taylor et al., eds (2003). *Globalization in Historical Perspective*. Chicago: National Bureau of Economic Research/Chicago University Press.

Boyer, R. and D. Drache, eds (1996). *States against Markets*. London, Routledge.

Brenner, N. (2004). *New State Spaces: Urban Governance and the Rescaling of Statehood*. Oxford and New York: Oxford University Press.

Bruff, I. (2005). 'Making Sense of the Globalization Debate when Engaging in Political Economy Analysis', *British Journal of Politics and International Relations*, 7(3): pp. 261–80.

Callinicos, A. (2003). *An Anti-Capitalist Manifesto*. Cambridge: Polity.

Campbell, J. (2004). *Institutional Change and Globalization*. Princeton: Princeton University Press.

Castells, M. (2000). *The Rise of the Network Society*. Oxford: Blackwell.

Cowen, T. (2004). *Creative Destruction: How Globalization is Changing the World's Cultures*. Princeton: Princeton University Press.

Dicken, P. (1998). *Global Shift*. London: Paul Chapman.

Dicken, P. (2000). *Global Shift*, 2nd edn. London: Paul Chapman.

Dollar, D. (2005). 'Globalization, Poverty and Inequality', in *Globalization: What's New?*, ed M. M. Weinstein. New York: Columbia University Press, pp. 96–128.

Eschele, C. (2005). 'Constructing the Antiglobalization Movement', in *Critical Theories, International Relations and the 'AntiGlobalization Movement': The Politics of Resistance*, ed. C. Eshele and B. Maiguashia. London: Routledge, pp. 17–35.

Falk, R. (2002). *Predatory Globalization*. Cambridge: Polity.

Ferguson, N. (2005). 'Sinking Globalization', *Foreign Affairs*, 84(2): pp. 64–77.

Frank, A. G. (1998). *Re-Orient: Global Economy in the Asian Age*. New York: University of California Press.

Garrett, G. (1998). 'Global Markets and National Politics.' *International Organization*, 52.

Garrett, G. (1999). *Partisan Politics in the Global Economy*. Cambridge University Press: Cambridge.

Garrett, G. (2000). 'The Causes of Globalization', *Comparative Political Studies*, 33(6): pp. 945–91.

Giddens, A. (1990). *The Consequences of Modernity*. Cambridge: Polity.

Gill, S. (2003). *Power and Resistance in the New World Order*. Basingstoke: Palgrave.

Gilpin, R. (2002). *The Challenge of Global Capitalism*. Princeton: Princeton University Press.

Hannerz, U. (1992). *Global Complexity*. New York: Columbia University Press.

Hannerz, U. (1996). *Transcultural Connections: Culture, People, Places*. London: Routledge.

Hardt, M. and A. Negri (2000). *Empire*. Cambridge, Mass.: Harvard University Press.

Harvey, D. (1989). *The Condition of Postmodernity*. Oxford: Blackwell.

Harvey, D. (2003). *The New Imperialism*. Oxford: Oxford University Press.

Hay, C. (2004). 'Globalization and the State', in *Global Political Economy*, ed. J. Ravenhill. Oxford: Oxford University Press.

Hay, C. and M. Watson (1998). *Rendering the Contingent Necessary: New Labour's Neo-Liberal Conversion and the Discourse of Globalization*. Cambridge, Mass: Center for European Studies, Harvard University.

Hay, C. and M. Watson (2000). 'Globalization and the British Political Economy', Mimeo.

Held, D. (2004). *Global Covenant*. Cambridge: Polity.

Held, D. and A. Kaya, eds (2006). *Global Inequality*. Cambridge: Polity.

Held, D., A. McGrew et al. (1999). *Global Transformations*. Cambridge: Polity.

Held, D. and A. McGrew (2002). *Globalization/Anti-globalization*. Cambridge: Polity.

Hirst, P. and G. Thompson (1999). *Globalization in Question*. Cambridge: Polity.

Hoffmann, S. (2002). 'The Clash of Globalizations', *Foreign Affairs* (July).

Holton, R. (2005). *Making Globalization*. Basingstoke: Palgrave.

Hoogvelt, A. (1997). *Globalization and the Post-Colonial World*. Basingstoke: Macmillan.

Hopkins. A. (2002). *Globalization in World History*. London: Pimlico.

James, H. (2001). *The End of Globalization*. Cambridge, Mass: Harvard University Press.

James, P. (2005). 'Globalism, Nationalism, Tribalism: Bringing Theory Back', in James and Nairn, eds (2005).

James, P. and T. Nairn, eds (2005). *Global Matrix: Nationalism, Globalization, and Terrorism*. London: Routledge.

Keane, J. (2003). *Global Civil Society*. Cambridge: Cambridge University Press.

Kearney, A. T. (2003). 'Globalization Index 2003', *Foreign Policy* (January).

Kearney, A. T. (2005). 'Globalization Index 2005', *Foreign Policy* (January).

Kennedy-Pipe, C. and N. Rengger (2006). 'Apocalypse Now? Continuities or Disjunctions in World Politics after 9/11', *International Affairs*, 82(3): pp. 539–52.

Keohane, R. and J. Nye (2003). Globalization: What's New? What's Not? (And So What?), in *The Global Transformations Reader*, ed. D. Held and A. McGrew. Cambridge: Polity, pp. 75–84.

Khor, M. (2001). *Rethinking Globalization*. London: Zed Press.

Lawrence, R. (1996). *Single World, Divided Nations? International Trade and OECD Labour Markets*. Washington, DC: Brookings Institution.

Mandelbaum, M. (2004). *The Ideas that Conquered the World: Peace, Democracy, and Free Markets in the Twenty-first Century*. New York: *Public Affairs*.

Mann, M. (1986). *The Sources of Social Power*, vol. 1. Cambridge: Cambridge University Press.

Mann, M. (2001). 'Globalization after September 11th', *New Left Review*, 12 (Nov/Dec): pp. 51–72.

Mittleman, J. (2000). *The Globalization Syndrome*. Princeton: Princeton University Press.

Mosley, L. (2003). *Global Capital and National Governments*. Cambridge: Cambridge University Press.

Naimi, M. (2002). 'Post-terror surprises'. September. Retrieved June 2003, from www.foreignpolicy. com/issue_september_2002/ml.html.

Noonan, J. (2003). *Critical Humanism and the Politics of Difference*. Montreal: McGill–Queens University Press.

Ohmae, K. (1990). *The Borderless World*. London: HarperCollins.

Ohmae, K. (1995). *The End of the Nation State*. New York: Free Press.

Olesen, T. (2005). International Zapatismo. London: Zed Books.

Petersen, V. S. (2004). 'Plural Processes, Patterned Connections', *Globalizations* 1(1): pp. 50–68.

O'Rourke, K. H. and J. G. Williamson (2000). *Globalization and History*. Boston, Mass: MIT Press.

Phillips, N. (2005). 'Whither IPE?', in *Globalizing International Political Economy*, ed. N. Phillips. Basingstoke: Palgrave, pp. 246–70.

Pogge, T. W., ed. (2001). *Global Justice*. Oxford: Blackwell.

Ritzer, G. (1995). *The McDonaldization of Society*. Thousand Oaks, Calif.: Pine Forge Press.

Robertson, R. (1992). *Globalization: Social Theory and Global Culture*. London: Sage.

Rosamond, B. (2001). 'Discourses of Globalization and European Identities', *The Social Construction of Europe*. ed. T. Christiansen, K. Jorgensen and A. Wiener. London: Sage, pp. 158–76.

Rosamond, B. (2003). 'Babylon and on? Globalization and International Political Economy', *Review of International Political Economy*, 10(4): pp. 661–71.

Rosamond, B. (2004). *Globalization and the European Union*. Basingstoke: Palgrave.

Rosenau, J. (1990). *Turbulence in World Politics*. Princeton: Princeton University Press.

Rosenau, J. (1995). *Along the Domestic Foreign Frontier*. Cambridge: Cambridge University Press.

Rosenau, J. (2003). *Distant Proximities*. Princeton: Princeton University Press.

Rosenau, J. (2004). 'Many Globalizations, One International Relations', *Globalizations*, 1(1), September: pp. 7–14.

Rosenberg, J. (2000). *The Follies of Globalisation Theory*. London: Verso Press.

Rosenberg, J. (2005). 'Globalization Theory: A Post Mortem', *International Politics*, 42: pp. 2–74.

Rugman, A. (2000). *The End of Globalization*. New York, Random House.

Sandel, M. (1996). *Democracy's Discontent*. Cambridge, Mass.: Harvard University Press.

Sassen, S. (1996). *Losing Control? Sovereignty in an Age of Globalization*. New York: Columbia University Press.

Saul, J. R. (2005). *The Collapse of Globalism*. London: Atlantic Books.

Scholte, J. A. (1999). *Globalization: A Critical Introduction*. Houndmills, Basingstoke: Palgrave.

Scholte, J. A. (2005). *Globalization: A Critical Introduction*, 2nd edn. Houndmills, Basingstoke: Palgrave.

Shaw, M. (2002). 'Globality and Historical Sociology: State, Revolution and War Revisited', in *Historical Sociology of International Relations*, ed. S. Hobden and J. M. Hobson. Cambridge: Cambridge University Press, pp. 82–99.

Shaw, M. (2003). 'The Global Transformation of the Social Sciences', in *The Global Civil Society Yearbook*, ed. M. Kaldor et al. London: Sage, pp. 35–44.

Stiglitz, J. (2002). *Globalization and its Discontents*. New York: Norton.

Stiglitz, J. P. (2005). 'The Overselling of Globalization', in *Globalization – What's New?* ed. M. M. Weinstein. New York: Columbia University Press, pp. 228–62.

Swank, D. (2002). *Global Capital, Political Institutions, and Policy Change in Developed Welfare States*. Cambridge: Cambridge University Press.

Taylor, Peter J. (1995). 'Beyond Containers: Internationality, Interstateness, Interterritoriality', *Progress in Human Geography*, 19 (March): pp. 1–15.

Tomlinson, J. (2007). 'Globalization and Cultural Analysis', in *Globalization Theory: Approaches and Controversies*, ed. D. Held and A. McGrew. Cambridge: Polity, ch. 7.

Tormey, S. (2004). *Anticapitalism*. Oxford: Oneworld.

UNCTAD (2003, 2005). World Investment Report 2003 (2005). Geneva: UNCTAD.

Urry, J. (2003). *Global Complexity*. Cambridge: Polity.

Wallerstein, I. (1979). *The Capitalist World Economy*. Cambridge: Cambridge University Press.

Weiss, L. (1998). *The Myth of the Powerless State*. Cambridge: Polity.

Wolf, M. (2004). *Why Globalization Works*. New Haven and London: Yale University Press.

Wood, E. M. (2003). *Empire of Capital*. London: Verso.

WTO (World Trade Organization) (2005). *World Trade Report*. Geneva: WTO.

Part I

The Making of Globalization

1
Organized Violence in the Making (and Remaking) of Globalization
Anthony McGrew

Introduction

Studies of globalization, with some exceptions, have given little more than passing attention to the subject of organized violence (Modelski, 1972; Held, McGrew et al., 1999; Hirst, 2001).[1] The primacy of economism and the 'cultural turn' discouraged a focus upon the coercive or, as some would have it, the 'dark side' of globality. In the aftermath of 9/11, however, few can ignore the fact that, as Keane observes, 'Violence seems to be back and here to stay, in a big and destabilizing way' (Keane, 2004, p. 7). Recognizing this, recent studies of globalization have sought to come to terms with collective violence just as theorists of international relations have sought to come to terms with globalized non-state violence. Such developments reflect complementary intellectual gaps: while the former have tended to overlook the centrality of violence in the making of a globalized world, the latter have tended to associate globalization primarily with 'low politics' as opposed to the 'high politics' of state security and survival. Taking both globalization and violence seriously involves, to paraphrase Charles Tilly, understanding 'how violence makes globalization and globalization makes violence' (Tilly, 1990). This is the principal, although not the sole, task of this chapter.

In his original and now classic account of globalization, George Modelski concluded that, 'One striking feature of the process of globalization has been the quality of arrogance and violence that fuelled it' (Modelski, 1972, p. 49). From the Chinese armadas of the thirteenth century, through the medieval Crusades, to the New Imperialism of the late nineteenth century, military conquest and force have been vital instruments in drawing the world's distant regions and discrete civilizations into tightening webs of recursive interaction. Of course, trade and capital played a primary role in driving this process but collective violence, contrary to much liberal thinking, has always been integral to it. Reflecting upon the introduction of breakfast in seventeenth-century Europe, the historian Christopher Bayly highlights the ways in which even this daily social practice was intimately connected, through Atlantic trading circuits, to an extraordinary system of 'brutality and subjugation in the Caribbean' (Bayly, 2004, p. 84). How organized violence, state and non-state, has contributed to both the unification and division of the modern world is the subject of the first section of the chapter. It draws upon the established genre of world history to explicate the role of force, warfare and conquest in the construction of the modern world order. This provides a historical context for critically exploring, in the second section, the unique features of contemporary globalized violence. The third section locates this discussion in related theoretical controversies within international relations concerning the causal significance and structural consequences of globalization for security, the state, and world order. The chapter concludes with some reflections upon the normative issues posed by the contemporary globalization of violence with particular emphasis given to the cosmopolitan project. In short, the chapter argues that, historically, organized violence has been constitutive of globalization – although it is theoretically neither a necessary element nor the sole determinant – while the current phase of globalized violence represents a significant challenge to orthodox thinking about security, the state and world order. Clausewitz's well rehearsed dictum that 'war is a continuation of politics by other means' might today more fittingly be reformulated as 'globalization is a continuation of violence by new means'.

The Globalization of Organized Violence: From World Civilizations to *Schicksalsgemeinschaft*[2]

Conventional histories of how the world's major civilizations came to be incorporated within a singular global system have largely followed a 'rise of the West' narrative. This narrative is premised principally upon a logic of innate European superiority whether cultural, economic or especially military (W. H. McNeill, 1963). As Kennedy argues, the story of Europe's rise to global dominance can be traced to endogenous factors in so far as 'Possessing fewer obstacles to change, European societies entered into a constant upward spiral of economic growth and enhanced military effectiveness which, over time, was to carry them ahead of all other regions of the globe' (Kennedy, 1988, p. xviii). Its growing military capability, a consequence of the transformation in the organization and technology of warfare, encouraged and enabled European global expansion. According to the military historian Geoffrey Parker,

> 'the rise of the West' depended on the exercise of force, upon the fact that the military balance between the Europeans and their adversaries overseas was steadily tilting in favour of the former . . . the key to the Westerner's success in creating the first truly global empires between 1500 and 1750 depended upon precisely those improvements in the ability to wage war which have been termed the military revolution. (Parker, 1988, p. 4)

Europe's multiple imperial projects, for they were uncoordinated, arose out of the dynamics and displacement of continental military competition, not to mention commercial imperatives. In the decades following the Berlin Conference of 1884, which sanctioned the 'Scramble for Africa', Europe's global rule expanded to embrace some 84 per cent of the world's territory by comparison with 35 per cent some two centuries earlier (Parker, 1988, p. 121). For many, the principal guarantor of the ascendancy of these emerging global empires can be located in the accelerating 'firepower gap' between Europe and the Rest which transformed the West's capacity for conquest by coercive means (Modelski, 1972; Headrick, 1981; Parker, 1988).

In his classic essay on European expansion, Michael Howard asserts that 'one way in which the ascendancy of European culture was manifested, and by no means the least important, was through military confrontation and conquest' (Howard, 1984, p. 34). He identifies three phases of this European expansion: the period of seaborne empires (fifteenth to seventeenth centuries); the emergence of gunpowder empires (1700–1850); and the global empires of the industrial age (1830s–1918). In each of these phases organized violence played a distinctive and oftentimes critical role. Although 'Old World' diseases, along with the Aztec's indigenous enemies, contributed much to the destruction of Aztec civilization by Cortes and 315 conquistadores, the crucial role of organized violence cannot be underestimated (Fernandez-Armesto, 1995, p. 195; McNeill and McNeill 2003, p. 172). As Cortes himself admitted, the conquistadores massacred more than 3,000 Indians in one single campaign of terror alone (Fernandez-Armesto 1995, p. 195). From the New World to Asia the major European powers defended and consolidated their early colonial settlements through the deployment of seaborne power and the construction of military garrisons. To some extent the technological and logistical limits to the projection of this coercive power restrained the colonization process in so far as overseas settlements relied ultimately upon seapower for their security and reinforcement. With the supremacy of European seapower, however, came the capacity to control essential trade routes such that force became a key factor in the expansion of world trade. Black emphasizes how, in this early period, organized violence 'was employed to influence or even dictate the terms of trade rather to gain territory'(Black, 1998, p. 32). Even so it was the military revolution of the late seventeenth century, by transforming Europe's capacity to wage war on land as well as by sea, that 'decisively accelerated the progress of Europe's expansion overseas' (Parker, 1988, p. 8). Technological change, in the form of firearms, combined with the formation of permanent military forces and the absolutist state, capable of extracting societal resources for the prosecution of war, dramatically altered the global balance of coercive power in Europe's favour. By the Peace of Passarowitz in 1718, when Austria defeated the Turks, 'the military balance between the "West" and the "East" had reversed' (Black, 1994, p. 14).

Alongside this military revolution came a decisive consolidation of European imperial projects on the Indian subcontinent, Africa, the Americas and subsequently the Antipodes. British, French, Dutch and Spanish military forces pushed further into the hinterlands beyond their coastal settlements through a combination of superior military firepower and organization (Howard, 1984). By the end of the eighteenth century European powers had acquired some 35 per cent of the world's territory although the efficacy of their substantive, as opposed to nominal, control varied considerably (Headrick, 1981). This proved a distinctly bloody process not only because military encounters became more unequal but also because there were fewer political and moral constraints upon imperial violence. For instance, the 1780 Peruvian 'intifada' claimed 10,000 lives with no public outcry in the Spanish metropole while in 1761 the British adopted a 'scorched earth policy' against the Cherokees simply as a matter of course (Black, 2002, p. 92). In this period, as Bayly caustically observes, 'Crudely, Europeans became much better at killing people', a fact underlined by Tilly's estimate that battlefield deaths increased tenfold in the five decades from 1750 to 1800 (Tilly, 1990, p. 165; Bayly, 2004, p. 62).

Europe's killing machine was not purely the business of the state either. Throughout this early phase of imperial expansion European states continued to rely, sometimes very significantly, upon the private provision of the means of violence. Indeed war at the time, as it was to become later in the twentieth century, was one of the biggest industries in

Europe. Louis de Geer, a seventeenth-century Amsterdam merchant, profited considerably from arranging and supplying to the Swedish monarch a complete navy, from sailors
to even a Vice-Admiral (Ferguson and Mansbach, 2004, p. 259). Although the medieval
condottieri system (in which private military companies, such as the Great Company
which commanded 10,000 troops, hired out their forces to rulers in return for capital, privileges or tribute) was being eclipsed by the creation of standing armies, states still
depended upon purchasing professional military forces (Singer, 2003, pp. 23–34). In the
American War of Independence, for instance, the British hired 30,000 soldiers from
Hesse-Kassel to fight the revolutionaries. Indeed it was quite common for European
standing armies to rely on 20–65 per cent foreign military personnel (Singer, 2003).
Furthermore, in the colonies private organizations, such as the English and Dutch East
India companies, commanded their own military forces, engaged in warfare and policed
their own territory. By 1782 the English East India Company had a 100,000-strong army,
greater than that of the British army at the time, and controlled territory which dwarfed
considerably that of the entire British Isles (Singer, 2003, p. 35). This was a period in
which the European state had yet to assert a monopoly over the means of organized violence or to nationalize its military forces. In effect, public and private agencies shared substantive control over, as well as participated in the globalization of, organized violence.
Especially at the beginning of this period private enterprise was evident too in a global
trade in arms, as Dutch colonizers traded arms for slaves (at the rate of 12 for 1 respectively) in Africa and merchants sold European weapons to Tokugawa Japan and the
American revolutionaries (Headrick, 1981, pp. 121 and 144). Despite this burgeoning
trade the firepower gap between the 'West' and the 'Rest' was hardly redressed. A world
military order nevertheless was in the making as European military technology, paradoxically much of it borrowed from Chinese and Islamic civilizations, as well as military
organization began to set a world standard which states and warlords on other continents
sought to emulate for purposes of either defence or offence. As Howard comments,
despite the fitful extension of European 'gunpowder empires' in this period, by the early
nineteenth century it was widely accepted that the 'only way to beat the Europeans was
to imitate them' (Howard, 1984, p. 36). This was a period, according to Bayly, which witnessed the very first world wars with the deepening imbrication of European great power
competition and distant colonial wars such that Napoleon remarked that 'the Battle of
Waterloo had been lost in India' when British forces had defeated the French (Bayly, 2004,
p. 86).

Despite European ambitions the world at the end of the eighteenth century, according
to Watson, was still far from 'a single global system'(Watson, 1992, p. 227). In particular
much of Asia, including Japan and China, remained outside direct European control while
the outcomes of the French and American revolutions destabilized the metropoles,
demonstrating that European power was far from invincible. Coupled with the many other
significant setbacks to its expansion in Asia and Africa, European hegemony was far from
assured. What transformed this situation was the intersection of European power politics
with the rapid diffusion of the industrial revolution: in short, the industrialization of
warfare. At the Congress of Vienna in 1815 Europe's great powers sought to manage their
continental competition with the consequence that it was largely displaced into a struggle
for global mastery. Capitalist industrialization reinforced this process since it required

healthy supplies of raw materials and new markets while simultaneously revolutionizing the instruments, organization and lethality of warfare. With the industrialization of warfare an accelerating firepower gap between the 'West' and the 'Rest' enabled 'European forces . . . to conquer large parts of Asia and Africa – empires of Napoleonic proportions – at an astonishingly low cost' (Headrick, 1981, p. 83). By 1878 Europe's imperial powers had doubled the territory under their direct control, reaching deep into Africa and establishing international settlements as far east as China. Transformations in communications and transport technologies, from the steamship and railway to the telegraph, enhanced and accelerated the logistics of building, as well as the infrastructural capacity for ruling, empires of a global reach. Both the gunboat and the machine gun symbolized this accelerating firepower gap. While the gunboat *Nemesis* contributed to the Chinese Emperor's capitulation to the British Expeditionary Fleet in 1842, the advent of the Maxim gun and repeating rifles enabled the Royal Niger Company force of 539 men to defeat the 31,000-strong army of the Nupe Emirate of Sokoto (Headrick, 1981, pp. 53 and 117).

This 'New Imperialism' was accompanied by enormous destruction, ethnic cleansing, and a huge displacement of indigenous peoples as European settlers, backed by preponderant military force, extended their rule over much of the world's territory. By the outbreak of the First World War European capitals ruled over 84 per cent of the world's surface and thereby much of the world's peoples (Headrick, 1981, p. 3). This had been achieved, according to Parker, 'above all [by] their military superiority' (Parker, 1988, p. 154). In the process 'the settlement of new lands became gradually more aggressive and destructive for their original inhabitants' (Bayly, 2004, p. 434). Charles Tilly calculates that annual war fatalities almost doubled from the eighteenth through to the end of the nineteenth centuries, from 90 fatalities per million to over 150 (Tilly, 2003, p. 55). Between 1850 and 1864 the Taiping Rebellion, notes Barkawi, invited such a ferocious response that it devastated an area the size of France and Germany combined resulting in 20 million fatalities (Barkawi, 2006, p. 23). Little wonder then, as Howard observes, that the threat, rather than the deployment, of superior forces was sufficient in many contexts to advance the imperial project such that military power could be kept in reserve (Howard, 1984). In the 1840s the now Dominican Republic sought voluntary incorporation into Western rule while in 1874 Germany refused Togo's request for membership of the German empire (Doyle, 1986, p. 254). Captured by a geopolitical social imaginary, which portrayed world politics as a struggle for global hegemony through territorial acquisition, elites in Europe and beyond came to believe, by century's end, that the scope for such expansion was rapidly diminishing. Imminent 'global closure' accelerated and intensified the 'New Imperialism' as colonizers, and even the colonized, sought to ensure they were 'not left behind in the race for territory and influence' (Bartlett, 1984, p. 20). By the turn of the bloody twentieth century all the world's major regions and civilizations had become incorporated, under Western military tutelage, 'into a single set of economic and strategic relations'(Watson, 1992, p. 294).

If organized violence had been central to the construction of this singular global system, it was also the case, by the early twentieth century, that the social relations of organized violence had crystallized into an evolving world military order. There was a flourishing arms trade, dominated by huge corporations such as Krupps and Vickers, which was part of an emerging 'global, industrialized arms business'(W. McNeill, 1982,

p. 241). The technology of arms and military organization rapidly diffused across the globe while patterns of amity and emulation found expression in regularized and direct contacts between national military establishments. This was an era, as McNeill, labels it, of intensified global military–industrial interaction (W. McNeill, 1982, p. 274). As technologies shrank geographic space and time, potential enemies moved closer in so far as 'the easier it appeared to overcome distance the broader was the horizon that needed to be scanned for possible enemies and competitors' (Osterhammel and Petersson, 2003, p. 84). Preparation for war, and the transnational logistical and industrial production systems on which it depended, became permanent features of modern society and the world military order. Simultaneously, states increasingly sought both to monopolize control over, and to nationalize, the means and instruments of organized violence. Warfare became significantly more lethal, costly and potentially destabilizing. Britain recruited its last foreign mercenaries in the Crimean War while non-state organized violence, whether piracy or corporate military forces – such as those of the British East India or Royal Niger companies – were increasingly outlawed and subject to elimination (Black, 1998, pp. 203–05). In effect, the normative structure of this evolving world military order institutionalized the notion that modern states were defined principally by their claim to a monopoly over the instruments and the legitimate use of organized violence (Thompson, 1994).

By the twentieth century the world was strategically and economically integrated but politically divided into rival imperialisms. Relative peace and prosperity in Europe had been realized, in part, through military conquest and the subjugation, sometimes annihilation, of distant peoples. Yet for many liberal observers at the time, such as Norman Angell, this new *belle époque* represented a virtuous circle of growing interdependence, prosperity and the growing irrationality of war (Angell, 1933, orig. pubn. 1908). When conflict did break out in August 1914, the globalizing imperatives of industrial war soon became evident as the transnational mobilization for war bound together the existential security and fortunes of communities in both metropoles and colonies alike. If organized violence had principally been an instrument or means by which European states had manufactured a singular global system, the prosecution of total war constituted a dramatic medium through which the world's peoples came to recognize, and subsequently to contest, their shared fate. Whatever the historical partiality of the rise of the West narrative, there exists fairly broad agreement, paraphrasing Fernandez-Armesto, that 'Of all the influences . . . which brought the world's major civilizations into mutual touch, none was more dynamic than the impulsion to conquest, none more pervasive than war' (Fernandez-Armesto, 1995, p. 214).

Many contemporary histories of the global condition have revisited the interpretative framework and assumptions of the rise of the West narrative (Said, 1979; Fernandez-Armesto, 1995; Ferro, 1997; Frank, 1998; Cowen, 2001; Pagden, 2001; Black, 2002; Robertson, 2003; Bayly, 2004; Hobson, 2004). They have brought into question the Eurocentric view of the world which it presupposes, most especially since it ignores the central role of the East in the making of the modern world and the infrastructures of Western globalization, from trading networks to continental empires to trans-oceanic voyages of discovery. Rather than a linear narrative of the 'rise and rise' of the West, emphasis is given to the somewhat discontinuous and seriously contested nature of

European expansion in particular. Viewed from the *longue durée* Europe's global hegemony appears a process of secular territorial expansion. Yet, as Black and Fernandez-Armesto, among others, recount it was actually more than just fitful but suffered periods of major setbacks while at times its conquests were largely contingent, if not temporary (Fernandez-Armesto, 1995; Black, 2002). As Fernandez-Armesto notes, recent historiography suggests that 'European successes in the third quarter of our millennium, "western" world hegemony in the last . . . no longer seem the foregone conclusion for which they have been taken' (Fernandez-Armesto, 1995, p. 192–3). Nor too is the belief in Western technical and military superiority. Not only was much of this technology 'borrowed' from Chinese and Islamic civilizations but until the industrial age the West's economic, military and technical edge over other civilizations was far from conspicuous (Hobson, 2004). Well before Columbus had sailed, the Chinese Admiral Cheng-He commanded a fleet of 300 ships carrying 28,000 men to East Africa and Mecca (Rozamo, 2005, p. 150). Bayly too emphasizes that in the 1780s 'the Chinese Empire and the Ottoman Empire were still powerful, world-class entities' (Bayly, 2004, p. 2). Even as late as 1830 the East was still much more economically powerful and productive than the West: in 1750 China alone accounted for 33 per cent of world output compared to Europe's 23 per cent (Frank, 1998; Hobson, 2004, p. 76). Furthermore, in many parts of the world European conquest was achieved less through military superiority than as a consequence of local collaboration. At the zenith of European military power, 'In the last quarter of the century, when European imperialism was extended in earnest . . . it still depended almost everywhere on local abettors' (Fernandez-Armesto, 1995, p. 418). Microbes too played their part as soldiers and settlers spread 'Old World' diseases, decimating subject populations, with millions of fatalities in the Spanish Americas alone (Crosby, 2003, ch.2). By qualifying the rise of the West narrative, revisionist historians have demonstrated that the emergence of a singular global order was a much more polycentric, complex, and contingent historical process than many orthodox accounts suggest. Even so, there remains significant agreement, as Giddens notes, that it 'would be hard to exaggerate the significance for global history of the "armaments gap" which existed between the Western countries and the rest of the world throughout the nineteenth and early twentieth centuries' (Giddens, 1985, p. 226). Organized violence remains a vital component of the story even if Western military superiority only became decisive in the industrial age.

More controversial perhaps is identifying the primary impulses driving European conquest and expansion. Much has been written about the logics of empire and imperialism, and by implication historical globalization. Doyle makes a useful distinction between metrocentric, pericentric and systemic accounts (Doyle, 1986, pp. 22–35). Metrocentric accounts, whether economic or political, emphasize the endogenous sources of expansionism rooted in the socio-economic organization of metropolitan societies; pericentric accounts stress the endemic instability of the periphery – resulting from its structural location in the world economy – as a centripetal impetus for empire; and systemic accounts locate imperialism in the competitive structure of global power relations. Thus the 'New Imperialism' of the industrial age is variously explained as an inevitable consequence of (monopoly) capitalism (Hobson/Lenin), the product of an atavistic militarism (Schumpeter), crises on the periphery (Fieldhouse), or driven by the imperatives of hegemonic power politics (Kennedy; see

Doyle, 1986). Controversy thus abounds as to whether the globalization of organized violence is simply epiphenomenal (primarily an instrument of the expansionary imperatives of capitalism), a relatively autonomous militarist impulse, or one among other constitutive elements of a globalizing modernity. Within the historical sociology of international relations literature the emphasis is increasingly upon the latter, rejecting both cruder versions of historical materialism and realist power politics. The work of Mann, Giddens and Hobson, among others, considers organized violence and military power as one institutional cluster or power dynamic within (what Bayly refers to as) a complex parallelogram of social forces – economic, political, ideological – which can be said to have shaped the trajectory of world historical development (Bayly, 2004; Giddens, 1985; Mann, 1986; Hobson, 2002). For Giddens it is the interlocking dynamics of capitalism, industrialism, militarism, and statism which have given rise to a globalizing modernity while for Mann globality is conceived as a product of a complex configuration of social forces (Ideological–Economic–Military–Political) each with a distinctive logic (Mann, 1986; Giddens, 1990). This broadly neo-Weberian epistemology gives rise to a conception of globalization which stresses both its multiple forms – economic, political, military etc. – as well as multiple dynamics or complex causation. Organized violence is thereby understood not in epiphenomenal or instrumental terms, as solely a tool of capitalist globalization, but on the contrary as very much constitutive of it – a globalizing dynamic in its own right (Barkawi, 2004, 2006). This is readily apparent in the context of the barbarous twentieth century.

Commenting upon the history of organized violence, Tilly remarks that the twentieth century 'visited more collective violence on the world than any century of the previous 10,000 years' (Tilly, 2003, p. 55). From 1914, observes Hobsbawm, humankind has 'lived and thought in terms of world war, even when the guns were silent and the bombs were not exploding' (Hobsbawm, 1994, p. 12). Industrial war and geopolitical competition fuelled an unprecedented globalization of organized violence which claimed in excess of 187 million fatalities worldwide (Hobsbawm, 1994, p. 12). Modern warfare required permanent preparation for hostilities and the mobilization of entire empires and societies. Much later, with the arrival of the nuclear age, the ever present possibility that superpower confrontation could result in the annihilation of the entire planet reinforced the notion of humanity as a single, global community of fate – a *Schicksalsgemeinschaft*. The era of globalized conflict, or its ever present impending threat, had arrived.

The First World War demonstrated that war between great powers in the industrial age could no longer be confined exclusively to the combatants on the battlefield. As Klein remarks, 'war, once conducted by military geniuses on a battlefield of limited scope, had come to embrace whole continents and to involve citizens at the home front in the era of total warfare' (Klein, 1994, p. 55). Total war, even more so in the case of the Second World War, rapidly became a 'global human catastrophe' (Hobsbawm, 1994, p. 52). Hostilities raged across almost every single continent and ocean, while effectively few states could remain neutral since supplying the war effort of both the Axis (Germany, Italy and Japan) and the Allied powers (USA, Britain, France) required extensive worldwide sourcing. As McNeill confirms, 'transnational organization for war . . . achieved a fuller and far more effective expression during World War II than ever before' (1982, p. 356). Undoubtedly, the most profound consequence of this war was the demise of Europe's global hegemony as the USA and the Soviet Union asserted their global superpower status.

For nearly five decades following the end of the Second World War international politics was dominated by the rivalry between these two superpowers. World politics was fractured into two rival blocs each organized through competing systems of military alliances and regional security pacts. While the nuclear arms race made war between the two superpowers rationally unthinkable (but not necessarily improbable), East–West rivalry was displaced into Africa, Asia and Latin America. In turn, the process of decolonization and the struggle for national liberation became imbued with a Cold War military dynamic. Where direct intervention was eschewed, war by proxy ensued. As Europe's foreign military presence was reduced, that of the two superpowers expanded (see Harkavy, 1989). Even outer space and the underwater world of the oceans began to be colonized for military purposes. Technological advances in military logistics and communications systems delivered the possibility of rapid worldwide projection of enormous destructive power. Intercontinental missiles collapsed military decision times as war could be launched in hours rather than weeks or months. The Cold War constituted a unique system of global power relations which, paradoxically, both divided the globe into rival camps and yet unified it within a singular world military order. This involved extensive and intensive regional and global networks of military relations, surveillance and, for the superpowers at least, geographically extensive military infrastructures to project unparalleled destructive power across the globe. At the height of the Cold War, in the mid-1980s, world military expenditure (in constant 1987 US dollars) approached $1,000 billion per annum (almost $190 for every individual on the planet); spending on military hardware exceeded $290 billion, while the trade in arms amounted to over $48 billion (see Krause, 1992, p. 93; Sivard, 1991, p. 499). Some 120 countries were enmeshed in a global 'arms transfer and production system', producing, buying and transferring arms and military technology (Krause, 1992, p. 1). In his comprehensive study of technology and warfare, van Creveld concludes that this era 'differs from many previous ones in that a single, fairly homogeneous, military technology is recognized everywhere as dominant' (1989, p. 290). A 'global arms dynamic' developed as advances in military technology in the West and East diffused rapidly within the international system. Some forty years after Hiroshima there was not just one but at least six states with a nuclear weapons capacity. Moreover, with the proliferation of missile technology and the technology of weapons of mass destruction, many more states acquired a capacity to project unprecedented lethality. Both the evolution and diffusion of revolutionary military technologies eroded the distinctions between national and international security while simultaneously decoupling state security from human security. If the twentieth century marked the end of formal empires, it in no sense was associated with the demise or erosion of strategic globality – that is, the transworld projection, organization and social relations of organized violence. On the contrary, from the trade in Kalashnikovs to the threat of nuclear annihilation, the world appeared to constitute a singular *Schicksalsgemeinschaft*.

It would be seriously misleading, however, to argue that organized violence is associated solely with processes of global integration over the twentieth century. Ian Clark, among others, has written convincingly of the impact of world war and Cold War geopolitical rivalry on the dynamics of globalism (Clark, 1997). Not only has the globalization of organized violence been highly uneven, differentially integrating states and societies into the world system, but also both world wars were associated with the profound disruption, if not destruction, of global networks: a process of radical (if temporary) de-globalization (Clark, 1997; James, 2001). As James argues, the collapse of the first 'golden age' of globalization, the *belle époque*, was triggered signficantly, in part, by the First World War (James, 2001). In its aftermath the liberal order upon which this imperial globalization had been constructed succumbed to those social and political forces which had contested it all along; with the rush to autarky throughout the 1930s, this resulted in accelerated de-globalization (James, 2001). Subsequently the Cold War united the world strategically but divided it politically and economically, thereby containing and restricting both the pace and the scope of economic and other forms of globalization. It was not until after the collapse of the Berlin Wall, as Mandelbaum reminds us, that capital again acquired a truly global reach (Mandelbaum, 2004). This suggests a more complex or contingent association between organized violence and globalism in so far as the former may, under particular historical conditions, either facilitate or undermine the latter. Hardly surprising, then, that in the aftermath of 9/11 many concluded that this single act of transworld terrorism would trigger the end of globalism, or at least its most recent phase.

A New Dark Ages? Organized Violence and the End of Globalization

Writing after 9/11, John Gray proclaimed 'the era of globalization is over'(Naimi, 2002). Since then there has been a steady outpouring of works and commentary writing the obituary of globalism (Rosenberg, 2005; Saul, 2005). Much of this genre emphasizes the ways in which the advent of transnational terrorism, and the responses to it, prefigures a closing of borders, from the political to the cultural, as they increasingly become barriers to the mobility of goods, capital, and people. Since the same global infrastructures which enable the outsourcing of production also make possible the transnational organization of violence, it is hardly surprising that states will seek to limit their citizens' vulnerability by making borders, physical or virtual, more impermeable. This securitization of societies seems by definition to involve the reassertion of territorial power, thereby provoking a more generalized process of de-globalization: the end of globalism. Such a conclusion, however, presumes that globalization is a singular, rather than multidimensional, process and principally economically driven. It ignores the ways in which organized violence is itself constitutive of globality such that the events of 9/11 and the strategic response to them, especially in the form of the global war on terror, represent in Keohane's view a strengthening of 'one dimension of globalism – the networks through which the means of violence flow' (Keohane, 2002, p. 273). Moreover, even if measured in terms of trade, finance, production, migration or communication flows, there is considerable empirical evidence to suggest that economic globalization has proved much more resilient than many predicted, or even hoped. Composing an epitaph for globalization remains somewhat premature since in key respects 9/11 signally illustrated how orthodox assumptions about organized violence and territorial defence have become increasingly problematic (Keohane, 2002, p. 273; Rasmussen, 2002). In Keohane's view the 'barrier conception of geographical space, already anachronistic with respect to thermonuclear war . . . was finally shown to be thoroughly obsolete on September 11th (Keohane, 2002, p. 276).

A similar 'millenarianism' accompanied the demise of the Cold War. At the time there was a general presumption that it represented the end of strategic globality. Nye and Donahue comment that 'In the context of superpower bipolarity, the end of the Cold War represented military deglobalization' (Nye and Donahue, 2001). Regional rivalries reasserted themselves and the world appeared increasingly bifurcated into a zone of democratic peace and a pre-Hobbesian zone of state collapse and endemic violence (Goldeier and McFaul, 1992; Kaplan, 1994; Keohane, 1995). War, at least within the broadly Western core, appeared, as Mueller argued, virtually obsolete but beyond, in the borderlands or what Barnett refers to as 'the Gap' of exclusion and poverty, collective violence appeared an almost natural state of affairs (Barnett, 2004; Mueller, 1989; Keohane, 1995). For Kaplan, and van Creveld, among others, the world appeared to be on the brink of a new dark ages in so far as traditional interstate war was in decline but the deployment of organized violence, in the context of trans-state, intra-state and low-intensity conflicts, had reached historic levels (van Creveld, 1991; Kaplan, 1994). As van Creveld presciently observed in the early 1990s, 'As war between states exits through one side of history's revolving door, low intensity conflict among different organizations will enter through the other. Present day low intensity conflict is overwhelmingly confined to the so-called developing world. However, to think this will be so for ever or even for very long is almost certainly a great illusion' (van Creveld, 1991, p. 224). In the context of intensifying trans-regional flows of people, goods, arms and cultures, the notion that local conflicts or intra-state wars could simply be contained geographically has proved illusory, as the tragic events of 9/11 and 7/7 confirm. Rather than the emergence of a strategically bifurcated or regionalized world the post-Cold War era has been associated with the reassertion of a new narrative of strategic globality – in the form of the global war on terror – as well as awareness of global vulnerability.

Significantly, it was the assertion of US unilateral power, combined with the events of 9/11, that were critical factors in regenerating, despite the demise of the Cold War, a renewed awareness of the geopolitical unity of the world. As Cohen has remarked, 'The common fear of terrorism . . . had the effect of beginning to erode the divisions in the world geopolitical system that were so sharp during much of the last half of the twentieth century' (Cohen, 2003, p. 403). There are interesting parallels with the geopolitics of the early twentieth century in so far as the competition between the world's great powers for privileged access to, or control over, resources, markets and vital regions has acquired greater intensity in recent years. For some, especially in the wake of the invasion of Iraq and the various humanitarian interventions in the 1990s, this represents either a new imperialism or an intensified militarization of globalization. Yet such historical parallels require qualification since currently there is one sole military hyperpower, with the other major powers engaged in processes of bandwagonning and balancing, while power rivalries have been conducted (so far) without any direct challenge to the liberal world order, or resort to formal empire building. The attack of 9/11 and the responses to it have not fundamentally altered geopolitics, as some predicted, since it remains a struggle for advantage and dominance between the major powers rather than a clash of civilizations. There are good reasons to conclude that 'taken in the round . . . world politics does not seem to have been radically altered by 9/11' (Kennedy-Pipe and Rengger, 2006). That said, it is nevertheless evident that contemporary geopolitics, as in the late nineteenth century, is contributing to a heightened existential awareness of the world as a single arena of strategic competition. This has been reinforced by transformations in military organization and communications technologies.

Just as industrialization engendered a new mode of warfare, so too the communications revolution has been associated with a revolution in military affairs. Within the West strategic thinking has moved on from twentieth-century notions of total and limited war to fourth-generation or network-centric warfare emphasizing mobility, speed, accuracy, flexibility and lethality in the projection of force (Freedman, 2006). Although the friction of distance remains an important constraint upon the projection of force, 'it has been significantly undermined by revolutions in communications transport and military delivery systems' (Ferguson and Mansbach, 2004, p. 252). In the Kosovo campaign in 1999 the pilots of B2 bombers based in Missouri conducted their sorties abroad and returned to the comfort of their homes (Ferguson and Mansbach, 2004, p. 252). In the information age strategic globality has acquired a new meaning articulated in a new Western mode of warfare. Martin Shaw, inspired by Kaldor's earlier analyses of modes of warfare – the social relations and institutions which underpin the material production, organization, and deployment of military force – refers to it as 'global surveillance warfare' (Shaw, 2005, p. 62). Whereas industrialized total war in the twentieth century demanded or threatened the complete mobilization or destruction of societies, global surveillance war is conducted by largely de-militarized societies with limited objectives and precision force on the perimeters of the West (Shaw, 2005). It is a mode of warfare which, as evidenced in the campaigns in Kosovo and Afghanistan, relies upon global infrastructures of command, control, communication, logistics and military organization. It is a mode of warfare which has much in common with new globalized modes of post-Fordist production in terms of outsourcing, flexibility, just-in-time methods and decentralization. In many respects it represents not simply a response to military-technological change but also to transformations in the nature of strategic threats in a globalized world.

Paradoxically, the same global infrastructures which make it possible to organize production on a worldwide basis can also be exploited to lethal effect. Modern societies are extremely vulnerable to disruption of those complex systems which enable them to function effectively, from transport to banking. Although this has always been the case, it is perhaps compounded today because of greater reliance on vital foreign primary products (from food to oil), the transnationalization of production, and the critical role of communications and transport infrastructures. Whereas total war implied the 'destruction' of the enemy, and in the Cold War depended on maintaining a strategic deterrent, in contemporary circumstances modern societies are seriously vulnerable to those who, with minimal coercive capability, threaten or seek to disrupt, rather than destroy, them. Using the 'weapons of the weak', from box-cutters to home-made explosives, the potential for non-state groups to leverage their coercive power through the disruption, criminalization or terrorizing of societies presents a significant threat to civil and international order. Furthermore, the potential of this 'asymmetric warfare' is magnified for two reasons. First, because borders are no longer barriers, disruption of critical infrastructures by cyber-attacks or alternatively the perpetration of terrorist attacks can be organized effectively across distant regions of the globe (Lukasik, Goodman et al., 2003). Often the sources of collective violence are no longer necessarily rooted in the locales in which it is directly experienced, whether it be acts of terrorism in London or gang warfare on the streets of Chicago. Second, the proliferation of highly lethal weapons systems, not to mention technologies of mass destruction, radically alters the scale of potential threats. Asymmetric warfare, under conditions of globalization, transforms the potential threat environment confronting states such that distinctions between vital strategic regions and non-strategic regions no longer hold while orthodox notions of territorial security are made problematic. For if potential threats can be organized, resourced or directed from multiple sites across the globe, countering them requires more than simply domestic security measures but a global surveillance infrastructure. National security increasingly begins abroad, not at the border, since borders are as much carriers as barriers to transnational organized violence. Security, in different contexts, is being decoupled from a statist territoriality. This has become increasingly evident in relation to what Kaldor calls the 'new wars' – complex irregular warfare in the global South.

Organized violence remains a defining feature of the contemporary global condition. However, by comparison with previous epochs, particularly that of the early twentieth century, it has acquired a substantially different form and scale (Ferguson and Mansbach, 2004). Interstate war has been almost entirely supplanted by intra-state and trans-state conflict located in the global South, or on the perimeters of the West. If, as Mueller argues, interstate war is now obsolescent, organized violence nevertheless remains one of the principal sources of poverty, underdevelopment and civilian fatalities in areas throughout Africa, Asia and Latin America (Mueller, 2004). These so-called 'new wars' are primarily located in failing states and rooted in identity politics, local conflicts and rivalries. They involve complex irregular warfare between military, paramilitary, criminal and private forces which rages through, but often around and across, state borders with little discrimination between civilians and combatants (Duffield, 2001; Kaldor, 1999). The UN estimates, for instance, that 35 people die every hour across the globe as a consequence of irregular armed conflict (Keane, 2004, p. 8). This is a form of warfare which would be more readily recognizable to medieval warlords or shoguns than it is to a military schooled in total war. Yet these 'new wars', whether in Bosnia, Darfur or Venezuela, are curiously modern since they are sustained largely by the capacity of combatants to exploit global networks to provide finance, arms, émigré support, or aid as well as to facilitate profiteering, racketeering and shadow economies, such as the diamond trade, which pays for arms and influence (Duffield, 2001; Tilly, 2003; Kaldor, 1999).

Despite their apparently localized quality, 'new wars' are in fact a manifestation of the contemporary globalization of organized violence. They represent a mode of warfare which, according to Duffield, 'stands comparison with the manner in which Northern political and economic actors have similarly adapted to the pressures and opportunities of globalization' (Duffield, 2001, p. 14). The dynamics of such conflicts often generate complex humanitarian emergencies which rapidly draw in international and external agencies, fuelling demands for humanitarian intervention, as in Kosovo and Somalia in the 1990s. Significantly, as Duffield argues, 'the increasing interconnectedness of the global system has magnified the threat of the internationalization of instability in the South' (Duffield, 2001, p. 37). Several consequences flow from this interconnectedness: a convergence between global security and development objectives (as aid is tied to security, and security to development); and the emergence of global strategic complexes spanning the North–South divide in which the West seeks, through selective incorporation, the pacification of its turbulent frontiers. In effect, 'as disorder in one part of the world has combined with IT and the speed of travel to feed insecurity in another, security has become increasingly diffuse and borders more complicated to defend' (Avant, 2005, p. 33).

Global strategic complexes bind together the security of societies across the North–South divide. So too does the illicit global trade in arms, the operations of private security companies, organized crime, and transnational terrorist networks. Over the last five decades there has been a remarkable expansion in parallel transnational networks which operate alongside, through or beyond the formal military networks between states – the world military order. From the illicit trade in small arms or weapons technologies, such as the Khan network which supplied nuclear technology to Libya and Iran, to the operations of private security companies, such as Executive Outcomes which was employed by the central government in Sierra Leone in the 1990s to impose civil order, these parallel transnational networks represent the emergence of a burgeoning global market for force and the means of violence. Frederick the Great, as the commander of an army 50 per cent of whom were foreigners, would probably not find this a terribly novel situation. Historically such a market has always existed; however, as Singer and Avant among others emphasize, the end of the Cold War, the opportunities opened up by intensifying globalization, the privatization and commercialization of military production and services in the North, and the endemic disorder in several regions of the world, have combined to produce a huge expansion in the global market for force (Singer, 2003; Avant, 2005). In much the same way as production has been outsourced and globalized, so too have many aspects of organized violence. As Singer remarks, 'A new global industry has emerged. It is outsourcing and privatizing of a twenty-first century variety, and it changes many of the old rules of international politics and warfare' – and one might also add too the maintenance of peace (Singer, 2003, p. 9).

Globalization, commercialization and criminalization combined, it can be argued, highlight a major disjuncture between the distribution of formal military power and the distribution of effective coercive power in the world today. Al-Qaeda, the Triads, narcoterrorism and the illicit arms trade, which are very much part of what Keohane refers to as agencies of informal organized violence or what Ferguson and Mansbach call postinternational violence – that is, non-state, privatized, outsourced and globalized (Keohane, 2002; Ferguson and Mansbach, 2004). Transnational terrorist and criminal organizations, alongside those transnational social forces operating within the shadow global economy, have been able to exploit the infrastructures of globalization for their own illicit and destructive purposes. So much so that, some conclude, 'the transnational expansion of these dangerous trades has come to form part of the essential machinery of globalization' (Bhattcharya, 2005, p. 32). Domestic policing increasingly has a transnational dimension. Deadly violence on the streets of the world's major cities can often be traced to the distant actions of trans-state organized criminal and gang networks. Among realists and liberals schooled in Weber's classic understanding of the state as 'a human community that claims the monopoly of the legitimate use of violence within a given territory' this is profoundly unsettling (quoted in Ferguson and Mansbach, 2004, p. 232). Keohane poses the issue starkly: 'States no longer have a monopoly on the means of mass destruction: more people died in the attacks on the World Trade Centre and the Pentagon than in the Japanese attack on Pearl Harbor in 1941' (Keohane, 2002, p. 284).

In her historical study of the modern state and organized violence Janice Thompson describes both how, by the early twentieth century, states had purposively acquired a monopoly of force and how this became an international norm (Thompson, 1994). Although this was a generalized historical process, it was never entirely universal so that significant exceptions remained, while even the most advanced states relied upon the private sector for the production of the means of violence. Indeed, as Victoria Hui has recently written, the modern Western state historically has lacked the kind of centralized control of organized violence which defined the ancient Chinese state (Hui, 2005). Caution is therefore required in interpreting contemporary developments as necessarily denoting the generalized erosion or demise of the state monopoly of organized violence, which historically is the exception rather than the norm (Singer, 2003).

That there are in the order of 30,000 non-citizens in the US military or that private military companies have trained the military in 42 countries or that in 2004 there were 20,000 private security personnel from 60 different international firms operating in Iraq, are hugely significant facts. However, as Avant argues, the commercialization and globalization of organized violence compromises rather than erodes the state's monopoly of organized violence while its actual consequences vary among strong and weak states (Avant, 2005). Although in some contexts control over organized violence may be redistributed, in other contexts states are able to enhance the provision of security with no substantial diminution of control (Avant, 2005). Deudney makes a helpful distinction here in arguing that 'states have a monopoly on the ability to legitimize violence, but they do not have the ability to monopolize violence' (quoted in Clark, 1999, p. 119). Yet, as Leander makes clear, even the state's capacity to legitimize violence is partly conditional, witness the 2003 allied decision to intervene in Iraq, given international legal constraints and the growing contestation of such authority by non-governmental organizations (NGOs) and transnational social movements (Leander, 2002). Rather than automatically eroding the state's effective monopoly of force it is perhaps more accurate to conclude that a global market for force is both complicating the actual business of control while also normalizing the actual practice of private ownership of the means of destruction, that is, that organized violence is, or should no longer be, a public monopoly (Leander, 2002; Avant, 2004). One paradox is that this tends to erode the distinction between legitimate and illegitimate organized violence which is essential to the identity of the modern state and articulated every day in the global war on terror.

If the modern state's legitimate monopoly of organized violence is in question, then its autonomous capacity to produce the means of destruction, with the exception of a few cases, has become somewhat compromised in recent decades. Just as manufacturing production has become globalized so too has production of the means of violence, although in a more controlled and restrained manner due to the primacy of national security considerations. Sustaining or nurturing an autonomous national defence industrial base remains central to the very existence of the modern state yet in truth it is perhaps more the exception than the norm. Since the 1960s technologies of military production have become increasingly diffused around the globe, such that many more countries, beyond the USA and Europe, have developed the capability to produce missiles, advanced fighters and chemical and biological weapons systems. Moroever, with rapid industrialization has come the increased capacity of many states to manufacture an array of lethal weapons. The proliferation of technologies of weapons of mass destruction (nuclear, chemical or biological), whether to states or non-state organizations, remains too a critical global security problem because of the accelerated diffusion of knowledge and operation of illicit global networks. However, since the 1990s intensified rationalization and concentration within the defence industrial sector, in response to the end of the Cold War, has been accompanied by its significant transnationalization, such that, apart from the first tier arms producers (USA, UK, France, China) few other states can claim to sustain an autonomous defence industrial base (Skons 1994). As Bitzinger observes, 'The industry has undergone an unprecedented restructuring, both on a national and a global scale' (Bitzinger, 2003). A recent Swedish defence review acknowledged publicly that the country 'can no longer afford to sustain a national defence industry to the extent that this was possible in the past' while even Japan has recognized that *kokusanka* (autonomy) is unrealistic (Bitzinger, 2003, p. 53). For many countries beyond the first tier of high-tech arms production the national defence industrial base has become integrated into a broader global division of labour in arms production (Bitzinger, 2003). To a more limited extent this is also true of the first-tier producers, although they retain a singular capacity for military-defence innovation. Even so, as Bitzinger concludes, 'the bulk of arms production has become more of a global, integrated and hierarchical affair' (Bitzinger 2003, p. 81).

One popular metaphor for describing the current global condition is the 'new medievalism', or 'dark ages'. Drawn principally from Hedley Bull's classic analysis of the future of world order the 'new medievalism' describes for some the coming dystopia: a world unified in a struggle between opposing ways of life, in which political authority is highly fragmented, control over organized violence highly decentralized, and endemic conflict on the periphery steadily encroaching on the pacific core (Bull, 1977). This is the world of a globalizing modernity and resistance to it, in which control over the means of violence is becoming increasingly diffused, of permanent war for permanent peace, and in which states share political authority with public and private agencies astride, below, and aside from them. As a description, rather than explanation, of our times it captures elements of the current condition. But in several respects it exaggerates 'the coming anarchy' and overlooks the ways in which the zones of stability in the world are collectively managed and regulated without resort to violence or warfare. It leads to conservative and simplistic prescriptions for world order which stress the need for a single global Leviathan, or hegemon, to impose order, where necessary by the threat or use of force, or alternatively for some form of empire-lite. Moreover it interprets violence and disorder as an entirely novel consequence of globalization rather than as historically constitutive of it. New wars and terrorist violence may be unique manifestations of the globalization of organized violence but force and coercion historically have been integral to globalism from well before Genghis Khan and the conquistadores. What is perhaps historically distinctive is that distance no longer affords the kind of protection it once did for those in the citadels of global power from those who seek to resist or contest such power by violent means. In her cultural history of fear, Joanna Bourke remarks of the rise of combat fundamentalism 'the "new warfare" that had for many decades provoked terrorism in the Middle East, Africa and the former Soviet republics now threatened Americans and

Britons, fuelling a sense of fright that no one could avoid' (Bourke, 2005, p. 358). The world is neither witnessing the end of globalization nor does its apparently resurgent militarization prefigure a new 'dark ages' since historically globalism has always been constituted by and through organized violence.

Organized Violence and the Limits of Globalization Theory

Writing in the great age of Empire, Karl Marx commented that 'in actual historical conquest, enslavement, robbery, murder, in brief violence, notoriously play the great part' (quoted in Keane, 2004, p. 10). Classical theories of state expansionism or imperialism, whether liberal, realist or historical materialist, have a great deal to say about the centrality of organized violence to the making of the modern global order. By contrast many contemporary accounts of globalization tend to associate it with the making and diffusion of the democratic peace. Both literatures, in different ways, are deficient in explaining the unique historical configuration and the particular forms of contemporary globalized violence. A largely pacific core of capitalist states seems at odds with those classical and contemporary accounts which associate capitalist globalization with inter-imperialist rivalry and the inevitability of inter-capitalist conflict; military intervention on the periphery sits uneasily alongside liberal notions of the benign character of capitalist globalization, while the rise of globalized non-state violence and the decline of great-power war remain puzzling to realism. What is required, notes Barkawi, is a historical sociology of globalized violence: an account of organized violence which recognizes it as constitutive of globalization and vice versa (Barkawi, 2004). In short, an analysis which explicates the systemic interrelation of the dynamics of perpetual peace and perpetual war.

Classical accounts of imperialism have sought to explain the global social relations of organized violence. Hobson, Lenin and Bukharin identified monopoly capitalism as the principal source of imperialism, emphasizing the inevitability of great-power rivalry and war (Brewer, 1980). Others such as Kautsky, Hilferding, Angell and Schumpeter considered capitalism more pacific with the potential for generating zones of capitalist peace, or a form of ultra-imperialism (Brewer, 1980; Doyle, 1997). Central to these classical accounts, to varying degrees, is a certain economism in which war and peace are explained respectively either as the product of a militarized monopoly capitalism or a natural resultant of growing economic interdependence. This economism has left its mark on contemporary theorizing about globalization with liberal analyses tending to overlook globalized violence while historical materialists simply reinterpret economic globalization as a form of imperialism. Neither is satisfactory since organized violence, as already evidenced, is very much constitutive of globalization while, as Pieterse and Duffield among others argue, globalization and imperialism are distinctive transnational social formations (Duffield, 2001; Pieterse, 2004). As Pieterse comments, 'If the new imperialism of the late nineteenth century, the Cold War, neoliberal globalization and present times are all empire, in what resides the difference between these periods?' (Pieterse, 2004, p. 37). Globalization undoubtedly is a form of domination but even Bukharin recognized that not every form of domination could be considered imperialism (Bukharin 1917; (repr. 1976), p. 114).

Much contemporary theorizing about globalization replicates this economism. Orthodox liberal thinking, from democratic peace theory to liberal institutionalism, considers economic globalization as a primarily pacific force, generating conditions of systemic interdependence between democratic capitalist states and thereby democratic security communities within which organized violence becomes largely obsolescent (McGrew, 2002). The globalization of organized violence and the impact of economic (among other aspects of) globalization in provoking or exacerbating conflicts and violent struggles within different world regions remains largely unexplored (Barkawi and Laffey, 1999). By contrast, while much historical materialist, along with realist and neo-realist, scholarship has much to say about these latter issues, it provides a much less convincing account, or alternatively largely undertheorizes, the relationship between globalization and pacific capitalism, that is, the absence of great-power war (Brewer, 1980; Donnelly, 2000; Ikenberry, 2001). These complementary limitations reinforce the case for drawing upon other and more historical–sociological approaches to world politics which situate organized violence in its global systemic context, that is, a cogent historical sociology of contemporary globalized violence and warfare (Mann, 2001; Hobson, 2002; Shaw, 2005; Barkawi, 2006).

Within the historical sociology of international relations literature a strong case is presented for a multi-sectoral, multi-causal and structurationist account of global modernity or world historical development (Hobson, 2002; Hobson and Hobden, 2002). Drawing upon the work of, among others, Mann, Giddens and Tilly, global modernity is explained in neo-Weberian terms by rejecting the primacy of a singular determinate causal power, whether it be the forces of production or the forces of destruction, stressing instead its historical contingency, the product of a complex of causal forces – economic, political, technological, social, military etc. – crystallized in distinctive institutional contexts across space and time, thereby producing its distinctive national or cultural forms (Mann, 1986; Giddens, 1990; Tilly, 1990). This neo-Weberian ontology finds expression in many influential accounts of contemporary globalization in so far as they conceive it as a multi-centric, multidimensional and dialectical process which is a product of a complex parallelogram of social forces (Mann, 1997; Held, McGrew et al., 1999; Keohane and Nye, 2003; Bayly, 2004; Holton, 2005; Scholte, 2005). As such works argue, besides its vital economic, social, political and ecological dimensions, the martial or coercive dimension is central to explaining both the histories and dynamics of archaic and modern globalization. Organized violence, in its various statist and non-statist configurations, has been, and remains, constitutive of globalization. Moreover, understanding the globalization of organized violence requires understanding its relationship to other dimensions of globalization. Not only can one not simply be read off causally from the other but in different historical contexts one may well reinforce or alternatively constrain the development of the other. Thus organized violence was essential to the making of the *belle époque* but subsequently global warfare undermined it. Despite warnings to the contrary (to date) the global war on terror has little substantive impact on trade and capital flows (Scholte, 2005). Barkawi summarizes well this historical-sociological approach to the study of globalized organized violence: 'War is not only an example of globalization, it is one of the principal mechanisms of globalization, a globalizing force' (Barkawi, 2006, p. 92).

If organized violence is constitutive of contemporary globalization, it is also the case that economic, political and other dimensions of globalization are significant factors in the endemic disorder, conflict and violence which plagues many regions of the world. It appears somewhat curious to argue, as do many liberals, that economic globalization generates the conditions for a democratic peace among the affluent – although such a causal reading is probably spurious – but to ignore the ways in which either directly or indirectly it contributes to collective violence within global capitalism's borderlands. There is considerable evidence to suggest that economic globalization in particular has contributed significantly to the social, ethnic and political strains in many developing states and regions which have resulted in collective violence and 'new wars' (Duffield, 2001; Black, 2004; Kaldor, 1999). As Black concludes of collective violence on the periphery, 'Globalism . . . is one of the major causes, as it accentuates the possibility of conflict' (Black, 2004, p. 4). Equally, global infrastructures have undoubtedly sustained many such conflicts, from Zaire to Colombia, beyond what purely indigenous resources might permit. But in a globalized world such conflicts are difficult to contain, such that one of the contradictions of economic globalization may be to undermine the very conditions which sustain the democratic peace among the affluent. For, as Duffield observes, there is a growing 'fear of underdevelopment as a source of conflicts, criminalized activities and international instability' (Duffield, 2001, p. 37). Moreover, resistance to cultural globalization and Westernization has spawned considerable violence within and across states and societies North and South. To the extent that North and South are increasingly connected by flows of people, goods, images, weapons, microbes and illicit activities etc., the contingency and vulnerability of the democratic peace is robustly exposed. This is precisely why in recent years, even before the second Iraq war, the question of humanitarian and military intervention acquired such salience on the global political agenda (Wheeler, 2000).

Writing before 9/11, Scholte presciently observed that 'equations of globalization and peace might prove to be dangerously complacent' (Scholte, 2000, p. 211). As Kaldor, Duffield and Barnett, among others, argue, the long-term sustainability of the liberal peace depends upon recognizing the shared nature of security across the shifting borders of the North–South divide – the global political, economic and security complexes which bind together different human communities of fate (Duffield, 2001; Barnett, 2004; Kaldor, 1999). To date this has encouraged a securitization of development, especially in the wake of 9/11, as societies or social formations are selectively included or excluded from the formal infrastructures of globalization. The problem is that, even if excluded from these formal networks, it is almost impossible to exclude social forces from the parallel globalizations of informal and illicit networks. As Duffield observes, 'The networks that support war cannot be easily separated out and criminalized in relation to the networks that characterize peace; they are both part of a complex process' of global development (Duffield, 2001, p. 190). In key respects, precisely because of globalization, the zones of perpetual peace and perpetual war may be geographically discontinuous but materially, socially and existentially radically conjoined (Barkawi and Laffey, 1999). This leads to a 'recognition of the integral relations between developments in the (liberal democratic) core and elsewhere, and so prompts an analysis of the [global] system not as divided into zones of [liberal] peace and war but as a structured whole' (Barkawi and Laffey, 1999, p. 412) – a structured totality in which organized violence is deployed, by state and non-state forces, for 'the purposes of extending or defending liberal spaces both at home and abroad' or alternatively by those resisting and contesting such purposes, or advancing other ways of life (Barkawi and Laffey, 1999, p. 422). The globalization of organized violence and inherent violence of globalization remain, as in previous epochs, organically related.

New Rules for Waging War? Global Norms for Globalized Violence

The globalization of organized violence has reopened some of the principal normative questions surrounding the production, threat, means, deployment, or use of force in global politics. In particular the emergence of post-international violence raises issues of a substantive, procedural and institutional kind in respect of the continued relevance of established international norms regulating organized violence. Existing norms and laws of warfare, from just war to weapons prohibitions, were developed principally by, and applicable to, members of international society: namely states and their principal agents. Of course significant exceptions exist, such as the Nuremberg War Tribunals judgments which formally qualified the customary view that *raison d'état* provided a legitimate defence for individuals perpetrating war crimes or crimes against humanity. However, while elements of a cosmopolitan legal and normative structure can be identified in existing international juridical and normative regimes concerned with organized violence, structurally the order remains overwhelmingly state-centric. Globalization presents some significant challenges to this state-centrism most especially in relation to, among other matters, the agents, legitimacy, and control of organized violence, as well as posing fresh ethical dilemmas concerning the justified use of force. In certain respects, comment Ferguson and Mansbach, globalization has contributed to a legal and ethical paradox in so far as civilians have never been more protected by international legal and normative regimes yet the demise of formal wars means potentially they have never been so much at risk (Ferguson and Mansbach, 2004, p. 263).

One of most significant normative shifts is expressed in the institutionalization of the human security discourse – protecting and advancing the existential, material and developmental welfare of individuals and communities (Thomas, 2000; Newman, 2001). Human security, as a regulative principle of national and international order, represents a qualification to the claims of orthodox notions of state and international security. Since it privileges individuals and societies, it may not always cohere with the principles of national or state security while, in some circumstances, it may actually stand in opposition to them. Underlying the normative debate about human security, which has found institutional expression in the UN Commission on Human Security and in the global development–security complex, is a cosmopolitan philosophy which, as with the universal human rights regime, is in tension with the Westphalian statist principles which historically have informed the rules of world order. Cosmopolitanism privileges individuals and the conditions necessary for human flourishing. It emphasizes that in a densely interconnected world our ethical duties and responsibilities are not territorially bounded but on the contrary, given our shared fate, duties necessarily transcend borders. Innocuous as this may appear, it raises the profoundly difficult and controversial question as to whether such duties may require or can justify military intervention on humanitarian grounds: whether, in other words, globalization implies we have a moral duty to save strangers (Wheeler, 2000).

Humanitarian intervention sits uneasily with a Westphalian world order which privileges state sovereignty and territorial integrity. However, if in an interconnected world the problems of domestic insecurity, underdevelopment and violent conflict spill across borders and regions, the international community is necessarily confronted, as it was in Kosovo, Somalia and many other places, with the practical issue of whether or not to intervene. Similarly, globalization presents the international community with stark moral choices where governments may be engaged in crimes against humanity or significant abuses of their citizens. Although the ethical issue of duties beyond borders pre-dates contemporary globalization, it has become increasingly salient and pressing since complex emergencies are not only given immediacy by a globalized media but also the international capacity to intervene or ameliorate injustice is generally not in doubt. Globalization is not an ethical justification for saving strangers, since such duties can be said to exist irrespective of the intensity of worldwide interconnectedness, but it has undoubtedly made more urgent and politically salient the ethical debate concerning duties beyond borders, whether in relation to humanitarian intervention or global distributive justice (making poverty history) (Caney, 2005).

Beyond the matter of saving strangers the globalization of organized violence has destabilized other norms and regimes with respect to the regulation of force. In particular, the character of complex irregular warfare, such as that pursued by al-Qaeda, has generated ethical and legal uncertainty concerning the rationales and justification for preventive and pre-emptive war. Globalized informal violence also raises more fundamental questions concerning the normative and legal claims of states to a monopoly of legitimate violence, whether such claims are conditional or qualified, and whether or in what circumstances informal or non-state violence might be legitimate. Moreover the commercialization and privatization of organized violence raises serious questions about what norms and legal rules should apply to these forces and how they are to be governed (Singer, 2004; Avant, 2005). Already, in the absence of formal (national or international) public regulation, the governance of commercial military forces is developing independently within mixed (public–private) global regimes (Avant, 2005; Tripathi, 2005). One such regime is the Voluntary Principles on Security and Human Rights which has established and implemented a normative framework for the regulation of public and private security activities within the global extractive industry (Business Social Responsibility Council, 2005). The globalization and commercialization of organized violence combined with the rise of complex irregular warfare, not to mention transnational organized crime, are creating, some would argue, a radical decentralization of control over the use of force and with it the erosion of legal and normative restraints on collective violence (Leander, 2002; Ferguson and Mansbach, 2004, p. 245; Leander, 2004). Significantly, the indiscriminate use of violence which is eroding the effective distinction between combatants and non-combatants is but one major consequence of these developments. As Ferguson and Mansbach conclude, 'post international violence today commonly involves non-sovereign participants fighting for anything but reasons of state' and thus often effectively beyond normative and legal restraints on the use of force (Ferguson and

Mansbach, 2004, p. 272). In these respects the globalization of organized violence invites serious ethical deliberation about the substantive norms and legal principles which should inform the global regulation of collective violence and military force.

Conclusion: Bringing Organized Violence Back In

This chapter has sought to redress a significant silence in contemporary accounts of globalization, namely the general absence of any serious discussion of organized violence. It has argued that collective violence and military force have been integral to the making (and remaking) of globalization, both in the past and today. To paraphrase Charles Tilly, 'if war made globalization', as the discussion above has emphasized, 'globalization has also made war'. Organized violence is constitutive of contemporary globalization and globalization is constitutive of contemporary modes of organized violence. There can be no convincing account of the making and remaking of globalization without a recognition of the centrality of war and organized violence. Modes of production as well as modes of destruction are both essential to explaining the history and dynamics of globalism, from the archaic globalization of the seventeenth century to the polycentric globalization of the twenty-first. Bringing organized violence back onto the agenda of globalization studies is not so much a reaction to the events of 9/11 as an attempt to rectify the seriously distorted understanding of globalization produced by the primacy of economism and the cultural turn.

Understanding the globalization of organized violence is crucial to understanding the contemporary human condition. Whether that condition can be ameliorated or improved will depend significantly upon how the world community comes to terms with the globalization of organized violence. This, as Modelski identified many years ago, is the defining test of 'whether the large community, indeed the community of [human]kind, can be a good community' (Modelski, 1972, p. 56). To date, the prospects appear less than encouraging.

Notes

1 Organized violence refers here to the deployment and use of coordinated destruction or force ('acts of physical damage on persons and objects' (Tilly, 2003, p. 3), whether by state or non-state, military or civil organizations), while the globalization of organized violence refers to the trans or multicontinental production, projection, or diffusion of the instruments, organization, and threatened or actual use of coercive power.
2 A term borrowed from Osterhammel and Petersson referring to a global community of fate threatened by nuclear annihilation. See J. Osterhammel and N. P. Petersson (2003).

References

Angell, N. (1933; orig. pubn.1908). *The Great Illusion*. London: William Heineman.
Avant, D. (2004). 'The Privatization of Security and Change in the Control of Force,' *International Studies Perspectives*, 5: pp. 153–7.

Avant, D. (2005). *The Market for Force: The Consequences for Privatizing Security*. Cambridge: Cambridge University Press.

Barkawi, T. (2004). 'Connection and Constitution: Locating War and Culture in Globalization Studies', *Globalizations*, 1(2): pp. 155–70.

Barkawi, T. (2006). *Globalization and War*. Oxford: Rowman and Littlefield.

Barkawi, T. and M. Laffey (1999). 'The Imperial Peace: Democracy, Force and Globalization', *European Journal of International Relations*, 5(4): pp. 403–34.

Barnett, T. P. (2004). *The Pentagon's New Map: War and Peace in the Twenty-First Century*. New York: Putnam.

Bartlett, C. J. (1984). *The Global Conflict 1880–1970*. London: Longman.

Bayly, C. A. (2004). *The Birth of the Modern World*. Cambridge: Cambridge University Press.

Bhattcharya, G. (2005). *Traffick: The Illegal Movement of People and Things*. London: Pluto Press.

Bitzinger, R. A. (2003). *Towards a Brave New Arms Industry?* Adelphi Paper 356. London: IISS/Oxford University Press p. 102.

Black, J. (1994). *European Warfare 1660–1815*. London: University College London Press.

Black, J. (1998). *War and the World 1450–2000: Military Power and the Fate of Continents*. New Haven: Yale University Press.

Black, J. (2002). *Europe and the World 1650–1830*. London: Routledge.

Black, J. (2004). *War and the New Disorder in the Twenty First Century*. London: Continuum.

Bourke, J. (2005). *Fear: A Cultural History*. London: Virago.

Brewer, A. (1980). *Marxist Theories of Imperialism: A Critical Survey*. London: Routledge and Kegan Paul.

Bukharin, N. (1917; repr. 1976). *Imperialism and the World Economy*. London: Merlin Press.

Bull, H. (1977). *The Anarchical Society*. London: Macmillan.

Business Social Responsibility Council (2005). 'Voluntary Principles on Security and Human Rights.' Retrieved 15 January 2006, from www.bsr.org/voluntprincip.

Caney, S. (2005). *Justice Beyond Borders*. Oxford: Oxford University Press.

Clark, I. (1997). *Globalization and Fragmentation*. Oxford: Oxford University Press.

Clark, I. (1999). *Globalization and International Relations Theory*. Oxford: Oxford University Press.

Cohen, S. (2003). *Geopolitics of the World System*. New York: Rowman and Littlefield.

Cowen, N. (2001). *Global History*. Cambridge: Polity.

Crosby, A. W. (2003). *The Columbian Exchange: Biological and Cultural Consequences of 1492*. Westport, Conn.: Praeger.

Donnelly, J. (2000). *Realism and International Relations*. Cambridge: Cambridge University Press.

Doyle, M. (1986). *Empires*. Albany NY: Cornell University Press.

Doyle, M. (1997). *Ways of War and Peace*. New York: Norton.

Duffield, M. (2001). *Global Governance and the New Wars*. London: Zed Press.

Ferguson, Y. H. and R. W. Mansbach (2004). *Remapping Global Politics*. Cambridge: Cambridge University Press.

Fernandez-Armesto, F. (1995). *Millennium*. London: Bantam.

Ferro, M. (1997). *Colonization: A Global History*. London: Routledge.

Frank, A. G. (1998). *Re-Orient: Global Economy in the Asian Age*. New York: University of California Press.

Freedman, L. (2006). *The Transformation of Strategic Affairs*. Adelphi Papers 379. London: IISS/Oxford University Press.

Giddens, A. (1985). *The Nation-State and Violence*. Cambridge, Polity.

Giddens, A. (1990). *The Consequences of Modernity*. Cambridge: Polity.

Goldeier, J. M. and M. McFaul (1992). 'A tale of two worlds: core and periphery in the post-cold war era', *International Organization* 46(2): pp. 467–91.

Harkavy, R. E. (1989). *Bases Abroad: The Global Foreign Military Presence*. Oxford: Oxford University Press.

Headrick, D. R. (1981). *The Tools of Empire: Technology and European Imperialism in the Nineteenth Century*. Oxford: Oxford University Press.

Held, D., A. McGrew et al. (1999). *Global Transformations: Politics, Economics and Culture*. Cambridge: Polity.

Hirst, P. (2001). *War and Power in the 21st Century*. Cambridge: Polity.

Hobsbawm, E. (1994). *Age of Extremes: The Short Twentieth Century 1914–1991*. London: Michael Joseph.

Hobson, J. M. (2002). 'The Two Waves of Weberian Historical Sociology in International Relations', in *Historical Sociology of International Relations*, ed. S. Hobden and J. M. Hobson. Cambridge: Cambridge University Press, pp. 63–82.

Hobson, J. M. (2004). *The Eastern Origins of Western Civilization*. Cambridge: Cambridge University Press.

Hobson, J. M. and S. Hobden (2002). On the Road towards an Historicized World Sociology, in *Historical Sociology of International Relations*, ed. S. Hobden and J. M. Hobson. Cambridge: Cambridge University Press, pp. 265–86.

Holton, R. (2005). *Making Globalization*. Basingstoke: Palgrave.

Howard, M. (1984). 'The Military Factor in European Expansion', in *The Expansion of International Society*, ed. H. Bull and A. Watson. Oxford: Oxford University Press.

Hui, V. T. (2005). *War and State Formation in Ancient China and Early Modern Europe*. Cambridge: Cambridge University Press.

Ikenberry, G. J. (2001). *After Victory*. Princeton: Princeton University Press.

James, H. (2001). *The End of Globalization*. Princeton: Princeton University Press.

Kaldor, M. (1999). *New and Old Wars*. Cambridge: Polity.

Kaplan, R. (1994). 'The coming anarchy', *Atlantic Monthly*, 277: pp. 44–76.

Keane, J. (2004). *Violence and Democracy*. Cambridge: Cambridge University Press.

Kennedy-Pipe, C. and N. Rengger (2006). 'Apocalypse Now? Continuities or Disjunctions in World Politics after 9/11', *International Affairs*, 82(3): pp. 539–52.

Kennedy, P. (1988). *The Rise and Fall of the Great Powers*. London: Unwin Hyman.

Keohane, R. (1995). 'Hobbes' Dilemma and Institutional Change in World Politics: Sovereignty in International Society', in *Whose World Order?* ed H.-H. Holm and G. Sorensen. Boulder Colo.: Westview Press, pp. 165–86.

Keohane, R. O. (2002). 'The Globalization of Informal Violence, Theories of World Politics, and the "Liberalism of Fear"', in *Power and Governance in a Partially Globalized World*. London: Routledge, pp. 272–87.

Keohane, R. and J. Nye (2003). Globalization: What's New? What's Not? (And So What?), in *The Global Transformations Reader*, ed. D. Held and A. McGrew. Cambridge: Polity, pp. 75–84.

Klein, B. S. (1994). *Strategic Studies and World Order*. Cambridge: Cambridge University Press.

Krause, K. (1992). *Arms and the State: Patterns of Military Production and Trade*. Cambridge: Cambridge University Press.

Leander, A. (2002). 'Conditional Legitimacy, Reinterpreted Monopolies: Globalisation and the Evolving State Monopoly on Legitimate Violence'. Paper of Annual Convention of the International Studies Association – Panel on Legitimacy and Violence: Globalisation and the Displacement of the State.

Leander, A. (2004). *Eroding State Authority? Private Military Companies and the Legitimate Use of Force*. Rome: Centro Militare di Studi Strategici.

Lukasik, S. J., S. E. Goodman et al. (2003). *Protecting Critical Infrastructures against Cyber-Attack*. London: IISS/Oxford University Press.

McGrew, A. (2002). 'Liberal Internationalism: Between Realism and Cosmopolitanism', in *Governing Globalization*, ed. D. Held and A. McGrew. Cambridge: Polity, ch. 10.

McNeill, J. R. and W. H. McNeill (2003). *The Human Web: A Bird's-Eye View of World History*. New York: Norton.

McNeill, W. (1982). *The Pursuit of Power*. Oxford: Basil Blackwell.

McNeill, W. H. (1963). *The Rise of the West: A History of the Human Community*. Chicago: University of Chicago Press.

Mandelbaum, M. (2004). *The Ideas that Conquered the World: Peace, Democracy, and Free Markets in the Twenty-first Century*. New York: Public Affairs.

Mann, M. (1986). *The Sources of Social Power*, vol.1. Cambridge: Cambridge University Press.

Mann, M. (1997). 'Has Globalization Ended the Rise and Rise of the Nation-state?', *Review of International Political Economy*, 4(3): pp. 472–96.

Mann, M. (2001). 'Globalization after September 11th'. *New Left Review* 12(Nov./Dec.): pp. 51–72.

Modelski, G. (1972). *Principles of World Politics*. New York: Free Press.

Mueller, J. (1989). *Retreat from Doomsday: The Obsolescence of Major War*. New York: Basic Books.

Mueller, J. (2004). *The Remnants of War*. Ithaca, NY: Cornell University Press.

Naimi, M. (2002). 'Post-terror surprises'. *Foreign Policy*, 132: pp. 95–6.

Newman, E. (2001). 'Human Security and Constructivism', *International Studies Perspectives*, 2: pp. 239–51.

Nye, J. S. and J. D. Donahue. (2001). 'A World Interconnected by "Thick Globalism"'. *Working Knowledge*. Retrieved 18 May 2006, from www.hbswk.hbs.edu/item.jhtml?id=2571&t=globalization.

Osterhammel, J. and N. P. Petersson (2003). *Globalization: A Short History*. Princeton: Princeton University Press.

Pagden, A. (2001). *Peoples and Empires*. London: Weidenfeld and Nicolson.

Parker, G. (1988). *The Military Revolution*. Cambridge: Cambridge University Press.

Pieterse, J. N. (2004). *Globalization or Empire?* London: Routledge.

Rasmussen, M. V. (2002). 'A Parallel Globalization of Terror: 9–11, Security and Globalization', *Cooperation and Conflict*, 37(3): pp. 323–49.

Reddy, Sanjay G. and Thomas Pogge, 'How Not to Count the Poor' (29 October). Available at SSRN: http://ssrn.com/abstract=893159.

Robertson, R. (2003). *The Three Waves of Globalization: A History of Developing Global Consciousness*. London: Zed Press.

Robertson, R. (1992). *Globalization: Social Theory and Global Culture*. London: Sage.

Rosenberg, J. (2005). 'Globalization Theory: A Post Mortem', *International Politics*, 42(2): pp. 2–74.

Rozamo, P. (2005). *Zheng-He and the Treasure Fleet 1405–1433*. Singapore: SNP.

Said, E. (1979). *Orientalism*. London: Allen Lane.

Saul, J. R. (2005). *The Collapse of Globalism*. London: Atlantic Books.

Scholte, J. A. (2000). *Globalization: A Critical Introduction*. London: Macmillan.

Scholte, J. A. (2005). *Globalization: A Critical Introduction*. Houndmills, Basingstoke: Palgrave.

Shaw, M. (2005). *The New Western Way of War*. Cambridge: Polity.

Singer, P. W. (2003). *Corporate Warriors: the Rise of the Privatized Military Industry*, Albany, NY: Cornell University Press.

Singer, P. W. (2004). 'War, Profits, and the Vacuum of Law: Privatized Military Firms and International Law', *Columbia Journal of Transnational Law*, 42(2): 521–44.

Sivard, R. L. (1991). *World Military and Social Expenditures*. Washington: World Priorities.

Skons, H. W. (1994). 'The Internationalization of the Arms Industry', *American Annals of Political and Social Science*, 535 (Sept): pp. 43–57.

Thomas, C. (2000). *Global Governance, Development and Human Security*. London: Pluto Press.

Thompson, J. (1994). *Mercenaries, Pirates and Sovereigns: State-Building and Extraterritorial Violence in Early Modern Europe*. Princeton: Princeton University Press.

Tilly, C. (1990). *Coercion, Capital and European States AD 990–1992*. Oxford: Basil Blackwell.

Tilly, C. (2003). *The Politics of Collective Violence*. Cambridge: Cambridge University Press.

Tripathi, S. (2005). 'International Regulation of Multinational Corporations', *Oxford Development Studies*, 33(1): pp. 117–31.

van Creveld, M. (1989). *Technology and War: From 2000 BC to the Present*. New York: Free Press.

van Creveld, M. (1991). *The Transformation of War*. New York: Free Press.

Watson, A. (1992). *The Evolution of International Society*. London: Routledge.

Wheeler, N. J. (2000). *Saving Strangers*. Oxford: Oxford University Press.

2

Globalization as American Hegemony

G. John Ikenberry

Introduction

The post-1945 era is marked by two great developments: the emergence of an open world economy and the American construction of a hegemonic order. These global transformations in markets and geopolitics are deeply intertwined. Even before the end of World War II, American leaders championed the rebuilding of an open system of trade, investment, and currency convertibility. An open market system was seen as a necessary condition for stable peace and the realization of American interests – and, by the late 1940s, it was an important element of Cold War strategy. Likewise, the extraordinary explosion in trade and investment across the postwar advanced industrial world created a rising tide of prosperity and economic interdependence that reinforced the American-centered hegemonic order. It was a virtuous circle: America's postwar system of security alliances and multilateral institutions facilitated the expansion of world markets and, in turn, the expansion of world markets fueled growth and transformed the Western order into the dynamic and triumphant epicenter of world politics in the second half of the twentieth century.

That American hegemony and economic globalization are connected is not surprising. Economic relationships always bear the imprint of powerful states. At various historical junctures – such as after great wars and other upheavals in international relations – leading states are presented with unusual opportunities to shape the basic organization and rules of regional and global markets. Britain after the Napoleonic wars of the early nineteenth century and the United States after World War II are the most dramatic and far-reaching episodes of major states that have had the power and opportunity to build and manage the world economy. In very different ways, Japan and Germany in the 1930s also pursued strategies of building and asserting control over regional economic spheres. Whether the goal is to construct an open world economy or organize exclusive economic blocs, the economic goals that powerful states pursue tend to be closely tied to their more general political and security goals and wider geopolitical ambitions.

America certainly seized its moment of opportunity. In the years after World War II, the United States led the world in creating a far-flung liberal multilateral order and Cold War alliance system that still exists today. Between 1944 and 1951, American leaders engaged in the most intensive institution building the world had ever seen – global, regional, security, economic, and political. The United Nations, Bretton Woods, GATT, NATO and the US–Japanese alliance were all launched. The United States undertook costly commitments to aid Greece and Turkey and reconstruct Western Europe. It helped rebuild the economies of Japan and Germany. With the Atlantic Charter, the UN Charter, and the Universal Declaration of Human Rights, it articulated a new vision of a progressive international community. In all these ways, the United States took the lead in fashioning a world of multilateral rules, institutions, open markets, democratic community, and regional partnerships – and it put itself at the center of it all.

Sixty years after their rise, the two realms of order – American hegemony and an open world economy – remain linked even if their relationship is more complex and uncertain. The end of the Cold War and the rise of US unipolarity have reshaped the logic of American hegemony, while globalization has intensified and become less directly connected to the policies and geopolitical designs of Washington. American hegemony may or may not be a necessary support for an open world economy in the post-Cold War era. Indeed, it is possible that without the Cold War – which disciplined American power and tied capitalist states together in security alliances – the United States is today less willing or able to act in ways that reinforce the stability and openness of the world economy. In this sense, an open economy is less at risk from American hegemonic decline than from Washington's unipolar excesses.

This chapter examines the ways in which the United States – acting as a hegemonic power – shaped and influenced the emerging global economy and launched the world on a path of market globalization.[1] I argue that America's postwar hegemonic project was a decisive source of support for the reconstruction of an open world economy in the 1940s and the successive decades of expanding global economic integration. The United States had the interests and the tools to encourage the reopening of the world economy. The American dollar, security alliances, and institutional mechanisms for joint management of political economic relations have all been part of the hegemonic support for the world economy. American power was put at the service of creating a relatively open world economy but this was because an open world economy would in turn benefit the United States – its state, society, and national security.

I look first at the theoretical claims about the relationships between hegemony and the world economic system. I also look at the sources and manifestations of American hegemonic power as it relates to global market relations. After this, I explore a series of postwar episodes in which American power was brought to bear in the construction of the Western system and global markets. In the conclusion, I speculate on the changing – and increasingly uncertain – relationship between American unipolar power and a system of open markets supported by multilateral rules and institutions.

State Power and World Markets

Scholars have long been intrigued by the connections between powerful states and world markets. Charles Kindleberger's classic account of the origins of the Great Depression emphasizes the failure of the United States to provide the necessary leadership to keep markets open in the face of a spiral of protectionism and restrictive policies that shut down international trade and growth in the early 1930s. Britain's declining geopolitical and economic position meant that it was no longer capable of managing the world economy while the United States had the power to do so – but it did not yet recognize or act on its new role as leader and stabilizer. American leadership would have included resisting the protectionist temptation, opening domestic markets to distressed goods, providing counter-cyclical financing to trading partners, and making political and ideo logical appeals for economic openness (Kindleberger, 1986).

Building on Kindleberger's insights, Robert Gilpin provides the most elegant and systematic theoretical statement of this so-called hegemonic stability thesis. In surveys of British and American hegemonic eras, Gilpin traces the ways in which each of these leading states employed power to open markets and foster free trade. Britain in its era encouraged openness through reciprocal trade agreements, foreign investment, and ideological appeals backed by the gold standard and the Royal Navy (Gilpin, 1977).[2] The United States emerged from World War II in a stronger economic and military position – and rival industrial powers were defeated and lay in ruin. The United States was thus in a position to use the postwar settlement and the rebuilding and reintegration of industrial states to advance its vision of an open world economy. Gilpin also argues that the decline of hegemonic power tends to be associated with the unravelling of economic openness, as it appears to do in the case of the nineteenth-century Pax Britannica. This claim is widely debated in the literature – and in the case of the United States, it appears it is too early to tell.[3]

A central insight links hegemony to an open world economy. As Niall Ferguson summarizes it, the leading state "enhances its own security and prosperity by providing the rest of the world with generally beneficial public goods: not only economic freedom but also the institutions necessary for markets to flourish" (Ferguson, 2004, p. 34). In effect, a sort of grand bargain informs the relationship between the hegemonic state and other political-economic players in the system. The leading state opens its domestic market, constructs institutions and upholds rules, and seeks to manage crises and imbalances in the system. In the background, it provides security and stability. In return, other countries agree to operate within this order and provide resources and logistical support for the hegemon. Everyone is better off and world markets are open and integrated.

Seen in this light, the hegemonic construction of a system of market openness is part of a larger process in which power, order, and rules are reconciled.[4] Multilateral rules – across the realms of economics, politics, and security – become mechanisms by which the hegemon and other states can reach a bargain over the character of international order. The dominant state reduces its "enforcement costs" and it succeeds in establishing an order where weaker states will participate willingly – rather than resist or balance against the leading power.[5] It accepts some restrictions on how it can use its power. The rules and institutions that are created serve as an "investment" in the longer-run preservation of its power advantages. Weaker states agree to the order's rules and institutions and in return they are assured that the worst excesses of the leading state – manifest as arbitrary and indiscriminate abuses of state power – will be avoided, and they gain institutional opportunities to work and help influence the leading state (Ikenberry, 2001, ch. 3).

But why would the expansion of world market relations – and increased economic interdependence – serve the political and strategic interests of a leading state? There are several reasons. First, a leading state may calculate quite simply that an open world economy increases the nation's access to markets, technology, and resources, in turn fostering greater domestic economic growth and wealth and, ultimately, enhancing national security and state power. This basic logic informed the American proposals for rebuilding the world economy after 1945. The United States emerged from the war as the most advanced and productive economy in the world. Its leading industries were well positioned for global competition. An open world economy – organized around non-discriminatory multilateral rules – was an obvious national interest. American policy makers concerned with national economic advancement were drawn to a postwar agenda of trade barrier reduction and the promotion of global multilateral economic openness.

A second political-strategic interest that might prompt a leading state to pursue market openness and integration is the opportunity to influence the political and economic orientation of other states and regions. Specifically, a world economy divided into closed and rival regional blocs may be contrary to the economic and security interests of the leading state. During World War II, American postwar planners were in agreement that the United States could not remain a viable great power and be isolated within the Western hemisphere. The American economy would need to integrate itself into a wider pan-regional world economy. The war itself was in part a struggle over precisely this matter. German and Japanese military aggression was aimed at the creation of exclusive regional blocs in Europe and Asia. The American economy would thrive best in a world without blocs and its status as a leading great power depended on economic openness. World economic integration was a necessary condition for the American economy to prosper and open markets would prevent the return of 1930s-style economic blocs.[6]

Third, the promotion of open and integrated markets can also serve another political-strategic goal: creating close-knit or binding economic ties that help reduce power balancing and strategic rivalry. This might be called "strategic interdependence" – where the leading state purposefully tries to entangle itself and the other great powers in each other's economies. In its postwar policies toward Japan and Western Europe, the United States sought to foster stronger economic relations as a way to reduce the possibility that these states would become great power rivals. As the Cold War began to emerge, the United States was increasingly interested in stimulating economic growth in Japan and Europe – and it was willing to forgo full reciprocity in trade liberalization to see their economic prospects improve. But the United States also sought to influence the global pattern of trade and investment – particularly in regard to Japan – in a way that would tie these states more closely to the American economy. The United States wanted to bring non-communist Asia and Western Europe into the American-led "free world" and the promotion of economic linkages was part of this strategy (Gowa, 1993).[7]

Strategic interdependence was also pursued within Europe. The solution to the German problem after World War II was to economically integrate the allied zones of occupied Germany within the wider Western European economy. The celebrated European Coal and Steel Community – which created joint French and German ownership of basic war industries – embodied this strategic goal. Economic integration can create mutual dependencies that make autonomous and destabilizing security competition more difficult. The same logic reappeared more recently during the process of German unification when Germany agreed to tie itself even more fully to Europe through monetary union.

Finally, a leading state may promote economic openness and integration so as to promote the more general political evolution of states and international relations. American officials who embrace liberal beliefs about politics and economics had long anticipated that expanding world trade and investment would indirectly promote and reward movement by states toward liberal democracy – and a world of democratic states would reduce security threats and allow the United States to more fully realize its international goals. Trade and investment strengthen the private sectors of countries – empowering civil society as a counterweight to strong states – and creates vested interests within theses countries in favor of pluralistic political order and stable and continuous relations between states. This is the view most forcefully made by the American Secretary of State Cordell Hull during World War II. Free and open trade would not just stimulate economic growth but it would strengthen democratic regimes around the world and make war less likely. In Secretary Hull's words – "when trade crosses borders, soldiers don't."

These basic logics of grand strategy and economic openness and integration will be traced in the following sections as they were pursued by the United States and other great powers in the post-World War II era as well as today. What these episodes reveal is that the postwar construction of an open multilateral world economy was facilitated by American political and strategic goals that incorporated market tools and economic integration as part of the conduct of great power politics and postwar order building.

American Postwar Power and Interests

The United States emerged as a global power after World War II with both the opportunity and incentives to organize its environment in a way that would serve its long-term interests. Pre-eminent power gave it opportunities – other states were diminished by the war, the United States had grown more powerful. The old order had collapsed and its reigning ideas had been discredited. At the same time, the United States had new global interests. It was less able to secure its interests by isolating itself in the Western Hemisphere. It could rely on no other major state for protection or to uphold an open and stable order. Hence, American opportunities and interests.

Paul Kennedy nicely captures this new reality:

> Given the extraordinarily favorable economic and strategical position which the United States thus occupied, its post-1945 outward thrust could come as no surprise to those familiar with the history of international politics. With the traditional Great Powers fading away, it steadily moved into a vacuum which their going created; having become number one, it could no longer contain itself within its own shores, or even its own hemisphere. To be sure, the war itself had been the primary cause of this projection outward of American power and influence; because of it, for example, in 1945 it had sixty-nine divisions in Europe, twenty-six in Asia and the Pacific, and none in the continental United States. Simply because it was politically committed to the reordering of Japan and Germany (and Austria), it was "over there"; and because it had campaigned via island groups in the Pacific, and into North Africa, Italy, and western Europe, it had forces in those territories also. There were, however, many Americans (especially among the troops) who expected that they would be home within a short period of time, returning United States armed-forces deployments to their pre-1941 position. But while that idea alarmed the likes of Churchill and attracted isolationist Republicans, it proved impossible to turn the clock back. Like the British after 1815, the Americans in their turn found their informal influence in various lands hardening into something more formal – and more entangling; like the British, too, they found "new frontiers of

insecurity" whenever they wanted to draw the line. The "Pax Americana" had come of age. (Kennedy, 1987, p. 359)

The war itself had turned America into a global power with new internationalist interests. Its power now had global reach – and so it had opportunities to structure the wider world in a way few states ever do. At the same time, it confronted new geopolitical worries.

A profound American interest in an open, stable, and friendly geopolitical environment was made clear during the war within academic and postwar planning circles. The central foreign policy question that American experts wrestled with was defined by the specter of a world divided into competing great power blocs. The question was: could the United States remain a viable major state if its trade and access to resources were confined to the Western Hemisphere? From the perspective of the late 1930s – when Japan, Germany, Russia, and Britain each controlled or sought to control large portions of the world – this was a question of great urgency. In planning circles, the question was asked in terms of the "grand area" – that is, the minimum size of the world's territory that the United States would need to have access to and defend so as to remain a viable and growing great power (Santoro, 1992, pp. 92–6). The conclusion was that the United States could not remain isolated within its own region – it would need to be able to operate and defend sea lanes and outposts around the wider Eurasian landmass. The same judgment was reached by scholars, such as Nicholas Spykman, during the war as well (Spykman, 1942).

Operationally, this meant – at the very least – forging strategic relationships, building up democratic states, and balancing regional powers so as to ensure that no other major military state(s) dominated or gained hegemony in Asia or Europe. Importantly, this was a strategic goal the United States had – and its experts embraced – even before the Soviet Union emerged as a menace. It was America's globally updated version of Britain's centuries-old grand strategy of ensuring that no single great power dominated the European continent. In earlier decades – including in 1919 – the United States did not have the power, opportunity, or security imperative to reach out and organize Asia and Europe in this way.

Also during the war another group of American officials similarly defined the national interest in terms of the building of an open world economy. The most forceful advocate of this position was Secretary of State Cordell Hull. Throughout the Roosevelt presidency, Hull and other State Department officials consistently held the conviction that an open international trading system was central to American economic and security interests and fundamental to the maintenance of postwar peace. Hull agreed with the widespread view that bilateralism and economic blocs of the 1930s were the root cause of world political instability and the onset of war. Charged with responsibility for commercial policy, the State Department championed tariff reduction agreements, most prominently in the 1934 Reciprocal Trade Agreement Act and the 1938 US–British trade agreement. Trade officials at the State Department saw liberal trade as a core American interest that reached back to the Open Door policy of the 1890s.[8] In the early years of the war, this liberal economic vision dominated initial American thinking about the future world order and became the initial opening position as the United States engaged Britain and other states over the shape of the postwar international order.

From these various wartime perspectives, American officials articulated a common position. At the heart of the country's postwar grand strategy would be a systematic effort to open markets and integrate regions. The national interest necessitated the expansion and integration of the world economy. This was a view that united leading domestic business interests, liberal internationalists, and geopolitical strategists. How this goal would be achieved, however, remained highly contested at home and abroad – requiring political bargains with both European partners and American society.

American Hegemony and World Markets

America's pre-eminent position after World War II provided the structure and context in which a world economy took root and flourished. This power was manifest in many ways – military, political, and economic – and it was the not-so-hidden hand that built the liberal postwar order. The importance of American power in postwar order building was most evident in the occupation, rebuilding, and reintegration of Germany and Japan. American troops began as occupiers of the two defeated axis states and never left. Host agreements were negotiated that created a legal basis for the American military presence – effectively circumscribing Japanese and West German sovereignty – made necessary in the early 1950s by a growing Cold War. The Federal Republic was integrated into Europe and the Atlantic alliance. Japan was also brought into the American security and economic orbit during the 1950s. Japan and Germany were turned into twin junior partners of the United States – stripped of their military capabilities and reorganized as engines of world economic growth.

Behind the scenes, America's hegemonic position has been backed by the reserve and transaction-currency of the dollar. The dollar's special status gives the United States the rights of "seigniorage" – it could print extra money to fight wars, increase domestic spending, and go deeply into debt without fearing the pain that other states would experience. Other countries would have to adjust their currencies, which were linked to the dollar, when Washington pursued an inflationary course to meet its foreign and domestic policy agendas. Because of its dominance, the United States did not have to raise interest rates to defend its currency, taking pressure off its chronic trade imbalances. In the 1960s, French President Charles de Gaulle understood this hidden source of American hegemony all too well and complained bitterly. But most of America's Cold War allies were willing to hold dollars for fear that a currency collapse might lead the United States to withdraw its forces overseas and retreat into isolationism (Cohen, 1998).

In this "realist" postwar bargain, American security protection, its domestic market, and the dollar have bound the allies together and created institutional supports for a stable order and open world economy. Because the US economy dwarfed other industrial countries, it did not need to worry about controlling the distribution of gains from trade between itself and its allies. The United States has provided its partners with security guarantees and access to American markets, technology, and supplies within an open world economy. In return, East Asian and European allies have had incentives to be stable partners who provide diplomatic, economic, and logistical support for the United States as it leads the wider American-centered postwar order.

There is also a "liberal" bargain in the American hegemonic order. The array of multilateral institutions and security pacts are not simply functional mechanisms that generate collective action. They are also elements of political architecture that allow for states within the hegemonic order to do business with each other. In championing these postwar institutions and in agreeing to operate within them, the United States is, in effect, agreeing to open itself up to an ongoing political process with other democratic states. The liberal character of the hegemonic order provides access points and opportunities for political communication and reciprocal influence. The pluralistic and regularized way in which American foreign and security policy is made reduces surprises and allows other states to build long-term, mutually beneficial relations. By providing other states with opportunities to play the game in Washington, the United States draws them into active, ongoing partnerships that serve its long-term strategic interests. In effect, the political architecture gave the postwar order its distinctive liberal hegemonic character – networks and political relationships were built that – paradoxically – both made American power more far-reaching and durable but also more predicable and malleable (Deudney and Ikenberry, 1999).

Also behind the scenes, the American hegemonic order has been made more stable by nuclear weapons. Even if the other major powers were to lose interest in the postwar bargain, the possibility of seeking a wholesale reorganization of the system through great power war is no longer available. The costs are too steep. As Robert Gilpin has noted, great power war is precisely the mechanism of change that has been used throughout history to redraw the international order. Rising states depose the reigning – but declining – state and impose a new order (Gilpin, 1981). But nuclear weapons make this historical dynamic profoundly problematic. On the one hand, American power is rendered more tolerable because in the age of nuclear deterrence American military power cannot now be used for conquest against other great powers. Deterrence replaces alliance counterbalancing. On the other hand, the status quo international order led by the United States is rendered less easily replaceable. War-driven change is removed as a historical process, and the United States was lucky enough to be on top when this happened.

In these various ways, the United States urged upon the postwar world a hegemonic political structure that provided generalized stability, frameworks for cooperation, and the provision of security. The Bretton Woods system and the international role of the dollar provided the parameters around which trade liberalization and the re-establishment of market relations were launched. Within this emerging hegemonic order, the United States also took steps to help rebuild and integrate Western Europe and Japan. Cold War security imperatives and the establishment of an open Western world economy went hand in hand.

Promoting European Integration

American postwar strategic interests also led it to promotion of European political and economic integration – which at least indirectly provided further support for an open and integrated world economy. By 1947 it became clear that the Bretton Woods agreements would not be sufficient to get Europe on its feet and revive the world economy. Britain and the continental states were much more weakened by the war than American officials had realized and this meant that the United States would need to play a more direct role – and spend much more money – in supporting Europe than expected. At the same time, relations with the Soviet Union also deteriorated and this provided additional incentives to assist Europe and agree to more intensive economic and security relations. The Cold War served to draw the United States into a more active leadership of the world economy. It also gave the United States an additional reason to support European integration and agree to the building of Atlantic political and security institutions that in turn supported economic openness.

American support for a unified Europe emerged as early as 1947 as troubles with the Soviet Union grew and the vision of a "one world" order began to fade. As officials in the State Department began to rethink relations with Western Europe and the Soviet Union, a new policy emphasis emerged concerned with the establishment of a strong and economically integrated Europe – what some officials came to call a "third force" in postwar order. The idea was to encourage a multipolar postwar system, with Europe as a relatively independent center of power. The policy shift was not to a bipolar or spheres-of-influence approach with a direct and ongoing American military and economic presence in Europe. Rather, the aim was to build Europe into an independent center of military and economic power – overcoming the problem of postwar German power by integrating it into a wider unified Europe.

American officials championed the idea of a united Europe initially as the best way to strengthen the political and economic foundations of the postwar European states. The emphasis was not on the direct threat of Soviet activities in Western Europe, but on the war-ravaged economic, political, and social institutions of Europe that made communist inroads possible. An American effort to aid Europe would best be conducted not by directly fighting communism but by restoring European growth and living standards. State Department officials, for example, supported the creation of a multilateral clearing system in Western Europe which would encourage the reduction of trade barriers and eventually evolve into a customs union (Beugel, 1966, p. 43). The idea was to encourage the rise of a united and economically integrated Europe standing on its own apart from the Soviet sphere and the United States. "By insisting on a joint approach," Kennan later wrote, "we hope to force the Europeans to think like Europeans, and not like nationalists, in this approach to the economic problems of the continent" (Kennan, 1967, p. 337).

A unified Europe was also seen by American officials as the best mechanism for containing the revival of German militarism. Kennan held this view, arguing in a 1949 paper that, "we see no answer to German problem within sovereign national framework. Continuation of historical process within this framework will almost inevitably lead to repetition of post-Versailles sequence of developments . . . Only answer is some form of European union which would give young Germans wider horizon."[9] As early as 1947, John Foster Dulles was arguing that economic unification of Europe would generate "economic forces operating upon Germans" that were "centrifugal and not centripetal" – "natural forces which will turn the inhabitants of Germany's state toward their outer neighbors" in a cooperative direction. Through an integrated European economy, including the internationalization of the Ruhr valley, Germany "could not again make war even if it wanted to" (Pruessen, 1982, ch. 12). Likewise, the American high commissioner for Germany, John McCloy, argued that a "united Europe" would be an "imaginative and creative policy" that would "link Western Germany more firmly into the West and make the Germans believe their destiny lies this way" (Schwartz, 1991, p. 95). If Germany was to be bound to Europe, Europe itself would need to be sufficiently unified and integrated to serve as an anchor.

Encouraging European unity also appealed to State Department officials working directly on European recovery. In their view, the best way to get Europe back on its feet was through encouraging a strong and economically integrated Europe. The goal was also to increase the Western orientation of European leaders and to prevent a drift to the Left or the Right. This could be done not just by ensuring economic recovery but also by creating political objectives to fill the postwar ideological and moral vacuum. As one May 1947 document argued, "the only possible ideological content of such a program was European unity."[10] Other officials who were concerned primarily with a postwar open trading system were alarmed by the economic distress in Europe and saw American aid and European unity as necessary steps to bring Western Europe back into a stable and open system.[11] These views helped push the Truman administration to announce the Marshall Plan of massive American aid. The plan itself would be administered in a way to promote European unity. The idea of a united Europe was to provide the ideological bulwark for European political and economic construction. But disputes between the British and French over the extensiveness of supranational political authority and economic integration, as well as European unwillingness to establish an independent security order, left the early proposals for a European "third force" unfulfilled.

American support for European unification unfolded as the Cold War became a reality and Europe and the United States bargained over the shape of postwar order. In the first years after the war, American officials were eager to see the restarting of economic growth in Europe – which was important both as a hedge against political instability and support for communism and as a necessary step in the building of an open world economy. But to get growth in Europe, German industrial production and trade ties with the continent needed to be restarted. This in turn raised the question of how to reintegrate and reconstruct Germany without risking the revival of militarism and aggression. As conflict with the Soviet Union intensified, the rebuilding of the Western zones of Germany became all the more important. At each step, the answer was to bind Germany to the rest of the Western Europe. But to accept this solution to the Germany problem, the other states in Europe insisted that the United States play a direct security protection role. The reconstruction and integration of Germany and the American security commitment to Europe went together.

Britain and France both favored a direct security tie with the United States rather than make Europe into a "third force." The United States in turn argued that any American security commitment must be preceded by a European-wide security arrangement. The Brussels Pact established in 1948 among the Western European states set the stage for the North Atlantic Pact that followed a year later. But even this watershed agreement by the United States to make a solemn security commitment to Europe was seen by State Department officials as a way to bolster European confidence and willingness to unify. In this sense, American security support might best be seen as a continuation of the logic that was embodied in the Marshall Plan: the United States was encouraging the Europeans to build pan-regional political and economic institutions that would make Europe a more stable and peaceful pillar of world order.

Apart from containing the Soviet Union and rehabilitating Germany, the United States supported European integration because it would connect all the great powers of Europe together thereby undercutting nationalism and strategic competition. Regional integration would not only make Germany safe for Europe, it would also make Europe safe for the world. The Marshall Plan reflected this American thinking as did Truman administration support for the Brussels Pact, the European Defense Community, and the Schuman Plan. In the negotiations over the NATO treaty in 1948, American officials made clear to the Europeans that a security commitment hinged on European movement toward integration. American congressional support for the Marshall Plan was also premised, at least in part, on not just transferring American dollars to Europe but also on encouraging integrative political institutions and habits (Beugel, 1966; Lundestad, 1998).

The various elements of the settlement among the Atlantic countries fit together. The Marshall Plan and NATO were part of a larger institutional package. NATO was a security alliance, but it was also embraced as a device to help organize political and economic relations within the Atlantic area. The resulting European and Atlantic orders facilitated economic revival in Europe and expanding trade and investment between the two regions. American political and strategic interests continued to drive its policies toward the construction of a world economy but the bargains and institutional frameworks needed to make economic openness possible became increasingly elaborate and multilayered.

Bringing Japan into the World Economy

American officials traced the cause of war in Asia to Japan's forced establishment of a closed and restrictive economic bloc in East Asia. United States goals after the war were to eradicate Japanese militarism and regional domination and restore Nationalist China as a great power. As the Nationalist Chinese slowly lost their hold on the mainland, the United States shifted its strategy back to Japan. The occupation of Japan initially focused on introducing democracy and market reform to the country but, as the Cold War took hold in Asia after 1948, the emphasis shifted to policies that fostered economic growth and political stability. But throughout the early postwar years, American economic goals served larger political and strategic objects – and this was to integrate East Asia into an open world economy.

American diplomats did not entirely agree on how best to deal with Japan after the war. Some officials thought that militarism was only weakly rooted in Japan and therefore favored a relatively mild policy of eradicating militarism in the armed forces, constitutional reform, and reintegration into a multilateral world economy. But the actual American occupation force – led by General Douglas MacArthur – pursued a much more aggressive campaign to demilitarize and democratize Japanese politics and society and implant American-oriented principles and institutions.[12] The economic reform program focused on the dissolving of the *zaibatsu*, the highly concentrated financial and industrial combines that dominated the Japanese economy. In the American view, these giant industrial structures were directly behind both German and Japanese militarism and stood in the way of individual rights and liberties. The American occupation's attack on such structures – part of a broader campaign of the Truman administration to liberalize postwar economic institutions around the world – aimed to remove the economic sources of dictatorship and military aggression (Pollard, 1985, pp. 174–9).

In these early years, the American occupation did little to promote the integration of Japan into the world economy. Democratization and economic reform were pursued even as the domestic economy itself deteriorated. As late at 1947, industrial production and per capita income were still only half of the prewar level. The occupation forces also retained curbs of foreign trade and actually imposed more restrictions. The Cold War came later to Asia than to Europe and regional or global strategic objectives were less influential in the conduct of occupation policy than they were in Germany and Europe (Pollard, 1985, pp. 178–9).

The big shift in American policy occurred after 1948. The failure of economic reform in Japan, worries about political instability, the fall of China, and the growing strategic importance of Japan all contributed to a new policy orientation stressing economic growth and incorporation into the world economy. The State Department led the way in 1948 in stressing Japanese regional strategic importance and placing East Asia within the wider global containment order. George Kennan and other policy planners urged the relaxation of reparations, the easing of controls over political and economic institutions, and an end to efforts at industrial and financial deconcentration. In their view, the aggressive American reconstruction of Japanese politics and society was not working and it was risking political upheaval that could bring communists into power. The new emphasis was on encouraging economic growth and building the foundations for an ongoing American–Japanese security partnership.

In the following years, Japan was brought into the American security and economic orbit. The United States took the lead in helping Japan find new commercial relations and raw material sources in Southeast Asia to substitute for the loss of Chinese and Korean markets (Schaller, 1982). Japan and Germany were now twin junior partners of the United States – stripped of their military capacities and reorganized as engines of world economic growth. Containment in Asia would be based on the growth and integration of Japan in the wider non-communist Asian regional economy – what Secretary of State Dean Acheson called the "great crescent" in referring to the countries arrayed from Japan through Southeast Asia to India. Bruce Cummins captures the logic: "In East Asia, American planners envisioned a regional economy driven by revived Japanese industry, with assured continental access to markets and raw materials for its exports" (Cumings, 1993, p. 38). This strategy would link together threatened non-communist states along the crescent, create strong economic links between the United States and Japan, and lessen the importance of European colonial holdings in the area. The United States would actively aid Japan in re-establishing a regional economic sphere in Asia allowing it to prosper and play a regional leadership role within the larger American postwar order. Japanese economic growth, the expansion of regional and world markets, and the fighting of the Cold War went together.

The solidification of a strategic partnership between Tokyo and Washington drove American policy after the fall of China. Japanese officials arrived in San Francisco in September 1951 to sign a peace treaty with 48 countries and during the same visit Japan signed a bilateral security pact with the United States – anchoring the American security order in East Asia. It was only after the security partnership took shape that the economic integration of Japan into the world economy began. Throughout the last years of the Truman administration and into the Eisenhower years, American officials identified Japanese economic success with America's regional strategic interests. Unusual steps would be taken to boost Japan's economy and foreign trade. "The entry of Japanese goods into the United States should be facilitated," argued a National Security Council document in 1952. The United States was urged to "utilize Japan . . . as a source of supply on a commercial basis for equipment and supplies procured by US armed forces or under US aid programs for other countries."[13] Similar policies continued into the 1950s. The United States was willing to forgo fully reciprocal trade relations if it meant that Japan's economy would be bolstered and lead to the growth and stabilization of non-communist Asia.

It was only later that Japan was fully incorporated in the multilateral economic order. Despite American backing, Japan did not gain equal status in the General Agreement on Tariffs and Trade (GATT) from the European states until the late 1950s (Pollard, 1985, p. 187). Even more so than in Europe, the Cold War containment strategy drove the methods and terms by which the United States sought to expand and integrate markets in East Asia. The bilateral security partnership with Japan – and later a larger array of bilateral partnerships in the region – created incentives and a political framework in which the United States could stimulate economic growth and market relations. The United States identified its own national interest with the rising economic fortunes of its new allies. The Bretton Woods model of economic openness was supplemented – and to some extent replaced – by a world economy situated within regional security institutions and Cold War political partnerships.

The American military guarantee to partners in East Asia (and Western Europe) provided a national security rationale for Japan and the Western democracies to open their markets. Free trade helped cement the alliance, and in turn the alliance helped settle economic disputes. In Asia, the export-oriented development strategies of Japan and the smaller Asian tigers depended on America's willingness to accept their imports and live with huge trade deficits; alliances with Japan, South Korea, and other Southeast Asian countries made this politically tolerable.[14]

The alliance system – and the US–Japanese security pact in particular – has also played a wider stabilizing role in the region. The American alliance with Japan has solved Japan's security problems, allowing it to forgo building up its military capability, and thereby making itself less threatening to its neighbors. This has served to solve or reduce the security dilemmas that would otherwise surface within the region if Japan were to rearm and become a more autonomous and unrestrained great power. At the same time, the alliance makes American power more predictable and connected to the region. This too reduces the instabilities and "risk premiums" that countries in the region would need to incur if they were to operate in a more traditional balance of power order.[15] Even China has seen the virtues of the US–Japanese alliance. During the Cold War it was at least partially welcome as a tool to balance Soviet power – an objective that China shared with the United States. But even today, as long as the alliance does not impinge on China's other regional goals – most importantly the reunification with Taiwan – the alliance does reduce the threat of a resurgent Japan.

Germany and European Economic Integration

Political and security objectives also stood behind the building of the European Community and the push for regional economic integration throughout the postwar era. Many Europeans – and the United States as well – strongly believed that economic and political integration was essential if Europe was to prevent future war on the continent. This solution was seen to be particularly relevant to the relationship between Germany and France – the central great power antagonists in three European wars in less than a century. Economic integration and the construction of a regional political order were also seen by many as a way to safeguard postwar capitalism and democracy in Western Europe and ensure a stable role for the Federal Republic of Germany (FRG) after 1949. When the Cold War ended and Germany was posed for reunification, European leaders again emphasized economic and political integration as a means to stabilize the region in a new era of German dominance.

France's promotion of economic integration with Germany stood at the heart of its postwar security policy in Western Europe. French leaders had few strategic options. As it had after World War I, France again initially pursued a policy aimed at undermining the ability of Germany to rebuild its industrial and military capabilities. Reparations, disarmament, and permanent allied occupation of German industrial areas were elements of this balance of power strategy. But it was impossible to sustain such a policy – the onset of the Cold War, the necessities of economic integration to French revival, and pressures from allies all forced the search for an alternative security strategy. Tying Germany down in a web of European and Atlantic economic and security institutions emerged as the necessary solution to the problem of postwar European order.

This strategy of economic and political integration also appealed to German leaders of the new Bonn republic, including its first chancellor, Konrad Adenauer. By agreeing to bind itself to a regional economic organization and the Atlantic alliance, the FRG could create a more stable environment needed to foster domestic economic growth and the consolidation of democracy. German willingness to tie itself to its neighbors allayed fears within Europe of a resurgence of German militarism and aggression. Germany would not reconstruct itself as a traditional great power. It would be enmeshed in a web of regional economic and security ties that would institutionally restrain German power. A reconstructed and strong Germany would now be acceptable within Europe – something that became increasingly important as the Cold War heated up.

This strategy of binding Germany to Europe and creating an integrated European order unfolded in several steps. The European Coal and Steel Community (ECSC) – proposed by French foreign minister Robert Schuman in May 1950 and established in 1951 – was the earliest attempt at this strategy. Under this plan six countries – the FRG, France, Italy, Belgium, the Netherlands, and Luxembourg – agreed to put their coal and steel industry under supernational control. The short-term goal was to phase out the Allied control of the German coal and steel sectors managed by the International Ruhr Authority. But the longer-term goal was to tie postwar German industrial capacity to a wider European institutional structure. As Michael J. Baun notes, "Through the ECSC, the integration of rebuilding Germany into the Western community of democratic states could begin, and German industrial power could be harnessed to the anti-Soviet cause" (Baun, 1996, p. 12). Germany's heavy industries – the core of war-making capacity – were reconstructed in a European-controlled enterprise. Rather than balance against Germany or destroy its industrial base, France and Western Europe moved instead to bind Germany to the wider regional order.[16]

Just months after Schuman announced his plan for the ECSC, the French government came forward with a plan for a European defense community (EDC). The plan called for the integration of national defense forces and the creation of a European army under a unified command. The initiative embodied the same logic as the coal and steel community plan. France and other Europeans realized that German rearmament was increasingly inevitable under the strains of a mounting Cold War – in recent months , the Soviet Union had successfully tested an atomic bomb in 1950 and North Korea had invaded the South. The EDC was proposed to insure that German rearmament took place within a European institutional framework thereby making it less destabilizing or threatening to neighboring states. In the end, the EDC was never implemented and the French General Assembly voted it down in August of 1954. But an institutional framework was established with the founding of the North Atlantic Pact in 1949 and its subsequent evolution to include the permanent stationing of American troops in Europe, multinational forces, and an integrated command. As we noted earlier, this NATO framework provided the necessary binding assurances and commitments between Europe and the United States to allow German military rebuilding to proceed.

European economic integration took a decisive step forward in June 1955 when the six members of the ECSC met in Messina, Italy, and agreed to establish a Common Market through the elimination of all internal tariff barriers between them and the creation of a customs union for trade with non-members. This was the basis of the 1957 Treaty of Rome which established the European Economic Community (EEC). A tripartite institutional structure was put in place that built on the ECSC model consisting of an executive commission, a council of ministers, and a legislative assembly. The basic technique of economic integration that was pursued for most of the first two decades of the EEC was "negative integration" – it involved the creation of tighter economic links between member countries through the elimination of barriers to the movement of goods across national borders. Apart from the common external trade policy, the new economic organization did not pursue a significant "positive" integration strategy – involving the formation of common economic policies and the building of supranational institutions.[17] The Common Agricultural Policy, established in 1964 and entailing subsidies and a common external tariff on agricultural products, is a significant exception.

In the years that followed, the underlying logic of European integration – involving the stabilization of Franco-German relations – remained in the background as the member states maneuvered for advantage and negotiated over the terms of EEC enlargement. By 1968, the transition to the Common Market was complete. In 1973 Britain joined the EEC after over a decade of resistance by France. The following year, the members created the European Council to provide an intergovernmental mechanism for more direct and ongoing direction of EEC affairs by the heads of government. But during the 1970s the momentum of European economic integration was lost. The strategic goals that prompted the early economic links had been achieved.

Expanding the Democratic World Order

The relationship between American hegemony and a globalizing world economy evolved over the postwar decades. The direct connections between American geopolitical dominance and the management and expansion of the world economy loosened. American hegemony increasingly played simply a permissive role – reinforcing the overall stability of geopolitical relations among the major economic powers and removing security competition as a potential source of economic conflict. Conflicts between the United States and its European and Japanese partners did arise – such as those surrounding the oil shocks of the 1970s and trade disputes, particularly between the United States and Japan – but they were "contained" within postwar political institutions. The most significant way in which American hegemony facilitated global economic integration in the 1980s and after was in providing instrumentalities and strategic incentives for incorporating newly democratizing and liberalizing countries into the Western international order.

In the 1970s and 1980s, the alliance system and multilateral institutions remained intact but the rules and mechanisms for cooperation took new turns. Three shifts were most important. First, the breakdown of the Bretton Woods dollar–gold standard and the liberalization of capital markets opened the system to intensified foreign direct investment and capital flows. Foreign monetary rules declined in salience even as the volume of trade and capital flows continued to expand (James, 1996). Second, successive trade liberalization rounds – in particular the Tokyo and Uruguay Trade Rounds, conducted under the rules of the GATT – continued to reduce trade barriers and began to address non-tariff barriers to trade and investment. Third, the leading democratic states devised new institutional mechanisms to facilitate cooperation. The so-called G-7 process began in the 1970s as a regularized informal dialogue among finance ministers and heads of state and evolved over the decades into a more elaborate intergovernmental process (Hajnal, 1999; Fratianni et al., 2003).

The most dramatic expansion of the world economy during the 1980s was the rise and integration of the newly industrializing East Asian states – including South Korea, Taiwan, Singapore, Thailand, and the Philippines. Importantly, the rise and integration of these countries took place within an American-centered alliance system. The leading East Asian tigers were small, unthreatening, and (except Indonesia) allied to the United States. This American hegemonic framework was important in two respects. First, the growing prosperity of these countries was seen by American officials as a strategic interest rather than a threat. This meant that the United States was more likely to keep its own market open so that these countries could pursue export-led development. Economic gains in these small Asian states was seen as a positive-sum development, bolstering friends and allies and strengthening America's overall hegemonic position in the region (Gowa, 1993).

Second, the United States was in a position – as a security patron in the region – to help tip several of these countries toward democratic transitions. America's hegemonic position allowed it to give liberalization a push at critical moments. In South Korea in 1987, the military regime was facing mounting student demonstrations, and the United States persuaded the generals to hold their fire. In Taiwan in 1990, Washington signaled to the Kuomintang that if they held elections this would help relations with the United States.

In the Philippines in 1986, the Reagan administration helped get Marcos out of the country, paving the way for elections. To be sure, the United States has used its hegemonic security position to build partnerships with non-democratic states – and during the Cold War this was perhaps the dominant pattern. But the alliance relations do provide a special instrumentality that gave the United States leverage in countries and at moments when Washington wanted to restrain authoritarian governments or encourage democratization.

Overall, the Cold War-era relations and bargains remain critical to regional order – and they remain largely intact. The United States is even more powerful today than it was in the past, particularly with the ongoing economic malaise in Japan and the growth of America's new economy during the 1990s. The United States is still the world's leading military power. The United States also remains the leading destination for East Asian exports. (In the late 1990s, the United States passed Japan as ASEAN's largest trade partner). There is a wide array of regional vested interests – on both sides of the Pacific – in favor of open trade and investment. This creates powerful and ongoing incentives for the countries of the region to engage with the United States and encourage the United States to establish credible restraints and commitments on its power. The US government clearly is convinced that its security and political presence in the region is as important as in the past, despite the end of the Cold War.[18]

Conclusion

The global power structure and the globalized world economy are intertwined. In the postwar era, the American-centered security system served as the political foundation that supported the expansion of world markets. This hegemonic structure – liberal, institutionalized, open, and expansive – provided the political and strategic infrastructure for an explosion in trade and investment. It set the stage for remarkable shifts in the postwar world economic system. A defeated Japan rose from roughly 5 percent of American GNP in the late 1940s to almost 60 percent by the early 1990s. The smaller East Asia countries also grew rapidly, democratized, and integrated into the Western world economy. Europe integrated and pursued a decades-long project of political union – and it did so while continuing to expand trade and investment across the Atlantic. All of this took place inside the postwar American hegemonic system.

American hegemony facilitated economic globalization in a variety of ways. At one level, the United States provided security and stability across much of the non-communist world. Security dilemmas and rivalry were muted as the major industrial democracies bound themselves together in alliances under American auspices. Japan and Germany were transformed, integrated and rendered acceptable to the other democratic states in Asia and Europe. The Cold War struggle tended to reinforce and help legitimate American power – and so too did the economic success which followed. At another level, American hegemony mattered as it was manifest in the layer cake of multilateral institutions and functional regimes that were constructed in the 1940s and after. These institutions provided vehicles for the provision of public goods. They provided venues for negotiation, contracting, and the establishment of credible commitments – all necessary political processes as states attempt to open markets and integrate economies. At yet another level, American hegemony facilitated globalization in the specific and targeted ways in which it occupied defeated states and transformed trade and economic relations with Japan and the European great powers. The United States made costly commitments to Japan and Western Europe and leveraged its power to push these countries toward participation within an open and liberal international order.

Today American hegemony and globalization are entering a new phase. American hegemony has become more problematic and contested. The end of the Cold War made the United States and its allies less dependent on each other. The postwar bargains – both realist and liberal – are less robust. Likewise, globalization has in many ways transcended the postwar confines of the American political and security order. This is not to say that globalization no longer rests on a foundation of institutions, rules, and stable great power relations. But it is less clear today that American hegemony is the necessary provider of these institutions, rules, and stability. The global array of actors – states, firms, groups, and individuals – who have a vested interest in a stable and open world economy is massive and still growing.

But as hegemony and globalization decouple, two questions remain without certain answers. One concerns the importance of stable and non-competitive great power relations. One of the great functional features of the postwar American-led order was that security cooperation tied the major democracies together. The alliances ensured that the security of one was the security of all. Peace was indivisible. What happens if security competition returns in great power relations – that is, when peace becomes divisible? What happens if the alliance structure continues to erode and fall away? Under these more traditional great power relations – where balancing and security competition prevail – it could well mean that the rules and institutions that support globalization will also erode and fall away.

The other question concerns American hegemony. Without the Cold War, American power in the world is seen as more worrisome and less legitimate. The United States itself – as the world's only superpower – appears more ambivalent about its willingness to underwrite global rules and institutions. It appears tempted to go it alone more often or use its power to pursue narrow or parochial advantage. American hegemony may not be necessary to sustain globalization but a hegemonic state that rejects a rule-based international order can be a threat to globalization. These questions await the next cycle of history.

Notes

1 This chapter builds on arguments I present in Grieco and Ikenberry, 2003, ch. 5.
2 Gilpin generalizes this argument into a theory of international relations in *War and Change in World Politics*, 1981.
3 The larger literature on hegemonic stability theory argues that the presence of a single powerful state is conducive to multilateral regime creation. The hegemonic state – by virtue of its power – is able to act on its long-term interests rather than struggle over short-term distributional gains. This allows it to identify its own national interest with the openness and stability

of the larger global system. In Robert Keohane's formulation, the theory holds that "hegemonic structures of power, dominated by a single country, are most conducive to the development of strong international regimes whose rules are relatively precise and well obeyed." Such states have the capacity to maintain regimes that they favor through the use of coercion or positive sanctions. The hegemonic state gains the ability to shape and dominate the international order, while providing a flow of benefits to smaller states that is sufficient to persuade them to acquiesce (Keohane, 1980).

4   This argument is developed in Ikenberry, 2001.

5   For sophisticated arguments along these lines, see Martin, 1993; and Lake, 1999.

6   For recent explorations of the relationship between economic interdependence and great power politics, see Papayoanou, 1999; Skalnes, 2000; Barbieri, 2005; and Mansfield and Pollins, 2003.

7   Joanne Gowa argues that the United States had a Cold War strategic interest in promoting the growth of its allies so as to increase their ability to share the burdens of security competition with the Soviet Union.

8   On the State Department's commitment to a postwar open trading system, see Gardner, 1964 and 1969.

9   'Question of European Union', Policy Planning Staff Paper quoted in Schwabe, 1995, p. 133.

10 Quoted in Beugel, 1966, p. 45.

11 See 'The European Situation,' Memorandum by the Under Secretary of State for Economic Affairs, *Foreign Relations of the United States*, 1947, III, pp. 230–2.

12 For the definitive account of the American occupation of Japan, see Dower, 1999.

13 Quoted in Auerbach, 1993.

14 This argument is made in Gilpin, 2000, ch. 2.

15 I discuss this logic of 'security binding' in the next section.

16 French support for the ECSC was also driven by more practical and immediate commercial goals, such as gaining access to cheap German coal as an input to its steel production. The actual political and economic achievements of the ECSC are also widely questioned. See Gillingham, 1991; Milward, 1984, 1993; and Moravcsik, 1998, ch. 2.

17 On positive and negative integration, see Pinder, 1968.

18 See overview of US policies in economic and security areas during the 1990s in Mastanduno, 1998.

References

Auerbach, Stuart (1993). "The Ironies that Built Japan Inc." *Washington Post*, 18 July, A1.

Barbieri, Katherine (2005). *The Liberal Illusion: Does Trade Promote Peace?* Ann Arbor: University of Michigan Press.

Baun, Michael J. (1996). *An Imperfect Union: The Maastricht Treaty and the New Politics of European Integration*. New York: Westview Press.

Beugel, Ernst H. van der (1966). *From Marshall Plan to Atlantic Partnership*. Amsterdam: Elsevier Publishing Co.

Cohen, Benjamin (1998). *The Geography of Money*. Ithaca, NY: Cornell University Press.

Cumings, Bruce (1993). "Japan's Position in the World System." In A. Gordon, ed., *Postwar Japan as History*. Berkeley/London: University of California Press, pp. 34–63.

Deudney, Daniel and G. John Ikenberry (1999). "The Sources and Character of Liberal International Order." *Review of International Studies*, 25(2): pp. 179–96.

Dower, John (1999). *Embracing Defeat: Japan in the Wake of World War II*. New York: Norton.

Ferguson, Niall (2004). *Colossus: The Price of America's Empire*. New York: Penguin.

Foreign Relations of the United States (1947). III, pp. 230–2.

Fratianni, Michele, Paolo Savona and John J. Kirton (2003). *Sustaining Global Growth and Development*. Aldershot: Ashgate.

Gardner, Lloyd (1964). *Economic Aspects of New Deal Diplomacy*. Madison: University of Wisconsin Press.

Gardner, Richard (1969). *Sterling–Dollar Diplomacy: The Origins and the Prospects of our International Economic Order*. New York: McGraw Hill.

Gillingham, John (1991). *Coal, Steel, and the Rebirth of Europe, 1945–1955: The Germans and French from the Ruhr Conflict to Economic Community*. Cambridge: Cambridge University Press.

Gilpin, Robert (1977). "Economic Interdependence and National Security in Historical Perspective." In Klaus Knorr, ed., *Economic Issues and National Security*, Lawrence: Regents Press of Kansas.

Gilpin, Robert (1981). *War and Change in World Politics*. New York: Cambridge University Press.

Gilpin, Robert (2000). *The Challenge of Global Capitalism: The World Economy in the 21st Century*. Princeton: Princeton University Press.

Gowa, Joanne (1993). *Allies, Adversaries, and International Trade*. Princeton: Princeton University Press.

Grieco, Joseph and G. John Ikenberry (2003). *State Power and World Markets: The International Political Economy*. New York: Norton.

Hajnal, Peter I. (1999). *The G7/G8 System: Evolution, Role and Documentation*. Aldershot: Ashgate.

Ikenberry, G. John (2001). *After Victory: Institutions, Strategic Restraint, and the Rebuilding of Order after Major Wars*. Princeton: Princeton University Press.

James, Harold (1996). *International Monetary Cooperation since Bretton Woods*. New York: Oxford University Press.

Kennan, George (1967). *Memoirs: 1925–1950*. Boston: Little, Brown.

Kennedy, Paul (1987). *The Rise and Fall of the Great Powers: Economic Change and Military Conflict from 1500 to 2000*. New York: Random House.

Keohane, Robert (1980). "The Theory of Hegemonic Stability and Changes in International Economic Regimes, 1967–1977." In Ole R. Holsti, Randolph M. Siverson, and Alexander L. George, eds, *Change in the International System*, Boulder, Colo.: Westview Press, pp. 131–62.

Kindleberger, Charles (1986). *The World in Depression 1929–1939*. Berkeley: University of California Press (revised and enlarged edition).

Lake, David (1999). *Entangling Relations: American in its Century*. Princeton: Princeton University Press.

Lundestad, Geir (1998). *"Empire" by Integration: The United States and European Integration, 1945–1997*. New York: Oxford University Press.

Mansfield, Edward and Brian M. Pollins, eds (2003). *Economic Interdependence and International Conflict: New Perspectives on an Enduring Debate*. Ann Arbor: University of Michigan Press.

Martin, Lisa L. (1993). "The Rational State Choice of Multilateralism." In J. G. Ruggie, ed., *Multilateralism Matters: The Theory and Praxis of an Institutional Form*. New York: Columbia University Press, pp. 91–121.

Mastanduno, Michael (1998). "Economics and Security in Statecraft and Scholarship." *International Organization*, 52(4): pp. 825–54.

Milward, Alan S. (1984). *The Reconstruction of Western Europe, 1945–1951*. Berkeley: University of California Press.

Milward, Alan S. (1993). *The European Rescue of the Nation-State*. London: Routledge.

Moravcsik, Andrew (1998). *The Choice for Europe: Social Purpose and State Power from Messina to Maastricht*. Ithaca, NY: Cornell University Press.

Papayoanou, Paul A. (1999). *Power Ties: Economic Interdependence, Balancing, and War*. Ann Arbor: University of Michigan Press.

Pinder, John (1968). "Positive Integration and Negative Integration: Some Problems of Economic Union in the EEC." *World Today*, 24: pp. 88–110.

Pollard, Robert (1985). *Economic Security and the Origins of the Cold War, 1945–1950*. New York: Columbia University Press.

Pruessen, Ronald W. (1982). *John Foster Dulles: The Road to Power*. New York: Simon and Schuster.

Santoro, Carlo Maria (1992). *Diffidence and Ambition: The Intellectual Sources of U.S. Foreign Policy*. Boulder, Colo.: Westview Press.

Schaller, Michael (1982). "Securing the Great Crescent: Occupied Japan and the Origins of Containment in Southeast Asia." *Journal of American History*, 69 (September): pp. 392–414.

Schwabe, Klaus (1995). "The United States and European Integration: 1947–1957." in Clemens Wurm, ed., *Western Europe and Germany, 1945–1960*. New York: Oxford University Press.

Schwartz, Thomas A. (1991). *America's Germany: John J. McCloy and the Federal Republic of Germany*. Cambridge, Mass.: Harvard University Press.

Skalnes, Lars S. (2000). *Politics, Markets, and Grand Strategy: Foreign Economic Policies as Strategic Instruments*. Ann Arbor: University of Michigan Press.

Spykman, Nicholas J. (1942). *America's Strategy in World Politics: The United States and the Balance of Power*. Hamden, Conn.: Archon.

3

Globalization, Imperialism and the Capitalist World System

Alex Callinicos

Globalization: Transhistorical Process or Imperial Project?

The theme of globalization has already migrated from commentary on contemporary trends into more academic literatures. In the course of doing so, the tendency to treat it as a long-term historical process rather than a more immediate feature of the world at the end of the twentieth century has become more pronounced. Thus historians have sought to detach globalization from its original association with the progressive integration of the modern world economy and to trace the different forms in which human interactions have over the centuries transcended political boundaries, civilizations, and even continents.[1] Often these efforts have also aimed at decentring world history: C. A. Bayly, for example, has explored the theme of 'archaic globalization', by which he means the inter-regional and intercontinental impacts of the agrarian empires – Qing China, Mughal India, Togukawa Japan, Java, and the Ottoman, Romanov and Habsburg empires – that dominated much of the early modern world (Bayly, 2002 and 2004, ch. 1).

Such research is an instructive example of how present preoccupations may allow us to re-examine the past from a new, and often illuminating perspective. But the present also powerfully pulls us away from the idea of globalization as a transhistorical process. The specific geopolitical context in which globalization has come so to dominate both scholarly and more ephemeral discourse – the era since the Cold War drew to a close at the end of the 1980s – has provided a powerful impulse to conceive globalization, not as a secular tendency, but as a highly specific political and economic project represented notably by the neo-liberal policies of the Washington Consensus – deregulation, privatization, monetary and fiscal stability, etc. – and informed by the drive to maintain and even extend the position of the United States as the dominant global power. Already under the Clinton administration Peter Gowan developed a compelling interpretation of '[t]he American post-Cold War global project' as 'a search for new ways of brigading states under American leadership and of anchoring American economic ascendancy', including 'globalization: this involves the opening of a state's political economy to the entry of products, companies, financial flows and financial operators from the core countries, making state policy dependent upon developments and decisions taken in Washington, New York, and other main capitalist centres' (Gowan, 1999, pp. vii–viii).

The experience of the administration of George W. Bush, whose leading figures made no bones about their aim of entrenching US global primacy and their disdain for the constraints imposed by international institutions and coalition-building, has greatly reinforced the widespread perception of globalization as a technique of American imperial rule.[2] Such views are not confined merely to the left of the political spectrum. Niall Ferguson, an energetic Tory economic historian, has now devoted two books to the theme of what he calls 'Anglobalization'. The first celebrates the British Empire as 'an agency for imposing free markets, the rule of law, investor protection and relatively uncorrupt government on roughly a quarter of the globe' (Ferguson, 2004a, p. xxi). The second reiterates the case for 'liberal empire' (which Ferguson describes as 'the political counterpart to economic globalization'), namely that the 'only hope' for the 'failed states' of the world 'would seem to be intervention by a foreign power capable of constructing the basic institutional foundations that are indispensable for economic development' (Ferguson 2004b, p. 183). Ferguson considers the United States to be the only candidate for resuming the burden once borne by Britain of 'imperial globalization', even though he has doubts whether American political culture has the resources necessary to sustain such a role (Ferguson, 2004b, p. 193).[3]

Ferguson's 'case for liberal empire' depends on the major premise that 'economic openness – free trade, free labour movement and free capital flows – helps growth' and the minor one that such openness does not develop automatically but depends on the military and financial power of an imperial state (Ferguson, 2004b, pp. 183–4; see also Ferguson, 2004a, pp. xviii–xxiv). But, of course, many deny the major premise. Mike Davis, for example, has written a masterly historical study of the role played by the liberal imperialism steered from Whitehall and the City of London in producing the terrible famines that afflicted India, China and Brazil at the end of the nineteenth century (Davis, 2001). Nor is this merely of historical interest. The widespread perception that contemporary neoliberal economic policies have increased global poverty and injustice and accelerated the processes of environmental destruction has been the main motivation behind the emergence of a new movement against the contemporary forms of globalization at the very end of the twentieth century.[4]

Those who share this critique of neoliberalism are likely to view globalization as a less benign imperial project than that portrayed by Ferguson. Thus James Petras and Henry Veltmeyer argue that we must conceptualize globalization 'not in structural terms but as the outcome of a consciously pursued strategy, the political project of a transnational capitalist class, and formed on the basis of an institutional structure set up to serve and advance the interests of this class' (Petras and Veltmeyer, 2001, p. 11). The term 'globalization' should, they contend, be seen 'as an ideological tool used for prescription rather than accurate description. In this context it can be counterposed with a term that has considerably greater descriptive value and explanatory power: *imperialism*' (Petras and Veltmeyer, 2001, p. 12). The analytical virtues of the two concepts are indicated by what they respectively stress:

> The concept of globalization argues for the interdependence of nations, the shared nature of their economies, the mutuality of their interests, and the shared benefits of their exchanges. Imperialism, in contrast, emphasizes the domination and exploitation by imperial states and multinational corporations and banks of less-developed states and labouring classes. (Petras and Veltmeyer, 2001, pp. 29–30)

The course taken by world history since 11 September 2001 certainly confirms that any analytical framework that fails to find a proper place for conflict, domination and imperialism is of little use either intellectually or morally. Nevertheless, Petras's and Veltmeyer's suggestion that we effectively equate globalization and imperialism – or, more accurately, treat the former as an ideological construct that serves to mask the contemporary forms taken by the latter, while in many ways tempting, is unnecessarily restrictive. Two considerations serve to indicate why. First, Petras and Veltmeyer tend, in presenting globalization as an imperial project, to conceive it as 'intentional and contingent, subject to the control of individuals who represent and seek to advance the interests of a new international capitalist class':

> A survey of major events, world trade treaties and regional integration themes is enough to dispel any explanation based on technological determinism: it is the policy-makers of the imperial states who establish the framework for global exchanges. Within that shell, the major transactions and organizational forms of capital movements, supported by international financial institutions, whose personnel are appointed by the imperial states. (Petras and Veltmeyer, 2001, pp. 12, 30)

As in the case even of Gowan's more analytically sophisticated and empirically grounded interpretation, this view of globalization as 'a consciously pursued strategy' can easily lend itself to a conspiratorial view of world events. Now, as the manoeuvres of the neo-conservative wing of the administration of the younger Bush shows, conspiracies certainly do take place. But the conquest and occupation of Iraq amply demonstrate that conspiracies are liable go astray amid a concatenation of unforeseen consequences. To return to the case of globalization, the opening and integration of markets over the past generation undoubtedly has been made possible by the political interventions of networks of actors centred on what has come to be known as 'the Wall Street–Treasury–IMF Complex'.[5] Recognizing this is a crucial corrective to the commonplace view of globalization as an irresistible force of nature. But to *reduce* globalization to these interventions is surely to exaggerate the capabilities of undeniably powerful actors who are nevertheless dependent on structural conditions beyond their control or even understanding. This leads us to the second reason for refusing straightforwardly to equate globalization and imperialism, namely that this equation closes off any exploration of the ways in which long-term economic processes may facilitate or impede imperial projects. The rest of this chapter is, among other things, an attempt to show why such exploration may be of some help in understanding imperialism in its contemporary forms.

Capitalism and *la longue durée*

Before proceeding, however, some definitions are essential. 'Globalization' is understood here primarily as an economic process, increasing cross-border integration of production and markets. In adopting this definition, I do not intend to deny either the existence or the significance of the processes commonly described as political and cultural globalization: but, for my purposes here, economic globalization is what counts.[6] Michael Doyle succinctly defines empire or imperialism as 'effective control, whether formal or informal, of a subordinated society by an imperial society' (Doyle, 1986, p. 30). This broad defin-ition is intended to be of transhistorical scope. What brings together globalization and imperialism in the modern context is a third term – capitalism. My understanding of this concept derives from Marx's critical analysis of the capitalist mode of production in *Capital* – that is, of an economic system constituted by two fundamental features, the exploitation of wage labour by capital and the competitive accumulation of capital. In other words, under the capitalist mode, on the one hand, the immediate producers are denied direct access to the means of production and thereby compelled to sell their labour-power to the capitalists who do control these means on terms that lead to the workers' exploitation, and, on the other, the competitive interaction of rival capitals leads to the reinvestment of a large share of the profits that are fruits of this exploitation in the further development of the productive forces.[7]

From a Marxist perspective, the lens through which to view globalization is that of the historical development of capitalism as a world system. Immanuel Wallerstein offers a classic definition of the 'European world economy' that began to take shape in the late fifteenth and early sixteenth centuries:

> It was a kind of world system the world has not really known before and which is the dis-tinctive feature of the modern world system. It is an economic, but not a political entity, unlike empires, cities, and nation-states. In fact, it precisely encompasses within its bounds (it is hard to talk of boundaries) empires, city-states and the emerging 'nation-states'. It is a 'world' system, not because it encompasses the entire world, but because it is larger than any juridically defined political unit. And it is a 'world *economy*' because the basic linkage between the parts of the system is economic, although this was reinforced to some extent by cultural links and eventually . . . by political arrangements and even confederal structures. (Wallerstein, 1974, p. 15)

Despite the serious analytical weaknesses of Wallerstein's understanding of capitalism (to which I return below), he is quite right to underline the historical novelty of the modern capitalist world system. Various scholars have argued that this system was preceded by earlier world economies in which Asian societies played the dominant role. Janet Abu-Lughod, for example, has written a distinguished study of what she calls 'the Thirteenth-Century World System' – the circuits of trade and investment that between AD 1250 and 1350 bound together merchants and producers of luxury and manufacturing goods in a vast zone stretching from France to China, in which western Europe was a backward 'sub-system' peripheral to more advanced Asian civilizations (Abu-Lughod, 1989). One of the conclusions that Abu-Lughod draws is the error of portraying the subsequent 'rise of the West' as inevitable. This is certainly right: other historians have gathered powerful evi-dence that Europe and North America succeeded in economically outdistancing China, Japan and India only comparatively recently and for highly contingent reasons (see, for example, Pomeranz, 2000).[8]

It is, however, one thing to resist Eurocentrism, another to assert the existence of pre-modern world economies whose linkages were as powerful as those of the modern cap-italist system. An important question to be addressed in assessing the latter claim is whether the economic exchanges that bound together the great civilizations of medieval Eurasia had an intensity comparable to those that came to prevail with the irruption of modern capitalism. Robert Brenner offers one way of giving this question more precision. He argues that 'modern economic growth', that is, 'the presence in the economy of a *systematic* and *continuous* tendency or drive to transform production in the direction of greater efficiency', presupposes that economic actors, whether (in Marxist terms) exploiters or direct producers, are dependent on the market for their reproduction:

> It is only where the organizers of production and the direct producers (sometimes the same person) have been separated from direct access to the means of subsistence, that they *must* buy on the market the tools and means of subsistence they need to reproduce themselves. It is only where the producers must buy on the market their means of reproduction, that they must be able to sell *competitively* on the market, i.e. at the socially necessary rate. It is only in the presence of the necessity of competitive production – and the correlative absence of the possibility of cutting costs, or otherwise raising income, by forcefully squeezing the direct producers – that we can expect the systematic and continual pressure to increase efficiency of production which is the *sine qua non* of modern economic growth. (Brenner, 1986, pp. 24, 33)

Undoubtedly relatively large numbers of economic actors in Abu-Lughod's 'Thirteenth-Century World System' were market-dependent in the relevant respects. It is nevertheless open to question how deep these relationships went into the societies bound together by medieval trade circuits. Thus, to take a slightly later case, in Mughal India during the sixteenth and seventeenth centuries, undeniably an advanced civilization by the standards of the early modern world, in which local and international trade was comparatively developed, the dominant economic relationship was the extraction of tribute by the state from peasant smallholders – precisely the kind of forcible surplus-appropriation that Brenner argues gave pre-capitalist exploiting classes no incentive to promote greater economic efficiency (Habib, 1999; compare Brenner, 1986, pp. 27–32). Moving in the opposite direction chronologically, Chris Wickham sees the 'Roman world system' that economically bound together the Mediterranean in a web of exchanges during late antiquity as unified by the same kind of tributary relationship – more specifically, 'the fiscal spine' underpinning the flows of tax revenues and commodities to the imperial capitals of Rome and Constantinople: when this spine broke, in the fifth and sixth centuries AD in the West, and in the seventh century in the East, the Mediterranean world system fragmented, with many regions experiencing a decline in economic complexity. Consequently, as Wickham writes of the Byzantine empire, the state acted as 'a structuring device for all exchange activity, including commerce' (Wickham, 2005, ch. 11, quotation from p. 790). Held, McGrew and their collaborators suggest that pre-modern economic exchanges are best seen as a case of what they call 'thin globalization', characterized by '*high extensity, low intensity, low velocity, low impact*' (Held, McGrew et al., 1999, p. 25; see also pp. 22, 416). The qualitatively greater intensity and impact of modern globalization followed the incorporation of the great civilizations of Asia into the capitalist world system, with the catastrophic human consequences documented by Davis, as spreading market-dependence and Western colonial bureaucracies undermined the mechanisms for coping with dearth put in place by the pre-colonial tributary states and increased peasant producers' vulnerability to the fluctuations of weather systems and the global economy (Davis, 2001).

Giovanni Arrighi and his collaborators have developed the most compelling attempt to deploy the concept of the capitalist world system in a historically illuminating fashion.[9] Arrighi argues that history of this system is best understood as a succession of overlapping 'systemic cycles of accumulation', each characterized by 'the leadership of communities and blocs of governmental and business agencies' that promote specific 'strategies and structures' constituting a distinct 'regime of accumulation on a world scale' (Arrighi, 1994, p. 9). There have been four such cycles to date, each associated with the hegemony of a particular state – Genoa (1340s to $c.$1630), the Netherlands ($c.$1560 to 1780s), Britain ($c.$1740 to the 1930s), the United States (1870s to ?). Each systemic cycle has a universal form that Arrighi uses Marx's general formula of capital, M–C–M′ (the investment of money in the production of commodities that are then, thanks to the extraction of surplus-value in production, sold for a larger sum of money than that initially invested), to characterize:

> The central aspect of this pattern is the alternation of epochs of material expansion (MC phases of capital accumulation) with phases of financial rebirth and expansion (CM′ phases). In phases of material expansion money capital 'sets in motion' an increased mass of commodities (including commoditized labour power and gifts of nature); and in phases of financial expansion an increasing mass of money capital 'sets itself free' from its commodity form, and accumulation proceeds through financial deals (as in Marx's abridged formula MM′). Together, the two epochs or phases constitute a full *systemic cycle of accumulation*. (Arrighi, 1994, p. 6)

Within this framework, periods of financial speculation are 'a recurrent phenomenon' marking 'the transition from one regime of accumulation on a world scale to another', the decline of one hegemonic power and its regime and the ascent of their successors (Arrighi, 1994, pp. ix–x). Financial expansions replace material (or trade) expansions because the rate of profit on the production and sale of commodities inevitably falls, encouraging the investment of surplus money capital in speculation in financial markets. Each financial expansion begins and ends with a crisis of the dominant regime of accumulation, the first a 'signal crisis' announcing the beginning of a new cycle, the second the 'terminal crisis' marking the end of the old cycle. The US regime of accumulation experienced its signal crisis around 1970 (Arrighi, 1994, pp. 215–16). Arrighi now argues that the fatally misjudged invasion of Iraq in 2003 marked the beginning of the terminal crisis of this regime (Arrighi, 2005a and 2005b).

Arrighi and his collaborators have used this theory of systemic cycles of accumulation to develop some extremely rich analyses of specific conjunctures and patterns of development (for example, Arrighi, 1994, ch. 4, on 'The Long Twentieth Century'). Nevertheless, it is vulnerable to two criticisms applicable to all versions of world systems theory. The first was developed by Brenner in a classic essay (1977). He criticizes what he calls 'Neo-Smithian Marxism', which he associates not merely with Wallerstein but also with dependency theorists such as Andre Gunder Frank (for example, Frank, 1971). These theorists share the assumption, first stated by Adam Smith, that all that is required for a distinctively capitalist economic dynamic (involving the intensive development of the productive forces) to develop is the formation of a global market involving an international division of labour. One implication of this assumption is that what Brenner calls social property-relations (Marx's relations of production, i.e. relations of effective control over the productive forces) play only a secondary role in supporting this dynamic. Thus, for Wallerstein, the 'second serfdom' east of the Elbe and the slave plantations of the Caribbean – both forms of coerced labour producing for the world market – were simply 'modes of labour control' performing the same function in the 'periphery' as did wage-labour in the 'core' (Wallerstein, 1974, ch. 2).

It should be easy enough to see why Brenner should object to this conceptualization, given his argument cited earlier. Where exploitation is based on what Marx called 'extra-economic coercion', as it is in the case of slavery and serfdom, neither exploiters nor direct producers have an incentive to develop the productive forces, since they can gain access to the means of subsistence without having to go onto the market. Things change when both classes are dependent on the market. Capitalists have to compete to reproduce themselves and hence have an interest in reducing their costs of production (and there-fore the price of their products) through productivity-enhancing investments. But, even more important, it is only where the immediate producers themselves have no direct access to the means of subsistence – as is, above all, true of wage-labourers who have no control of the means of production – that they can be induced to cooperate in increasing pro-ductivity through a combination of market-based sanctions (ultimately, unemployment) and rewards (for example, higher wages for improved productivity). Hence the distinctive dynamic of 'modern economic growth' can only be sustained once, not merely the world economy, but capitalist property relations – and in particular the relationship between capital and wage-labour – have been fully constituted. Brenner accordingly argues that the decisive breakthrough came with the emergence of capitalist agriculture in early modern England: without the increases in food output that this made possible the factory labourers of the Industrial Revolution could not have been fed.[10]

The charge against world systems theory is, then, that, in reducing property (or production) relations to mere 'modes of labour control', it fails fully to grasp the histor-ical specificity of the capitalist world system, and in particular the way in which the market-dependence of exploiters and producers subjects them to the imperative of com-petitive accumulation. This helps to explain the tendency of this school to project world economies far back into the historical past – a tendency most fully realized by Frank, for whom world systems have existed for 5,000 years (for example, Frank, 1998). This is surely to stretch the concept of the capitalist world economy so far as to render it meaningless. The second major criticism explicitly thematizes this transhistorical quality of world systems theory: in portraying global history as the rise and fall of hegemonic powers world systems theory tends to efface the differences between distinct phases in the evolu-tion of the state system and impose a rigid pattern on contemporary history that is in fact absent.[11] One of the attractions of Arrighi's version of world systems theory is its sensitivity to the historical differences between the successive hegemonies it distinguishes (for example, Arrighi, Silver et al., 1999, ch. 2). Nevertheless, his commitment to the idea of cycles of systemic accumulation does confront him with difficulties when he considers the future of capitalism. Arrighi argues that American capitalism is on the way to a terminal crisis while a new regime of accumulation took shape in East Asia:

> Whether we are about to witness a change of guard at the commanding heights of the cap-italist world economy and the beginning of a new stage of capitalist development is still

unclear. But the displacement of an 'old' region (North America) by a 'new' region (East Asia) as the most dynamic centre of the processes of capital accumulation on a world scale is already a reality. (Arrighi, 1994, p. 332)

Initially Arrighi identified Japan as the driving force of this new 'dynamic centre': 'the Japanese multilayered subcontracting system has developed dynamically and expanded trans-nationally in a close symbiotic relation with the ascendant and highly competitive supply of labour of the East and Southeast Asian region' (Arrighi, 1994, p. 244: see also ibid., pp. 347–51). The obvious problem with this analysis is that in the 1990s Japanese capitalism sank into a protracted deflationary crisis while the US economy, supposedly on the way out, experienced an equally prolonged boom (Brenner, 1998 and 2002). Meanwhile, of course, the emergence of China as a major centre of capital accumulation has become one of the most salient facts of global political economy (Hore, 2004; Harvey, 2005, ch.5; Harman, 2006). In more recent versions of Arrighi's argument, the focus accordingly shifts away from Japan to 'the revitalization of the overseas Chinese business diaspora' (Arrighi, Silver et al., p. 149; see also ibid., ch. 4, and Arrighi, 2005b). As always, Arrighi has much of interest to say about the distinctive characteristics of East Asian capitalism, but the fact that his argument has to be reframed in this manner suggests a certain looseness of fit between his cyclical theory and the historical evidence – an impression that is reinforced when he seeks to explain away the Japanese crisis as a sign of strength rather than weakness (Arrighi, Silver et al., 1999, pp. 95–6).[12]

Arrighi himself identifies a further anomaly: 'Whereas previous transitions resulted in a greater *fusion* of world financial and military power under the jurisdiction of the rising hegemon than had been realized by the declining hegemon, the present transition has resulted in a *fission* under different jurisdictions of the two sources of world power' (Arrighi, Silver et al., p. 95). The following assessment of 'the peculiar configuration of world power that has emerged at the end of the US systemic cycle of accumulation' was written in the early 1990s, but it is as true of the presidency of the younger Bush as it was of the era of Reagan and Bush *père*:

On the one hand, the United States retains a near-monopoly of the legitimate use of violence on a world scale . . . But its financial indebtedness is such that it can continue to do so only with the consent of the organizations that control world liquidity. On the other hand, Japan and lesser 'islands' of the East Asia capitalist archipelago have gained a near-monopoly of world liquidity . . . But their military defencelessness is such that they can continue to exercise the near-monopoly only with the consent of the organizations that control the legitimate use of violence on a world scale. (Arrighi, 1994, pp. 352–3)

This 'bifurcation of military and financial power' (Arrighi, Silver et al., 1999, p. 96) is indeed one of the main features of contemporary global politics. But the fact that it marks an important deviation from the pattern that Arrighi claims to have discovered in earlier systemic cycles of accumulation suggests that this cyclical theory is too confining. The very rich concrete analyses that Arrighi and his collaborators have developed could be accommodated within a more roomy conceptual framework, one provided by the Marxist theory of imperialism.

Imperialism, its Phases and Future

From a Marxist perspective, imperialism is what happens when two forms of competition – the economic struggle among capitals and geopolitical rivalries between states –
fuse. Arrighi has drawn an analogous distinction between

> 'capitalism' and 'territorialism' as opposite modes of rule or logics of power. Territorialist
> rulers identify power with the extent and populousness of their domains and conceive of
> wealth/capital as a means or a by-product of the pursuit of territorial expansion. Capitalist
> rulers, in contrast, identify power with the extent of their command over scarce resources and
> consider territorial acquisitions as a means and a by-product of the accumulation of capital.
> (Arrighi, 1994, p. 33)

As a first approximation, these two logics of power can be seen as having their origins in
different modes of production. Marx argues that the 'laws of motion' of capitalism – the
tendencies distinctive to this mode of production, in particular, capital accumulation and
its consequences (greater economic concentration and recurrent crises of overproduction)
– become operative by virtue of the competitive struggle among rival capitals. Brenner
has suggested that, in pre-capitalist modes of production such as feudalism, the lords
could expand their income only by 'building up their *means of coercion* – by investment
in military men and equipment' that would allow them to seize land and peasants from
their rivals. 'Indeed, we can say the drive to *political accumulation*, to state-building, is the
pre-capitalist analogue to the capitalist drive to accumulate capital' (Brenner, 1986,
pp. 31, 32). In the politically fragmented conditions of late medieval Europe, political
accumulation provided the basic impulse behind the chronic condition of warfare, territorial expansion and political consolidation that provided the formative context of the
modern state system over five hundred years. But, as the capitalist world economy began
to take shape, economic and geopolitical competition increasingly intersected. Initially,
colonial ventures provided European rulers with resources to pursue their projects of
dynastic territorial aggrandizement. The first capitalist states, however, the United
Provinces and post-revolutionary England, enjoyed a selective advantage in these struggles thanks to their more dynamic economic bases, and thereby put the great absolute
monarchies under growing pressure to modernize, unleashing a destabilizing process of
political transformation that swept Europe into turmoil between 1789 and 1871.[13]

By the beginning of the twentieth century, two decisive changes had taken place. First,
a global economic space had been created that was increasingly dominated by capitalism
in its mature form – the industrial capitalism that, from its initial bases in northwestern
Europe and the North American Atlantic seaboard was spreading out to unify, dominate,
and transform the world (Hobsbawm, 1975). Secondly, political and capital accumulation
were now integrated into a single process. On the one hand, the 'industrialization of war'
compelled even the great European land empires – Germany, Austria-Hungary and
Russia – to promote the development of industrial capitalism within their domains if they
were to maintain their position in the state system (McNeill, 1983, chs 6–8). On the other
hand, the internationalization of trade and investment encouraged the increasingly large
and intertwined banks and corporations now dominating industrial capitalism to build

partnerships with their states in order to advance their global interests (Harman, 1991). As Arrighi puts it, 'the fusion of the territorialist and capitalist logics of power had gone so far among the three main contenders (Britain, Germany, and the United States) for world supremacy that is difficult to say which were the capitalist rulers and which were the territorialist' (Arrighi, 1994, p. 59).

Another way of thinking about these changes would be to say that competition among capitals now takes two forms – economic struggles for markets, investment sites, and resources, and military and diplomatic conflicts between states. It is important to understand this claim in a non-reductionist way: in other words, the thought is not that, with the advent of imperialism, states become instruments of capitalist firms. David Harvey puts it well when he calls 'capitalist imperialism' the 'contradictory fusion' of Arrighi's capitalist and territorialist logics:

> The relationship between these two logics should be seen therefore as problematic and often contradictory (that is, dialectical) rather than as functional or one-sided. This dialectical relationship sets the stage for an analysis of capitalist imperialism in terms of the intersection of these two distinct but intertwined logics of power. The problem for concrete analyses of actual situations is to keep the two sides of this dialectic simultaneously in motion and not to lapse into either a solely political or a predominantly economic mode of argumentation. (Harvey, 2003, pp. 26, 30) [14]

On the basis of this methodological injunction it is possible to distinguish three phases in the history of modern, that is to say capitalist, imperialism.[15] The first is that of what we might call classical imperialism (1875–1945). This is, of course, the era in which the European powers incorporated most of the rest of the world in their formal or informal empires. But this process of colonial expansion must be seen against the background of the more fundamental development highlighted by Arrighi: in this phase, economic and geopolitical competition were mutually reinforcing. By the beginning of the twentieth century, Britain, the European state with the strongest claim to be a global power, confronted Germany and the United States as both economic and geopolitical challengers: both countries had built up highly competitive manufacturing industries that broke Britain's position as the Workshop of the World, but both were also developing navies that threatened the key form of military power through which London knitted together its dispersed possessions and dependencies. Similarly, control over economic resources played a decisive military role in the two world wars that were the consequence of this triadic conflict: the importance of access to oil in shaping German and Japanese strategies during the Second World War is merely the most obvious illustration of this fact.

Allied victory in this gigantic conflict ushered in a second phase, what one might call superpower imperialism (1945–90). From a long-term perspective, the most important aspect of this era was a partial dissociation of economic and geopolitical competition. On the one hand, during the Cold War the world was effectively partitioned between two rival military and ideological blocs, led respectively by the United States and the Soviet Union. On the other hand, as Gowan emphasizes, this geopolitical struggle allowed the United States to brigade together the advanced capitalist states of Western Europe and Japan under its politico-military leadership. This allowed Washington to pursue its long-term strategic objective of preventing Eurasia from falling under the domination of a hostile state or coalition of states, but it also led to the formation of a transnational (though not yet geographically global) economic space (whose institutional conditions were secured by American-led bodies such as the International Monetary Fund – IMF) in which competition among capitals for markets did not, as it had in the previous era, lead to geopolitical rivalries. The growing competitive challenge to the United States from Japan and Germany brought an end to the long post-war boom at the end of the 1960s and ushered in a protracted crisis of profitability and overcapacity that continues till the present day (Harman, 1984; Brenner, 1998; Arrighi, 2003). The resulting political and economic tensions were not sufficient, however, to break up the Western bloc. This era also saw the end of the European colonial empires, but this transformation was facilitated by, and in turn promoted what Michael Mann has aptly called 'ostracizing imperialism' – the tendency for capital effectively to abandon large parts of Africa, Asia and Latin America as international trade and investment became increasingly concentrated within the advanced capitalist bloc itself (Mann, 2001, p. 54). The emergence of new centres of capital accumulation in East Asia and Latin America represented an exception to this trend. The growing size and weight of international trade and investment over the past generation – of which these rising economies have been major beneficiaries – have been the driving force behind greater economic globalization.

It is hard to find an apt name for the new imperialist phase ushered in by the end of the Cold War and the disintegration of the Soviet Union and its empire in 1989–91. 'Hyperpower imperialism' captures the most visible aspect, namely the unchallenged global hegemony of the United States. But, in many respects, this era involves an intensification of some of the trends that developed after 1945. The Western politico-economic space has become genuinely global with the incorporation of the former Communist states into market capitalism and institutions such as the WTO, NATO, and the European Union. The partial dissociation of economic and political competition within this space became even starker, as the eclipse of the USSR as the second (though always weaker) superpower and the information technology-driven 'Revolution in Military Affairs' gave the United States an overwhelming military advantage over all other powers singly or combined. But, as Arrighi's thesis of a 'bifurcation of military and financial power' underlines, the global economy is a genuinely multipolar field. Despite the hype about America's 'New Economy' during the 1990s, productivity levels in the United States and continental Western Europe are broadly comparable, and Brussels and Washington regularly clash over trade issues. China, Japan, and South Korea form a dynamic and increasingly interdependent economic region knitted together by huge flows of commodities and capital.

Probably the most critical question for the future of the planet is whether economic rivalries become geopolitical conflicts as well. Praise-singers for globalization have of course asserted the contrary since 1989, arguing that greater economic interdependence is washing away national antagonisms and proclaiming contemporary liberal democracy as 'the state without enemies'. But the very close links that bound together the world economy before 1914 were not enough to prevent the great powers unleashing a bout of hugely destructive wars and, in the interim, the partial disintegration of the world market during the Great Depression of the 1930s (James, 2001). Fortunately, nothing as terrible as this is in prospect. Nevertheless, 11 September 2001 and its aftermath have put paid to facile talk about the disappearance of national antagonisms.[16] Perhaps the best way to get the measure of the problem is to say that, while the end of the Cold War made possible the globalization of the Western-dominated transnational economic space, it also removed the most obvious reason why the United States should continue to be the hegemonic power within that space. Some American analysts have predicted that, with the discipline of the Cold War relaxed, Germany will assert itself as the regional hegemon in Europe, and China, if its economy continues its spectacular growth rate, in East Asia (for example, Mearsheimer, 2001). Gowan is right to argue that the policy of the Clinton administration was directed to containing these centrifugal tendencies, both by promoting neoliberal economic policies favourable to American investment banks and multinational corporations and by expanding NATO and the EU into East and Central Europe as a means of maintaining and extending the position of the US as the dominant power in Eurasia.[17]

The global strategy of the administration of the younger Bush is best seen as a different intervention in this same constellation of forces (Callinicos, 2003b). The seizure of Iraq in particular is a good example of how geopolitical and economic considerations tend to combine in imperial policy. In the first place, the demonstration of American military supremacy would serve to dramatize, not just for al-Qaeda and its sympathizers but also for potential geopolitical rivals, the high costs of contesting US hegemony. Secondly, a permanent American military presence in the Middle East would make it easier for Washington to address growing US dependence on imported oil and also give it an important geopolitical advantage. Harvey makes the point nicely:

> Europe and Japan, as well as East and South-East Asia (now crucially including China), are heavily dependent on Gulf oil, and these are regional configurations of political-economic power that now pose a challenge to US global hegemony in the world of production and finance. What better way for the United States to ward off that competition and secure its own hegemonic position than to control the price, condition, and distribution of the key economic resource upon which those competitors rely? And what better way to do this than to use the one line of force where the US remains all-powerful – military might? (Harvey, 2003, p. 25)

Thirdly, the polarization between 'Old' and 'New' Europe over the Iraq War seemed to reflect a significant policy shift, in which Washington now proclaimed the expanding and integrating EU as a potential rival that needed to be kept under control through the open use of divide-and-rule. It is probably this aspect of the Bush administration's policy that has been most strongly contested within the American establishment, particularly as it became clear that the military capabilities sufficient to seize Iraq were not the same as those required to hold it (see, for example, Mann, 2003). Zbigniew Brzezinski has been particularly forthright in his criticism of the geopolitical incompetence of Bush and his advisers and in his insistence that a stable US hegemony depended, not on trying to split the EU, but on incorporating it as Washington's junior partner in 'global leadership' (Brzezinski, 2004).[18] The outcome of these strategic debates depends on factors too concrete to be addressed at this level of generality, but Brzezinski's own analysis highlights the fragility of the present global conjuncture, not merely in the Middle East, but also in

East Asia, where a relatively minor shift in the regional balance of forces could unleash a nuclear arms race that would bring Japan, whose strategic partnership with the United States has grown stronger in recent years, into confrontation with China, with South Korea increasingly aligned with the latter, despite the economic flows that have drawn these four states together (Brzezinski, 2004, pp. 107–23).

The geopolitical fragility of East Asia is particularly telling when we consider that the symbiotic relationship between this region and the United States is critical to keeping the world economy afloat. China, Japan and South Korea export vast quantities of relatively cheap goods to the United States. These countries' governments then lend back many of the dollars they earn to the United States, allowing it to carry on buying their exports and keeping their own currencies relatively low against the dollar and thereby maintaining their ability to compete. This growth nexus then provides markets for the manufactured goods of Europe and the raw materials of Russia, the Middle East, Latin America, and Africa. But, not simply could interstate conflict within this region seriously escalate, but, despite the improvement in relations between Washington and Beijing since 9/11, many in the US security establishment continue to regard China as the most serious medium-term threat to American global interests – a judgement that is reflected in the Pentagon's policy of mounting huge naval exercises in the Pacific, such as 'Summer Pulse 04', which deployed an unprecedented 7 out of 12 US carrier strike groups off the Chinese coast.[19]

Such displays of American military power invite reflection on the sources of US global hegemony. In confronting America with a choice between 'global domination' and 'global leadership', Brzezinski interestingly (but presumably unconsciously) reproduces Antonio Gramsci's famous distinction between two dimensions of ruling-class hegemony – purely coercive 'domination' and the 'moral and intellectual leadership' without which stable class rule is unsustainable (Gramsci, 1971, pp. 55ff.). Various Marxist writers have sought to extend this distinction to the global scale. Arrighi, for example, argues that 'leadership in an international context' requires that 'a dominant state becomes the "model" for other states to emulate' and that it demonstrates that it has the capability and will to 'address system-level problems' (Arrighi, Silver et al., 1999, pp. 22, 27, 28; see also Harvey, 2003, pp. 36ff.). He has also suggested that the United States today is in a position of what Ranajit Guha has called 'domination without hegemony' (Arrighi, 2004, p. 12; see also Arrighi, 2005a and 2005b). Along somewhat parallel lines Walden Bello has argued that the dominant model of neoliberal capitalism – closely identified, of course, with US global hegemony – has been experiencing a 'crisis of legitimacy', which, inaugurated by the East Asian crisis of 1997–8, was intensified by the emergence of the anti-globalization movement, the collapse of the Clinton boom, the Enron scandal, and the Argentinian financial debacle (Bello, 2002).

It seems indisputable that the war on Iraq and the enormous popular opposition that it has provoked has further exacerbated this crisis of legitimacy and encouraged more extensive questioning of American hegemony, particularly in Europe (for example, Reynié, 2004). The resulting international isolation of the United States and the difficulty that the Bush administration has consequently faced in recruiting the assistance of states such as France, Germany and India, not to speak of Middle Eastern elites, in governing Iraq, have in turn set limits to the ability of American occupation forces to use their overwhelming firepower to destroy the Iraqi resistance (Callinicos, 2004a; and Bello, 2004). Unvarnished military power – domination without hegemony – has proved relatively ineffective.[20] The interesting question is what is likely to emerge from this crisis of empire. Is the best we can expect another turn in the long historical cycle, a new East Asian 'systemic cycle of accumulation'?[21] Or is there any chance of breaking out of this apparently eternal recurrence? Harvey observes: 'There are, of course, far more radical solutions lurking in the wings, but the construction of a new "New Deal" led by the United States and Europe, both domestically and internationally, in the face of the overwhelming class forces and special interests ranged against it, is surely enough to fight for in the present conjuncture' (Harvey, 2003, p. 210). Harvey does not specify what this New Deal might involve; presumably it would mean an attempt to reverse the neoliberal counter-revolution and return to a more regulated version of capitalism.[22] But, given the intense resistance that, as he acknowledges, even such relatively limited measures would evoke, might it not be more rational for the gigantic movements against neoliberal globalization and imperial war that emerged at the turn of the millennium to target, not just the American hegemony and the economic model closely identified with it, but the entire capitalist system that they sustain?

Notes

1 See, for example, the essays collected in Hopkins, 2002. The approach they represent is close to that taken by David Held, Anthony McGrew and their collaborators, who argue that, in pre-modern times, '[g]lobalization, defined in this context as inter-regional and inter-civilizational encounters, operated predominantly . . . through the domains of military and cultural power and human migrations – specifically, empires of domination, world religions, nomadic invasions and agrarian expansion, accompanied by the movement of human diseases', Held, McGrew et al., 1999, p. 416. For an earlier discussion of the globalization debate, see Callinicos, 2001a, ch. 1.

2 See, among a vast literature, Callinicos, 2003b; Chomsky, 2003. Mann, 2004 offers the best account to date of the leading personnel of the second Bush administration, while Bacevich, 2002 stresses the continuities between its policies and those of the Clinton presidency.

3 See Callinicos, 2004a for a review of Ferguson, 2004b.

4 For some contrasting political assessments of this movement, see Held and McGrew, 2002; Callinicos, 2003a; and Wolf, 2004.

5 See, for example, Wade and Veneroso, 1998, itself an example of the 'intentionalist' interpretation of contemporary political economy from which I am trying to distance my argument. For a typically robust defence of conspiracy theories, see Žižek, 2004, pp. 77–9.

6 But see the discussion of political globalization in Callinicos, 2001a, ch. 3; and Callinicos, 2002.

7 See Cohen, 1978 for a classic exposition of Marx's concepts.

8 But see Brenner and Isett, 2002 for a stringent theoretical and empirical critique of Pomeranz's central claim that Europe and China were at comparable levels of economic development as late as 1800.

9 See esp. Arrighi, 1994; Arrighi, Silver et al., 1999; Arrighi, 2004; and Arrighi, 2005a and 2005b. Arrighi, like Wallerstein, acknowledges the influence of the great historian Fernand Braudel: see esp. Braudel, 1981, 1982, 1984.

10 See Aston and Philpin, 1985; and Hoppenbrouwers and Van Zanden, 2001. Compare also Marx, 1976, pp. 1025–34. Note that Brenner distinguishes separation from the means of subsistence –

above all, land – from separation from the means of production, which comprises tools and other instruments of production as well: according to him, only the latter constitutes proletarianization in Marx's sense, but the former is sufficient for the market-dependence required to support a capitalist economic dynamic; see Brenner, 2001, p. 278 n. 1 and 310 n. 16.

11 For a version of this criticism that is applied also to theories of hegemonic stability in mainstream International Relations, see Nye, 1991, ch. 1.

12 Arrighi, 2004, responds to criticisms particularly of the cyclical aspect of his theory, for example in Hardt and Negri, 2000, pp. 238–9.

13 For theoretical discussion of this highly compressed history, see Callinicos, 1989, and Carling, 1991, part 1.

14 Arrighi has pointed out that his version of the two logics distinguishes between kinds of state policy, whereas Harvey in effect contrasts economic and (geo)political forms of power: Arrighi, 2005a, p. 28 n. 15. For further discussion of this point see Ashman and Callinicos, forthcoming. This chapter follows Harvey's rather than Arrighi's usage.

15 See, for much supporting analysis, Callinicos, 1991; 2001b; 2002; 2003a, pp. 50–65; 2003b, esp. ch. 5; 2004b; 2005; and Harman, 2003.

16 Not all this talk has come from the boosters of neoliberal globalization: see Hardt and Negri, 2000.

17 The latter strategy is expounded by its architect in Brzezinski, 1997.

18 For a stimulating attempt to place contemporary debates on US global strategy in historical perspective, see Gaddis, 2004.

19 For a vivid account of the 'symbiotic relationship between Asian savers and American spenders', see Ferguson, 2004b, pp. 279–85 (quotation from p. 282). I explore further the nature of contemporary great power rivalry in Callinicos, 2005.

20 For a characteristically incisive (though much more pessimistic) use of Gramscian categories to analyse the contemporary global conjuncture, see Anderson, 2002.

21 This is one of the three alternatives discussed by Arrighi, 1994, pp. 355–6; and 2004, passim (the other two are a US-imposed 'world empire' and 'systemic chaos').

22 Harvey seems a little ambivalent about this strategy: elsewhere he warns that 'it is by no means sure that this would really work in the face of the overwhelming excess capacity in the global system. It is salutary to remember the lessons of the 1930s: there is little evidence that Roosevelt's "New Deal" solved the problems of the Depression' (2003, p. 76).

References

Abu-Lughod, J. L. (1989). *Before European Hegemony*. New York: Oxford University Press.

Anderson, P. (2004). 'Force and Consent', *New Left Review*, 2(17): pp. 5–30.

Arrighi, G. (1994). *The Long Twentieth Century*. London: Verso.

Arrighi, G. (2003). 'Tracking Global Turbulence', *New Left Review*, 2(20): pp. 5–71.

Arrighi, G. (2004). 'The Rough Road to Empire', www.nu.ac.za/ccs/.

Arrighi, G. (2005a). 'Hegemony Unravelling–1', *New Left Review*, 1(32): pp. 23–80.

Arrighi, G. (2005b). 'Hegemony Unravelling–2', *New Left Review*, 1(33): pp. 83–116.

Arrighi, G., B. Silver et al. (1999). *Chaos and Governance in the Modern World System*. Minneapolis: University of Minnesota Press.

Ashman, S. and A. Callinicos (forthcoming). 'Capital Accumulation and the State System: Assessing David Harvey's *The New Imperialism*', *Historical Materialism*.

Aston, T. H. and C. H. E. Philpin, eds (1985). *The Brenner Debate*. Cambridge: Cambridge University Press.

Bacevich, A. J. (2002). *American Empire*. Cambridge, Mass.: Harvard University Press.

Bayly, C. A. (2002). '"Archaic" and "Modern" Globalization in the Eurasian and African Arena, *c*.1750–1850', in Hopkins, 2002, pp. 47–73.

Bayly, C. A. (2004). *The Birth of the Modern World 1780–1914*. Oxford: Blackwell.

Bello, W. (2002). *Deglobalization*. London: Zed.

Bello, W. (2004). 'Empire and Resistance Today', www.zmag.org.

Braudel, F. (1981, 1982, 1984). *Civilization and Capitalism 15th–18th Century*, 3 vols. London: Collins.

Brenner, R. (1977). 'The Origins of Capitalist Development', *New Left Review*, 1(104): pp. 25–92.

Brenner, R. (1986). 'The Social Basis of Economic Development', in J. Roemer, ed., *Analytical Marxism*. Cambridge: Cambridge University Press, pp. 23–53.

Brenner, R. (1998). 'The Economics of Global Turbulence', *New Left Review*, 1(229): pp. 1–265.

Brenner, R. (2001). 'The Low Countries in the Transition to Capitalism', in P. Hoppenbrouwers and J. L. Van Zanden, eds, *Peasants into Farmers?* Brepols: Turnhout, pp. 270–338.

Brenner, R. (2002). *The Boom and the Bubble*. London: Verso.

Brenner, R. and C. Isett (2002). 'England's Divergence from the Yangzi Delta: Property Relations, Microeconomics, and Patterns of Development', *Journal of Asian Studies*, 61: pp. 609–62.

Brzezinski, Z. (1997). *The Grand Chessboard*. New York: Basic Books.

Brzezinski, Z. (2004). *The Choice: Global Domination or Global Leadership*. New York: Basic Books.

Callinicos, A. (1989). 'Bourgeois Revolutions and Historical Materialism', *International Socialism*, 2(43): pp. 113–71.

Callinicos, A. (1991). 'Marxism and Imperialism Today', *International Socialism*, 2(50): pp. 3–48.

Callinicos, A. (2001a). *Against the Third Way*. Cambridge: Polity.

Callinicos, A. (2001b). 'Periodizing Capitalism and Analysing Imperialism', in R. Albritton et al., eds, *Phases of Capitalist Development*. Houndmills: Palgrave, pp. 230–45.

Callinicos, A. (2002). 'Marxism and Global Governance', in D. Held and A. McGrew, eds, *Governing Globalization*. Cambridge: Polity, pp. 249–66.

Callinicos, A. (2003a). *An Anti-Capitalist Manifesto*. Cambridge: Polity.

Callinicos, A. (2003b). *The New Mandarins of American Power*. Cambridge: Polity.

Callinicos, A. (2004a). 'Spectre of Defeat', *Socialist Review*, 287: pp. 26–8.

Callinicos, A. (2004b). 'Marxism and the International', *British Journal of Politics and International Relations*, 6: 426–33.

Callinicos, A. (2005). 'Imperialism and Global Political Economy', *International Socialism*, 2(108): pp. 109–27.

Carling, A. (1991). *Social Division*. London: Verso.

Chomsky, N. (2003). *Hegemony or Survival: America's Quest for Global Dominance*. London: Hamish Hamilton.

Cohen, G. A. (1978). *Karl Marx's Theory of History*. Oxford: Clarendon Press.

Davis, M. (2001). *Late Victorian Holocausts*. London: Verso.

Doyle, M. W. (1986). *Empires*. Ithaca, NY: Cornell University Press.

Ferguson, N. (2004a). *Empire: How Britain Made the Modern World*. London: Penguin.

Ferguson, N. (2004b). *Colossus: The Rise and Fall of the American Empire*. London: Allen Lane.

Frank, Andre Gunder (1971). *Capitalism and Underdevelopment in Latin America*. Harmondsworth: Penguin.

Frank, Andre Gunder (1998). *ReORIENT: Global Economy in the Asian Age*. Berkeley: University of California Press.

Gaddis, J. L. (2004). *Surprise, Security, and the American Experience*. Cambridge, Mass.: Harvard University Press.

Gowan, P. (1999). *The Global Gamble*. London: Verso.

Gramsci, A. (1971). *Selections from the Prison Notebooks*. London: Lawrence and Wishart.

Habib, I. (1999). *The Agrarian System of Mughal India*. New Delhi: Oxford University Press.

Hardt, M. and A. Negri (2000). *Empire*. Cambridge, Mass.: Harvard University Press.

Harman, C. (1984). *Explaining the Crisis*. London: Bookmarks.

Harman, C. (1991). 'The State and Capitalism Today', *International Socialism*, 2(51): pp. 3–54.

Harman, C. (2003). 'Analysing Imperialism', *International Socialism*, 2(99): pp. 3–81.

Harman, C. (2006). 'The Dragon's Fire: China's Economy and Europe's Crisis', *International Socialism*, 2(109): pp. 69–90.

Harvey, D. (2003). *The New Imperialism*. Oxford: Oxford University Press.

Harvey, D. (2005). *A Short History of Neo-Liberalism*. Oxford: Oxford University Press.

Held, D. and A. McGrew (2002). *Globalization/Anti-Globalization*. Cambridge: Polity.

Held, D., A. McGrew et al. (1999). *Global Transformations*. Cambridge: Polity.

Hobsbawm, E. J. (1975). *The Age of Capital 1848–1875*. London: Weidenfeld and Nicolson.

Hopkins, A. D., ed. (2002). *Globalization in World History*. London: Pimlico.

Hoppenbrouwers, P. and J. L. Van Zanden, eds (2001). *Peasants into Farmers?* Brepols: Turnhout.

Hore, C. (2004). 'China's Century?', *International Socialism*, 2(103): pp. 3–48.

James, H. (2001). *The End of Globalization*. Cambridge, Mass.: Harvard University Press.

McNeill, W. H. (1983). *The Pursuit of Power*. Oxford: Basil Blackwell.

Mann, J. (2004). *The Rise of the Vulcans*. New York: Viking Penguin.

Mann, M. (2001). 'Globalization and September 11', *New Left Review*, 2(12): pp. 51–72.

Mann, M. (2003). *Incoherent Empire*. London: Verso.

Marx, K. (1976). *Capital*, I. Harmondsworth: Penguin.

Mearsheimer, J. J. (2001). *The Tragedy of Great Power Politics*. New York: Norton.

Nye, J. S. (1991). *Bound to Lead*. New York: Basic Books.

Petras, J. and H. Veltmeyer (2001). *Globalization Unmasked: Imperialism in the 21st Century*. London: Zed.

Pomeranz, K. (2000). *The Great Divergence: China, Europe, and the Making of the Modern World Economy*. Princeton: Princeton University Press.

Reynié, D. (2004). *La Fracture occidentale*. Paris: La Table Ronde.

Wade, R. and F. Veneroso (1998). 'The Asian Crisis: The High-Debt Model versus the Wall Street–Treasury–IMF Complex', *New Left Review*, 1(228): pp. 3–23.

Wallerstein, I. (1974). *The Modern World System*, I. New York: Academic Press.

Wickham, C. (2005). *Framing the Early Middle Ages: Europe and the Mediterranean, 400–800*. Oxford: Oxford University Press.

Wolf, M. (2004). *Why Globalization Works*. New Haven: Yale University Press.

Žižek, S. (2004). *Iraq: The Borrowed Kettle*. London: Verso.

4

The Places and Spaces of the Global: An Expanded Analytic Terrain

Saskia Sassen

The organizing proposition in this chapter is that the global – whether an institution, a process, a discursive practice, or an imaginary – simultaneously transcends the exclusive framing of national states yet partly inhabits national territories. Seen this way, globalization is more than its common representation as growing interdependence and the formation of self-evidently global institutions. Further, this proposition also implies somewhat different methodological and theoretical challenges to state-centric social sciences from the challenges posed by the notion of the global as that which transcends the state. Each of these two perspectives on the global is a necessary part of the larger effort to theorize and research globalization. But the second has dominated discussion and interpretation. This chapter can then be read as an experiment in expanding the analytic terrain for understanding and representing what we have come to name globalization.

If, as I argue, the global partly inhabits the national, it becomes evident that globalization in its many different forms directly engages a key assumption in the social sciences: the implied correspondence of national territory and national institutions with the national, that is, if a process or condition is located in a national institution or in national territory, it must be national. This assumption describes conditions that have held, albeit never fully, throughout much of the history of the modern state, especially since World War I, and to some extent continue to do so. What is different today is that these conditions are partly but actively being unbundled. Different also is the scope of this unbundling.

We might reformulate this proposition as a research project. The fact that a process or entity is located within the territory of a sovereign state does not necessarily mean it is a national process or entity; it might be a localization of the global. Today it is an empirical question. While most such entities and processes are likely to be national, there is a growing need for empirical research to establish this for what is in turn a growing range of localizations of the global. Much of what we continue to code as national today may well be precisely such a localization. Developing the theoretical and empirical specifications that allow us to accommodate such conditions is a difficult and collective effort. This chapter seeks to contribute to this collective effort by mapping an analytic terrain for the study of globalization predicated on this more complex understanding.

A brief introduction discusses critical conceptual and empirical elements in this effort to expand the analytic terrain for understanding the global. The chapter's first half then proceeds to elaborate on these elements. The chapter's second half examines the implications of this type of understanding of the global for the state, the critical enactor and legitimator of the national and hence in some ways a critical agent in enabling global structurations inside the national.

Conceptual and Empirical Elements

Expanding the analytic terrain within which to locate the global can, in principle, incorporate a variety of domains. We might include digital and subjective domains, two areas which remain understudied. The critical one in this chapter is the complex aggregate that is the national, which is to say a geographic terrain and institutional environment that has been encased in an elaborate set of national laws and administrative capacities. The embeddedness of the global in the national points to necessary re-negotiations of this encasement – whether in the form of at least a partial lifting of these national encasements as might be the case with the deregulations of trading regimes of the 1990s, or in more elusive processes that are actually denationalizing what continues to be represented as national.

The empirical dimensions of these renegotiations of national encasements of territories and institutions are diverse and numerous: they constitute research agendas within each of the social sciences. Some aspects of this empirical work are well under way. One example is global cities research; the category of the global city captures a complex type of economic embeddedness of the global in the national and opens up a rather vast agenda for empirical research, given all that takes place in cities. Another, very different type of example is the research on the expanded use since 1998 of international human rights instruments in national courts; this points to a gradual filtering of these norms into, and their eventual stabilizing as, components of national law. What matters to the analysis in this chapter is that in both of these cases the renegotiation at work is one that denationalizes particular dimensions of national institutions without constituting a self-evidently novel global institution.

The focus then shifts away from self-evidently global institutions and growing interdependence among countries to a far more specific type of inquiry: the structurations of the national insofar as inhabited, and/or transformed by the global and what this entails for national state authority and practice, and more generally for the spaces and institutional framings of the national. Expanding the analytic terrain for the global along these lines has the effect of adding a growing range of partial and often highly specialized processes and conditions that denationalize the national as historically constructed. This denationalizing is typically obscured by the fact that it continues to be represented, coded and experienced as national. Thus part of the effort of expanding the analytic terrain for researching the global is understanding what is actually national in what continues to be understood as such. While most of it may indeed correspond to the longer historical condition of the national, some of it does not and is a type of global.

One critical articulating nexus in this theoretical and empirical research agenda is the question of the national state as the enactor and legitimator of what has historically been produced as the national. Thus expanding the analytic terrain of the global to include the national implies a necessary participation by the state in the process of globalization, even when it concerns the state regulating its own withdrawal from domains such as the national economy. One question this raises is whether this participation might entail the formation of a specific type of authority/power for the state in global systems – both for the state as such and/or for the particular state institutions involved. Does the weight of private, often foreign, interests in this specific work of the state become constitutive of that authority and indeed produce a hybrid that is neither fully private nor fully public?

My argument is that, indeed, we are seeing the incipient formation of a type of authority and state practice that entail a partial denationalizing. This denationalizing consists of several specific processes, including, importantly, the reorienting of national agendas towards global ones, and the circulation of private agendas inside the state apparatus where they get dressed up as public policy. Such a conceptualization introduces a twist in the analysis of private authority because it seeks to detect the presence of private agendas inside the state, rather than the more common focus on the shift of state functions to the private sector, including private forms of authority. It differs from an older scholarly tradition on the captured state which focused on cooptation of states by private actors. In contrast to this older tradition, I emphasize the privatizing of norm-making capacities that were once part of state authority and the enactment of private norms in the public domain.

The purpose here is, then, to understand and specify a particular aspect of globalization and the state which is lost in what are typically rather dualized accounts of this relation; in such accounts, the spheres of influence of respectively the national and the global, and of state and non-state actors, are seen as distinct and mutually exclusive. Even if many components of each of these spheres are separate and mutually exclusive, I argue that this still leaves a specific set of conditions or components that does not fit in this dual structure. Key among these are some components of the work of ministries of finance, central banks, and the increasingly specialized technical regulatory agencies, such as those concerned with finance, telecommunications, and competition policy. In this regard, then, my position is not comfortably subsumed under the proposition that nothing has much changed in terms of sovereign state power, nor can it be subsumed under the proposition of the declining significance of the state.

The first half of this chapter will introduce a number of conceptual issues about the mix of processes we have come to group under the term globalization. Using a multi-scalar analytics allows us to see that subnational processes and institutions are also critical sites for globalization. Accepting the proposition that the global is multi-scalar leads to its conceptualizing as at least partly consisting of the denationalizing of specific forms of state authority which results from the location of particular components of global processes in national institutional orders and the development of global agendas inside the national. This is the subject of the second half of the chapter. Mapping this conceptualization against the mainstream scholarship on the state and globalization, the argument moves on to sketch out the particular substance and conditionality of what I argue is a new mode of state authority that remains insufficiently recognized and theorized. Though housed or located in national state capacities and institutions, this mode of authority is not national in the way we had come to understand this feature of states over the last century. The empirical focus for much of the examination is confined to states under the so-called rule of law, and especially the United States.

Globalization and Denationalization

What is it we are trying to name with the term globalization? In my reading of the evidence it is actually two distinct sets of dynamics. One of these involves the formation of explicitly global institutions and processes, such as the World Trade Organization (WTO), global financial markets, the new cosmopolitanism, the War Crimes tribunals. The practices and organizational forms through which these dynamics operate are constitutive of what are typically thought of as global scales.

But there is a second set of processes that does not necessarily scale at the global level as such, yet, I argue, is part of globalization. These processes take place deep inside territories and institutional domains that have largely been constructed in national terms in much, though by no means all, of the world. What makes these processes part of globalization even though localized in national, indeed subnational, settings is that they involve transboundary networks and formations connecting or articulating multiple local or "national" processes and actors. Among these processes I include particular aspects of the work of states, the subject of the second half of this chapter. Examples are specific monetary and fiscal policies critical to the constitution of global markets that are hence being implemented in a growing number of countries as these become integrated into global markets. Other instances are cross-border networks of activists engaged in specific localized struggles with an explicit or implicit global agenda, as is the case with many human rights and environmental organizations; the use of international human rights instruments in *national* courts; non-cosmopolitan forms of global politics and imaginaries that remain deeply attached or focused on localized issues and struggles yet are part of global lateral networks containing multiple other such localized efforts. A particular challenge in the work of identifying these types of processes and actors as part of globalization is the need to decode at least some of what continues to be experienced and represented as national.

Here I want to focus particularly on these types of practices and dynamics and conceptualize them as constitutive of global scalings we do not usually recognize as such. When the social sciences focus on globalization – still rare enough – it is typically not on these types of practices and dynamics but rather on the self-evidently global scale. And although the social sciences have made important contributions to the study of this self-evident global scale by establishing the fact of multiple globalizations (e.g. Gereffi et al., 2005; Ferguson and Jones, 2002; Appadurai, 1996; Eichengreen and Fishlow, 1996; Aman, 1998), only some of which correspond to neoliberal corporate economic globalization, there is much work left. At least some of this work entails distinguishing: (a) the various scales that global processes constitute, ranging from supranational and global to subnational (Brenner and Keil, 2005; Taylor, 2004; Swyngedouw, 1997; Amin and Thrift, 1994), and (b) the specific contents and institutional locations of this multiscalar globalization (e.g. Bartlett, 2007; Massey, 1993; Howitt, 1993; Jonas, 1994). It is the latter two that concern me in this chapter. Geography more than any other of the social sciences today has contributed to a critical stance toward scale, recognizing the historicity of scales and resisting the reification of the national scale so present in most of social science.

The Locational and Institutional Embeddedness
of the Global Economy

There are three features of the global economy I want to emphasize here. First, the geography of economic globalization is strategic rather than all-encompassing and this is especially so when it comes to the managing, coordinating, servicing, and financing of global economic operations. This geography differs from that of the world system perspective, which defines a global economy by a continuous division of labor between states (Wallerstein, 1974). Differentiation between center and periphery now involves less a differentiation between different production processes or places in commodity chains; rather, the differentiation is largely functional, and cuts across the spatialities presupposed in Wallerstein's framework. By defining the world economy basically as a relationship between territorial states, Wallerstein forecloses the possibility of conceptualizing globalization as anything but the expansion of the world economy to include new states; the possibility of a reconstitution of the spatiality of global capitalism is rendered invisible (Brenner, 1999, pp. 57–60). The fact that this geography is strategic is significant for a discussion about the possibilities of regulating and governing the global economy. Second, the center of gravity for managing the transactions that we refer to in an aggregate fashion as the global economy lies in the North Atlantic region. This facilitates the development and implementation of convergent regulatory frameworks and technical standards and enables a convergence around "Western" standards. If the geography of globalization were a diffuse condition at the planetary scale, and one involving equally powerful countries and regions with a much broader range of differences than those evident in the North Atlantic, the question of its regulation might well be radically different. Third, the strategic geography of globalization is partly embedded in national territories, namely global cities and "Silicon Valleys".

The combination of these three characteristics suggests that states may have more options to participate in governing the global economy than much of the focus on the loss of regulatory authority allows us to recognize. Research by Gereffi (1994, 1999) emphasizing the cross-border organization of production and marketing seems at first to transcend some of the limitations of the classical world system perspective. Not only does he conceptualize production as taking place across multiple borders, but the primary axes of differentiation are *functional*. However, the basic positions of structural differentiation are static – e.g. assembly, manufacturing, retailing, each are located in a country with a distinct world-system location. To the extent that new possibilities for relocation emerge, they are seen as a function of technological change (e.g. information technology allowing dispersal of production) and changes in market demand structure (mass production vs. flexible specialization). Since these are defined as pre-given conditions of ongoing economic activities, the most the state can do is attempt to maximize its position within a given hierarchy – it can try to "upgrade" its position. It remains relatively difficult in this analysis to grasp the constitutive role of the state vis-à-vis the global economy, and hence its potential capacities for global economic governance.

There are sites in this strategic geography where the density of economic transactions and the intensity of regulatory efforts come together in complex, often novel configurations. Two of these are the focus of this section. They are foreign direct investment, which mostly consists of cross-border mergers and acquisitions, and the global capital market, undoubtedly the dominant force in the global economy today. Along with trade, they are at the heart of the structural changes constitutive of globalization and the efforts to regulate it. These two processes also make evident the enormous weight of the North Atlantic region in the global economy. Both foreign direct investment and the global capital market bring up specific organizational and regulatory issues.[1] There is an enormous increase in the complexity of management, coordination, servicing, and financing for firms operating worldwide networks of factories, service outlets, and/or offices, and for firms operating in cross-border financial markets. For reasons I discuss in greater detail elsewhere (2001, Preface to the new edition, ch. 5) this has brought about a sharp growth in control and command functions, and their concentration in a cross-border network of global cities. This in turn contributes to the formation of a strategic geography for the management of globalization. Nowhere is this as evident as in the structure of the global capital market and the network of financial centers within which it is located. Elsewhere I have examined this institutional order as the site of a new type of private authority (1996, ch. 2; 2006, ch. 5).

The empirical patterns of foreign direct investment and global finance show to what extent their centers of gravity lie in the North Atlantic region, and, but to a far lesser extent, in China. The northern transatlantic economic system (specifically the links among the European Union, the United States and Canada) is the major concentration of these processes of economic globalization in the world today. This holds whether one looks at foreign direct investment flows generally, at cross-border mergers and acquisitions (M&As) in particular, at overall financial flows or at the new strategic alliances among financial centers. At the turn of the millennium this region accounts for two-thirds of worldwide stock market capitalization, 60 percent of inward foreign investment stock and 76 percent of outward stock, 60 percent of worldwide sales in M&As, and 80 percent of purchases in M&As. There are other major regions in the global economy: Japan, Southeast Asia, and Latin America. But except for some of the absolute levels of capital resources in Japan, they are dwarfed by the weight of the northern transatlantic system.

This heavy concentration in the volume and value of cross-border transactions raises a number of questions. One concerns its features, such as the extent to which there is interdependence, and in that sense, the elements of a cross-border economic system. The weight of these transatlantic links needs to be considered against the weight of established zones of influence for each of the major powers – particularly, the Western Hemisphere in the case of the United States, and Africa, Central, and East Europe for the European Union.

The United States and individual European Union members have long had often intense economic transactions with their zones of influence. Some of these have been reinvigorated in the new economic policy context of opening to foreign investment, privatization, and trade and financial deregulation. In my reading of the evidence, both the relations with their respective zones of influence and the relations within the northern transatlantic system have changed. We are seeing the consolidation of a transnational economic system that has its center of gravity in the North Atlantic system both in terms of the intensity and value of transactions, and in terms of the emerging system of rules and standards. This system is articulated with the rest of the world through a growing network of sites for investment, trade, and financial transactions. It is through this incorporation in a hierarchical global network that has its center in the North Atlantic that the relations with their zones of influence are being reconstituted. Thus, while the United States is still a dominant force in Latin America, several European countries have become major investors in Latin America, on a scale far surpassing past trends. And while several European Union countries have become leaders in investment in Central and Eastern Europe, US firms are playing a role they never played before.

What we are seeing today is a new grid of economic transactions superimposed on the old geoeconomic patterns. The latter persist to variable extents, but they are increasingly submerged under this new cross-border grid which amounts to a new, though partial, geoeconomics. The decline of the import substitution model of development can be seen as symptomatic of this shift. Under this model, the state, as interface between the national and the international economy, set up a number of protections for infant industries until they were ready to compete. High position in the global hierarchy was associated with high value-added manufacturing work, and the goal was a complete development of national space. By contrast, the advent of export-led development resulted in the creation of specialized spaces within national territories – Export Processing Zones and so forth – which only imperfectly aligned with the old categories of national and international economies. The paradigmatic cases of this form of development in East Asia did not accomplish this solely through acquiescence to market logic; rather, the strong role of the state has been well documented. From these local innovations within an old economic-spatial hierarchy, traces of the new order emerged. Analysis of these hierarchies cannot be satisfied with identifying its structure and the occupants of the various positions: rather, we must know how it is produced, reproduced, and transformed. In my own research I have found that these new configurations are particularly evident in the organization of global finance, and, though to a lesser extent, in direct foreign investment, especially cross-border mergers and acquisitions.

Worldwide networks and central command functions

There are, clearly, strong dispersal trends contained in the patterns of foreign investment and capital flows generally. These include the off-shoring of factories, the expansion of global networks of affiliates and subsidiaries, and the formation of global financial markets with a growing number of participating countries. What is left out of this picture is the other half of the story. This worldwide geographic dispersal of factories and service outlets takes place as part of highly integrated corporate structures with strong tendencies towards concentration in control and profit appropriation. As discussed above, the North Atlantic system is the site for most of the strategic management and coordination functions of the new global economic system.

Elsewhere (2001) I have shown that when the geographic dispersal of factories, offices, and service outlets through cross-border investment takes place as part of integrated corporate systems, mostly multinational corporations, there is also a growth in central functions; we can see a parallel trend with financial firms and markets. One way of saying it is that the more globalized firms become, the more their central functions grow – in importance, in complexity, in number of transactions.[2] The specific forms assumed by globalization over the last decade have created particular organizational requirements. The emergence of global markets for finance and specialized services, and the growth of investment as a major type of international transaction have contributed to the expansion in command functions and in the demand for specialized services for firms.[3]

We can make this more concrete by considering some of the staggering figures involved in this worldwide dispersal and imagining what it entails in terms of coordination and management for parent headquarters (Sassem, 2006). For instance, by 2004 there were almost half a million foreign affiliates of firms worldwide, most of them belonging to firms from North America and Western Europe.[4] There has been a greater growth in foreign sales through affiliates than through direct exports: the foreign sales through affiliates were US$11 trillion in 1999, and through worldwide exports of goods and services US$8 trillion. This has of course also fed the intra-firm share of so-called free cross-border trade. The data on foreign direct investment show clearly that the United States and the EU are the major receiving and sending areas in the world. Finally, the transnationality index of the largest transnational corporations (TNCs) shows that many of the major firms from these two regions have over half of their assets, sales, and workforces outside their home countries.[5] Together these types of evidence provide a fairly comprehensive picture of this combination of dispersal and the growth of central functions.

The globalization of a firm's operations brings with it a massive task of coordination and management. Much of this has been going on for a long time but has accelerated over the decades. This dispersal does not occur under a single organizational form – rather, behind these general figures lie many different organizational forms, hierarchies of control, degrees of autonomy. The globally integrated network of financial centers is yet another form of this combination of dispersal and the growing complexity of central management and coordination.

Of importance to the analysis here is the dynamic that connects the dispersal of economic activities with the ongoing weight and often growth of central functions. In terms of sovereignty and globalization this means that an interpretation of the impact of globalization as creating a space economy that extends beyond the regulatory capacity of a single state is only half the story; the other half is that these central functions are disproportionately concentrated in the national territories of the highly developed countries.

By central functions I do not only mean top-level headquarters functions; I am referring to all the top-level financial, legal, accounting, managerial, executive, planning functions necessary to run a corporate organization operating in more than one country, and increasingly in several countries. These central functions are partly embedded in headquarters, but also in good part in what has been called the corporate services complex, that is, the network of financial, legal, accounting, advertising firms that handle the complexities of operating in more than one national legal system, national accounting system, advertising culture, etc., and do so under conditions of rapid innovations in all these fields. Such services have become so specialized and complex, that headquarters increasingly buy them from specialized firms rather than producing them in-house. These agglomerations of firms producing central functions for the management and coordination of global economic systems are disproportionately concentrated in the highly developed countries – particularly, though not exclusively, in the kind of cities I call global cities. Such concentrations of functions represent a strategic factor in the organization of the global economy.

One argument I am making here is that it is important to analytically unbundle the fact of strategic functions for the global economy or for global operation, and the overall corporate economy of a country. These global control and command functions are partly embedded in national corporate structures but also constitute a distinct corporate subsector. For the purposes of certain kinds of inquiry this distinction may not matter; for the purposes of understanding the global economy, it does. This subsector can be conceived of as part of a network that connects global cities across the globe. These networks are not defined by a division of labor in the production of commodities and resulting market-based trade transactions; rather, the "members" of these networks divide up the work of reproducing the global economy, that is, the structures of global domination. In a similar way as the state could once be seen as institutionally central to the reproduction of a regime of accumulation, in other words as pivotal to a mode of regulation, the distribution of strategic functions to global cities can be seen as the rearticulation of a mode of regulation reproducing a new global regime of accumulation. Regulation theory, basically as a form of institutionalism, would likely have difficulties grasping this form of global regulation, for two reasons. First, the spatialities comprising these modes of regulation are not easily matched with specific institutional scales. Second, absent the emergence of a single global institutional frame capable of structuring world economic relations, it is unclear that this perspective is capable of detailing the actual mechanisms whereby structure is reproduced. So far, only potential elements of such a system have emerged, largely from relatively "local" practices in these "central" areas. Regulation theory is better equipped to detail the functioning of an already-existing institutional structure; it is less well equipped to explain the constitution of that structure.

The distinction between a national and a global corporate sector also matters for questions of regulation, notably regulation of cross-border activities. If the strategic central functions – both those produced in corporate headquarters and those produced in the specialized corporate services sector – are located in a network of major financial and business centers, the question of regulating what amounts to a key part of the global economy is not the same if the strategic management and coordination functions were as distributed geographically as are the factories, service outlets and affiliates. However, regulation of these activities is becoming more specialized and international than most current state-centric national systems can comfortably accommodate today. In my reading a crucial issue for understanding the question of regulation and the role of the state in the global capital market is the ongoing embeddedness of this market in these networks of financial centers operating within national states; these are not offshore markets. The North Atlantic system contains an enormous share of the global capital market through its sharp concentration of leading financial centers.[6] Further, as the system expands through the incorporation of additional centers into this network – from East Europe, Latin America, etc. – the question of regulation also pivots on the existence of dominant standards and rules, that is, those produced by the economies of the North Atlantic. Studies that emphasize deregulation and liberalization do not sufficiently recognize an important feature, and one which matters for the analysis here: the global financial system has reached levels of complexity that require the existence of a cross-border network of financial centers to service the operations of global capital. Each actual financial center represents a massive and highly specialized concentration of resources and talent; and the network of these centers constitutes the operational architecture for the global capital market.

It might be interesting at this point to recall Arrighi's (1994) argument that the restarting of a cycle of accumulation derives from local entrepreneurial innovations. As a local system manages to draw profits toward itself, it becomes a model for other systems in the world economy – it exercises a hegemonic leadership function. Power accrues to this territorial region due to its superior performance, not because of its strategic positioning within a global capitalist system. Hence, the basic dynamics of the world economy remain stable, and spatial differentiation is primarily a function of market and competitive efficiency. Without attention to the conditions of production and reproduction of these structural dynamics, the level of change which may be theorized within a system is limited.[7] In examining the structuring of key features of the current global economy, I emphasize on the one hand the production of strategic resources and capabilities, and on the other, the fact that these cities do not simply compete with each other. Together they provide a critical networked infrastructure for the management and control of the global economy, with considerable specificity of functions. This leads to division of highly specialized functions and corresponding positioning in the global economy.

State regulatory capacities

The fact of such a strategic geography for the organizational side of the global economy is a significant factor for the question of how the state can and does participate in the implementation of the global corporate economy. Regulation is one angle into this question. The orders of magnitude and the intensity of transactions in the North Atlantic system facilitate the formation of standards even in the context of what are, relatively speaking, strong differences between the United States and continental Europe in their legal, accounting, anti-trust, and other rules. It is clear that even though these two regions have more in common with each other than with much of the rest of the world, their differences matter when it comes to the creation of cross-border standards. The fact of shared Western standards and norms, however, in combination with enormous economic weight, has facilitated the circulation and imposition of US and European standards and rules on transactions involving firms from other parts of the world. There is a sort of globalization of Western standards. Much has been said about the dominance of US standards and rules, but European standards are also evident, for instance in the new antitrust rules being developed in Central and Eastern Europe.

Foreign direct investment and the global capital market are each at the heart of a variety of regulatory initiatives. The growth of foreign direct investment has brought with it a renewed concern with questions of extraterritoriality and competition policy, including the regulation of cross-border mergers. The growth of the global capital market has brought with it specific efforts to develop the elements of an architecture for its governance: international securities regulation, new international standards for accounting and financial reporting, and various EU provisions. Each has tended to be ensconced in fairly distinct regulatory frameworks: foreign direct investment in antitrust law and global finance in national regulatory frameworks for banking and finance.[8]

In my current research on the United States I am extricating from what has been constructed as "US legislative history" a whole series of legislative items and executive orders that can be read as accommodations on the part of the national state and as its active participation in producing the conditions for economic globalization. It is a history of micro-interventions, often minute transformations in regulatory or legal frameworks that facilitated the extension of cross-border operations of US firms. This is clearly not a new history, neither for the United States nor for other Western former imperial powers (e.g. the "concessions" to trading companies under British, Dutch, and other colonial regimes). Yet, I argue that we can identify a new phase, one which has very specific instantiations of this broader feature.[9]Among the first of these new measures in the United States, and perhaps among the best known, are the tariff items passed to facilitate the internationalization of manufacturing, which exempted firms from import duties on the value added of reimported components assembled or manufactured in offshore plants. I date this microhistory of legislative and executive interventions to the late 1960s, with a full crystallization of various measures facilitating the global operations of US firms and the globalization of markets in the 1980s, and work continuing vigorously in the 1990s. The Foreign Investment Act of 1976, the implementation of International Banking Facilities in 1981, the various deregulations and liberalizations of the financial sector in the 1980s, and so on are but the best known landmarks in this microhistory.

Further, the new types of cross-border collaborations among specialized government agencies concerned with a growing range of issues emerging from the globalization of capital markets and the new trade order are yet another aspect of this participation by the state in the implementation of a global economic system. A good example is the heightened interaction in the last three or four years among competition policy regulators from a large number of countries. This is a period of reinvigorated competition policy work because economic globalization puts pressure on governments to work towards convergence, given the diversity of competition laws or enforcement practices (Portnoy, 2000). This convergence around specific competition policy issues can coexist with ongoing, often enormous differences among these countries when it comes to laws and regulations about components of their economies which do not intersect with globalization. There are multiple other instances of this highly specialized type of convergence: regulatory issues concerning telecommunications, finance, the Internet, etc. It is, then, a very partial type of convergence among regulators of different countries who often begin to share more with each other than they do with colleagues in their home bureaucracies.

What is of particular concern here is that today we see a sharp increase in the work of establishing convergence.[10] We can clearly identify a new phase in the last ten years. In some of these sectors there has long been an often elementary convergence, or at least coordination of standards. For instance, central bankers have long interacted with each other across borders, but today we see an intensification in these transactions which becomes necessary in the effort to develop and extend a global capital market. The increase of cross-border trade has brought with it a sharpened need for convergence in standards, as is evident in the vast proliferation of regulatory standards issued by the International Standards Organization (ISO).

While this strategic geography of globalization is partly embedded in national territories, this does not necessarily entail that existing national regulatory frameworks can regulate those functions. Two trends are evident, one recognized, the other not. Much attention has gone to the fact that regulatory functions have shifted increasingly towards a set of emerging or newly invigorated cross-border regulatory networks and the development of a whole array of standards to organize world trade and global finance. Specialized, often semi-autonomous regulatory agencies and the specialized cross-border networks they are forming are taking over functions once enclosed in national legal frameworks, and standards are replacing rules in international law. The question for research and theory is whether this mode of regulation is sufficient and whether state participation may not emerge again as a more significant factor for the ultimate workability of some of these new regulatory regimes. The second trend, discussed below, is that, while the state does participate in this new regulatory apparatus, it does so under very specific conditions.

The Subnational: A Site for Globalization

Studying the global, then, entails not only a focus on that which is explicitly global in scale, but also a focus on locally scaled practices and conditions articulated with global dynamics and a focus on the multiplication of horizontal cross-border connections among various localities. Further, it entails recognizing that many of the globally scaled dynamics, such as the global capital market, actually are partly embedded in subnational sites and move between these differently scaled practices and organizational forms. For instance, the global capital market is constituted both through electronic markets with global span, and through locally embedded conditions, that is, financial centers.

A focus on such subnationally based processes and dynamics of globalization requires methodologies and theorizations that engage not only global scalings but also subnational scalings as components of *global* processes, thereby destabilizing older hierarchies of scale and conceptions of nested scalings. Studying global processes and conditions that get constituted subnationally has some advantages over studies of globally scaled dynamics, but it also poses specific challenges. It does make possible the use of long-standing research techniques, from quantitative to qualitative, in the study of globalization. It also gives us a bridge for using the wealth of national and subnational data sets as well as specialized scholarships such as area studies. Both types of study, however, need to be situated in conceptual architectures that are not quite those held by the researchers who generated these research techniques and data sets, as their efforts mostly had little to do with globalization.

One central task we face is to decode particular aspects of what is still represented or experienced as "national" which may in fact have shifted away from what had historically been considered or constituted as national. This is in many ways a research and theorization logic that is the same as that developed in the economics of global city studies. But there is a difference: today we have come around to recognize and code a variety of components in global cities as part of the global. What I am trying to focus on here engages a range of conditions and dynamics that are to be distinguished from those global city components in that they are still coded and represented as local and national; further, my concern here is largely the realm of the political rather than economic.

As the preceding section indicated, three types of cases serve to illustrate some of the conceptual, methodological, and empirical issues in this type of study. One of these addresses the role of place in many of the circuits constitutive of economic and political globalization. A focus on places allows us to unbundle globalization in terms of the multiple specialized cross-border circuits on which different types of places are located.[11] Yet another example is that of global cities as subnational places where multiple global circuits intersect and thereby position these cities on several structured cross-border geographies, each typically with distinct scopes and constituted in terms of distinct practices and actors.[12] This type of analysis produces a different picture about globalization from one centered on global firms and markets, international trade, or the pertinent supranational institutions. It is not that one type of focus is better than the other, but rather that the latter focus, the most common focus by far, is not enough.

A second type of case, partly involved in that described above, is the role of the new interactive technologies in repositioning the local, thereby inviting us to a critical examination of how we conceptualize the local. Through these new technologies a financial services firm becomes a microenvironment with continuous global span. But so do resource-poor organizations or households: they can also become microenvironments with global span, as might be the case with activist organizations. These microenvironments can be oriented to other such microenvironments located far away, thereby destabilizing both the notion of context, which is often imbricated with that of the local, and the notion that physical proximity is one of the attributes or markers of the local. A critical reconceptualization of the local along these lines entails an at least partial rejection of the notion that local scales are inevitably part of nested hierarchies of scale running from the local to the regional, the national, the international.

A third type of case concerns a specific set of interactions between global dynamics and particular components of national states. The crucial conditionality here is the partial embeddedness of the global in the national, of which the global city is perhaps emblematic. My main argument here is that insofar as specific structurations of the global inhabit what has historically been constructed and institutionalized as national territory, this engenders a variety of negotiations. One set of outcomes evident today is what I describe as an incipient, highly specialized, and partial denationalization of specific components of national states.

In all three instances the question of scaling takes on very specific contents in that these are practices and dynamics that, I argue, pertain to the constituting of the global yet are taking place at what has been historically constructed as the scale of the national. With few exceptions, most prominently among which is a growing scholarship in geography, the social sciences have not had critical distance, that is, historicized the scale of the national. The consequence has been a tendency to take it as a fixed scale, reifying it, and, more generally, to neutralize the question of scaling, or at best to reduce scaling to a hierarchy of size. Associated with this tendency is also the often uncritical assumption that these scales are mutually exclusive, most pertinently for my argument here, that the scale of the national is mutually exclusive with that of the global. A qualifying variant which allows for mutual imbrications, though of a very limited sort, can be seen when scaling is conceived of as a nested hierarchy.[13]

Finally, the three cases described above go against those assumptions and propositions that are now often captured through the concept of methodological nationalism. But they do so in a distinct way. Crucial to the critique of methodological nationalism is the need for transnationalism because the nation as container category is inadequate given the proliferation of transboundary dynamics and formation (e.g. Taylor, 2000; Beck, 2000). What I am focusing on here is a set of reasons other than transnationalism for supporting the critique of methodological nationalism: the fact of multiple and specific structurations of the global inside what has historically been constructed as national. Further, I posit that because the national is highly institutionalized and thick, structurations of the global inside the national entail a partial, typically highly specialized and specific denationalization of particular components of the national.[14]

The Destabilizing of Older Hierarchies of Scale

Various components of globalization bring with them a destabilizing of older hierarchies of scale – scales and hierarchies constituted through the practices and power projects of past eras, with the national scale eventually emerging as the pre-eminent one. Most notable today is what is sometimes seen as a return to older imperial spatialities for the economic operations of the most powerful actors: the formation of a global market for capital, a global trade regime, and the internationalization of manufacturing production. It is, of course, not simply a return to older forms: it is crucial to recognize the specificity of today's practices and the capabilities enabling these practices. This specificity partly consists of the fact that today's transboundary spatialities had to be produced in a context where most territory is encased in a thick and highly formalized national framework marked by the exclusive authority of the national state. This is, in my reading, one of the key features that distinguishes the current phase of globalization from earlier ones. It entails the necessary participation of national states in the formation of global systems (Sassen, 1996, chs 1 and 2; 2006).[15]

The global project of powerful firms, the new technical capabilities associated with information and communications technologies, and some components of the work of states have together constituted scales other than the national as strategic. Most important among these are subnational scales such as the global city, and supranational scales such as global markets. These processes and practices also contained a destabilizing of the scale hierarchies that expressed the power relations and political economy of an earlier period. The latter were, and to a good extent continue to be, organized in terms of institutional size and territorial scope: from the international, down to the national, the regional, the urban, and the local, with the national functioning as the articulator of this particular configuration. That is to say, the crucial practices and institutional arrangements that constituted the system occurred at the national level. Notwithstanding multiple different temporal frames, the history of the modern state can be read as the work of rendering national just about all crucial features of society: authority, identity, territory, security, law, capital accumulation. Earlier periods to that of the ascendance of the national state saw rather different types of scalings, with territories typically subject to multiple systems of rule rather than the exclusive authority of the state.

Today's rescaling dynamics cut across institutional size and across the institutional encasements of territory produced by the formation of national states. This does not mean that the old hierarchies disappear, but rather that rescalings emerge alongside the old ones, and that the former can often trump the latter. Older hierarchies of scale constituted as part of the development of the nation-state continue to operate, but they do so in a far less exclusive field than they did in the recent past, even when we factor in the hegemonic power of a few states, which meant and continues to mean that most national states were in practice not quite sovereign.

Existing theory is not enough to map today's multiplication of practices and actors constitutive of these rescalings. They include a variety of non-state actors and forms of cross-border cooperation and conflict, such as global business networks, the new cosmopolitanism, NGOs, diasporic networks, and spaces such as global cities and transboundary public spheres. International Relations (IR) theory is the field that to date has had the most to say about cross-border relations. But current developments associated with various mixes of globalization and the new information and communications technologies point to the limits of IR theory and data. Several critical scholars (Taylor, 2000; Cerny, 2000; Ferguson and Jones, 2002; Hall and Biersteker, 2002) have shown us how its models and theories remain focused on the logic of relations between states and the scale of the state at a time when we see a proliferation of non-state actors, cross-border processes, and associated changes in the scope, exclusivity, and competence of state authority over its territory. Theoretical developments in other disciplines may prove important; especially relevant is, as I mentioned above, geography and its contributions to critical analyses of scale, unlike other social sciences which tend to take scale as a given and the national scale as a naturalized condition.

A second feature is the multi-scalar character of various globalization processes that do not fit into older conceptions of hierarchies of scale or conceptions of nested hierarchies. Perhaps most familiar here is, again, the bundle of conditions and dynamics that marks the model of the global city. In its most abstract formulation this is captured in what I see as one of the key organizing hypotheses of the global city model, to wit, that the more globalized and digitized the operations of firms and markets, the more their central management and specialized servicing functions (and the requisite material structures) become strategic and complex, thereby benefiting from agglomeration economies.[16] To variable extents these agglomeration economies are still delivered through territorial concentrations of particular resources. This points to multiple scales that cannot be organized as a hierarchy or a nested hierarchy: for example, far-flung networks of affiliates of multinational firms along with the concentration of strategic functions in a single or in a very limited number of locations (e.g. Taylor et al., 2002; GAWC). This is a multiscalar system, operating across scales and not merely scaling upward because of new communication capabilities.[17]

Some of these issues assume particular contents and locations when it comes to the political domain. This is the focus next.

The Partial Denationalizing of State Work

The scholarship on the state and globalization contains three basic positions: one finds the state is victimized by globalization and loses significance; a second one finds that nothing much has changed and states basically keep on doing what they have always done; and a third, a variant on the second, finds that the state adapts and may even be transformed, thereby ensuring that it does not decline and remains the critical actor. There is research to support critical aspects of each one of these three positions, partly because much of their difference hinges on interpretation. But notwithstanding their diversity these scholarships tend to share the assumption that the national and the global are mutually exclusive.

Given the effort in this chapter to expand the analytic terrain within which to map the question of globalization, the larger research and theorization agenda needs to address aspects of globalization and the state which are lost in these dualized accounts about their relationship. Even when the spheres of influence of respectively the national and the global are seen as mutually exclusive, there is a growing, often specific set of components that does not fit in this dual structure. This is evident, for instance, with critical components in the work of ministries of finance and central banks (called, respectively, the Treasury and the Federal Reserve in the United States), and with the increasingly specialized technical regulatory agencies, such as those concerned with finance, telecommunications, and competition policy.

Factoring in these types of conditions amounts to a fourth position alongside the three referred to above. While this fourth type of approach does not necessarily preclude all propositions in the other three, it is nonetheless markedly different in its foundational assumptions. For instance, in my own research I find that far from being mutually exclusive, the state is one of the strategic institutional domains where critical work for developing globalization takes place. This does not necessarily produce the decline of the state but neither does it keep the state going as usual, or produce merely adaptations to the new conditions. The state becomes the site for foundational transformations in the relation between the private and the public domains, in the state's internal balance of power, and in the larger field of both national and global forces within which the state now has to function (Sassen, 2006, chs 4 and 5).

A number of scholars have addressed various dimensions of the state's participation in global processes. Some (e.g. Krasner, 1999; Fligstein, 2001; Evans, 1997) argue that globalization is made possible by states and that hence not much has changed for states and the interstate system. The present era is merely a continuation of a long history of changes that have not altered the fundamental fact of state primacy (Mann, 1997). Both the "strong" and the "weak" version of neo-Weberian state theory (Skocpol, 1985; Evans, 1997) share certain dimensions of this conceptualization of the state. While acknowledging that the primacy of the state may vary given different structural conditions between state and society, these authors tend to understand state power as basically denoting the same conditions throughout history: the ability successfully to implement explicitly formulated policies. A second type of literature (Panitch, 1996; Gill, 1996; Mittelman, 2000) interprets deregulation and privatization as the incorporation by the state of its own shrinking role. In its most formalized version this position emphasizes the state's constitutionalizing of its own diminished role. In this literature economic globalization is not confined to capital crossing geographic borders, as is captured in measures of international investment and trade, but is in fact conceptualized as a politico-economic system. A third, growing literature emphasizes the relocation of national public governance functions to private actors both within national and global domains (e.g. Hall and Biersteker, 2002). Key institutions of the supranational system, such as the World Trade Organization, are emblematic of this shift. Cutting across these types of literature are the issues raised earlier as to whether states are declining, are remaining as strong as they have ever been, or have changed, but as part of an adaptation to the new conditions rather than a loss of power.

Sociologists such as those briefly discussed above have not focused on the question of globalization and the state. But much in their work can illuminate critical aspects of the state helpful in developing a more sociological approach to that question. The focus developed in this chapter emphasizes the work of states in the development of a global economy, and to a lesser extent other forms of globalization. The consequences for the state associated with such work are diverse and can be interpreted in more than one way – for instance, some interpretations might conceive of these as intended and others as unintended consequences. Here I will focus particularly on types of state work that I interpret as producing a denationalizing of particular components of state authority, which, nonetheless, remain inside the state rather than shifting to the private or global institutional domains, as is typically emphasized in the pertinent scholarship. Tilly's distinction of the national state from "the state" as such is helpful in this regard. While states are "coercion-wielding organizations that are distinct from households and kinship groups and exercise clear priority in some respects over all other organizations within substantial territories," *national* states are distinguished by "governing multiple contiguous regions and their cities by means of centralized, differentiated, and autonomous structures" (Tilly, 1990, pp. 1–2). Reification of this form of state distorts our recognition of incipient processes of denationalization. The centralized national state acts as an interface between national and supranational forces, and acts as a "container" for the former (Brenner, 1999; Agnew, 1993; O'Riain, 2000). Delimiting the national state as one particular form of state allows more analytic freedom in conceptualizing these processes.

A first step in establishing the state's positioning is to recover the ways in which the state participates in governing the global economy in a context increasingly dominated by deregulation, privatization, and the growing authority of non-state actors. A key organizing proposition is the embeddedness of much of globalization in national territory, that is to say, in a geographic terrain that has been encased in an elaborate set of national laws and administrative capacities. The embeddedness of the global requires at least a partial lifting of these national encasements and hence signals a necessary participation by the state, even when it concerns the state's own withdrawal from regulating the economy. Like Tilly, nearly all sociological definitions of the state from Weber forward emphasize a territorial dimension of state power. To the extent that this entails a conception of territory familiar from the "national state," we must assume that existing state capacities are oriented toward a univocally national society. Even Mann (1986, pp. 26–7), who is otherwise enormously sensitive to the multiple spatialities of the exercise of power in social life, defines the state largely as an organization exercising political power and enforcing cooperation within a bounded territory. This territorial dimension means that as states participate in the implementation of the global economic system they have, in many cases, undergone significant transformations. The accommodation of the interests of foreign firms and investors entails a negotiation. At the heart of this negotiation is the development inside national states – through legislative acts, court rulings, executive orders – of the mechanisms necessary for the reconstitution of certain components of national capital into "global capital," and necessary to accommodate new types of rights/entitlements for foreign capital in what are still national territories in principle under the exclusive authority of their states.[18]

This has the effect of denationalizing particular, often highly specialized institutional orders inside the state. Such an approach is one way of expanding the analytic terrain for mapping globalization – it extends that terrain deep into highly specialized components of the national state. These particular transformations inside the state are partial and incipient but strategic. For instance, such transformations can weaken or alter the organizational architecture for the implementation of international law insofar as the latter depends on the institutional apparatus of national states. Further, they have also created the conditions whereby some parts of national states actually gain relative power (Sassen, 1996, chs 1 and 2; 2006) as a result of that participation in the development of a global economy. Certain wings of the state become more powerful due to their functional importance for the global economy. This must be distinguished, on the one hand, from Skocpol's position which emphasizes the structural independence of the various components of the state and their internal rationalization and, on the other hand, from a world-system perspective which would treat "state power" as monolithically resulting from placement in the world-economic structural hierarchy. States do not meekly confront their changing environments; rather, they actively engage with them and try to maintain their position of power. This involves both the modification of existing capacities to new situations (Weiss, 1998), and potentially the attempt by state actors to link into the global economy, to claim jurisdiction over the various tasks involved in globalization, thereby securing their own power (for an illuminating model of this process involving professional groups, see Abbott, 1988). As particular components of national states become the institutional home for the operation of some of the dynamics that are central to globalization they undergo change that is difficult to register or name. In my own work I have found useful the notion of an incipient denationalizing of specific components of national states, that is, components that function as such institutional homes. The question for research then becomes what is actually "national" in some of the institutional components of states linked to the implementation and regulation of economic globalization. The hypothesis here would be that some components of national institutions, even though formally national, are not national in the sense in which we have constructed the meaning of that term over the last hundred years.

This partial, often highly specialized or at least particularized, denationalization can also take place in domains other than that of economic globalization, notably the more recent developments in the human rights regime which allow national courts to sue foreign firms and dictators or that grant undocumented immigrants certain rights. Denationalization is, thus, multivalent: it endogenizes global agendas of many different types of actors, not only those of corporate firms and financial markets, but also human rights objectives. In discussing the state as a site for the pursuit and articulation of strategies, Jessop (1990, ch. 9) argues that any coherence to the state can only be temporary and grounded in a hegemony of particular groups. Due to this, numerous compromises with subaltern groups are necessary, and there exists the possibility of entrenchment of non-dominant groups within certain components of the state apparatus.

These trends towards a greater interaction of national and global dynamics are not unidirectional. There have been times in the past when they may have been as strong in certain aspects as they are today. For instance, there was a global capital market at the turn of the twentieth century. Further, in many ways state sovereignty was never absolute but rather always subject to significant fluctuations. Thus Arrighi and Silver (1999, pp. 92–4) argue that historically "each reaffirmation and expansion of legal sovereignty was nonetheless accompanied by a curtailment of the factual sovereignty that rested on the balance of power" (p. 93). "The crisis of national sovereignty is no novelty of our time. Rather, it is an aspect of the stepwise destruction of the balance of power that originally guaranteed the sovereign equality of the members of the Westphalian system of states" (p. 94).

Nonetheless, after almost a century of the strengthening of the national state, beginning in the late 1980s and continuing today, we saw a considerable institutionalizing of the "rights" of non-national firms, the deregulation of cross-border transactions, and the growing influence/power of some of the supranational organizations. If securing these rights, options, and powers entailed an even partial relinquishing of components of state authority as constructed over the last century, then we can posit that this sets up the conditions for a necessary engagement by national states in the process of globalization. Further, we need to understand more about the nature of this engagement than is represented by concepts such as deregulation. It is becoming clear that the role of the state in the process of deregulation involves the production of new types of regulations, legislative items, court decisions (Picciotto, 1992; Cerny, 1990; Panitch, 1996), in brief, the production of a whole series of new "legalities." The background condition here is that the state remains as the ultimate guarantor of the "rights" of global capital, namely the protection of contracts and property rights, and, more generally, a major legitimator of claims.[19] (See also Fligstein, 1990, 2001; Datz, 2007.)

The state can, then, be conceived of as representing a technical administrative capacity enabling the implementation of a corporate global economy. It is a capacity which cannot be replicated at this time by any other institutional arrangement; furthermore, this is a capacity backed by military power, albeit not in all cases (see e.g. Williams, 2000), with global power in the case of some states. To use the phraseology of Skocpol, and apply it to the global domain, we can say that the state maintains its level of capacity (albeit with some transformations), even as it may lose some of its autonomy. We might want to research whether these capacities are being deployed in accordance with the functional logic of capital, or with that of projects articulated within the state. From the perspective of firms and investors operating transnationally, the objective is to enjoy the protections traditionally exercised by the state in the national realm of the economy for national firms. How this gets done may involve a range of options. To some extent this work of guaranteeing is becoming privatized, as is signaled by the growth of international commercial arbitration (Dezalay and Garth, 1996), and by key elements of the new privatized institutional order for governing the global economy (Cutler, 2002).

There is a second articulation of the state and globalization, predicated on the sharply unequal power of states. It is in fact some states, particularly the United States and the United Kingdom, which are producing the design for the new standards and legalities needed to ensure protections and guarantees for global firms and markets. The United States and the United Kingdom are by far the most powerful producers of such standards and legalities insofar as most of them are derived from Anglo-American commercial law and accounting standards. Hence it is a limited number of states, often functioning through the supranational system, which are imposing these standards and legalities. This creates and imposes a set of specific constraints on states participating in the global economy.[20] Yet, legislative items, executive orders, adherence to new technical standards, and so on, will have to be produced through the particular institutional and political structures of each of these states. In terms of research and theorization this is a vast uncharted terrain: it would mean examining how that production takes place and gets legitimated in different countries. This signals the possibility of cross-national variations (which then would need to be established, measured, and interpreted). To some extent, we may describe this as the production of instances of "institutional isomorphism" (see the essays in Powell and DiMaggio, 1991). While work such as that collected in Powell and DiMaggio (1991) analyzes the structural causes for the emergence of formal similarities among organizations across widely separated areas, and the mechanisms of power and legitimation underlying these causes, it tends to assume that organizations already exist within a shared structural field. Once these organizations are mutually relevant, structural forces can act on each to shape them to a common mold. In the situations under analysis here, it is not immediately clear that the various relevant organizations exist within the same organizational fields, and much of the work performed is oriented specifically toward making them co-present with a common (global) field/space. Here it is important to emphasize that the emergent, often imposed, consensus in the community of states to further globalization is not merely a political decision: it entails specific types of work by a large number of distinct state institutions in each of these countries. This is an under-researched process, one which would lend itself to comparative cross-national studies. Clearly, the role of the state will vary significantly depending on the power it may have both internally and internationally.

A crucial part of the argument is the fact of the institutional and locational embed-dedness of globalization discussed in the first half of this chapter. Specifying this emb-eddedness has two purposes. One is to provide the empirical specification underlying my assertion that the state is engaged in the implementation of global processes, rather than being a "victim" of these; establishing embeddedness of the global in the national in turn feeds the proposition about the denationalizing of particular state functions and capaci-ties as this engagement by the state proceeds. The second purpose is to signal that, given this embeddedness, the range of ways in which the state might be involved could, in prin-ciple, be far more diverse than today's, largely confined to furthering economic global-ization. Jessop (1990), though not necessarily focused on globalization, provides an extraordinary theoretical perspective for conceptualizing how these various possibilities are either reinforced or selected against by the structures of the state. Conceivably state involvement could address a whole series of global issues, including the democratic deficit in the multilateral system governing globalization.[21]

Conclusion

This chapter focused on critical global structurations inside national domains. Such a perspective expands the analytic terrain within which to understand the global. In so doing it constitutes distinct objects of study, some of which have not typically been seen as part of the research and theorization agenda of the global.

We can distinguish very broadly three major types of objects of study. One consists of the endogenizing or the localizing of global dynamics, producing a concrete and situated object of study such as particular types of places. A second consists of formations which although global are articulated with particular actors, cultures, or projects, producing an object of study that requires negotiating a global and a local scale, such as global markets and global networks. A third consists of the denationalizing of what had historically been constructed as national and may still continue to be experienced, represented, and coded as such; this produces an object of study that is contained within national frames but needs to be decoded, such as state institutions that are key producers of instruments needed by global economic actors. These three types capture distinct social entities and have diverse origins. However, they are not necessarily mutually exclusive. They may well come together in some of the conditions or processes we might want to construct as objects of study.

Cutting across these diverse processes and domains is a research and theorization agenda. This agenda brings together different strands of a rapidly growing scholarship in several different disciplines, some focused on self-evidently global processes/conditions and others on local or national processes/conditions. This agenda is driven by at least some of the following major concerns. At the most general level a first concern is establishing novel or additional dimensions of the spatiality of the national and the global. Specific structurations of what we have represented as the global are actually located deep inside states and other national institutions, and, more generally, in territories encased by national legal, administrative, and cultural frames. In fact, what has been represented (and to some extent reified) as the scale of the national contains a simultaneity of scales, spaces, and relations, some national in the historic sense of the term, some denationalized or in process of becoming so, and some global.

A second major concern is with critical examinations of how we conceptualize the local and the subnational in ways that allow us to detect those instances – even when these might be a minority of all instances – that are in fact denationalized and multi-scalar even when represented and experienced as "simply local." The multi-scalar versions of the local have the effect of destabilizing the notion of context, often predicated on that of the local, and the notion that physical proximity is one of the attributes or markers of the local. Further, a critical reconceptualizing of the local along these lines entails an at least partial rejection of the notion that local scales are inevitably part of nested hierarchies of scale running from the local to the regional, the national, the international. Because of new communication capabilities, localities can constitute multi-scalar systems operating horizontally across borders and not merely scaling upward.

A third major concern is how to conceptualize the national, particularly the specific interactions between global dynamics and particular components of the national. The crucial conditionality here is the partial embeddedness of the global in the national, of which the global city is perhaps emblematic and one of the most complex instances. My main argument here is that this engenders a variety of negotiations insofar as specific structurations of the global inhabit, and partly contribute to constituting what has historically been constructed and institutionalized as national. One set of outcomes evident today is an incipient, highly specialized, and partial denationalization of specific components of national states. This type of focus brings to the fore the particularities of each state when it comes to its interaction with global forces. Even though most states have wound up implementing policies that support economic globalization, this does not preclude institutional differences in the process of accommodation. Some states will have resisted, and others promptly acquiesced. Understanding this interaction of global and national forces demands detailed studies of the particular ways in which different countries have handled and institutionalized this negotiation. But this also signals that the denationalized participation of states could be oriented towards agendas for the public good and shared commons.

Notes

1 For a detailed examination of these two aspects see Sassen, 2001, chs 4, 5 and 7.
2 This process of corporate integration should not be confused with vertical integration as conventionally defined. See as well Gereffi, 1995 on commodity chains and Porter's (1990) value-added chains, two constructs that also illustrate the difference between corporate integration at a world scale and vertical integration as conventionally defined.
3 A central proposition here is that we cannot take the existence of a global economic system as a given, but rather need to examine the particular ways in which the conditions for economic globalization are produced. This requires examining not only communication capacities and the power of multinationals, but also the infrastructure of facilities and work processes necessary for the implementation of global economic systems, including the production of those inputs that constitute the capability for global control and the infrastructure of jobs involved in this production. The emphasis shifts to the *practice* of global control: the work of producing and reproducing the organization and management of a global production system and a global marketplace for finance, both under conditions of economic concentration. The recovery of place and production also implies that global processes can be studied in great empirical detail.
4 Affiliates are but one form of operating overseas and hence their number under-represents the dispersal of a firm's operations. There are today multiple forms, ranging from new temporary partnerships to older types of subcontracting and contracting.
5 This index is an average based on ratios of the share that foreign sales, assets, and employment represent in a firm's total of each. If we consider the world's top 100 TNCs, the EU has 48 of these firms and the US, 28; many of the remaining are from Japan. Thus together the EU and the US account for over 2/3 of the world's 100 largest TNCs. The US, the UK, France, Germany, and Japan together accounted for 3/4 of these 100 firms in 1997; this has been roughly so since 1990. The average transnationality index for the EU is 56.7 percent compared to 38.5 percent for the US (but 79.2 for Canada). (See OECD, 2000 for the full listing.)
6 Two major developments that can alter some of the features of the present configuration: the growth of electronic trading and the growth of the Eurozone. The creation of an enormous consolidated capital market in the Eurozone raises serious questions about the feasibility of maintaining the current pattern with as many international financial centers as there are member countries; some of these markets may lose top international functions and get repositioned in complex and hierarchical divisions of labor. Secondly, electronic trading is leading to a distinct

shift towards setting up strategic alliances among major financial centers, producing a combination of a cross-border digital market embedded in a set of specific city-based financial markets. I have examined this at greater length in Sassen, 2006, chs 5 and 7.

7 Hence, for Arrighi, the geography of power in the contemporary cycle of accumulation is marked by a situation unique within the history of capitalism: military and financial hegemony are not exercised by the same state. Rather, they are held respectively by the US and East Asia. While Arrighi sees a unique situation within the contemporary world-system, the spatiality of the world-system itself has remained relatively unmodified. Power remains distributed among core and peripheral regions, not among points in a global network. The primary difference is that the world is now multipolar instead of unipolar, for the main military power has become ineffcient relative to the main economic power.

8 It is quite possible that globalization may have the effect of blurring the boundaries between these two regulatory worlds.

9 I am trying to distinguish current forms from older notions of the state as a tool for capital, comprador bourgeoisies, or neocolonialism. Further, there are important parallels in this research with scholarship focused on the work of the state to produce the distinction between private and public law (see Cutler, 2002), and with scholarship on the work of the state in setting up the various legal and administrative frameworks that gave the modern state its shape (see e.g. Novak, 1996 for a review of the case of the US).

10 I use the term convergence for expediency. In the larger project (2006), I posit that conceptualizing these outcomes as convergence is actually problematic and often incorrect. Rather than a dynamic whereby individual states wind up converging, what is at work is a global dynamic that gets filtered through the specifics of each "participating" state. Hence what is of central concern is not so much the outcome, "convergence," but the work of producing this outcome.

11 Elsewhere I examine the emergence of forms of globality centered on localized struggles and actors that are part of cross-border networks; this is a form of global politics that runs not through global institutions but through local ones (2006, chs 6 and 7).

12 For instance, at least some of the circuits connecting São Paulo to global dynamics are different from those of Frankfurt, Johannesburg, or Mumbai. Further, distinct sets of overlapping circuits contribute to the constitution of distinctly structured cross-border geographies: for instance, the intensifying of older hegemonic geographies, e.g., the increase in transactions between New York and Miami, Mexico City, and São Paulo (e.g. Schiffer, 2002; Parnreiter, 2002), as well as newly constituted geographies, e.g. the articulation of Shanghai with a rapidly growing number of cross-border circuits (Gu and Tang, 2002).

13 In my early research on the global city I began to understand some of these questions of reified scales. Much of the literature on global and world cities has a critical appraisal of questions of scaling, but with important exceptions (Taylor, 1995; Brenner, 1998) this appraisal tends to be in embryo, undertheorized and not quite explicated. On the other hand, the scholarship on "glocalization" recognizes and theorizes questions of scale but often remains attached to a notion of nested scalings (e.g. Swyngedouw, 1997). I find that among the literatures in geography that come closest in their conceptualization, albeit focused on very different issues, to what I develop in this chapter are those on first-nation peoples' rights claiming (e.g. Howitt, 1993; Silvern, 1999; Notzke, 1995). Clearly, there is a particularly illuminating positioning of the issues in this case because from the outset there is: (a) the coexistence of two exclusive claims over a single territory; and (b) the endogeneity of both types of claims – that of the modern sovereign and that of the indigenous nation. In this chapter it is the coexistence of the claim of the historical sovereign and the claim of the global as endogenized in the reconstituted sovereign. For a full development of this somewhat abstract statement, please see Sassen, 2006.

14 I have developed this at greater length in Sassen, 1996 and 1999. I should clarify that when I

first developed the construct 'de-nationalization' in the 1995 Memorial Schoff Lectures (1996) I intended it to denote a specific dynamic. I did *not* intend it as some general notion that can be used interchangeably with post-national, global, or other such terms. In this regard see the debate in *Indiana Journal of Global Legal Studies* (2000).

15 Diverging somewhat from what has emerged as the main proposition in globalization research – growing interdependence – I argue that the marking condition for globalization is the way in which the national has been constructed over the last century (with different temporal frames in different countries). From here then comes my emphasis on denationalization: the necessity to denationalize specific structurations inside this thickly constructed and highly formalized national context. This type of focus allows us to capture the enormous variability across countries in terms of incorporation/negotiation/resistance, since these are partly shaped by the specifics, both de facto and de jure, of each country; at the same time, it avoids the trap of comparative studies in that it introduces the thesis that the conditionalities of a global system need to be partly met through specific structurations in multiple countries.

16 For what I define as the organizing hypotheses of the global city model please see the Preface to the new edition (Sassen, 2001). In preparing this new edition I was far more able to formulate these nine hypotheses than I was in writing the first edition, partly thanks to the enormously rich and varied literature produced during the 1990s and the equally rich and varied (though not always as enjoyable) criticisms the first edition provoked.

17 Thus I would distinguish this from the case of illegal traffickers of people who have now been able to go global, where before they were regional, because of the infrastructure for communications and money transfers brought about by globalization. For a development of this argument please see Sassen, 2000.

18 Two very different bodies of scholarship which develop lines of analysis that can help in capturing some of these conditions are represented by the work of Rosenau, particularly his examination of the domestic "frontier" inside the national state (1997), and by the work of Walker (1993) problematizing the distinction inside/outside in international relations theory.

19 While it is well known, it is worth remembering that this guarantee of the rights of capital is embedded in a certain type of state, a certain conception of the rights of capital, and a certain type of international legal regime: it is largely embedded in the state of the most developed and most powerful countries in the world, in Western notions of contract and property rights, and in new legal regimes aimed at furthering economic globalization, e.g. the push to get countries to support copyright law.

20 This dominance assumes many forms and does not only affect poorer and weaker countries. France, for instance, ranks among the top providers of information services and industrial engineering services in Europe and has a strong though not outstanding position in financial and insurance services. But it has found itself at an increasing disadvantage in legal and accounting services because Anglo-American law and standards dominate in international transactions. Anglo-American firms with offices in Paris do the servicing of the legal needs of firms, whether French or foreign, operating out of France (Sassen, 2001). Similarly, Anglo-American law is increasingly dominant in international commercial arbitration, an institution grounded in continental traditions of jurisprudence, particularly French and Swiss (Dezalay and Garth, 1996).

21 Elsewhere (2006, ch. 6) I examine how these dynamics also position citizens (still largely confined to national state institutions for the full execution of their rights) vis-à-vis these types of global struggle. My argument is that state participation creates an enabling environment not only for global corporate capital but also for those seeking to subject the latter to greater accountability and public scrutiny. But unlike what has happened with global corporate capital, the necessary legal and administrative instruments and regimes have not been developed. The tradeoffs and the resources that can be mobilized are quite different in the case of citizens

seeking to globalize their capacities for governing compared to those of global capital seeking to form regimes that enable and protect it.

References

Abbott, Andrew (1988). *The System of Professions*. Chicago: University of Chicago Press.

Agnew, John (1993). "Representing Space: Space, Scale and Culture in Social Science." In *Place/Culture/Representation*, ed. J. Duncan and D. Ley. London and New York: Routledge, pp. 251–71.

Aman, Alfred C. (1998). "The Globalizing State: A Future-Oriented Perspective on the Public/Private Distinction, Federalism, and Democracy." *Vanderbilt Journal of Transnational Law*, 31: pp. 769–870.

Amin, A. and N. Thrift (1994). *Globalization, Institutions and Regional Development in Europe*. Oxford: Oxford University Press.

Appadurai, Arjun (1996). *Modernity at Large*. Minneapolis: University of Minnesota Press.

Arrighi, Giovanni (1994). *The Long Twentieth Century*. New York: Verso.

Arrighi, Giovanni and Beverly Silver (1999). *Chaos and Governance in the Modern World System*. Minneapolis: University of Minnesota Press.

Bartlett, Ann (2007). "The City and the Self: The Emergence of New Political Subjects in London." In *Deciphering the Global: Its Spaces, Scales and Subjects*, ed. S. Sassen. New York and London: Routledge.

Beck, Ulrich (2000). *What is Globalization?* Cambridge: Polity.

Brenner, Neil (1998). "Global Cities, Glocal States: Global City Formation and State Territorial Restructuring in Contemporary Europe." *Review of International Political Economy*, 5(2): pp. 1–37.

Brenner, Neil (1999). "Beyond State-Centrism? Space, Territoriality, and Geographical Scale in Globalization Studies." *Theory and Society*, 28(1): pp. 39–78.

Brenner, Neil and Roger Keil (2005). *The Global Cities Reader*. New York and London: Routledge.

Cerny, Philip G. (1990). *The Changing Architecture of Politics*. London and Newbury, Calif.: Sage.

Cerny, Philip G. (2000). "Structuring the Political Arena: Public Goods, States and Governance in a Globalizing World." In *Global Political Economy: Contemporary Theories*, ed. Ronen Palan. London: Routledge, pp. 21–35.

Cutler, A. Claire (2002). "The Politics of 'Regulated Liberalism': A Historical Materialist Approach to European Integration." In *Historical Materialism and Globalization*, ed. Mark Rupert and Hazel Smith. London: Routledge, pp. 230–56.

Datz, Giselle (2007). "Global–National Interactions: Toward a Theory of Sovereign Debt Restructuring Outcomes." In *Deciphering the Global: Its Spaces, Scales and Subjects*, ed. S. Sassen. New York and London: Routledge.

Dezalay, Yves and Bryant G. Garth (1996). *Dealing in Virtue: International Commercial Arbitration and the Construction of a Transnational Legal Order*. Chicago: University of Chicago Press.

Eichengreen, Barry and Albert Fishlow (1996). *Contending with Capital Flows*. New York: Council of Foreign Relations.

Evans, Peter (1997). "The Eclipse of the State? Reflections on Stateness in an Era of Globalization." *World Politics*, 50(1): pp. 62–87.

Ferguson, Yale H. and R. J. Barry Jones eds (2002). *Political Space: Frontiers of Change and Governance in a Globalizing World*. Albany, NY: SUNY Press.

Fligstein, Neil (1990). *The Transformation of Corporate Control*. Cambridge, Mass.: Harvard University Press.

Fligstein, Neil (2001). *The Architecture of Markets*. Princeton: Princeton University Press.

GAWC (Globalization and World Cities: Study Group and Network). Website: www.lboro.ac. uk/gawc/.

Gereffi, Gary (1994). "The Organization of Buyer-Driven Commodity Chains." In *Commodity Chains and Global Capitalism*, ed. Gary Gereffi and Miguel Korzeniewicz. Westport, Conn.: Praeger, pp. 95–122.

Gereffi, Gary (1995). "Global Production Systems and Third World Development." In *Global Change, Regional Response: The New International Context of Development*, ed. Barbara Stallings. New York: Cambridge University Press, pp. 100–42.

Gereffi, Gary (1999). "International Trade and Industrial Upgrading in the Apparel Commodity Chain." *Journal of International Economics*, 48: pp. 37–70.

Gereffi, Gary, John Humphrey and Timothy Sturgeon (2005). "The Governance of Global Value Chains." *Review of International Political Economy* (Special Issue: *Aspects of Globalization*), 12(1): pp. 78–104.

Gill, Stephen (1996). "Globalization, Democratization, and the Politics of Indifference." In *Globalization: Critical Reflections*, edited by James Mittelman. Boulder, Colo.: Lynne Rienner Publishers, pp. 205–28.

Gu, Felicity Rose and Zilai Tang (2002). "Shanghai: Reconnecting to the Global Economy." In *Global Networks/Linked Cities*, ed. Saskia Sassen. New York and London: Routledge, pp. 273–307.

Hall, Rodney Bruce and Thomas J. Biersteker (2002). *The Emergence of Private Authority in Global Governance*. Cambridge and New York: Cambridge University Press.

Howitt, Richard (1993). "A World in a Grain of Sand: Towards a Reconceptualization of Geographical Scale." *Australian Geographer*, 24(1): pp. 33–44.

Indiana Journal of Global Legal Studies (2000). *The State of Citizenship, Special Issue*, 7(2).

Jessop, Bob (1990). *State Theory*. University Park: Pennsylvania State University Press.

Jonas, Andrew (1994). "The Scale Politics of Spatiality." *Environment and Planning D: Society and Space*, 12(3): pp. 257–64.

Krasner, Stephen D. (1999). "Globalization and Sovereignty." In *Globalization and the Asian Pacific*, ed. K. Olds et al. London: Routledge, pp. 34–52.

Mann, Michael (1986). *The Sources of Social Power, Vol 1*. Cambridge: Cambridge University Press.

Mann, Michael (1997). "Has Globalization Ended the Rise and Rise of the Nation State?" *Review of International Political Economy*, 4(3): pp. 472–96.

Massey, Doreen (1993). "Politics and Space/Time." In *Place and the Politics of Identity*, ed. M. Keith and S. Pile. London and New York: Routledge, pp. 141–6.

Mittelman, James H. (2000). *The Globalization Syndrome: Transformation and Resistance*. Princeton: Princeton University Press.

Notzke, Claudia (1995). "A New Perspective in Aboriginal Nature Resource Management: Co-Management." *Geoforum*, 26(2): pp. 187–209.

Novak, William J. (1996). *The People's Welfare: Law and Regulation in Nineteenth-Century America*. Chapel Hill: University of North Carolina Press.

OECD (Organization for Economic Cooperation and Development) (2000). *International Direct Investment Statistics Yearbook 1999*. Paris: OECD.

O'Riain, Sean (2000). "States and Markets in an Era of Globalization." *Annual Review of Sociology*, 26: pp. 187–213.

Panitch, Leo (1996). "Rethinking the Role of the State." In *Globalization: Critical Reflections*, ed. James Mittelman. Boulder, Colo.: Lynne Rienner Publishers, pp. 83–113.

Parnreiter, Christof (2002). "Mexico: The Making of a Global City." In *Global Networks/Linked Cities*, ed. Saskia Sassen. New York and London: Routledge, pp. 145–82.

Picciotto, Sol (1992). *International Business Taxation: A Study in the Internationalization of Business Regulation*. New York: Quorum Books.

Portnoy, Brian (2000). "Constructing Competition: The Political Foundations of Alliance Capitalism." Ph.D. dissertation, University of Chicago.

Porter, Michael E. (1990). *The Competitive Advantage of Nations*. New York: Free Press.

Powell, Walter and Paul DiMaggio, eds (1991). *The New Institutionalism in Organizational Analysis*. Chicago: University of Chicago Press.

Rosenau, James N. (1997). *Along the Domestic–Foreign Frontier: Exploring Governance in a Turbulent World*. Cambridge and New York: Cambridge University Press.

Sassen, Saskia (1996). *Losing Control? Sovereignty in an Age of Globalization*. New York: Columbia University Press.

Sassen, Saskia (1999). *Guests and Aliens*. New York: New Press.

Sassen, Saskia (2000). "Territory and Territoriality in the Global Economy." *International Sociology*, 15(2): pp. 372–93.

Sassen, Saskia (2001). *The Global City*, 2nd edn. Princeton: Princeton University Press.

Sassen, Saskia (2005). "Electronic Markets and Activist Networks: the Weight of Social Logics in Digital Formations". In *Digital Formations: IT and New Architectures in the Global Realm*, ed. Robert Latham and Saskia Sassen. Princeton: Princeton University Press.

Sassen, Saskia (2006). *Territory, Authority, Rights: From Medieval to Global Assemblages*. Princeton: Princeton University Press.

Schiffer, Sueli Ramos (2002). "São Paulo: Articulating a Cross-Border Region." In *Global Networks/Linked Cities*, ed. Saskia Sassen. New York and London: Routledge, pp. 209–36.

Silvern, Steven E. (1999). "Scales of Justice: Law, American Indian Treaty Rights and Political Construction of Scale." *Political Geography*, 18: pp. 639–68.

Skocpol, Theda (1985). "Bringing the State Back In: Strategies of Analysis in Current Research." In *Bringing the State Back In*, ed. Peter Evans, Dietrich Rueschemeyer, and Theda Skocpol. Cambridge and New York: Cambridge University Press.

Swyngedouw, Erik (1997). "Neither Global nor Local: "Glocalization" and the Politics of Scale." In *Spaces of Globalization: Reasserting the Power of the Local*, ed. Kevin Cox. New York: Guilford Press, pp. 137–66.

Taylor, Peter (1995). "World Cities and Territorial States: The Rise and Fall of their Mutuality." In *World Cities in a World-System*, ed. Peter Taylor and P. L. Knox. Cambridge: Cambridge University Press, pp. 28–62.

Taylor, Peter (2000). "World Cities and Territorial States under Conditions of Contemporary Globalization." *Political Geography*, 19(5): pp. 5–32.

Taylor, Peter J. (2004). *World City Network: A Global Urban Analysis*. London: Routledge.

Taylor, Peter, D. R. F. Walker, and J. V. Beaverstock (2002). "Firms and their Global Service Networks." In *Global Networks/Linked Cities*, ed. Saskia Sassen. New York and London: Routledge, pp. 93–115.

Tilly, Charles (1990). *Coercion, Capital, and European States*. Oxford: Basil Blackwell.

Walker, R. B. J. (1993). *Inside/Outside: International Relations as Political Theory*. Cambridge: Cambridge University Press.

Wallerstein, Immanuel (1974). *The Modern World-System*. New York: Academic Press.

Weiss, Linda (1998). *The Myth of the Powerless State*. Ithaca, NY: Cornell University Press.

Williams, M. (2000). *Contesting Global Governance: Multilateral Institutions and Global Social Movements*. Cambridge: Cambridge University Press.

5

The Political Economy of Globalization

Layna Mosley

What are the politics that underlie, and that result from, the contemporary wave of economic globalization? While the trend toward greater economic interdependence draws partly from technological change, in terms of firms' and investors' ability to disregard political boundaries, it also results from deliberate decisions by political leaders to embrace more open markets. In some cases, these decisions reflect a long-standing "compromise of embedded liberalism," in which European governments paired increased openness to international trade with increased domestic protection for those dislocated by trade (Rodrik, 1997; Ruggie, 1982). These governments embraced neoclassical economists' claim that economic openness improved overall national welfare; at the same time, though, their awareness of the distributional consequences of growing openness led them to a model of "openness plus compensation."

In other cases, and particularly in the developing world, governments' moves toward openness reflect a later embrace, in the 1980s and 1990s, of neoliberal-oriented development strategies. The success of export-oriented industrialization in Southeast Asia, as well as the shortcomings of import-substitution industrialization in Latin America, facilitated this embrace. And, in at least some cases, citizens of developing nations began to privilege low inflation and economic stability, despite the painful adjustment process associated with economic reform (Armijo, 1996; Weyland, 1996). Of course, for developing nations in particular, the political causes of economic openness were external as well as internal. In many cases, the reduction of trade barriers and the liberalization of capital markets were mandated by IMF structural adjustment programs (e.g. Stone, 2002; Vreeland, 2003). And even when this was not the case, explicit pressure from the US government, private financial markets, the IMF, and the World Bank, as well as the diffusion of neoliberal economic ideas, helped to drive governments toward greater economic openness.[1]

The relative impact of external and internal factors, or of political versus economic considerations, is a central topic in the academic fields of comparative and international political economy. Are democracies, for instance, less likely to liberalize trade than nondemocracies? Or do countries under IMF adjustment programs succeed to a greater degree in economic reform and liberalization? While these types of issues are important, both to scholars and to policymakers, this chapter focuses on the reverse question: how does economic globalization affect government policymaking? Specifically, to what extent, and in what ways, does economic interdependence affect national policymaking and policy outcomes? More broadly, does economic globalization alter the capabilities of national governments, thereby rendering impossible many welfare-oriented policies?

Or do governments retain some measure of policymaking autonomy, despite economic globalization?

After briefly summarizing trends in economic globalization, this chapter discusses the potential incompatibility between welfare states and economic globalization, exemplified in the "race to the bottom" claim. It presents the causal logic behind this claim, as well as the main theoretical objections to it. It then turns to empirical evidence regarding recent government policymaking, as a means of assessing the correlation between economic openness and policy outcomes, in both developed and developing nations. From this review of economic globalization's general effects, I move to a consideration of the specific effects of financial globalization. To what extent does the increased velocity and volume of global financial flows render governments the slaves, rather than the masters, of capital markets? The main argument presented is that, while capital market openness does influence some aspects of government policymaking, this influence is by no means omnipotent or omnipresent. In some areas, governments retain significant "room to move." This is more the case in developed than in developing nations; but even in the developing world, we should be careful not to overstate the influence of foreign investors. The chapter concludes with an assessment of why, despite pronounced empirical evidence against it, the "race to the bottom" hypothesis remains firmly in the public eye.

Contemporary Economic Openness

While there is debate regarding the extent to which today's economic globalization is historically unprecedented, or the extent to which today's globalization falls short of "full openness,"[2] most observers would agree that contemporary trade and financial markets exhibit a significant degree of openness. During the last three decades, governments have reduced legal barriers to the movements across national borders of capital, goods and services (e.g. Garrett, 2000). They have lowered taxes (tariffs) on international trade, attempted to create common international standards for services and products, and often have liberalized rules regarding investment inflows and outflows. In tandem with these policy changes, advances in technology and reductions in transportation costs have facilitated a growing interdependence of national economies. Interest rate changes in one country, for instance, quickly spread to other countries; changes in US monetary policy affect Latin American markets, and European Union monetary policy impacts markets in the former Soviet Union, North Africa, and the Middle East. Even if governments wanted to retain legal barriers to the mobility of capital, they probably would have difficulty in enforcing capital account restrictions. Similarly, the effects of national business cycles are felt globally, as they generate changes in demands for imports, in the prices of exports, and in exchange rates. Recent history also has witnessed the development and intensification of global production networks, in which the value chain of production is spread across multiple, often distant, locations (e.g. Gereffi and Korzeniewicz, 1994).

Figure 5.1a illustrates the overall trend toward economic openness, from 1970 to 2002; it plots flows of trade and capital, each as a proportion of gross domestic product, for low-, middle-, and high-income nations.[3] Figure 5.1b reports gross private capital flows, which include shorter-term, more speculative investment, as well as longer-term direct investment. Figure 5.1a reports imports and exports; it demonstrates that, in terms of overall trade openness, developed countries were most open during the 1970s and 1980s. Wealthy nations' average level of trade openness continued to rise in recent years but, by 1990, middle-income countries were even more open, at least in terms of product flows. This reflects the use of export-oriented development strategies in many middle-income nations, as well as the increased integration of these countries into global production networks. Trade openness also rose dramatically in low-income countries during the 1990s and after. On the finance side (figure 5.1b), capital flows are most important to high-income nations throughout the period, with the exception of the 1978–83 period. Although capital flows to middle-income countries declined in the wake of the 1980s debt crisis, the 1990s saw a recovery of investment in middle-income nations, particularly in nations like Brazil and China. The importance of different types of flow to developing nations varies across time, particularly in response to financial market crises and concerns about creditworthiness. In 2003 total net capital flows, from both official and private sources, were equivalent to 3.6 percent of developing country GDP; for some nations, however, the ratio of flows to income was much higher. Of the private capital flows, foreign direct investment (FDI) accounted for 68 percent, with equities, bonds and bank loans accounting for the rest.

Greater economic openness offers governments the promise of improved economic outcomes. At the aggregate national level, many economists have argued that higher levels of openness to trade are associated with higher rates of economic growth (e.g. Bhagwati, 1998). Despite recent critiques of this finding (see Garrett, 2000; Rodrik and Rodriguez, 2001), governments have tended to embrace it, lowering tariffs and other trade barriers in recent decades. While reductions in protectionist barriers have a negative impact on firms, sectors, or factors lacking a comparative advantage, this impact is offset by gains for those with comparative advantages.[4] Nations, particularly those with democratic governments, may elect to spend part of the trade-related economic gains on compensating the losers from freer trade (Adserá and Boix, 2001; Cameron, 1978; Rodrik, 1997).

On the finance side, openness again could offer benefits, including higher rates of growth, poverty alleviation, and greater macroeconomic policy discipline. Empirical analyses of the relationship between capital flows and growth offer a mixed and complicated picture, sometimes finding small or even non-existent effects on growth in developing nations.[5] The mixed pattern is due partly to the varying effects of different types of capital flow. Studies that distinguish among portfolio flows, bank lending, and direct investment find that FDI has the greatest positive impact on growth (Agénor, 2001; Dobson and Hufbauer, 2001).

Global capital flows also are concentrated in a narrow set of middle-income recipients; many lower-income developing nations continue to receive less capital than an efficient (and risk adjusted) global allocation suggests. In a recent survey, *The Economist* (2003) reported that, at the end of 2001, less than 8 percent of the worldwide stock of cross-border bank loans ($9 trillion total) were directed to developing-country borrowers; and developing countries accounted for only $600 billion of the $12 trillion in global cross-border securities investment. Similarly, during the 1989–2002 period, the top eight recipients of portfolio equity investment accounted for 84 percent of total flows; and the top ten recipients of FDI comprised 70 percent of developing-country direct investment in 2002 (World Bank, 2004). While the latter is an improvement (from 79 percent in 2000), the general pattern persists: China, Mexico, Brazil, South Africa, and other middle-income

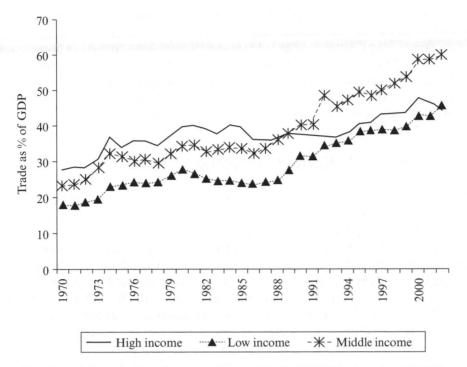

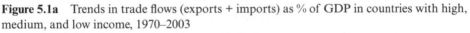

Figure 5.1a Trends in trade flows (exports + imports) as % of GDP in countries with high, medium, and low income, 1970–2003

Source: World Bank, *World Development Indicators* database.

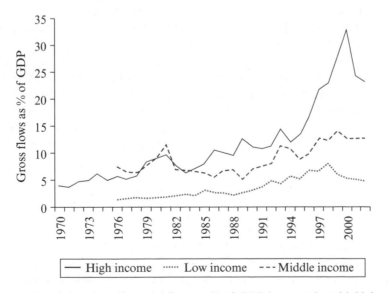

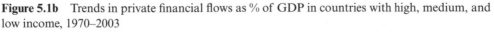

Figure 5.1b Trends in private financial flows as % of GDP in countries with high, medium, and low income, 1970–2003

Source: World Bank, *World Development Indicators* database.

nations may do well at attracting capital, but smaller, poorer nations have much less success. Moreover, financial openness, especially to shorter-term instruments, brings risks, including increased volatility and the abrupt reversals of flows, as well as banking crises (World Bank, 2001). These risks stem partly from domestic policy mistakes, but also from instability in capital markets. Investment flows to developing nations tend to be volatile, with some periods of great enthusiasm and availability of funds, and other periods of pessimism and credit rationing. These issues are discussed later in the chapter.

Economic Globalization and National Government Policies

While the contemporary trend toward economic globalization is, in some respects, unique historically, scholars and policymakers long have been interested in the relationship between national governments and private economic actors. International economic relations, in one mode or another, always have affected the control and authority of national states (Krasner, 1999). In the *Wealth of Nations* (1776), Adam Smith points out that the imposition of taxes by national governments can provoke capital flight (book II, sections 373–9). And in *The Great Transformation,* published in the mid-1940s, Karl Polanyi argues that high levels of international economic openness are politically sustainable only when governments insulate and compensate vulnerable groups in society, by embedding market relations in a set of social institutions. Without such intervention, societies choose to close their economic borders, as they did in the 1920s.

So, despite the recent intensification of economic globalization, concerns about the autonomy and centrality of the nation-state have long characterized international relations scholarship. For instance, writing in 1971, Robert Keohane and Joseph Nye argued that the growing importance of transnational actors to the conduct of international relations necessitated the development of an alternative to the state-centric paradigm (Keohane and Nye, 1971). They pointed out that greater economic interdependence – perhaps the 1970s equivalent of "globalization" – signified changes in the capacity and roles of national states. Along these lines, national policymakers were less able to exercise authority over political and economic outcomes than they were in the 1950s and 1960s (Keohane and Nye, 1977). In such an environment, the cross-national coordination of economic policies seemed a functional imperative. The ability of firms to relocate production overseas, for example, limited governments' choices over economic policies.

A race to the bottom?

In recent years, scholars and policymakers have again questioned the extent to which the nation-state – and, specifically, the modern welfare state, marked by intervention and publicly provided social protection – is compatible with economic globalization. A theoretical divide emerged in the 1990s, pitting theories that predict cross-national policy convergence against theories that expect sustained cross-national divergence.[6] The empirical evidence, reviewed below, suggests that, while transnational actors – including multinational corporations, institutional investors, banks, and non-governmental organization – undoubtedly influence contemporary national policymaking, they have not brought about the demise of the nation-state. Nor have the pressures generated by such actors resulted in the elimination of cross-national differences in policy outcomes and political institutions. In the face of economic globalization, governments retain "room to move," particularly in the developed world, but also in developing nations. Before reviewing evidence in support of the "race to the bottom" claim – or in support of the contending "divergence" or "room to move" claim – we examine the theoretical logic behind each.

Many popular discussions of economic globalization invoke the "race to the bottom" hypothesis, which is grounded in the imperatives of cross-national competition (in markets for goods, capital, and services) and economic efficiency.[7] Nations benefit, in aggregate terms, from trade and financial openness, but this openness forces them into competition with one another. Competition reduces governments' abilities to provide goods and services to their citizens, and it renders governments more accountable to external economic agents than to citizens of the polity. The driving force behind convergence accounts is efficiency: traditional welfare state policies are economically uncompetitive, so governments are quick to abandon them. Governments become leaner, embracing a neoliberal model of state-economy relations; they abandon the post-World War II "compromise of embedded liberalism," which involved generous social protection for states exposed to the global economy. In these accounts, the prognosis is particularly dim for left-of-center governments which, the story goes, receive the most unfavorable evaluations from financial asset holders (e.g. Helleiner, 1994; Cerny, 1999). At the extreme, global markets become masters of governments, eviscerating the authority of national states. Along these lines, Susan Strange maintains that "the impersonal forces of world markets . . . are now more powerful than the states to whom ultimate political authority over society and economy is supposed to belong. Where states were once the masters of markets, now it is the markets which, on many crucial issues, are the masters over the governments of states" (Strange, 1996, p. 4).

The "race to the bottom" (RTB) hypothesis implies not only a convergence of national policies, but also convergence toward the lowest common denominator. It has become a rallying point for various anti-globalization protestors, as well as a favorite straw man of comparative and international political economists. As many of these divergence-oriented scholars have argued, there are myriad reasons to be skeptical of the claim that the competitive pressures set off by economic openness will lead all nations to pursue a similar, bare-bones set of economic and social policies. As a result, cross-national differences in economic and social policies are likely to persist.

First, literature grounded in comparative politics has established that domestic institutions play an important role in mediating pressures from the global economy, and that these institutions often are resilient in the face of global economic pressures. In his 1985 analysis of small, trade-dependent European states, Peter Katzenstein suggested that, while small states are constrained substantially by the international economy, in that they have little choice but to trade, historical differences in these states' domestic institutions generate cross-national variation in political-economic strategies. More recently, the "varieties of capitalism" literature argues that there are different ways of organizing production in capitalist economies (e.g. Hall and Soskice, 2001; Huber and Stephens, 2001). Varying complexes of institutions can generate similar levels of overall economic performance, and these different sets of business practices, training systems, and worker organizations provide comparative advantages to particular countries and sectors. Accounts based on institutional diversity have at their heart a Tiebout-type model, in which specialization is possible – and beneficial — within globalization (e.g. Rogowski, 2003). Assuming that citizens and firms have different preferences over public services, taxation, and regulation, governments will offer different combinations of these goods, and firms and citizens will locate in the jurisdiction that best matches their preferences. Interestingly, this argument applies the logic of Smith and Ricardo, in which economic openness increases incentives for specialization, to economic and social policies. It also suggests that – contrary to some extreme views of economic globalization, but consistent with endogenous growth theory – some firms will favor some government interventions in domestic economies (Mares, 2003; Pitruzzello, 2004).

The second main objection to the RTB model is, again, rooted in domestic politics. Economic openness may spur citizens to demand increased, rather than decreased, levels of public sector intervention, as a means of compensating them for the volatility induced by the international economic system. As globalization heightens economic insecurity (Rodrik, 1997; Scheve and Slaughter, 2004), demands for government intervention persist, or increase. In a process that recalls the post-World War II compromise of embedded liberalism, governments have domestic incentives to insulate citizens from exogenously generated insecurity and volatility. While governments may pay an economic price (via higher interest rates, for instance) for maintaining welfare state policies, this price is offset by the internal political benefits of compensatory policies (see Adserá and Boix, 2001; Garrett and Mitchell, 2001). While overall trade openness may spur demands for compensation, specific openness to low-wage imports – which increase insecurity for lower-skilled workers – appear even more strongly associated with expansions in public welfare (Burgoon, 2001).

The empirical record

These theoretical doubts about the RTB logic, raised by "divergence" theories, give rise to an empirical prediction: despite increases in trade and financial openness during the last two decades, national economic and social policies should continue to display a good deal of diversity, reflecting differences in citizens' and firms' preferences, in political institutions, and in traditional welfare state policies. These domestically driven policies should be resistant to external pressures. How well does the existing evidence support this prediction?

Among developed democracies, aggregate fiscal and monetary policies (government budget deficits and rates of inflation) converged in the 1990s, reflecting a trend toward lower inflation rates and smaller budget deficits (and, in Europe, reflecting efforts to meet the Maastricht criteria for monetary union by 1997). At the same time, though, substantial cross-national diversity remains in areas such as government consumption spending, government transfer payments, public employment, and public taxation.[8] Despite the substantial convergence in overall fiscal and monetary policies, motivated at least in part by economic globalization, domestic politics and institutions continue to be the most important determinants of the overall size of government and the distribution of government spending across programmatic areas. In the realm of capital taxation, Hays (2003) finds a reduction of variation among OECD nations, but toward an intermediate level of taxation; capital-poor consensus democracies tend to raise rates of capital taxation in response to increased globalization, while capital-rich majoritarian democracies are inclined to lower their rates of capital taxation. And Swank points out that reductions in corporate tax rates often come hand-in-hand with a broadening of the tax base, as governments close various loopholes in their tax codes.

Turning to the developing world, economic globalization has generated greater pressures and incentives for cross-national policy divergence, particularly in the direction of neoliberal economic reform. Again, however, some room for government autonomy – and, therefore, for cross-national diversity in policies – remains. The "compensation hypothesis" is borne out in studies that find a positive association between trade openness and the size of the public sector in developing nations; this pattern has long existed in richer democracies as well (e.g. Rodrik, 1998). In their study of the relationship between trade openness and public spending, for instance, Adserá and Boix (2001) find a positive and significant relationship between trade openness and public sector spending in developing nations. This effect is most pronounced in democracies; the combination of democracy and openness pushes spending even further upward, possibly reflecting the incentives of governments to compensate citizens exposed to volatility (and the absence of these incentives in non-democratic polities). They conclude, then, that developing nations – especially those with competitive export sectors – may be able to sustain a policy of high compensation (generous welfare state policies), especially if the public goods provided generate future improvements in competitiveness and economic growth. Similarly, Rudra and Haggard (2005) posit that the effect of trade openness on social policy spending depends on the political regime; again, authoritarian nations tend to reduce spending as globalization increases, but democracies do not.

Case study evidence for Latin America also bears out the claim regarding the role of domestic politics. To take an example, Kurtz's (2002) study of social policies in Chile and Mexico demonstrates that, despite the general espousal of neoliberal reforms, and the presence of external constraints, in both countries in the 1980s and 1990s, there was significant variation in their social welfare regimes, in terms of efforts to integrate the poor into the market economy and in terms of the use of means-testing versus universal provision in the distribution of benefits. While the global economy and the dominant neoliberal ideology narrowed the policy space for these governments, there remained substantial room for variation, and this variation flowed from political alliances, the degree of organization of the poor in society, and the competitiveness of the political party system. Along slightly different lines, in her study of the determinants of social security reform in a variety of countries, Brooks (2002) reports that pressures from international financial markets play a role in the occurrence and nature of reform. At the same time, though, the type of political regime, as well as the distribution of political power and the structure of previous social security arrangements, also influences the reform process.

This mixed pattern also emerges in Wibbels and Arce's (2003) analysis of the nature of taxation in Latin America in recent decades; they find that higher levels of short-term capital flows and of foreign direct investment place downward pressure on capital's share of taxation. These relationships, however, are not statistically significant, while the relationship between tax policy and the extent of left government and labor policy is. At the same time, though, dependence on international financial institutions (the IMF and the World Bank) predicts that labor will bear an increased share of the tax burden. Rudra

(2002) shares this pessimism about the continued capacity for domestically determined economic policies. She analyzes the determinants of social policy in 53 developing nations; she considers the impact of labor's domestic strength, as well as of trade and financial openness, on welfare spending. Rudra argues that, while labor in developing nations should, as the abundant factor, benefit from increased openness, workers in developing nations have been unable to prevent reductions in welfare state policies. While labor in the developed world has been able to mobilize politically to demand sustained compensation, labor in developing nations has been much less able to do so.

For developing nations, then, a more mixed picture has emerged: as in the advanced democracies, political institutions and domestic interests continue to play a role in the determination of social and economic policies. But, in some cases, the role of domestic factors is rivaled by the pressures emanating from economic globalization. The story scholars tell about globalization's impact in such countries depends heavily on the dependent variable they choose; Kaufman and Segura-Ubiergo's (2001) quantitative analysis of total social spending in Latin America during the 1970s, 1980s, and 1990s finds that trade integration has a consistent, negative impact on social spending, and that this effect is exacerbated by financial openness. But a more complex picture emerges when they use as their dependent variable particular types of social spending – social security transfers, health care, and education. Globalization's negative effect on social programs obtains in the area of social security transfers, but much less so for health and education spending. And each type of spending is influenced markedly by domestic political variables.

Global Capital Markets and Government "Room to Move"

When we turn from the general impact of economic globalization to the specific influence of international capital markets on government policymaking, the same mixed patterns – in which international forces affect government policymaking, but not to the exclusion of domestic factors; and in which developing nations are more constrained than developed ones – emerge. In the realm of capital markets, investors' capacity for exit, and the political voice it confers, is central to convergence- (or "race to the bottom") oriented accounts (e.g. Cerny, 1995; Hirshman,1970; Kurzer, 1993). While capital market openness provides governments with greater access to capital, it also subjects them to external (or "market") discipline. Governments must sell their policies not only to domestic voters, but also to international investors. Because investors can respond swiftly and severely to actual or expected policy outcomes, governments must consider financial market participants' preferences when selecting policies. Again, this generates dire predictions when it comes to governments' capacity for domestically driven policymaking; as financial openness increases, the capacity to spend and tax, and the more general ability to pursue divergent policies, should diminish markedly.

Has this happened? As the evidence reviewed above suggests, some cross-national convergence has occurred, leading to lower average rates of inflation and smaller fiscal deficits in both advanced and developing nations. But, when we move beyond these macro-policy indicators, we find less evidence for convergence, particularly in developing nations. For instance, Burgoon's (2001) study of social policy in the OECD finds that openness to foreign direct and portfolio investment has a generally positive effect on spending for worker training and relocation, but a negative effect on total social spending. He also reports smaller, negative relationships between financial openness and health care and family benefits. But the size and the statistical robustness of these relationships is modest. In the developing world, there appear to be greater pressures for policy convergence, and these pressures extend beyond macro-policies, to more micro-policies, such as the specific structure of tax systems (the balance of the burden between labor and capital) and the provision of education, health, and social security policies. Of course, as the above review indicates, these pressures do not fully determine policy choices.

What explains the difference in the financial market constraints faced by developed versus developing (or "emerging market") nations? Mosley (2003) addresses these issues in a recent analysis of the influences of global capital markets on government policy-making, with a specific focus on the government bond market, suggesting that, because of professional investors' incentives and information needs, financial market pressures will vary across groups of countries. In the advanced capitalist democracies, market participants consider key macroeconomic indicators, but not supply-side or micro-level policies. The result is a "strong but narrow" financial market constraint in the developed world. Governments that conform to capital market pressures in select macroeconomic areas, such as overall government budget deficits and rates of inflation, are relatively unconstrained in supply-side and microeconomic policy areas. And for the most important developed nations, the constraint may not be very strong: the archetypal current case is the continued ability of the US government to borrow at relatively low rates of interest, despite its large and growing budget deficits.[9]

For developing nations, however, the scope of financial market influence often extends to cover both macro- and micro-policy areas. Market participants, concerned with default risk, consider many dimensions of government policy when making asset allocation decisions. Domestic policymaking in these nations will tend more toward the convergence view, as the financial market constraint is both strong and broad. Empirical support for these assertions comes from interviews and surveys of professional investors, as well as quantitative analyses. Mosley finds that, as a result of their concerns with default risk, financial market participants treat emerging markets differently from – and more stringently than – developed ones.

The consequences of strong and broad financial market influence for developing country governments *could* be rather severe. Because the interest rates charged to governments are related directly to a wide range of economic policies, social policies, and institutional features, governments that want to please international market participants can find themselves highly constrained. Investors can easily punish governments, and their grounds for punishment include both macro- and supply-side policies, as well as political outcomes. Ultimately, then, those societies most in need of egalitarian redistribution may have, in terms of external financial market pressures, the most difficulty achieving it. And, yet, even in developing nations, many governments seem to have some room for policy autonomy. Argentina's 2005 decision to offer a "take it or leave it" deal on its defaulted sovereign debts is an extreme case; to the surprise of many market observers, approximately 90 percent of bondholders agreed to accept only 30 cents on the dollar (rather than the more standard 50 to 60 cents) from the government.

To understand less extreme instances of developing nations resisting financial market pressures, it is important to note that financial market influence varies over time, as well as across groups of countries. Investment, especially on the shorter-term end, surges when the global economy booms and contracts when global recession looms. Reduced barriers to capital flows mean not only that foreign investors can come and go, but also that domestic capital owners in developing countries also are free to take their assets elsewhere. Often, the global market environment is a normal one, and country-specific factors dominate; governments' costs of borrowing are tightly correlated with their economic policies and their political conditions, either prospectively or retrospectively. In such periods, variations in the cost and availability of credit are due largely to country- or region-specific "pull factors" (e.g. Agénor, 2001; World Bank, 2004). But, at other points in time, investors are motivated by factors external to borrowing nations ("push factors"), such as the rate of return in major developed markets, investors' appetite for risk, and the general perception of "emerging markets." Global markets, then, are characterized either by mania (risk acceptance) or by panic (risk aversion). In these market environments, developing countries find their access to capital to be either very easy (mania) or very difficult (panic). In the former, even nations with poor policies can access capital at low rates, and constraints are meager; in the latter, even nations with good policies have difficulty in attracting investment (see Mosley, 2003). Variation in market moods can accentuate pressures for convergence (in the wake of panics, governments may try even harder to please investors) or for divergence (when global liquidity is high, governments will be more able to pursue divergent policies).

The volatility that characterizes international capital markets can reduce the benefits to governments of liberalization. While financial globalization offers developing countries greater access to resources and higher levels of growth, it also brings with it a higher likelihood of crisis. Conceição (2003) reports that between 1975 and 1998, there were 116 currency crises, 42 banking crises, and 26 twin (banking and currency) crises in emerging market countries. These crises were associated with cumulative output losses between 5 and 19 percent of annual GDP. Similarly, Dobson and Hufbauer (2001) estimate that banking and financial crises cost Latin America 2.2 percent of annual GDP during the 1980s, and cost East Asia 1.4 percent of annual GDP during the 1990s. More generally, several recent studies hint at a strong, negative relationship between financial volatility and economic growth. And, as the East Asian crisis demonstrated, it is the poor – who lack social safety nets and personal savings – who often bear the brunt of financial crises and post-crisis contractions.

Analytical Challenges and the Persistence of the "Race to the Bottom"

The race continues?

The evidence presented in the previous two sections offers grounds for caution about the empirical validity of the "race to the bottom" claim. And, yet, despite the accumulation of evidence against the RTB logic, this argument continues to characterize popular debates. Pundits claim that the global economy has placed governments, particularly in the developing world, in a "golden straightjacket"; they must compete in order to survive, and the only means of competing is reducing government intervention, lowering taxes, and steadfastly pruning environmental, health and safety, and labor regulations. Developed nations also are not immune, according to these observers; US firms and employees must worry not only about the flight of multinational production to developing nations, but also about the outsourcing of jobs to low-wage locales. What explains this apparent disconnect between social science research on the subject and the claims of politicians and pundits? To begin, the developing world shows us that, while a full RTB process is not occurring, there are stronger pressures on some governments than on others.

But two additional elements also are important. The first is ideological. For many, the RTB, and the possibility of constraints on government autonomy, is seen favorably. An important normative question often underlies, but rarely is made explicit in, positive treatments of the relationship between economic openness and national government policymaking: is the market or the government more able to make the correct policy choices? Economists, as well as political scientists in the public choice tradition, usually assume that the market is a more legitimate arbiter of value – and of values. If there are constraints on governments that result from financial globalization, they are welcome ones; they will pull governments back from the precipice of distorting policies. On the other hand, many political scientists worry about the failures of markets to provide public goods and to improve overall welfare. For them, constraints on governments are unwelcome ones, as they inhibit the ability of governments to protect their citizens from the vagaries and volatilities of markets. Of course, this is an old debate, reflected in debates regarding the value of pre-World War I laissez-faire capitalism versus post-World War II "embedded liberalism."[10]

The RTB claim, then, can be used to justify the delegation of decision-making away from governments, toward the private sector. It is plausible to argue that "market discipline" provides benefits to citizens.[11] If investors' threats of exit prevent governments from engaging in corrupt practices, or in promoting policies that could lead to hyperinflation, then citizens will benefit from the constraining effects of financial openness. But this claim requires an assumption that market decision-making criteria are consistent over time, and that investors' preferences over policies are similar to citizens' wants. Financial bubbles and busts, however, call the former into question; and investors' short time horizons are reason to question the latter. As a result, a more politically expedient argument might be not that markets *should* pressure governments (and should be the ones to which governments are accountable), but that markets inevitably *will* pressure and constrain governments.

In other words, if a policymaker's claim is not only that governments *should not* intervene in the domestic economy, but that they also *cannot* do so, he or she may be better able to convince voters of the necessity of making certain policy changes. The global economy, then, becomes a useful scapegoat for leaders who would like, for domestic reasons, to reduce government spending, lower the rate of inflation, or enact tax and social security reform (e.g. Vreeland, 2003). This may assume that voters lack sophistication: they do not realize that the pressures being invoked are more imagined than real; and policymakers are able to fool them.

According to this logic, changes in national policies during the last fifteen years may reflect a shift in ideology domestically – a change in what governments *want* to do (e.g. Garrett, 2000) – rather than an increase in pressures internationally – a change in what governments *are able* to do. It is, of course, difficult to separate governments' desires over a menu of policies from their capacity to pursue a certain set of policies. Perhaps governments of a more neoliberal stripe had electoral successes in the late 1980s and early 1990s because they were more appealing, generally, to voters. But what was behind their appeal? Might it have been the case that voters believed that these parties could best guide their nation through an era of increased economic openness? Here, again, we get to the murkiness of the relationships between domestic policymaking and the global economy, and we are reminded that correlation is quite different from causation.

Of course, policymakers who scapegoat the global economy generally, or international capital markets specifically, do so not necessarily out of ideological bias; sometimes, the global economy is a convenient cover for the negative consequences of past policy mistakes. Reform is necessary, leaders might argue, not because past governments have consistently mismanaged the public economy, but because domestic firms are threatening to exit and locally produced goods are no longer competitive on world markets. Leaders also may attempt to provoke a shift in ideas regarding the appropriate relationship between state and market; in at least some instances, this promotion reflects strategic behavior, rather than learning or ideational change (e.g. Blyth, 2002; Notermans, 2000). For instance, in the face of steeply rising rates on government borrowing, Sweden underwent a significant amount of welfare state retrenchment in the 1990s. For some, this was evidence that the Swedish welfare state model was incompatible with trade and financial globalization. But the real roots of Sweden's problems appear to have been domestic: once Sweden addressed its domestic fiscal crisis (which included a deficit/GDP ratio of 16 percent in 1993), it experienced an economic recovery. At the end of the 1990s and the beginning of this decade, Sweden addressed pressures on its welfare state by trimming and modifying existing programs, rather than by making fundamental changes to its universalistic welfare state principles (Mosley, 2003). And it was once again able to pursue many of the social policies that have been its hallmark.

The second element contributing to the persistence of RTB is methodological: it is quite easy to find instances of governments cutting social programs or lowering taxes, or to find cases in which workers in developing nations are treated poorly. In some instances, especially in the developing world, governments have enacted policy changes in an effort to attract investment or to promote export industries. Portraying the plight of a textile worker in Vietnam, or of a firm that has moved from the United States to Mexico, and again from Mexico to China, may make for appealing journalism. But such anecdotal evidence (or "anecdata") may not be representative of broader empirical patterns; there may not be a real connection between alleged causes (economic globalization) and apparent effects (a lack of labor rights in poor nations).

For instance, if we look at collective labor rights ("core" rights, including the rights to form unions, to strike, and to bargain collectively) over time, we see an increase in violations of rights, which seems to coincide with increases in economic globalization. Figure 5.2 summarizes trends, at the regional level, in violations of collective labor rights. This figure is based on annual, country-level data, which reports total violations in six broad categories (and 37 subcategories) of collective labor rights, in terms of the provision of legal rights, as well as their observance in practice. Reports of violations, then,

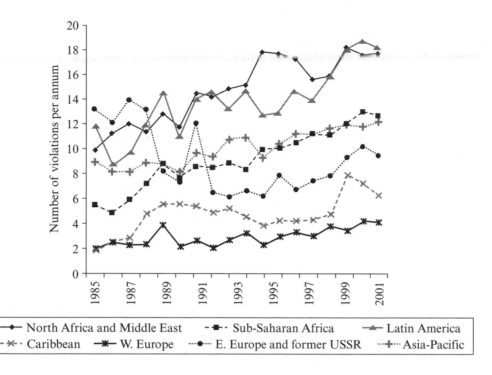

Figure 5.2 Annual collective labor rights violations, by region (regional numbers for each year are unweighted averages of country-level scores)

cover the areas of freedom of association and collective bargaining-related liberties; the right to establish and join worker and union organizations; other union activities; the right to bargain collectively; the right to strike; and rights and export processing zones. The coding of these violations is based on three annual reports: the US State Department *Annual Reports on Human Rights Practices*; the ILO Committee of Experts on the Applications of Conventions and Recommendations (CEACR) and the Committee on Freedom of Association (CFA) reports; and the International Confederation of Free Trade Unions (ICFTU) *Annual Survey of Violations of Trade Union Rights*. A country's total score for a given year is based on the total number of violations, with each of the 37 types of violations weighted according to its severity (for more information, see Mosley and Uno, 2007). Higher scores, then, indicate less respect for (more violations of) collective labor rights.

As figure 5.2 suggests, labor rights are most respected in Western Europe, and least respected in the Middle East, North Africa and Latin America. There also are changes over time; for instance, we see a worsening of labor rights in Latin America and sub-Saharan Africa. These broad patterns suggest that, as economic integration has increased, so have violations of collective labor rights; this picture is consistent with concerns that financial globalization has deleterious consequences for workers.

At first glance, this figure might suggest that economic openness – and, perhaps specifically, the rise in multinational activity in the developing world – has generated downward pressures on labor standards, just as the "race to the bottom" claim would predict. The sweatshop model might then seem to apply broadly, not only to production in labor-intensive sectors (such as textiles) but also to production in capital-intensive and service industries. But this first glance can be misleading; initial quantitative analyses of determinants of labor rights outcomes suggest that domestic factors are the most important correlates of labor rights outcomes, and that the association between inflows of direct investment and labor rights practices is, if anything, a positive one. So, while globalization and labor rights may trend in the same direction, the ultimate determinants of workers' rights (or, to take another example, of anti-inflation policies) may well be internal.

This second element behind the persistence of the RTB logic reveals not only a failing of journalists and policymakers to absorb the findings of academic research, but also of academic researchers to study systematically some of the key – but empirically difficult – questions regarding the effects of economic openness on societies. That is, disentangling causal relationships remains a difficult task, and one that demands a combination of approaches, both quantitative and qualitative. It also demands a constant awareness of the distinction between correlation and causation. For instance, we might assume that changes to welfare state policies and employment patterns in developed nations reflect pressures emanating from increased economic openness, as these trends move in tandem. But there has been another trend in the developed world – the shift away from the manufacturing sector and toward the service sector. It could be this change, and the broader menu of technological changes in advanced economies, that gives rise to many of the pressures facing contemporary governments (Iversen and Cusack, 2000; Iversen and Wren, 1998).

Varieties of constraints and varieties of capitalists?

In addition to resisting the temptation to rely on "anecdata," we should be specific in our studies of the impact of "globalization" on states' policymaking capacity. It is not sufficient to assume that economic globalization is a unidimensional concept. Rather, nations are integrated differently into the global economy (Garrett, 2000). Some have high levels of trade openness, but lower levels of capital market openness. High trade openness may present governments with one set of pressures, while high capital market openness may expose them to a different – and perhaps contradictory – set of demands. For instance, as Rodrik (1997) and others have suggested, increased trade openness may enhance public demands for compensation, while increased reliance on short-term capital flows may reduce governments' capacity to accumulate large debts and to run substantial budget deficits.

Additionally, trade flows and capital flows have different impacts on domestic economies: trade can result in increased output volatility, while capital flows can induce greater volatility in investment, but also can allow for consumption smoothing. Moreover, different types of flows can generate different types of shocks. Some nations attract mostly long-term investment (FDI), while others are more reliant on shorter-term portfolio flows. This difference – a "variety of capitalists" – generates different vulnerabilities and opportunities for governments. There is stronger econometric evidence, for instance, that FDI has a positive effect on economic growth than that short-term investment promotes growth. Along these lines, a recent study by Shambaugh (2004) investigates the effect of investors on exchange rate regime choice in developing countries. Shambaugh argues that different types of capital – commercial bank loans, FDI, and portfolio investment – have different effects on governments' preferences over exchange rate regimes. And, even within FDI, there probably is variation across sectors (e.g. labor-intensive textile production versus capital-intensive pharmaceutical industries), in terms of investors' preferences and pressures on national policies (see Mosley and Uno, 2007).

Thus, it is useful to consider the specific causal mechanisms through which capital market openness – as opposed to economic openness in general – can affect government policymaking autonomy. As Wibbels and Arce have noted, "the manner in which a nation is plugged in has implications for the constraints domestic policymakers will encounter" (2003, p. 130). Tying this to the point above about the temptation to rely on anecdotal evidence, when we hear assertions about the impact of globalization on the nation-state, we must always ask, "what type of globalization," and "what kind of state?" Or, "under what conditions does economic openness leave governments with reduced room to move . . . and under what conditions does state autonomy persist?" Only by specifying how varying dimensions of globalization matter for government policy choices can we begin to gauge the overall – and often contending – effects of economic openness on policymaking. And the extant evidence suggests that these overall effects are likely to be diverse, with some sorts of openness associated with a growth in public sector intervention, and other types associated with a decline in public sector intervention. Finally, in order to understand fully the linkages between economic globalization and national governments, we need to connect events in global markets with changes in government policy, and we must consider how various domestic institutions and ideologies mediate these changes. In other words, under what conditions do governments accede to financial market influence, resist financial market influence, or attempt to insulate themselves from financial market influence?

Conclusion

This chapter has considered one aspect of the political economy of globalization, namely, the extent to which trade and financial openness lead to changes in processes of national policymaking, and to a reduction of the influence of domestic variables on national policy outcomes. The evidence presented suggests that, despite the continued popularity of the "race to the bottom" notion in public debate and in the popular press, a cross-national, downward convergence of national policies has not occurred. Although there are some pressures for convergence in both developed and developing nations, there also are forces leading to cross-national divergence. These forces include domestic institutions, which mediate influences emanating from the global economy, and domestic interests, which may push for compensatory policies in some nations, but not in others. The result, then, is a narrowing of cross-national differences in *some* policy areas, but not in others.

This chapter also suggests that the political economy of globalization varies across types of countries. Developing nations, which are more dependent on global investment flows and are characterized by higher levels of default risk, face stronger pressures from global capital markets and, as a result, are more likely locations for races to the bottom. As Robert Keohane and Joseph Nye write, borrowing from commentator Thomas Friedman, "the problem is that, in many countries, some citizens get more of the gold while others feel more of the [straight]jacket" (2001, p. 255). Even in the developing world, though, the key determinants of national policy outcomes often remain internal, rather than external.

In analyzing the impact of globalization on political decisions, then, students of politics must demand causal, not simply correlative, evidence. That is, it is important to uncover, and to assess, the causal mechanisms linking the global economy with government policy choices. In some cases, these mechanisms will be found to be in operation, and governments will engage in a competitive lowering, or at least narrowing, of standards – just as the "race to the bottom" logic predicts. In many other cases, though, these mechanisms will not obtain, and governments will retain their "room to move."

Notes

1 On the role of the IMF, see Blustein, 2001; Stiglitz, 2003. Simmons and Elkins (2004) explore the diffusion of neoliberal policy reforms, including capital account liberalization, while Simmons (2001) discusses the role of major financial centers in the push toward financial openness.
2 See Bordo et al., 2003; Garrett, 2000; and Mosley, 2003 for comparisons between contemporary and historical financial globalization.
3 Data for this figure are from the World Development Indicators, 2004.
4 On the conditions under which trade-related domestic politics occur at the sectoral (by industry) versus the factoral (capital, labor, and land) level, see Hiscox, 2002.
5 For instance, see Agénor, 2001; Durham, 2002.
6 Cohen, 1996; Garrett, 1998; and Mosley, 2003 provide reviews of this literature.
7 See Drezner, 2001 for a review of the "race to the bottom" argument, and Garrett and Mitchell, 2001 for a summary of the "race to the bottom" logic.
8 See Burgoon, 2001; and Mosley, 2003 for reviews of this literature. Examples include Garrett and Mitchell, 2001; Huber and Stephens, 2001; Scruggs and Lange, 2002; Swank, 2002. Allan and Scruggs (2004) point out, however, that using programmatic qualities of welfare states (replacement rates, coverage ratios) rather than spending data paints a different picture. In their analyses, the welfare state is affected by global financial markets, as well as by government partisanship, and some retrenchment has occurred.
9 Of course, continued borrowing at low rates is, to some extent, facilitated by the willingness of foreign central banks to hold large stocks of US Treasury bills and bonds as part of their foreign reserves. And, while rates on US government bonds have not reacted negatively to persistent deficits, the US dollar has declined markedly.
10 See Pitruzzello, 2004 for a review of the historical roots of this debate.
11 For contending views on market discipline, see Obstfeld, 1998 and Sasken, 1996.

References

Adserá, Aliciá and Carles Boix (2001). "Trade, Democracy and the Size of the Public Sector: The Political Underpinnings of Openness." *International Organization*, 55.
Agénor, Pierre-Richard (2001). "Benefits and Costs of International Financial Liberalization: Theory and Facts." Paper prepared for World Bank conference, Financial Globalization: Issues and Challenges for Small States, March 2001.

Allan, James P. and Lyle Scruggs (2004). "Political Partisanship and Welfare State Reform in Advanced Industrial Societies." *American Journal of Political Science*, 48(3): pp. 493–512.

Armijo, Leslie Elliott (1996). "Inflation and Insouciance: The Peculiar Brazilian Game." *Latin American Research Review*, 31: pp. 7–45.

Bhagwati, Jagdish (1998). "The Capital Myth: The Difference between Trade in Widgets and Dollars." *Foreign Affairs* (May/June): pp. 7–12.

Blyth, Mark (2002). *Great Transformations: Economic Ideas and Political Change in the Twentieth Century*. Cambridge: Cambridge University Press.

Blustein, Paul (2001). *The Chastening: Inside the Crisis that Rocked the Global Financial System and Humbled the IMF*. Washington: PublicAffairs.

Bordo, Michael D., Alan M. Taylor, and Jeffrey Williamson, eds (2003). *Globalization in Historical Perspective*. Chicago: University of Chicago Press.

Brooks, Sarah M. (2002). "Social Protection and Economic Integration." *Comparative Political Studies*, 35: pp. 491–523.

Burgoon, Brian (2001). "Globalization and Welfare Compensation: Disentangling the Ties that Bind." *International Organization*, 55(3): pp. 509–51.

Cameron, David (1978). "The Expansion of the Public Economy: A Comparative Analysis." *American Political Science Review*, 72: pp. 1243–61.

Cerny, Philip G. (1995). "Globalization and the Changing Logic of Collective Action." *International Organization*, 49: pp. 595–626.

Cerny, Philip G. (1999). "Globalization and Erosion of Democracy." *European Journal of Political Research*, 36: pp. 1–26.

Cohen, Benjamin (1996). "Phoenix Risen: The Resurrection of Global Finance." *World Politics*, 48: pp. 268–96.

Conceição, Pedro (2003). "Assessing the Provision Status of Global Public Goods." In Inge Kaul, Pedro Conceição, Katell Le Goulven, and Ronald U. Mendoza (2003). *Providing Global Public Goods: Managing Globalization*. Oxford: Oxford University Press, pp. 152–79.

Dobson, Wendy and Gary Clyde Hufbauer (2001). *World Capital Markets: Challenge to the G-10*. Washington: Institute for International Economics.

Drezner, Daniel W. (2001). "Globalization and Policy Convergence." *International Studies Review*, 3(1): pp. 53–78.

Durham, J. Benson (2002). "The Effects of Stock Market Development on Growth and Private Investment in Lower-Income Countries." *Emerging Markets Review*, 3: pp. 211–32.

Garrett, Geoffrey (1998). *Partisan Politics in the Global Economy*. New York: Cambridge University Press.

Garrett, Geoffrey (2000). "The Causes of Globalization." *Comparative Political Studies*, 33: pp. 941–91.

Garrett, Geoffrey and Deborah Mitchell (2001). "Globalization and the Welfare State." *European Journal of Political Research*, 39(2): pp. 145–77.

Gereffi, Gary and Miguel Korzeniewicz, eds (1994). *Commodity Chains and Global Capitalism*. New York: Praeger.

Hall, Peter and David Soskice, eds (2001). *Varieties of Capitalism: The Institutional Foundations of Comparative Advantage*. Oxford: Oxford University Press.

Hays, Jude (2003). "Globalization and Capital Taxation in Consensus and Majoritarian Democracies." *World Politics*, 56 (October): pp. 79–113.

Helleiner, Eric (1994). "Editorial. The World of Money: The Political Economy of International Capital Mobility." *Policy Sciences*, 27: pp. 295–8.

Hirschman, Albert (1970). *Exit, Voice, and Loyalty*. Cambridge, Mass.: MIT Press.

Hiscox, Michael (2002). *International Trade and Political Conflict: Commerce, Coalitions and Factor Mobility*, Princeton: Princeton University Press.

Huber, Evelyne and John D. Stephens (2001). *Development and Crisis of the Welfare State: Parties and Policies in Global Markets*. Chicago: University of Chicago Press.

Iversen, Torben and Thomas Cusack (2000). "The Causes of Welfare State Expansion: Deindustrialization or Globalization?" *World Politics*, 52: pp. 313–49.

Iversen, Torben and Anne Wren (1998). "Equality, Employment and Budgetary Restraint: The Trilemma of the Service Economy." *World Politics*, 50: pp. 507–46.

Kaufman, Robert and Alex Segura-Ubiergo (2001). "Globalization, Domestic Politics, and Welfare Spending in Latin America: A Time-Series Cross-Section Analysis, 1973–1997." *World Politics*, 53(4): pp. 551–85.

Keohane, Robert O. and Joseph S. Nye, Jr. (1971). "Transnational Relations and World Politics: An Introduction." *International Organization*, 25(3): pp. 329–49.

Keohane, Robert O. and Joseph S. Nye (1977). *Power and Interdependence: World Politics in Transition*. Boston: Little, Brown.

Krasner, Stephen D. (1999). *Sovereignty: Organized Hypocrisy*. Princeton: Princeton University Press.

Kurtz, Marcus J. (2002). "Understanding the Third World Welfare State after Neoliberalism: The Politics of Social Provision in Chile and Mexico." *Comparative Politics* (April): pp. 293–313.

Kurzer, Paulette (1993). *Business and Banking in Europe*. Ithaca, NY: Cornell University Press.

Mares, Isabela (2003). "The Sources of Business Interest in Social Insurance: Sectoral versus National Differences." *World Politics*, 55(2): pp. 229–58.

Mosley, Layna (2003). *Global Capital and National Governments*. Cambridge: Cambridge University Press.

Mosley, Layna and Saika Uno (2007). "Racing to the Bottom or Climbing to the Top? Foreign Direct Investment and Collective Labor Rights." *Comparative Political Studies*, forthcoming.

Notermans, Ton (2000). *Money, Markets and the State: Social Democratic Economic Policies since 1918*. Cambridge: Cambridge University Press.

Obstfeld, Maurice (1998). "The Global Capital Market: Benefactor or Menace?" *Journal of Economic Perspectives*, 12: pp. 9–30.

Pitruzzello, Salvatore (2004). "Trade Globalization, Economic Performance, and Social Protection: Nineteenth-Century British Laissez-Faire and Post-World War II U.S.-Embedded Liberalism." *International Organization*, 58: pp. 705–44.

Rodrik, Dani (1997). *Has Globalization Gone Too Far?* Washington: Institute for International Economics.

Rodrik, Dani (1998). "Why Do More Open Economies Have Bigger Governments?" *Journal of Political Economy*, 106(5): pp. 997–1033.

Rodrik, Dani and Francisco Rodriguez (2001). "Trade Policy and Economic Growth: A Skeptic's Guide to the Cross-National Evidence." In Ben Bernanke and Kenneth S. Rogoff, eds, *Macroeconomics Annual 2000*. Cambridge, Mass. MIT Press for NBER.

Rogowski, Ronald (2003). "International Capital Mobility and National Policy Divergence." In Miles Kahler and David A. Lake, eds, *Governance in a Global Economy: Political Authority in Transition*. Princeton: Princeton University Press, pp. 255–73.

Rudra, Nita (2002). "Globalization and the Decline of the Welfare State in Less Developed Countries." *International Organization*, 56 (Spring): pp. 411–45.

Rudra, Nita and Stephan Haggard (2005). "Globalization, Democracy and Welfare Spending in the Developing World." Unpublished manuscript, University of Pittsburgh.

Ruggie, John Gerard (1982). "International Regimes, Transactions and Change: Embedded Liberalism in the Postwar Economic Order." *International Organization*, 36(2): pp. 379–415.

Sassen, Saskia (1996). *Losing Control? Sovereignty in an Age of Globalization*. New York: Columbia University Press.

Scheve, Kenneith and Matthew J. Slaughter (2004). "Economic Insecurity and the Globalization of Production." *American Journal of Political Science* (October).

Scruggs, Lyle and Peter Lange (2002). "Where Have All the Members Gone? Globalization and National Labor Market Institutions." *Journal of Politics*, 64.

Shambaugh, George (2004). "The Power of Money: Global Capital and Policy Choices in Developing Countries." *American Journal of Political Science*, 48(2): pp. 281–95.

Simmons, Beth A. (2001). "The International Politics of Harmonization: The Case of Capital Market Regulation." *International Organization*, 55(3): pp. 589–620.

Simmons, Beth A. and Zachary Elkins (2004). "The Globalization of Liberalization: Policy Diffusion in the International Economy." *American Political Science Review*, 98(1).

Stiglitz, Joseph (2003). *Globalization and Its Discontents*. New York: Norton.

Stone, Randall (2002). *Lending Credibility: The IMF and the Post-Communist Transition*. Princeton: Princeton University Press.

Strange, Susan (1996). *The Retreat of the State: The Diffusion of Power in the World Economy*. New York: Cambridge University Press.

Swank, Duane (1998). "Funding the Welfare State: Global Taxation of Business in Advanced Market Economies." *Political Studies*, 46: pp. 671–92.

Swank, Duane (2002). *Global Capital, Political Institutions, and Policy Change in Developed Welfare States*. Cambridge: Cambridge University Press.

Vreeland, James Raymond (2003). *The IMF and Economic Growth*. Cambridge: Cambridge University Press.

Weyland, Kurt (1996). "Risk Taking in Latin American Economic Restructuring: Lessons from Prospect Theory." *International Studies Quarterly*, 40: pp. 185–208.

Wibbels, Erik and Moisés Arce (2003). "Globalization, Taxation and Burden-Shifting in Latin America." *International Organization*, 57: pp. 111–36.

World Bank (2001). *Finance for Growth: Policy Choices in a Volatile World*. Oxford: Oxford University Press and the World Bank.

World Bank (2004). *Global Development Finance*. Washington: World Bank.

6

Social Constructivism Meets Globalization

Thomas Risse

1 Introduction

Writing about what social constructivism contributes to the study of globalization represents a challenging task. The main reason for this difficulty is that the meanings of both "social constructivism" and of "globalization" are far from clear. Both have become common catchwords that can be interpreted rather differently. First, social constructivism is often treated as a theory of international relations making substantive claims about the real world. In the following, however, I use social constructivism as a social ontology, a meta-theory about the social world and our knowledge about it (see also Adler, 1997, 2002; Fearon and Wendt, 2002). As a result, there cannot be a "social constructivist theory of globalization" as, for example, there could be a Marxist approach to globalization. Rather, as I will argue in the following, social constructivism provides a particular view on globalization processes, a lens which allows us to interpret globalization in distinctive ways and which leads us to ask specific questions about it.

If social constructivism is an unclear term, this is even more true for "globalization," as a brief look at the usage of the concept immediately reveals (see e.g. Beisheim and Walter, 1997; Held et al., 1999; Kofman and Youngs, 2003). For some, globalization means the internationalization of financial markets and of production networks. Others understand globalization as the erosion of borders and the end of the nation-state as we know it. Last not least, some focus on the global diffusion of norms and other cultural scripts. These are very different social and political processes that might or might not be causally linked. If the concept of globalization is used in very different ways, explanations for its origins as well as its consequences are equally varied.

So, what can social constructivism add to this? I suggest two ways in which social constructivism can enlighten our understanding of globalization. First, it allows a critical view on the taken-for-grantedness of many globalization discourses. "Globalization" itself is far from an innocent concept, but contains a particular discourse about international reality which can be uncovered if one cares about the social construction of reality. Second, on more substantive grounds, a social constructivist understanding of globalization emphasizes the non-material forces at work here and focuses on processes of meaning construction and interpretation as constitutive for globalization. A social constructivist lens also helps to bring the political back into the globalization discourse by emphasizing the potential for change rather than the inevitability of global processes.

This chapter proceeds with the following steps. It begins with a clarification of social constructivism as a meta-theoretical approach and some initial thoughts on what this means for the study of globalization. I then proceed with discussing three contributions of social constructivism to understanding globalization. The first contribution focuses on the globalization of culture and norms from a sociological perspective. The second value-added concentrates on language and the discursive construction of globalization. A third perspective focuses on deliberative global governance as a political response to globalization. I conclude with a short summary of the argument.

2 What Is Social Constructivism?

There is considerable confusion in the field on what precisely constitutes social constructivism and what distinguishes it from other approaches to international relations.[1] As a result, it has become fairly common to introduce constructivism as yet another substantive theory of international relations, such as realism, liberalism, or institutionalism. Yet, it should be emphasized at the outset that social constructivism as such does not make any particular claims about international politics, let alone globalization. Constructivists may adhere to an institutionalist reading of international regimes and institutions as the central way to understand global politics. They may equally join the liberal crowd emphasizing domestic politics and domestic institutions as central explanatory variables for great power politics. Many social constructivists would also feel comfortable as critical theorists in favor of various emancipatory projects.

It is equally misleading to claim, as some have argued, that social constructivism subscribes to a "post-positivist" epistemology (how can we know something?), while conventional approaches are wedded to positivism and the search for law-like features in social and political life. Unfortunately, terms such as "positivism" are often used as demarcation devices to distinguish the "good self" from the "bad other" in some sort of disciplinary tribal warfare (for an excellent discussion of this tendency in International Relations theory see Wight, 2002). However, if "post-positivism" means,

1 a healthy skepticism toward a "covering law" approach to social science irrespective of time and space and instead a strive toward middle-range theorizing;
2 an emphasis on interpretive understanding as an intrinsic, albeit not exclusive, part of any causal explanation; and
3 the recognition that social scientists are part of the social world which they try to analyse ("double hermeneutics" – see Giddens, 1982, but first and foremost Habermas, 1968)

– is anybody still a "positivist" then (to paraphrase an article by Legro and Moravcsik, 1999)?

In sum, while there are some radical constructivist positions denying the possibility of intersubjectively valid knowledge claims in the social sciences, this view is by no means a defining and unifying characteristic of social constructivism as a meta-theoretical approach to the study of social phenomena (on this point see also Adler, 2002; Ruggie, 1998).

Defining social constructivism

So, what then is "social constructivism" (for the following see e.g. Adler, 1997, 2002; Checkel, 1998; Fearon and Wendt, 2002; Wendt, 1999)? It is a truism that social reality does not fall from heaven, but that human agents construct and reproduce it through their daily practices – "the social construction of reality" (Berger and Luckmann, 1966). Yet while this is a core argument of social constructivism, as a truism it does not provide us with a clear enough conceptualization. Therefore, it is probably more useful to describe constructivism as based on a social ontology which insists that human agents do not exist independently from their social environment and its collectively shared systems of meanings ("culture" in a broad sense). This is in contrast to the methodological individualism of rational choice according to which "(t)he elementary unit of social life is the individual human action" (Elster, 1989, p. 13). The fundamental insight of the structure–agency debate, which lies at the heart of many social constructivist works, is not only that social structures and agents are mutually co-determined. The crucial point is to insist on the mutual *constitutiveness* of (social) structures and agents (Adler, 1997, pp. 324–25; Wendt, 1999, ch. 4; see also Giddens, 1984). The social environment in which we find ourselves, defines ("constitutes") who we are, our identities as social beings. "We" are social beings, embedded in various relevant social communities. At the same time, human agency creates, reproduces, and changes culture through our daily practices. Thus, social constructivism occupies a – sometimes uneasy – ontological middleground between individualism and structuralism by claiming that there are properties of structures and of agents that cannot be collapsed into each other.

This claim has important, if often overlooked, repercussions for the study of globalization processes. Many approaches to globalization are committed to an overly structuralist ontology. Structuralists tend to argue that some anonymous forces – be they financial markets, be they global production networks – command the global economy as a result of which states and political decision-making have lost almost all autonomy and freedom of choice (e.g. Ohmae, 1990; Gill, 1995; Gill and Law, 1993; Altvater and Mahnkopf, 1996; also Strange, 1996; for an excellent review of this literature see Beisheim and Walter, 1997). All they can do is to adapt and to conform to the forces of the neoliberal world economy. These trends result into a "race to the bottom" with regard to social policies and to the end of the welfare state as we knew it. Some praise these forces in line with the neoliberal discourse itself; others try to save as much of the welfare state as possible by propagating a "third way." Finally, globalization critics paint such a fundamentally negative picture of globalization that only revolutionary changes appear to present a way out. Yet, it is interesting to note that many authors take "globalization" as a given – as the dominant social structure of the contemporary international system.

From a social constructivist viewpoint, there is very little "given" about economic globalization. First, one would emphasize that the globalization discourse constitutes itself as a social construction in the sense that making economic globalization inevitable serves particular purposes and interests (see below). Depriving anonymous market forces of human agency overlooks, for example, that the liberalization of capital markets occurred at certain points in time by concrete political decisions; that is, human agency was involved here. This is not to imply that these decisions can easily be taken back. But it is to suggest that globalization is reinforced and reproduced by and through social and political practices. And these practices can change as a result of which the course of globalization will change.

Second, at a deeper level, social constructivists would probably insist that the concept of "globalization" itself constitutes a particular interpretation of a social reality which is itself being interpreted and reinterpreted by social agents. Moreover, the concept has long lost its analytical innocence (if it ever had one) and has become part of the standard interpretations of the global reality which political, economic, and social actors routinely use to make sense of their world. In that sense, "globalization" as a discourse reifies globalization as a social structure. Describing the international system as "globalized" not only overlooks the fragmented and uneven nature of globalization (is the world economy globalized, or rather "OECDized?"; see Zürn, 1998). The consensual knowledge generated by the concept of "globalization" also constitutes our worldviews. If we construct the world as globalized, we focus on interconnectedness, networks, and complex interdependence (Keohane and Nye, 1977). At the same time, we de-emphasize those forces in the current world order that contribute to fragmentation and (cultural) difference. Furthermore, one does not have to be a realist to notice that globalization and the interconnectedness of the world cannot be reconciled easily with a worldview of unipolarity emphasizing American hegemony. How can a global order with one single state sitting at the top of the international pecking order be described as "globalized" at the same time without the concept losing much of its meaning (see also chapter 2 above, by G. John Ikenberry)?

Agency, structure, and the constitutive effects of norms and rules

If we try to analyze the reality of globalization, social constructivists would probably take issue with an overly structuralist account as criticized above. In contrast, when it comes to the *impact* of globalization on the nation-state and its domestic polities, politics, and policies, the target of constructivist attack is likely to be the methodological individualism emphasized by rational choice and its overly agency-centered approach. The reason for this can be found in the way in which social constructivists conceptualize how social structures impact on agents and their behavior. Rationalist institutionalism ("neoliberal" institutionalism in International Relations jargon, see Keohane, 1989) views social institutions as primarily constraining the behavior of actors with given identities and preferences. These actors follow a "logic of consequentialism" (March and Olsen, 1989, 1998) enacting given identities and interests and trying to realize their preferences through strategic behavior. The goal of action is to maximize or to optimize one's interests and preferences. Institutions constrain or widen the range of choices available to actors to realize their interests. In a similar vein, economic globalization and global market forces can be analyzed as rearranging the distribution of power among domestic political and social actors (see e.g. Keohane and Milner, 1996). Globalization would lead to a redistribution of resources available to actors as a result of which some gain and some lose. Some authors analyze this process as a global shift in the power balance between labor and capital.

In contrast, social constructivism and sociological institutionalism emphasize a different logic of action, which March and Olsen have called the "logic of appropriateness": "Human actors are imagined to follow rules that associate particular identities to particular situations, approaching individual opportunities for action by assessing similarities between current identities and choice dilemmas and more general concepts of self and situations" (March and Olsen, 1998, p. 951). Rule-guided behavior differs from strategic and instrumental behavior in that actors try to "do the right thing" rather than maximizing or optimizing their given preferences. The logic of appropriateness entails that actors try to figure out the appropriate rule in a given social situation. It follows that social institutions can no longer be viewed as "external" to actors. Rather, actors including corporate actors such as national governments, firms, or interest groups are deeply embedded in and affected by the social institutions in which they act.

This relates to what constructivists call the *constitutive* effects of social norms and rules (Onuf, 1989; Kratochwil, 1989). Many social norms not only regulate behavior, they also constitute the identity of actors in the sense of defining who "we" are as members of a social community. The norm of sovereignty, for example, not only regulates the interactions of states in international affairs, it also defines what a state *is* in the first place. Constructivists concentrate on the social identities of actors in order to account for their interests (e.g. Wendt, 1999, particularly ch. 7; also Checkel, 2001a). Constructivism maintains that collective norms and understandings define the basic "rules of the game" in which they find themselves in their interactions. This does not mean that constitutive norms cannot be violated or can never change. But the argument implies that we cannot even describe the properties of social agents without reference to the social structure in which they are embedded.

What does this mean for our understanding of the impact of globalization? If we treat globalization as a global social structure, social constructivists would first insist that globalization consists not only of global material (mostly economic) forces, but also of whole sets of collective understandings which need to be investigated as part of it (see below). Material and economic factors do not exist and emerge in an ideational vacuum. Rather, collective understandings and meaning structures offer interpretations to make sense of the material world. The concept of "globalization" itself is a prime example for such collective understandings that offer a peculiar interpretation of the international economy. I have also mentioned already the neoliberal globalization discourse which is to be further examined below. In addition, sociological institutionalists in particular focus on processes of cultural globalization, namely the emergence of global normative structures with constitutive effects on nation-states and their domestic environments (see below).

Second, constructivists would focus on the constitutive effects of the various globalization processes. Economic globalization, for example, constitutes social actors in reference to their position in the global economy which shapes their interests and even identities. Notions such as "global players," for example, imply particular understandings and self-understandings of the companies in question as incorporating a global outlook and, as a result, global interests. There is an interesting twist to these notions in recent years. Transnational corporations who want to become "global players" these days not only have to recognize their global corporate interests, but also responsibilities for the global public good. The globalization of culture and norms reconstitutes political and other social actors in the sense that they have to accept these norms in order to be recognized as "good global citizens," and the like.

Communication, discourse, and knowledge

The emphasis on communicative and discursive practices constitutes a final characteristic feature of social constructivist approaches.[2] If we want to understand and explain social behavior, we need to take words, language, and communicative utterances seriously. It is through discursive practices that agents make sense of the world and attribute meaning to their activities. Moreover, as Foucault reminds us, discursive practices establish power relationships in the sense that they make us "understand certain problems in certain ways, and pose questions accordingly" (Diez, 2001, p. 90). And further, "(a)lthough it is 'we' who impose meaning, 'we' do not act as autonomous subjects but from a 'subject position' made available by the discursive context in which we are situated" (ibid., referring to Foucault, 1991, 58).

There are at least two ways in which the study of communicative practices might contribute to our understanding of globalization processes (see section 4 below). First, scholars have started applying the Habermasian theory of communicative action to international relations (Habermas, 1981, 1992; Müller, 1994; Risse, 2000). They focus on arguing and reason-giving as an agency-centered mode of interaction which enables actors to challenge the validity claims inherent in any causal or normative statement and to seek a communicative consensus about their understanding of a situation as well as justifications for the principles and norms guiding their action, rather than acting purely on the basis of strategic calculations. Argumentative rationality means that the participants in a discourse are open to be persuaded by the better argument and that relationships of power and social hierarchies recede in the background. Argumentative and deliberative behavior is as goal-oriented as strategic interactions, but the goal is not to attain one's fixed preferences, but to seek a reasoned consensus. As Keohane put it, persuasion "involves changing people's choices of alternatives independently of their calculations about the strategies of other players" (Keohane, 2001, p. 10). Actors' interests, preferences, and the perceptions of the situation are no longer fixed, but subject to discursive challenges. Where argumentative rationality prevails, actors do not seek to maximize or to satisfy their given interests and preferences, but to challenge and to justify the validity claims inherent in them – and are prepared to change their views of the world or even their interests in light of the better argument.

Advocates of deliberative democracy on a global scale tend to emphasize arguing and persuasion as mechanisms by which cosmopolitan values can be furthered in an age of globalization (see David Held's contribution to this volume, ch. 12). While this work focuses on the normative potential of communicative rationality and persuasion for increasing the legitimacy of global governance, a more analytical approach to arguing and persuasion focuses on those institutional sites in the international system that allow for the contestation and exchange of ideas and normative beliefs. The various UN world conferences, for example, can be analyzed in a traditional way as simply representing interstate negotiation platforms. But they can also be looked at as arenas for global delib-eration of issues of common concern involving the various public and private stakehold-ers. We can then investigate under which conditions these discourse arenas are actually suitable for increasing the legitimacy and problem-solving capacity of global governance in response to, but also as part of, globalization processes.

The second way in which discursive practices can be studied with regard to globaliza-tion focuses not so much on arguing and reason-giving, but on discourse as a process of meaning construction allowing for certain interpretations while excluding others. In other words, this work follows Michel Foucault rather than Jürgen Habermas (Foucault, 1973, 1991, 1996; overview in Howarth, Norval, and Stavrakakis, 2000; for an application to international relations see Litfin, 1994) and focuses on discursive practices as means by which power relationships are established and maintained. Who is allowed to speak in a discursive arena, what counts as a sensible proposition, and which meaning constructions become so dominant that they are being taken for granted? The neoliberal discourse on globalization, for example, had become so all-pervasive during the mid-1990s that it estab-lished itself almost as strong as Maggie Thatcher's TINA ("There Is No Alternative"). Of course, this discourse then gave rise to a counter-discourse put forward by the so-called "anti-globalization" movements (which is a misnomer insofar as these transnational social movements are part and parcel of a globalization process, only "globalization from below" this time). In sum, this constructivist emphasis on communicative practices contributes to alternative understandings of power relationships in the process of globalization.

The three contributions of social constructivism to the study of globalization

In sum, social constructivism as a meta-theory of social action and interaction does not as such produce a substantive "theory of globalization." Yet there are at least three ways in which social constructivism contributes to a better understanding of globalization processes and their impact on the nation-states. First, accepting the mutual constitutive-ness of agency and structure allows for a deeper analysis of the social construction of globalization than conventional and overly structuralist approaches. Second and related, emphasizing the constitutive effects of international social order enables us to study how globalization processes shape social identities and interests of actors. And vice versa! Third, focusing on communicative practices permits us to examine more closely how globalization processes are constructed discursively and how actors try to come to grips with their meanings.

In the following, I use these theoretical insights to discuss three substantive contribu-tions to the study of globalization informed by a social constructivist ontology. The first stems from sociological institutionalism and adds ideational and social factors to our understanding of globalization. The second contribution emphasizes the discursive dimensions of globalization processes. Emphasizing communicative processes also enriches our understanding of the power dimensions of globalization. Last not least, con-structivism contributes to a fuller account of global governance as a political response to globalization processes.

3 Sociological Understandings: The Globalization of Culture and Norms

Contemporary understandings of globalization often focus on the transnationalization of economic production, the globalization of financial markets, and the like. It is thereby overlooked, however, that globalization processes entail a lot more than material and economic forces and equally include cultural phenomena and the spread of consensual knowledge as well as principles and norms. Long before globalization became a catchword in the social sciences and beyond, sociological institutionalists such as John Meyer and his colleagues at Stanford University pointed out, against world systems theory of the Immanuel Wallerstein variety (Wallerstein, 1974, 1980, 1989), that modernity entails not only the global spread of capitalism, but also the global diffusion of cultural standards as well as collective understandings and identities (see e.g. Meyer, 1987; Meyer, Boli, and Thomas, 1987; Meyer et al., 1997; Thomas et al., 1987; Boli and Thomas, 1997, 1998). They argued essentially that the history of modernity constitutes the gradual spread of Western cultural standards of rationality on a global scale. John Meyer and his colleagues pointed out, for example, that modern statehood as an institution entails a lot more than territory, control over people, and sovereignty. Rather, modern states come with a whole set of cultural understandings about how states and governments are supposed to look, what constitute "public" as opposed to "private" affairs, and so forth. Moreover, they were able to show empirically that particular cultural scripts have been enacted worldwide in processes of state-building. For example, any new state these days is supposed to have a ministry of science, irrespective of whether the country in question actually has a university or other research institutions to speak of. The Stanford school showed that national school curricula worldwide follow certain cultural scripts prescribing what is appropriate to teach children at the various levels of educational systems. Calculus, for example, entered elementary school curricula worldwide irrespective of whether the country actually was able to educate teachers in mathematics (overviews in Finnemore, 1996b; Jepperson, 2002; see also Finnemore, 1996a).

John Meyer and his colleagues argued, therefore, that a world polity is in the making, based on Western cultural standards. Moreover and more recently, sociological institutionalists tried to substantiate empirically theoretical arguments about the emergence of a global civil society (see e.g. Keane, 2003) by pointing to the emergence of global social movements as well as transnationally operating (International) Non-Governmental Organizations (INGOs) that are strikingly similar as to their organizational structures, material and ideational resources, and action strategies (see e.g. Boli and Thomas, 1999; Ramirez, 1987). This argument has been taken up in the meantime by scholars researching social movements who have increasingly begun to focus on transnational movements and their activities (e.g. Smith, Chatfield, and Pagnucco, 1997; Tarrow, 2005; Keck and Sikkink, 1998).

Moreover, international relations scholars inspired by sociological institutionalism have pointed out that globalization not only entails the the global spread of capitalism and the global diffusion of Western cultural values and scripts, but also the emergence of global norms and behavioral standards enshrined in international institutions. Over the past twenty years, for example, we can observe what Martha Finnemore and Kathryn

Sikkink called a "norm cascade" in many issue-areas of international politics (Finnemore and Sikkink, 1998). "Norm cascade" refers to the tipping point where international norms become global standards of appropriate behavior in the sense that a growing number of states subscribe to them. Once the tipping point is reached, international norms tend to exert constitutive effects on the states in the sense that it becomes the "normal" and appropriate thing to do to sign up to and to ratify the respective treaties. If you want to be a member of international society "in good standing," a civilized member of the international community, you had better sign up to the treaty at this point.

The globalization of international legal norms can be observed across a whole variety of issue-areas in world politics. Today, there is not a single issue-area in international affairs which is not regulated by at least some international norms and rules. In the fields of international human rights (including gender and social rights) as well as in international environmental politics in particular, there has been a mind-boggling increase in international agreements and treaties. Of course, the emergence of many of these international norms is directly linked to the agenda-setting role of transnational social movements, advocacy networks, and INGOs (see e.g. Florini, 2000; for the human rights area see Korey, 1998). These norm cascades have resulted in a situation in which there is not a single state left in the international system today which has not signed and ratified at least one of the major instruments of international human rights law or international environmental treaties (for the human rights area see Liese, 2006; Schmitz and Sikkink, 2002; for the international environment see e.g. Haas, Keohane, and Levy, 1993; Mitchell, 2002). This further contributes to what sociological institutionalists call an emerging world polity insofar as human rights and environmental protection norms not only set standards of appropriate behavior worldwide, but also constitute states in the world system as members of the international community. States which want to be "in" rather than "out" (or rogue states), are expected to subscribe to international human rights and environmental norms.

While the trend described so far pertains mostly to states as the main subjects of international law, a more recent tendency extends international norms as standards of appropriate behavior to the private sector. Once again, advocacy networks and global transnational movements have been at the origins of these developments by denouncing transnational corporations as violating human rights and damaging the global environment. Transnational campaigns such as the global mobilization against the sports firm Nike and its use of sweatshops and child labor in the Philippines and elsewhere were only the beginning of global efforts to raise consciousness that private actors such as multinational firms can violate human and social rights, too. These campaigns have led to the extension of international human rights and environmental norms to the private sector, the catchword being "global corporate social responsibility" as one aspect of a new global public policy (see Reinicke, 1998; Reinicke and Deng, 2000). Take the UN's Global Compact, for example: it asks multinational corporations to voluntarily subscribe to a list of international human rights and environmental standards and to regularly report on their progress in implementing these norms. While the Global Compact is entirely voluntary and does not entail any enforcement mechanism, other instruments of "Global Corporate Social Responsibility" use market incentives to induce norm compliance or entail elaborate monitoring and rating mechanisms (see e.g. the Dow Jones Sustainability

Index). Thus, we can currently observe a process by which private non-state actors are increasingly involved in and subject to the regulations of global norms of appropriate behavior. If you want to be a socially accepted "global player" these days, you had better subscribe at least to some international human rights and environmental standards, and you had better report about your efforts at implementing these norms through changes in management and production rules. Thus, norms of corporate social responsibility are starting to exert similar constitutive effects on transnational corporations as international human rights or environmental rules did on states about ten years earlier. We currently observe a mainstreaming of these norms into corporate practices which is again similar to the process by which states started instituting, say, specialized human rights agencies and commissions some time ago.

In sum, sociologist institutionalists and international relations scholars interested in the study of international norms and institutions have produced sufficient data to support the claim that a globalization of cultural standards, norms, and rules has taken place in parallel to the well-known globalization of markets. This process has occurred both informally through diffusion and emulation, but also more formally through international law-making and institution-building. It is noteworthy that this argument pre-dates the contemporary populist literature on "McWorld" and the Americanization/Westernization of global culture (Barber, 2003). This latter literature also argues that the diffusion of cultural values constitutes one important aspect of globalization. Yet there is an important difference between the sociological institutionalist argument and the more popular literature on the globalization of Western (or US-American) values and cultural standards. Those who complain about the Westernization of culture around the globe suggest that the global diffusion of cultural scripts inevitably leads to cultural homogeneity and the erosion of local or indigenous values and understandings – in line with popular arguments about the effects of economic globalization. We are all going to eat at McDonald's, drink CocaCola, listen to American Rock 'n' Roll, and watch Hollywood movies in the end – from Kampala to Shanghai to Paris.[3]

Sociological institutionalists, however, would disagree. Local values are not just being washed away by cultural globalization. Cultural differences continue to matter.[4] Rather, the more globalized cultural standards and institutionalized norms are incompatible or do not resonate with local standards, the more we will observe what sociologists called "decoupling" (Powell, 1991; DiMaggio and Powell, 1991; Jepperson, 2002): you talk the talk, but you do not walk the walk. In other words, cultural scripts will be enshrined in standard operating procedures and institutional norms because this is the culturally appropriate thing to do if one wants to be or become a member of the global society or the world polity. But the actual social practice is likely to deviate from these standards. People will continue to enact their local scripts and follow local norms of appropriate behavior. Moreover, hybrid cultures are likely to emerge which incorporate some global scripts into the local habits, while rejecting others. "Glocalized" cultures are the likely result.

"Decoupling" also explains why it is that simply signing up to international norms and rules – by states and increasingly so by transnational corporations – does not necessarily lead to improved compliance with these norms (as a brief look into the annual reports by Amnesty International, Human Rights Watch, Greenpeace, or Friends of the Earth will tell us immediately). Several studies have shown considerable variation in the degree to which states comply with international norms and rules, even with those treaties that they have signed and ratified – including obligatory reporting mechanisms (see e.g. Liese, 2006; Keith, 1999; Raustiala and Slaughter, 2002). Unfortunately, sociological institutionalism is not particularly good at explaining the variation in the extent to which states – and private actors – comply with these norms. This school of thought is so much concerned with demonstrating the structural homogeneity of corporate actors – including states in the contemporary world system – that it has little to offer about the degrees of decoupling. Focus on the global dissemination of cultural scripts and norms has led to a somewhat apolitical approach to the study of international standards and their diffusion (see Finnemore, 1996b on this point). In other words, politics and norm contestation has to be brought in, in order to explain variation in the degree of norm compliance. A comparative study of the domestic compliance with international human rights norms showed, for example, that transnational as well as domestic mobilization is necessary to pressure governments "from above and from below" toward rule-consistent behavior (Risse, Ropp, and Sikkink, 1999; Risse, Jetschke, and Schmitz, 2002).

This study also demonstrated that communicative processes are a crucial part of processes of norm diffusion and implementation. This begins with the agenda-setting phase for emerging international norms, during which framing processes and other strategic constructions play a crucial role in order to persuade actors that something has to be done about the respective global problem. Strategic constructions such as "naming and shaming" are also crucial when it comes to stigmatizing violators of international norms. In sum, we need to focus on communicative processes if we want to understand the microfoundations of cultural globalization. This leads to another contribution of social constructivism to the study of globalization.

4 Globalization as Communicative Practice: Discourses and Counter-Discourses

Irrespective of their various theoretical differences and disagreements, social constructivists tend to stress the significance of communicative practice and language as the processes by which meanings are constructed, interpretations are given to social phenomena, and, ultimately, social order is being established. As argued above, there are two ways in which the study of communicative practices can be brought to bear on globalization. One follows primarily a Foucaultian line and views the discursive construction of meanings as a process by which power relationships are established. The other approach follows essentially a Habermasian concept of communication and views discourses as reasoning processes of challenges and counter-challenges to arguments and justifications.

Starting with a Foucaultian concept of discourse, one has to keep in mind the intimate relationship between meaning construction and power. It is important to note that power is understood here as a social structure rather than an interactive relationship in which somebody establishes her will against others (a Weberian understanding of power, cf. Baldwin, 2002). Rather, the "power of discourse" refers to a structure of domination and subordination in which meanings and interpretations impose themselves on the subjects by defining how certain problems are to be viewed and which questions are to be asked (for an excellent review of these various concepts of power see Barnett and Duvall, 2005). In a way, discourses establish structures of ideational "soft power" without which systems of rules cannot function (on "soft power" see Nye, 1990 and 2004).

Take the notion of "globalization" from such a critical discourse-oriented perspective, for example (see also Steger, 2003). First, as the word itself implies, it is about universal rather than regional, national, or local processes. Thus, everybody is affected, no matter where you reside on the globe. Something is going on globally, we are all part of it, and it concerns everybody. But are we all "affected," and by what? Even in the global North, not everybody is immediately and directly affected by the trillions of US dollars moved daily through the world financial centers. At least, the causal mechanisms by which the world's capital markets affect the lives of ordinary citizens around the globe are more complex than the social construction of "globalization" seems to imply.

Second, "globalization" implies some sort of interconnectedness of everybody with everybody else, at least in theory. The term and the discourse accompanying it seem to suggest the absence of hierarchies in global networks of communication and information. What about the winners and losers of "globalization"? What about the global North and the global South? What about cultural globalization as a process of Westernization (see above) or even Americanization (see chapter 2 above by G. John Ikenberry)? What about simultaneous processes of fragmentation and increasing divergences? The globalization discourse also suggests a whole range of simultaneous economic, technological, political, and cultural processes that are all lumped together as "globalization." But does it really make sense to talk about "global civil society" as part of the same overall process as "global production networks"? As if there is one big causal factor behind it all?

Third, there seems to be something inevitable and irreversible about "globalization." One might discuss how and under what condition the process can be politically managed and how much political autonomy states continue to possess under "globalization." But the discourse is no longer about radical alternatives to "globalization." (Remember the 1970s and the development discourse about "self-sufficiency and autonomous development" in response to structural dependency?) Today, we discuss "managing globalization" rather than altering its course radically (and what is "it" anyway?). Where does politics come in here? Is "global governance" nothing more than a clean-up process to smoothe over some negative externalities of globalization?

Fourth, globalization processes appear to come without actors. They are all structure and no agency, just anonymous forces that decide our fate. Discourse theorists remind us, however, that references to anonymous forces constitute rhetorical constructions which often serve to cover up underlying power structures. What about US power in all of this? To what extent does "globalization" coincide with American hegemony in the world system? What about the structural power of capital and of transnational corporations in this process? What about international organizations, such as the International Monetary Fund, the World Bank, and the World Trade Organization? To what extent does the "globalization" discourse represent a strategic construction by powerful actors in the world system?

To be sure, this is not to suggest a conspiracy theory of globalization that would simply replace a structuralist view of global processes by an equally problematic "agentist" approach according to which global forces can be traced back to some concrete evil (economic) power interests of individual actors. Conspiracy theories serve to simplify a complex world, but, unfortunately, they rarely provide good causal explanations. Social constructivists would also have difficulties buying into a (Marxist) analysis by which discourse simply constitutes a super-structure which reinforces an underlying economic and material base, such as transnational capitalism.

Rather, the main task of a critical deconstruction of the globalization discourse is to uncover the structure of power as a structure of domination and subordination that this discourse itself establishes and reproduces. This might help the interests of transnational corporations as a side effect (no doubt about that). But to simply argue that globally oriented capitalists are the sole sources of a globalization discourse would reduce the complex story of social and intersubjective meaning construction to an almost mono-causal account. Rather, the constructivist reading of the globalization discourse presented here shows some similarities to a Neo-Gramscian approach to the international political economy, as represented in International Relations theory by Robert Cox and others (Cox, 1986, 1987; Cox and Sinclair, 1996; Gill, 1993). Neo-Gramscians analyze international power structures as configurations of economic forces, (political) institutions, and ideational constructions ("discourses" in my usage). But unlike traditional Marxists, they would insist on the relative autonomy of institutions and ideas from underlying economic configurations.

The critical analysis of the "globalization" discourse presented here also applies to the so-called "neoliberal discourse" which many have identified as the dominant discourse of globalization processes. Of course, this discourse is all about market liberalization, deregulation, and the global integration of markets. It contains some of the same ingredients – inevitability, irreversability, anonymous forces, etc. – as the globalization discourse itself. Yet, the "neoliberal discourse" also serves as a good example of how a discursive construction of reality, which some already took for reality itself, has generated its own counter-discourse in the meantime. Transnational social movements started challenging the assumptions behind the neoliberal and monetarist constructions of globalization. Through a process of deconstructing and reframing, they established an alternative construction of global processes.

It is ironic, of course, that some have called these activists "anti-globalization" forces. To some extent, the transnational social movements challenging neoliberal globalization have been as interconnected and networked and as dependent on modern information technologies as the forces they try to challenge. If interconnectedness, network organizations, and modern communication technologies are characteristics of globalization processes, "anti-globalization" movements are part and parcel of them. Which only serves to show, once again, how vaguely defined and unclear the concept of "globalization" remains to this day.

The main achievement of activists and transnational social movements opposing neoliberal economic globalization has been to open up the discursive space of the meaning structure constituted by "globalization" and to contest some of its hitherto dominant interpretations. At this point, we can move from a Foucaultian emphasis on the "power of discourse" to a Habermasian focus on the "power of the better argument." While a dominant discourse establishes structural power in the sense that it defines what the world does and ought to look like, what are the relevant questions to be asked, and who is considered a legitimate and authoritative voice, it is always open to agency in the sense that communicative practices and justifications can be challenged. To the extent that the globalization discourse as identified above contains universal truth claims, it is open to contestation. For example, the claim that economic liberalization and market integration benefits everybody from the global North to the global South, has been successfully challenged by transnational activists. These groups contested almost every single claim by globalization proponents and, thus, established a counter-discourse. They suggested an alternative vision of the world that included alternative causal knowledge claims and alternative views of a justice and fairness in the global order. This counter-discourse succeeded in persuading enough audiences in the North and the South of the globe so that we can no longer speak of neoliberalism as the "dominant discourse" of globalization.

The establishment of a (neoliberal) globalization discourse and the rise of a counter-discourse focusing on global justice can be better understood if we take the mutual constitutiveness of agency and structure into consideration – the mantra of social constructivism. While discourses establish systems of meanings and interpretation and, thus, a structure of power, these communicative structures are being produced and re-produced by agents. The agents are not freewheeling autonomous subjects who can change structures of power at will (no methodological individualism here!), but they are also not communicative robots that must always reproduce the dominant discourse. Rather, their communicative practices not only reproduce structures, but also (re-)interpret them. Thus, the ability to change and to contest dominant discourses is built into communicative practices, as Habermas reminds us.

A social constructivist reading of globalization as the discursive construction of interpretations and challenges to these interpretations and to established meanings, therefore, provides a better understanding of the contested nature of these processes than conventional readings that concentrate only on the material forces at play. Moreover, a social constructivist understanding allows us to "bring politics back in," that is, to challenge overly structuralist accounts of globalization that leave no room for agency and for political change. At the same time, it helps us to avoid voluntarist accounts, as if global social and material structures can be altered at will, "if we only want to."

5 Deliberative Global Governance as a Response to the Legitimacy Deficit of Globalization?

A final contribution of social constructivism to the study of globalization processes concerns their normative implications and particularly the question of how these processes can be subjected to political steering. The emphasis on the constructed nature of globalization discourses implies, of course, that globalization does not mean the end of politics, but its transformation (see e.g. Beck, 1997 and 2002). *Global Governance* has become the catchword for efforts at dealing with the political consequences of globalization and subjecting them to political intervention (see e.g. Commission on Global Governance, 1995). More recently, some scholars have suggested Global Public Policy and tripartite policy networks – so-called public–private partnerships – to steer globalization processes politically and to include private actors – companies and advocacy networks alike – in these processes (e.g. Reinicke, 1998; Reinicke and Deng, 2000; for a critical review see Börzel and Risse, 2005). The idea is that the inclusion of stakeholders is likely to make global governance both more legitimate and more effective in terms of enhancing its problem-solving capacity. The theoretical underpinnings of these ideas build, once again, on Habermasian notions of communicative action and discourse ethics (see e.g. Habermas, 1992, 1996), which are then used to develop the concept of deliberative democracy.

Its proponents claim that deliberation constitutes a significant means to increase the democratic legitimacy of governance mechanisms, particularly in situations in which democratic representation and/or voting mechanisms are not available options (see particularly Held, 1995; Wolf, 2000; Bohman and Regh, 1997; Elster, 1998; Joerges and Neyer, 1997; for the following see Risse, 2006). Deliberation is based on arguing and persuasion as non-hierarchical means of steering to achieve a reasoned consensus rather than a bargaining compromise. The general idea of this literature is that democracy is ultimately about involving the stakeholders, that is, those concerned by a particular social rule, in a deliberative process of mutual persuasion about the normative validity of particular rules. Once actors reach a reasoned consensus, this should greatly enhance the legitimacy of the rule, thus ensuring a high degree of voluntary compliance in the absence of sanctions. As Ian Hurd put it, "(w)hen an actor believes a rule is legitimate, compliance is no longer motivated by the simple fear of retribution, or by a calculation of self-interest, but instead by an internal sense of moral obligation" (Hurd, 1999, p. 387). Such an internal sense of moral obligation that accepts the logic of appropriateness behind a given norm requires some measure of moral persuasion. Advocates of deliberative democracy argue, therefore, that deliberation and arguing not only tackle the participatory deficit of global governance, but also increase voluntary compliance with inconvenient rules by closing the legitimacy gap.

However, institutional solutions in transnational governance to increase the deliberative quality of decision-making face obstacles which need to be addressed. There are several tradeoffs between deliberation, accountability, and legitimacy to be considered. First, selecting the relevant stakeholders for transnational rule-setting processes is difficult. It is often unclear who the stakeholders are and whom they represent. While the actors involved in trisectoral networks rarely face serious internal accountability problems (see above), external accountability remains an issue. Deliberation requires participation of those in the policymaking process that are potentially affected by the rules. Take the World Commission on Dams, for example – a trisectoral body designed to develop rules for the construction of large dams. It was set up institutionally by the World Bank as a deliberative body to maximize arguing and learning. It produced a policy report, but there is little agreement in the literature and the policy world alike whether it actually achieved its goal of reaching a reasoned consensus that would allow the World Bank to construct a sustainable policy toward large dams without antagonizing the various stakeholders (see e.g. Khagram, 2000; Dingwerth, 2003).

Second, and related to the first problem, decisions about selection of members in deliberative bodies with policymaking authority are about inclusion and exclusion. Whom to include, whom to exclude, and who decides about inclusion and exclusion represent, therefore, most contentious processes in the establishment of trisectoral public policy networks. This problem is exacerbated by the fact that specific stakeholder interests can usually be organized and represented much more easily than diffuse stakeholder interests.

Third, once the stakeholders have been selected, how can deliberation and arguing be framed, so as to improve the quality of the negotiations? Specific institutional settings are required that enable actors to engage in the reflexive processes of arguing. These settings must provide incentives for actors to critically evaluate their own interests and preferences, if the arguing process is supposed to go beyond just mutual information and explicating one's preferences to others. At this point, a tradeoff between transparency and argumentative effectiveness in deliberative settings has to be considered. Many negotiation systems show that arguing and persuasion work particularly well behind closed doors, that is, outside the public sphere (see Checkel, 2001b). A reasoned consensus might be achievable more easily if secrecy of the deliberations prevails and actors are not required to justify their change of position and the like in front of critical audiences. Behind closed doors, negotiators can freely exchange ideas and thoughts more easily than in the public sphere where they have to stick to their guns. Yet transparency is usually regarded as a necessary ingredient for increasing the democratic legitimacy of transnational governance. If we can only improve the deliberative quality of global governance by decreasing the transparency of the process even further, the overall gain for legitimacy and external accountability might not be worth the effort.

This leads to a final point, namely potential tensions between accountability and deliberation. Negotiators – be they diplomats or private actors in trisectoral networks – usually have a mandate from their principals to represent the interests of their organizations and are accountable to whoever sent them to the negotiating body. As a result, there are limits in the extent to which they are allowed to engage in freewheeling deliberation. What if negotiators change sides in the course of negotiations because they have been persuaded by the better argument? Of course, it makes no sense to consider negotiators as nothing but transmission belts of their principals' preferences with no leeway at all. But it does raise issues of accountability if negotiators are so persuaded by the arguments of their counterparts that they change sides. At least, one would have to require that they engage in a process of "two-level arguing," that is, of trying to persuade their principals that they should change their preferences, too.[5] It is not enough to institutionalize deliberative processes in multilateral negotiations including trisectoral public policy networks. There needs to be a communicative feedback loop into the domestic and other environments to which negotiating agents are accountable. Otherwise, one would sacrifice accountability and legitimacy for efficiency. "Two-level arguing" might also be necessary to overcome the tension between effectiveness of deliberation in secrecy, on the one hand, and ensuring the transparency of the process, on the other.

6 Conclusions

I have argued in this chapter that social constructivism contributes to our understanding of globalization in several significant ways. First, an emphasis on norms and cultural understandings identifies the global diffusion of cultural scripts and norms as part and parcel of globalization. Yet, this globalization remains incomplete in terms of both its global reach horizontally and its vertical penetration into national and/or local cultures. As a result, we do not observe increasing cultural homogeneity across the globe, but varying degrees of hybrid and "glocalized" cultures linking the different local systems of meanings to the global in various ways.

Second, social constructivism emphasizes the discursive construction of globalization. A Foucaultian perspective demonstrates how globalization discourses constitute power structures of domination and subordination. This view allows us to critically examine the various systems of meanings involved when we talk the "globalization talk." At the same time, a Habermasian perspective on discourse as reasoning introduces transformative potential into the alleged inevitability of globalization. Transnational social movements have successfully challenged the dominant neoliberal view of globalization and have introduced a counter-discourse focusing on fairness, justice, and legitimacy.

Finally, if we treat global governance as a political response to globalization to enhance the legitimacy and problem-solving capacity of multilateral institutions, social constructivism helps us to critically examine some of the claims put forward by proponents of deliberative democracy on a global scale. A Habermasian perspective, once again, allows us to discuss some of the tradeoffs involved in making global governance more legitimate and more effective.

In sum, social constructivism does not offer yet another theory of globalization, if a theory of something as unspecified is possible at all. Yet, it serves as a critical perspective that allows students of globalization processes to challenge the conventional wisdom in the scholarly as well as the wider public discourse on these questions. Social constructivists are likely to share the approach of critical theorists asking about the winners and losers of globalization. They will also share the skepticism of those pointing to the fragmented and uneven nature of many processes identified with globalization. Last not least, social constructivists are likely to point out that globalization as a dominant discourse in world politics tends to reify existing power structures.

Notes

1 This part builds on Risse, 2002, 2003.
2 For an excellent review of the linguistic turn in international relations theory see Holzscheiter, 2004.
3 Of course, this only applies if you have access to electricity, if you have enough money to go to McDonald's occasionally, or if you are able to read and write.
4 There is a whole literature on cultural difference which is impossible to review here. See e.g. Robertson, 1993; Drechsel, Schmidt, and Götz, 2000.
5 "Two-level arguing" is analogous to Putnam's "two-level games," see Putnam, 1988. I thank Mathias Koenig-Archibugi and David Held for alerting me to this point.

References

Adler, Emanuel (1997). "Seizing the Middle Ground. Constructivism in World Politics." *European Journal of International Relations*, 3(3): pp. 319–63.

Adler, Emanuel (2002). "Constructivism in International Relations." In *Handbook of International Relations*, ed. Walter Carlsnaes, Thomas Risse, and Beth Simmons. London: Sage, pp. 95–119.

Altvater, Elmar and Birgit Mahnkopf (1996). *Grenzen der Globalisierung. Ökonomie, Ökologie und Politik in der Weltgesellschaft*. Münster: Westfälisches Dampfboot.

Baldwin, David A. (2002). "Power and International Relations." In *Handbook of International Relations*, ed. Walter Carlsnaes, Thomas Risse, and Beth Simmons. London: Sage, pp. 177–191.

Barber, Benjamin R. (2003). *Jihad vs. McWorld: Terrorism's Challange to Democracy*, London: Corgi.

Barnett, Michael and Raymond Duvall (2005). "Power in International Politics," *International Organization*, 59(1): pp. 39–75.

Beck, Ulrich (1997). *Was ist Globalisierung?* Frankfurt/Main: Suhrkamp, tr. as *What is Globalization?* Cambridge: Polity, 1999.

Beck, Ulrich (2002). *Macht und Gegenmacht im globalen Zeitalter*. Frankfurt/Main: Suhrkamp.

Beisheim, Marianne and Gregor Walter (1997). "'Globalisierung' – Kinderkrankheiten eines Konzeptes." *Zeitschrift für Internationale Beziehungen*, 4(1): pp. 153–80.

Berger, Peter L. and Thomas Luckmann (1966). *The Social Construction of Reality: A Treatise in the Sociology of Knowledge*. New York: Doubleday.

Bohman, James and William Regh (1997). *Deliberative Democracy: Essays on Reason and Politics*. Cambridge, Mass.: MIT Press.

Boli, John and George M. Thomas (1997). "World Culture in the World Polity." *American Sociological Review*, 62: pp. 171–190.

Boli, John and George M. Thomas, eds (1998). *World Polity Formation since 1875*. Stanford, Calif.: Stanford University Press.

Boli, John and George M. Thomas, eds (1999). *Constructing World Culture: International Nongovernmental Organizations since 1875*. Stanford, Calif.: Stanford University Press.

Börzel, Tanja A. and Thomas Risse (2005). "Public–Private Partnerships: Effective and Legitimate Tools of International Governance?" In *Complex Sovereignty: Reconstituting Political Authority in the Twenty-First Century*, ed. Edgar Grande and Louis W. Pauly. Toronto: University of Toronto Press.

Checkel, Jeffrey T. (1998). "The Constructivist Turn in International Relations Theory." *World Politics*, 50(2): pp. 324–48.

Checkel, Jeffrey T. (2001a). "Social Construction and Integration". In *The Social Construction of Europe*, ed. Thomas Christiansen, Knud Erik Jørgensen, and Antje Wiener. London: Sage, pp. 50–64.

Checkel, Jeffrey T. (2001b). "Why Comply? Social Learning and European Identity Change." *International Organization*, 55(3): pp. 553–88.

Commission on Global Governance (1995). *Our Global Neighbourhood*. Oxford: Oxford University Press.

Cox, Robert W. (1986). "Social Forces, States, and World Orders: Beyond International Relations Theory." In *Neorealism and its Critics*, ed. Robert O. Keohane. New York: Cambridge University Press.

Cox, Robert W. (1987). *Production, Power, and World Order*. New York: Columbia University Press.

Cox, Robert W. and Timothy J. Sinclair (1996). *Approaches to World Order*. Cambridge: Cambridge University Press.

Diez, Thomas (2001). "Speaking 'Europe': The Politics of Integration Discourse." In *The Social Construction of Europe*, ed. Thomas Christiansen, Knud Erik Jørgensen, and Antje Wiener. London: Sage, pp. 85–100.

DiMaggio, Paul J. and Walter W. Powell (1991). "The Iron Cage Revisited: Institutional Isomorphism and Collective Rationality in Organizational Fields". In *The New Institutionalism in Organizational Analysis*, ed. Walter W. Powell and Paul J. DiMaggio. Chicago: University of Chicago Press, pp. 63–82.

Dingwerth, Klaus (2003). "Globale Politiknetzwerke und ihre demokratische Legitimation." *Zeitschrift für Internationale Beziehungen*, 10(1): pp. 69–111.

Drechsel, Paul, Bettina Schmidt, and Bernhard Götz (2000). *Kultur im Zeitalter der Globalisierung – von Identität zu Differenzen*. Frankfurt/Main: IKO-Verlag für interkulturelle Kommunikation.

Elster, Jon (1989). *Nuts and Bolts for the Social Sciences*. Cambridge, Mass.: MIT Press.

Elster, Jon, ed. (1998). *Deliberative Democracy*. Cambridge: Cambridge University Press.

Fearon, James D. and Alexander Wendt (2002). "Rationalism v. Constructivism: A Skeptical View." In *Handbook of International Relations*, ed. Walter Carlsnaes, Thomas Risse, and Beth Simmons. London: Sage, pp. 52–72.

Finnemore, Martha (1996a). *National Interests in International Society*. Ithaca, NY: Cornell University Press.

Finnemore, Martha (1996b). "Norms, Culture, and World Politics: Insights From Sociology's Institutionalism". *International Organization*, 50(2): pp. 325–47.

Finnemore, Martha and Kathryn Sikkink (1998). "International Norm Dynamics and Political Change." *International Organization*, 52(4): pp. 887–917.

Florini, Ann, ed. (2000). *The Third Force: The Rise of Transnational Civil Society*. Tokyo/ Washington DC: Japan Center for International Exchange/Carnegie Endowment for International Peace.

Foucault, Michel (1973). *The Order of Things*. New York: Vintage Books.

Foucault, Michel (1991). "Politics and the Study of Discourse." In *The Foucault Effect: Studies in Governmentality*, ed. Graham Burchell, Colin Gordon, and Peter Miller. Hemel Hempstead: Harvester Wheatsheaf, pp. 53–72.

Foucault, Michel (1996). *Diskurs und Wahrheit. Berkeley-Vorlesungen 1983*, trans. Mira Köller, ed. Joseph Pearson. Berlin: Merve Verlag.

Giddens, Anthony (1982). "Hermeneutics and Social Theory." In *Profiles and Critiques in Social Theory*, ed. Anthony Giddens. Berkeley: University of California Press, pp. 1–17.

Giddens, Anthony (1984). *The Constitution of Society: Outline of the Theory of Structuration*. Berkeley: University of California Press.

Gill, Stephen, ed. (1993). *Gramsci, Historical Materialism, and International Relations*. Cambridge: Cambridge University Press.

Gill, Stephen (1995). "Globalization, Market Civilization, and Disciplinary Neoliberalism." *Millennium: Journal of International Studies*, 24(3): pp. 399–423.

Gill, Stephen and David Law (1993). "Global Hegemony and the Structural Power of Capital." In *Gramsci, Historical Materialism, and International Relations*, ed. Stephen Gill. Cambridge: Cambridge University Press, pp. 93–124.

Haas, Peter M., Robert O. Keohane, and Marc A. Levy, eds (1993). *Institutions for the Earth: Sources of Effective International Environmental Protection*. Cambridge, Mass.: MIT Press.

Habermas, Jürgen (1968). *Erkenntnis und Interesse*. Frankfurt/Main: Suhrkamp.

Habermas, Jürgen (1981). *Theorie des kommunikativen Handelns*. 2 vols. Frankfurt/M.: Suhrkamp.

Habermas, Jürgen (1992). *Faktizität und Geltung. Beiträge zur Diskurstheorie des Rechts und des demokratischen Rechtsstaats*. Frankfurt/M.: Suhrkamp.

Habermas, Jürgen (1996). *Die Einbeziehung des Anderen*. Frankfurt/Main: Suhrkamp.

Held, David (1995). *Democracy and the Global Order: From the Modern State to Cosmopolitan Governance*. Cambridge: Cambridge University Press.

Held, David, Anthony McGrew, David Goldblatt, and Jonathan Perraton (1999). *Global Transformations: Politics, Economics, and Culture*. Stanford, Calif.: Stanford University Press.

Holzscheiter, Anna (2004). PolitikON Modul: Sprache, Diskurs, kommunikatives Handeln. PolitikON Module, Berlin: Otto Suhr Institut für Politikwissenschaft.

Howarth, David A., Aletta J. Norval, and Yannis Stavrakakis, eds (2000). *Discourse Theory and Political Analysis*. Manchester: Manchester University Press.

Hurd, Ian (1999). "Legitimacy and Authority in International Politics." *International Organization*, 53(2): pp. 379–408.

Jepperson, Ronald L. (2002). "The Development and Application of Sociological Neo-institutionalism." In *New Directions in Contemporary Sociological Theory*, ed. Joseph Berger and Morris Zelditch Jr. Lanham, Md.: Rowman & Littlefield, pp. 229–66.

Joerges, Christian and Jürgen Neyer (1997). "Transforming Strategic Interaction into Deliberative Problem-Solving: European Comitology in the Foodstuffs Sector." *Journal of European Public Policy*, 4: pp. 609–25.

Keane, John (2003). *Global Civil Society?* Cambridge: Cambridge University Press.

Keck, Margret and Kathryn Sikkink (1998). *Activists beyond Borders: Transnational Advocacy Networks in International Politics*. Ithaca, NY: Cornell University Press.

Keith, Linda Camp (1999). "The United Nations International Covenant on Civil and Political Rights: Does it Make a Difference in Human Rights Behavior?" *Journal of Peace Research*, 36(1): pp. 95–118.

Keohane, Robert O. (1989). *International Institutions and State Power*. Boulder, Colo: Westview.

Keohane, Robert O. 2001. "Governance in a Partially Globalized World." *American Political Science Review*, 95 (March); pp. 1–13.

Keohane, Robert O. and Helen Milner, eds (1996). *Internationalization and Domestic Politics*. Cambridge: Cambridge University Press.

Keohane, Robert O. and Joseph S. Nye (1977). *Power and Interdependence*. Boston: Little, Brown.

Khagram, Sanjeev (2000). "Toward Democratic Governance for Sustainable Development: Transnational Civil Society Organizing around Big Dams." In *The Third Force. The Rise of Transnational Civil Society*, ed. Ann M. Florini. Tokyo/Washington DC: Japan Center for International Exchange/Carnegie Endowment for International Peace, pp. 83–114.

Kofman, E. and G. Youngs, eds (2003). *Globalization: Theory and Practice*, 2nd edn. London: Continuum.

Korey, William (1998). *NGOs and the Universal Declaration of Human Rights. 'A Curious Grapevine'*. New York: St Martin's Press.

Kratochwil, Friedrich (1989). *Rules, Norms, and Decisions*. Cambridge: Cambridge University Press.

Legro, Jeffrey W. and Andrew Moravcsik (1999). "Is Anybody Still a Realist?" *International Security*, 24(2): pp. 5–55.

Liese, Andrea (2006). *Staaten am Pranger. Zur Wirkung internationaler Regime auf die innerstaatliche Menschenrechtspolitik*. Opladen: VS Verlag für Sozialwissenschaften.

Litfin, Karen (1994). *Ozone Discourses: Science and Politics in Global Environmental Cooperation*. New York: Columbia University Press.

March, James G. and Johan P. Olsen (1989). *Rediscovering Institutions*. New York: Free Press.

March, James G. and Johan P. Olsen (1998). "The Institutional Dynamics of International Political Orders." *International Organization*, 52(4): pp. 943–69.

Meyer, John M. (1987). "The World Polity and the Authority of the Nation State." In *International Structure: Constituting State, Society and the Individual*, ed. George M. Thomas, John W. Meyer, Francisco O. Ramirez, and John Boli. London: Sage.

Meyer, John W., John Boli, and George Thomas (1987). "Ontology and Rationalization in the Western Cultural Account." In *Institutional Structure: Constituting State, Society, and the Individual*, ed. George Thomas et al. Newbury Park, Calif.: Sage, pp. 12–37.

Meyer, John W., John Boli, George M. Thomas, and Francisco O. Ramirez (1997). "World Society and the Nation-State." *American Journal of Sociology*, 103(1): pp. 144–81.

Mitchell, Ronald B. (2002). "International Environmental Policy." In *Handbook of International Relations*, ed. Walter Carlsnaes, Thomas Risse, and Beth Simmons. London: Sage, pp. 500–17.

Müller, Harald (1994). "Internationale Beziehungen als kommunikatives Handeln. Zur Kritik der utilitaristischen Handlungstheorien." *Zeitschrift für Internationale Beziehungen*, 1(1): pp. 15–44.

Nye, Jr, Joseph S. (1990). *Bound to Lead: The Changing Nature of American Power*. New York: Basic Books.

Nye, Jr, Joseph S. (2004). *Soft Power: The Means to Succeed in World Politics*. New York: Public Affairs Press.

Ohmae, Kenichi (1990). *The Borderless World: Power and Strategy in the Interlinked Economy*. New York: Harper.

Onuf, Nicholas (1989). *World of our Making: Rules and Rule in Social Theory and International Relations*. Colombia: University of South Carolina Press.

Powell, Walter W. (1991). "Expanding the Scope of Institutional Analysis". In *The New Institutionalism in Organizational Analysis*, ed. Walter W. Powell and Paul J. DiMaggio. Chicago: Chicago University Press, pp. 183–204.

Putnam, Robert (1988). "Diplomacy and Domestic Politics: The Logic of Two-Level Games." *International Organization*, 42(2): pp. 427–60.

Ramirez, Francisco O. (1987). "Comparative Social Movements." In *Institutional Structure: Constituting State, Society and the Individual*, ed. George M. Thomas, John W. Meyer, Francisco O. Ramirez, and John Boli. London: Sage, pp. 290–4.

Raustiala, Kal and Anne-Marie Slaughter (2002). "International Law, International Relations, and Compliance." In *Handbook of International Relations*, ed. Walter Carlsnaes, Thomas Risse, and Beth Simmons. London: Sage, pp. 538–58.

Reinicke, Wolfgang H. (1998). *Global Public Policy: Governing without Government?* Washington, DC: Brookings Institution.

Reinicke, Wolfgang H. and Francis Deng (2000). *Critical Choices: The United Nations, Networks, and the Future of Global Governance*. Ottawa: International Development Research Centre.

Risse, Thomas (2000). "'Let's Argue!' Communicative Action in International Relations." *International Organization*, 54(1): pp. 1–39.

Risse, Thomas (2002). "Constructivism and International Institutions: Toward Conversations across Paradigms." In *Political Science: The State of the Discipline*, ed. Ira Katznelson and Helen V. Milner. New York: Norton, pp. 597–623.

Risse, Thomas (2003). "Social Constructivism and European Integration." In *European Integration Theory*, ed. Thomas Diez and Antje Wiener. Oxford: Oxford University Press.

Risse, Thomas (2006). "Transnational Governance and Legitimacy." In *Governance and Democracy: Comparing National, European and International Experiences*, ed. Arthur Benz and Ioannis Papadopoulos. London: Routledge.

Risse, Thomas, Anja Jetschke, and Hans Peter Schmitz (2002). *Die Macht der Menschenrechte. Internationale Normen, kommunikatives Handeln und politischer Wandel in den Ländern des Südens, Weltpolitik im 21. Jahrhundert*. Baden-Baden: Nomos.

Risse, Thomas, Stephen C. Ropp, and Kathryn Sikkink, eds (1999). *The Power of Human Rights: International Norms and Domestic Change*. Cambridge: Cambridge University Press.

Robertson, Roland (1993). *Globalization. Social Theory and Global Culture* (1992). Repr. as *Theory, Culture and Society*. London: Sage.

Ruggie, John Gerard (1998). "What Makes the World Hang Together? Neo-Utilitarianism and the Social Constructivist Challenge." *International Organization*, 52(4): pp. 855–85.

Schmitz, Hans Peter and Kathryn Sikkink (2002). "International Human Rights." In *Handbook of International Relations*, ed. Walter Carlsnaes, Thomas Risse, and Beth Simmons. London: Sage, pp. 517–37.

Smith, Jackie, Charles Chatfield, and Ron Pagnucco, eds (1997). *Transnational Social Movements and Global Politics: Solidarity Beyond the State*. Syracuse, NY: Syracuse University Press.

Steger, Manfred B. (2003). *Globalization: A Very Short Introduction*. Oxford: Oxford University Press.

Strange, Susan (1996). *The Retreat of the State: The Diffusion of Power in the World Economy*. Cambridge: Cambridge University Press.

Tarrow, Sidney (2005). *The New Transnational Activism*. Cambridge: Cambridge University Press.

Thomas, George M., John W. Meyer, Francisco Ramirez, and John Boli, eds (1987). *Institutional Structure: Constituting State, Society, and the Individual*. Newbury Park Calif.: Sage.

Wallerstein, Immanuel (1974, 1980, 1989). *The Modern World-System*, 3 vols, vol. 1. San Diego: Academic Press.

Wendt, Alexander (1999). *Social Theory of International Politics*. Cambridge: Cambridge University Press.

Wight, Colin (2002). "Philosophy of Science and International Relations." In *Handbook of International Relations*, eds Walter Carlsnaes, Thomas Risse, and Beth Simmons. London: Sage, pp. 23–51.

Wolf, Klaus Dieter (2000). *Die Neue Staatsräson – Zwischenstaatliche Kooperation als Demokratieproblem in der Weltgesellschaft*. Baden-Baden: Nomos.

Zürn, Michael (1998). *Regieren jenseits des Nationalstaates. Globalisierung und Denationalisierung als Chance*. Frankfurt/Main: Suhrkamp.

7

Globalization and Cultural Analysis

John Tomlinson

1 The Cultural Dimension of Globalization

To begin with let us agree – on this we *can* all probably agree – that 'globalization' is a rather unsatisfactory term for the phenomena we are attempting to describe and to understand. The reasons why globalization is such an unfortunate word are several. Because it invites overstatement and smacks of an overweening tendency to universalize, or at least to over-generalize. Because most of the processes and experiences it describes, though vastly wide and growing in their distribution, are hardly ever actually, *literally* global in their reach. And therefore because it invites close analysis to point out all the exceptions rather than to see the force of the trajectories involved. And because, as a response to this, the élan of the term quickly becomes dissipated once it is hedged about by necessary qualifications – for instance its general pairing with the opposing tendency to 'localization'. More significantly, because it seems to many to articulate – and even to distribute and enforce – the dominant cultural, economic and political discourses of the West. But most of all because it has been a victim of its own success: hardly mentioned before 1990, it is now a word, as Zygmunt Bauman (1998, p. 1) says, 'on everybody's lips, a fad word fast turning into a shibboleth'.

This proliferation of the discourse naturally leads to oversimplifications and confusions and these are not least evident in the sphere of culture – the focus of this discussion. Here one of the chief problems has been that the term initially presented itself as what language teachers call a *faux ami*. In it many cultural critics mistakenly recognized something familiar: Western cultural imperialism or, more directly, Americanization. This initial critical reception of the concept was understandable – for, albeit in a superficial sense, the most visible fruits of cultural globalization have been the increasing distribution of Western and specifically American popular cultural products and forms. And indeed there has been much in the implicit cultural stance of the United States' administration in recent years – catalysed by the events of 11 September 2001 – that apparently vindicates an interpretation based in the self-conscious project of American cultural-political hegemony. It was entirely predictable, then, that questions of the dominance of Western culture wedded to political-economic power came to dominate the discussion of cultural globalization.

Yet, for all this, it was and is a mistake to confuse the broader phenomenon of cultural globalization with cultural imperialism; and not only because this has been responsible for a good deal of rather tedious raking over of old ground. For what is sure is that globalization, vexed term though it be, grasps a process of huge significance which, without exaggeration, may be said to define the cultural condition of our times. The challenge to a theory of cultural globalization is to generate interpretations and understandings of this process at a sufficient level of analysis to do justice to it. And this may mean standing back somewhat from the most immediate manifestations of the process – that is to say, from particular contexts of cultural-political power relations, even from questions of where cultural-political-economic power happens to be concentrated in the world at present – in order to try to understand the underlying dynamics of the process.

But how to understand these dynamics – and what theoretical resources can we call upon to help in this understanding? Well, this depends very much on the *way* in which we want to understand things. Globalization has without doubt prompted some radical critiques of extant theory in the social sciences. John Urry articulates a common perception of its implications for the discipline of sociology when he argues:

> The study of the global disrupts many conventional debates and should not be viewed as merely an extra level or domain that can be 'added' to existing sociological analyses that can carry on regardless. 'Sociology' will not be able to sustain itself as a specific and coherent discourse focused upon the study of given, bounded or 'organized' capitalist societies. It is irreversibly changed. (Urry, 2003, p. 3)

Ulrich Beck puts the point even more forcefully in his critique of the adequacy of 'normal social science concepts' to the analysis of the rapid and perplexing changes set in train by globalization. Citing Kant's dictum, 'Observations without concepts are blind; concepts without observations are empty', Beck writes, 'Normal social science categories are becoming *zombie* categories, empty terms in the Kantian meaning. Zombie categories are living dead categories, which blind the social sciences to the rapidly changing realities inside the nation-state containers and outside as well' (Beck, 2002, p. 24)

There is, then, a distinct conceptual iconoclasm implicit in globalization. It may not be of the same order as the self-conscious rug-pulling dismissal of grand narratives that characterized postmodernism. Nonetheless, the conceptual challenge which globalization presents is both profound and extensive. What both Beck and Urry are pointing to is the rather obvious inadequacy – once you come to think about it – of some key intellectual assumptions about the social, economic and cultural order developed in the nineteenth and the early part of the twentieth centuries – to a world that is rapidly revealing its complicated, fluid and dynamic interconnectedness.

It seems to me that there are at least two general ways of responding to this state of affairs. The first is what might be described as the 'back to the drawing board' approach. This insists that not only can we not understand the globalized world we live in without generating new concepts, but that globalization reveals fundamental misconceptions at the heart of the theoretical project of the social sciences as presently conceived. Nothing short of a general theoretical revision will answer. This is in different ways the implication of both Beck's and Urry's comments. In Beck's case this involves a systematic re-visioning of fundamental sociological concepts – interrogating the relevance of the concept of class, the nature of power, the category of modernity and so forth from the perspective of globality. Urry, by contrast, responds at a meta-theoretical level, by confronting the inherent *complexity* and fluidity of global interconnectedness, and he turns to theories of complexity derived from the physical sciences to understand a social order which is now 'always on the edge of chaos' (Urry, 2003). These are major and, it has to be said, bold and exciting undertakings.

However, the second available response approaches the instabilities and fluidities of the global order more modestly. Instead of insisting on wholesale theoretical revision, it tries to generate concepts and find descriptive categories and analytic strategies adequate to the immediate state of affairs that complex connectivity presents us with. This response is recognizable most obviously in the hermeneutic tradition of cultural analysis which attempts to interpret and contextually understand rather than systematically to explain the social world. Such an approach operates close to the cultural and the phenomenological data of everyday experience and is more heuristically inclined, less given to theoretical system building (or dismantling). Its empirical project is close to the Geerzian/Rylian style of 'thick description', and its theoretical aims might be described as middle-order ones – to generate sets of conceptual categories capable of grasping and interpreting new orders of experience.

This is the broad approach I shall take in addressing the cultural agenda of globalization, and in section 2 I will offer some interpretive categories through which to think about the complex connectivity of globalization in its cultural dimension. However, even in this more pragmatic mood, we cannot avoid confronting two rather fundamental theoretical issues in relation to culture.

The consequentiality of culture

The first is by way of a caution against such frequently used formulations as 'the *impact* of globalization on culture' or 'the cultural *consequences* of globalization'. Such phrases are, no doubt, often used casually as a reference to the way in which the connectivity and fluidity of globalization makes itself felt within the sphere of culture. Yet the trouble with these phrases is that, taken literally, they imply globalization to be a process which somehow has its sources and its sphere of operation *outside* of culture. This is important because it betrays some rather stubborn preconceptions about both the driving forces of globalization and also the nature of 'culture' itself.

Pretty much everyone today would give at least broad assent to the general proposition that globalization is a multidimensional process, taking place simultaneously within the spheres of the economy, of politics, of the environment, of the institutionalization of technologies, and of culture. But this agreement probably masks a good many tacit assumptions as to the relative importance of each of these dimensions. And it is clear that chief among these assumptions is that it is the economic sphere, the institution of the global capitalist market that is the crucial element, the *sine qua non* of global connectivity.

The validity of this assumption is not, in fact, that easily determined, because we are not dealing here with straightforward empirical judgements, but also with questions of the constitution of categories: to what extent are economic practices also, intrinsically, cultural ones? But it is the force of the assumption on the way in which cultural globalization is perceived that is the issue. One major reason why it seems natural to speak of globalization's 'impact' on culture is that global market processes – say, the distribution of consumer goods – are relatively easy to understand as having a potential influence on people's cultural experience. This, indeed, is at the core of the interpretation of cultural globalization as Americanization or Westernization or as the spread of a global-capitalist monoculture (Tomlinson, 1997, 1999). In all such readings 'culture' seems to be a peculiarly inert category.[1] Much has been written from the semiotic-hermeneutic perspective of cultural (and particularly media) analysis in response to this, demonstrating the active, transformative nature of the appropriation of cultural goods (Morley, 1992; Moores, 1993; Lull, 2000). But despite this critique, the idea of culture as being intrinsically *constitutive* of globalization – as being a dimension which has consequences for other domains – remains relatively obscure.

This is to some extent a problem of the self-understanding of culture as an area of academic study, perhaps most forcefully from the semiotic tradition. 'Culture is not a power, something to which social events can be causally attributed', says Clifford Geertz (1973, p. 14), and this is surely right to the extent that we should think of cultural processes *primarily* as oriented towards the construction of socially shared meanings. Meaning is, as it were, an end in itself for culture. And this has, quite justly, shaped the way in which culture has been typically studied: as representation, as lived experience, as text and as context.

The notion of 'causality' sits awkwardly within this discourse. However, this does not mean to say that culture is not *consequential*. It is certainly so in that the processes of meaning construction inform, inspire and direct individual and collective actions which are *themselves* consequential. Culture is thus not only 'a context in which [events] may be meaningfully interpreted' (Geertz, 1973, p. 14) it is *the* context in which agency arises and takes place. Cultural signification and interpretation constantly orients people, individually and collectively, towards particular actions. Actions which seem to be fairly instrumental ones, following a logic of practical or economic necessity, are nonetheless always undertaken within that set of self-understandings, plans, hopes or aspirations which we can think of as the constitutive elements of the individual's lifeworld. Even the most basic instrumental actions of satisfying bodily needs are not in this sense outside of culture: in certain circumstances (slimming, eating disorders, religious fasting, hunger strikes) the decision to eat or to starve is a cultural decision.

One way to think about the consequentiality of culture for globalization, then, is to grasp how culturally informed 'local' actions can have globalizing consequences. The complex connectivity of globalization is not just the ever tighter integration of social institutions, it is at the same time the integration of individual agency into the workings of institutions. Thus cultural connectivity discloses the increasing *reflexivity* of global-modern life (Giddens, 1990).

Uprooting culture

The second theoretical issue concerns the way we are to understand the concept of 'culture'. For the globalization process disturbs a rather deep-seated intuition that culture has a special and almost defining relationship to geographical place.

Culture has long held connotations tying it to the idea of a fixed locality. The idea of 'a culture' implicitly connects meaning construction with particularity and location. In the sociological treatment of culture, particularly in the functionalist tradition where collective meaning construction was seen largely as serving the purposes of social inte-gration, there has been a tacit assumption that culture is a spatially bounded entity, somehow paralleling the bounded, integrated entity of the 'society' (Mann, 1986). The notion of societal subcultures – even where these are ethnically defined – in fact does nothing to disturb this identification of culture with territory. Culture in this under-standing either binds individual meaning constructions into the circumscribed social, political space of the nation-state, or places obstacles – in the form of competing territo-rially defined attachments – in the way of this integrative process.

The connectivity of globalization is clearly threatening to such conceptualizations, not only because the multiform penetration of localities disrupts this binding of meanings to place, but also because it undermines the thinking through which culture and fixity of location are originally paired.

This has perhaps been most evident in anthropology where, for a notable example, James Clifford's work on 'travelling cultures' (Clifford, 1992 and 1997) has focused on prising culture apart from location. Clifford challenges one of the grounding assumptions of traditional anthropological fieldwork that, 'authentic social existence is, or should be, centred in circumscribed places – like the gardens where the word "culture" derived its European meanings'. (1997, p. 3) He goes on to demonstrate how the practices of field-work have contributed to the localizing of the concept of culture: 'centering the *culture* around a particular locus, the *village*, and around a certain spatial practice of dwelling/research which itself depended on a complementary localization – that of the *field*' (1997, p. 20). So the traditional research methods of anthropology – the practice of ethnography as 'dwelling' with the community – have contributed to a synecdoche in which location is taken for culture. And this assumption continues in contemporary ethnography where the locations may be 'hospitals, labs, urban neighbourhoods, tourist hotels' rather than remote villages.

Clifford's challenge to this tradition is to think of culture as *mobile* rather than static, to treat 'practices of displacement . . . as constitutive of cultural meanings', to pay more attention to 'routes' than to 'roots'. This is close to the conceptual challenge globaliza-tion makes to culture. However, it is not, as Clifford allows, that we have to *reverse* the priority between 'roots and routes', insisting on the essence of culture as restless nomadic movement. Rather, globalization changes the texture of lived experience both in mobility and in dwelling. Though it promotes much more physical mobility than ever before, the key to globalization's cultural dimension is not primarily grasped in the trope of travel, but in the transformation of localities themselves. In the following section, I deploy the concept of 'deterritorialization' to understand this weakening of the ties of culture to place,[2] and in the process return to the question of mobilities and the particular role of media and communications technologies in the globalization process.

2 Deterritorialization

If globalization, in its rawest description, is the proliferation of complex connectedness across distance, then deterritorialization refers to the reach of this connectivity into the localities in which everyday life is conducted and experienced. This is at once a perplexing and disruptive, and an exhilarating and empowering phenomenon, involving the simultaneous penetration of local worlds by distant forces, and the dislodging of everyday meanings from their 'anchors' in the local environment. It is also undoubtedly an uneven and often contradictory business, involving winners and losers, felt more forcibly in some places than others, and often met by countervailing tendencies to re-establish the power of locality (Castells, 1997). But deterritorialization, for all its various and ambiguous entailments, is surely a feature of all societies in the twenty-first century and, without doubt, a phenomenon of the greatest consequence for both cultural practices and experience.

Perhaps the thrust of the idea is most succinctly captured in Nestor Garcia Canclini's phrase, 'the loss of the "natural" relation of culture to geographical and social territories' (1995, p. 229). Garcia Canclini says 'loss', but, of course, the loss is not a total one – it is not as though localities, and the particularities and differences they generate, suddenly and entirely disappear.

Indeed, we all live in places that retain a high degree of distinctiveness. This applies not only to remote corners and backwaters, but to capital cities and great metropolitan centres – the most concentrated locations of global connectivity: Birmingham clearly has its own cultural 'feel' quite different from Berlin, Buenos Aires or Beijing. But the point is that this particularity is no longer – as it may have been in the past – the single most important determinant of our cultural experience. Globalized culture is less determined by location because location is increasingly penetrated by 'distance' – by the integration of structures of global connectivity. So, deterritorialization is more a question of the *attenuation* of the hold that local particularities have on our cultures, combined with the increasing significance of distant places, processes and events in our lives.

Deterritorialization and dystopias

It follows from this that deterritorialization should not be confused with those dystopian visions which predict the end of local culture and its replacement by an undifferentiated homogenized global culture.[3] If deterritorialization does not signal the end of locality on account of a creeping cultural uniformity, neither does it imply that the 'loss' of local determinations must result in a more generally diminished culture. Marc Augé's otherwise suggestive anthropology of the 'non-places' of the late twentieth century provides just such a pessimistic account of the transformation of localities. What is lost, for Augé, is the communal intimacy and the culturally nourishing everyday routines of the 'anthropological places' of an earlier era – what he calls, in a resonant phrase, the era of 'Baudelairian modernity'. Such places – interactionally-suffused locales – are typified for Augé by the slow pace of small French provincial towns – 'where a few words are exchanged and solitudes momentarily forgotten, on the church steps, in front of the town hall, at the café counter or in the baker's doorway' (1995, pp. 66–7). These have not quite disappeared, but where they exist today they do so as mere survivals – contrasting starkly with Augé's description of 'non-lieux' – 'the real measure of our time', calculated:

by totalling all the air, rail and motorway routes. . . . The airports and railway stations, hotel chains, leisure parks, large retail outlets and finally the complex skein of cable and wireless networks that mobilize extraterritorial space for the purposes of a communication so peculiar that it often puts the individual in contact only with another image of himself. (1995, p. 79)

Non-places are the bleak archetypal locales of contemporary modernity – places of silence, transience, instrumentality and contractual interactions – the apotheosis of *Gesellschaft* – lifted out of organic relation with communal dwelling extended in time.

Well, there is undeniably something striking in this comparison – and I think Augé is correct to say that what he calls 'non-places' *are* a distinctive anthropological phenomenon of contemporary modernity. But his account risks misrepresenting things by this rather stark and tendentious dualism between 'anthropological places' and 'non-places'. Quite apart from the dangers of nostalgia, it seems to me that the transformation of localities is a more intrinsically ambiguous business than Augé allows. Non-places: hypermarkets, shopping malls, airports, petrol filling stations, multiplex cinemas, bank lobbies filled with automatic cash dispensers. These all, at first glance, particularly with the passing glance of the consumer (or the anthropologist) in transit, suggest a level of abstraction, impersonality and even alienation. But of course, all such places inevitably generate, or become colonized by, their own cultural interactions. The supermarket check-out is not only the site of contractual relations, but of chat, pleasantries, observations, jokes, arguments. Itineraries intersect and acquaintances are struck during the *longeurs* endured in airport departure lounges. Even the cashpoint becomes the favoured post of the enterprising beggar (nobody said that 'genuine' cultural interactions have to be comfortable ones). Nothing in this endorses the pessimism of Augé's conclusion: 'So there will soon be a need – perhaps there is already a need – for something that may seem a contradiction in terms: an ethnology of solitude' (1995, p. 120).

Yet this insistent, upwelling flow of interaction into newly created locales is not the main criticism to be made of the notion of non-places. Indeed, if this is taken to suggest that nothing has changed, that it is traditional cultural business as usual, this is even more misleading. No. The point is that deterritorialization means we cannot maintain a clear distinction between non-places and anthropological places, because even the locales which appear on the surface to retain local cultural thickness – the 'real places' of a supposed undisturbed locality – are in fact penetrated and transformed by globalization. All locales – our workplaces, 'local' bars and restaurants, schools, shops, market places, community centres and village halls – even the most intimate recesses of our private homes – now to varying degrees conjoin the local and the distant in new – and not necessarily abstract, culturally thin, or alienating – ways. Deterritorialized localities have their own sort of cultural texture. To be sure, they may lack something of the existential security – what Heidegger might have called the 'thereness' – of pre-modern locales; they may depend on systems of expertise and abstractions which lift the control of experience out of local relations of presence. And this may introduce new problems of cultural identity, new uncertainties and new ambiguities to life – what Zygmunt Bauman (2000) describes as a new 'liquidity' to culture. But these perplexities are also mixed with benefits and exhilarations – from the enormously expanded flow of commodities and cultural experiences afforded by the global capitalist market, to the expansion of cultural horizons – a greater everyday 'openness to the world' – made possible by either physical or electronically mediated 'mobility'.

The cultural analysis of deterritorialization, then, is primarily concerned with how life is lived in these transformed, connected and penetrated, 'phantasmagoric' (Giddens, 1990) localities of everyday life. It attempts to understand how we construct meanings in places that we are linked to in respect of routine, quotidian life, but in which the elements of a fixed locality have ceased to be the definitive mark of our experience.

Situatedness and mobility

It might be objected, however, that this view of deterritorialization is rather conservative in continuing to focus on life as it is lived in localities. Has not everyday life become so much more inherently *mobile* that it in some senses now transcends locality? Is a deterritorialized culture better regarded as a culture inherently 'on the move'? What is involved here can be encapsulated in James Clifford's phrase 'dwelling-in-travel'. Clifford, of course, as we saw in the previous section, means us to take this phrase as a general cultural statement, as 'a view of human location as constituted by displacement as much as by stasis' – 'Everyone's on the move and has been for centuries' (1997, p. 2). But might not the idea of 'dwelling-in-travel' be the more radical focus of a cultural sociology of deterritorialization? At stake is the sense in which our specifically global-modern forms of human mobility alter the centrality of sedentary dwelling to cultural meaning. This is an important question to which I have two responses.

The first is fairly conservative. It is to defend the continuing relevance of locality. There are some obvious demographic and material factors to be considered here. In the first place, physical translocation – on either a permanent or an extended basis – is still a comparatively rare case for the human population as a whole. Current estimates suggest that less than 3 per cent of the world's population live outside the country of their birth (Stalker, 2002). Moreover, even where deterritorialization does refer to actual physical displacement – as, for instance, in the case of diasporic communities, labour migrants, refugees and asylum seekers – locality continues to exercise its influence in the cultural imagination. Either seen as the hope for a new settlement, or as the (perhaps nostalgically) remembered locale of original belonging, 'the concept of home often remains as the uninterrogated anchor or alter ego of all this hyper-mobility' (Morley, 2000, p. 3).

And in the second place, the human condition, and the forces of material circumstance keep most of us, most of the time, locally situated. The sheer biological constitution of human beings dictates that some form of local dwelling necessarily persists as the norm of globalized everyday life. As embodied creatures we dwell for shelter, for security, and for all the routines of everyday material existence. These necessities no doubt established the primordial cultural attachments to localities – to land, to home and homeland – that deterritorialization is now breaking down. The trajectory of culture may be changing, but the material – indeed the existential – condition, it might be argued, remains.

However, notwithstanding these basic material-existential considerations, a second response must be to recognize that the massive increase in everyday mobility has indeed changed the cultural environment for most people at the beginning of the twenty-first century. How to conceptualize these changes?

One important step is to acknowledge that mobilities to a great extent now *integrate* with local dwelling. There is a deep-seated cultural dualism to be overcome here between notions, on the one hand, of the 'authenticity' (or, on a different judgement, the 'narrowness') of settlement and sedentary habitation, and, on the other, of the emancipations (or alienations) of movement, of cultural detachment, of 'nomadism'.[4] There is certainly something of this dualism which colours Augé's analysis and it is there, if in a more complex manner, in Heidegger's metaphysical ruminations on the existential 'authenticity' of building and dwelling (Heidegger, 1971). But, as John Urry shows, even in a Heideggerian-derived analysis, 'contemporary forms of dwelling almost always involve diverse forms of mobility' (Urry, 2000, p. 132).[5] Mundane mobility – long- and short-distance commuting, shopping, leisure pursuits, family visits – combine with an ever increasing degree of routine overseas travel in altering the experience of local dwelling for steadily growing numbers in developed societies. Against this background it becomes increasingly difficult to regard the experience of local dwelling as in any sensible way, culturally bounded, self-contained, 'gemeinschaftlich'. To this extent, to study the transformation of localities by deterritorialization is inevitably also to study the mobility which characterizes them.

There is moreover a rather specialized case of 'mobility in the locality' to be accounted for, particularly given the constraints of embodiment noted earlier. This concerns the influence of globalizing media and communications technologies, to which I now turn.

Telemediatization and the culture of immediacy

By telemediatization I understand the increasing implication of electronic communications and media systems in both the reach of global connectivity into everyday experience, and the 'accessing of the world' by locally situated individuals. This is to understand the primary role of media and communications systems as modes – both technologies and institutions – of time–space bridging.[6] Telemediatization can thus be considered as a distinct *mode* of deterritorialization – of lifting cultural experience out of its anchoring in localities. Often this distinction is described in terms of a peculiar form of *mobility* that does not involve actual corporeal mobility. Typically, the use of the Internet, and even to some degree of television, is described as a form of 'virtual travel' and popular expressions often employ metaphors of mobility (surfing, channel hopping, going online, navigating, and so on). While there is some force in these metaphors, there are also some obvious obscurities involved. In fact it seems more useful to think of telemediatization, not as a form of mobility, but rather, on its own terms, as a specific phenomenological mode. Telemediated practices and experiences – watching television, typing, scrolling, clicking and browsing at the computer screen, talking, texting or sending and receiving pictures on a mobile phone – are best regarded as unique cultural practices and ways in which experience is presented to consciousness. They occupy a space in the everyday flow of experience within the individual's lifeworld that is distinct, yet integrated with face-to-face interactions of physical proximity. And indeed they are increasingly integrated with the sort of experiences afforded by actual travel – the routine corporeal mobility of modern cultures.

Perhaps the first step in understanding the increasing significance of communications and media technologies in our lives, then, is to recognize that these are, in fact, worthy of analysis. Telemediated practices and experiences are now so much a routine and taken-for-granted aspect of everyday life in developed societies that they can appear almost transparent. And yet just a moment's reflection reveals a good deal of both variety and complexity in our interaction with these technologies. Consider, for example, the differences between these three everyday media practices: solitary, concentrated web-browsing in your study; casual, half-attentive television viewing of a soap opera with the family; the interruption of a face-to-face conversation when one person breaks off to answer their mobile phone. Each of these utterly mundane occurrences reorders the experience of 'presence' in quite different ways: as a sense of the instant and infinite availability of the world's resources; as a sort of familiar representational-imaginary annexe to domestic life; as the dissolution of the exclusivity of corporeal presence. None of these experiences has any counterpart beyond the last few decades of world history, and each of them helps to define what it is to exist as a social being in the modern world. The agenda for cultural analysis which telemediatization establishes is thus an extensive one, including its transformation of taken-for-granted contexts of experience and interaction in time and space; its implications for shifts in our emotional sensibilities and perhaps the extension of our ethical horizons; its applicability to debates about the transformation of the public sphere and the possibility of the development of cosmopolitan cultural dispositions; along with a whole range of anxieties over our growing dependence on 'virtual' modes of experience. And yet, curiously, comparatively little systematic work has been done to date on describing, let alone analysing, this aspect of deterritorialization.[7]

In the space available here, I want to select just one item from this agenda – the question of whether telemediatization may be associated with a shift in wider cultural sensibilities evident in developed, global-modern societies. To put it briefly, whether the instant and ubiquitous connectivity supplied by new media and communications technologies may be changing routine assumptions and expectations about how life is to be lived, and what we may expect it to deliver.[8]

One significant feature of mediated connectivity to be considered here is the pretty universal assumption that the *speed* of communication is both an unremarkable regularity of modern societies and an undisputed good. This quintessentially modern cultural assumption that all sorts of communication (in particular, the exemplary concept of 'news') should be delivered *as fast as possible* defines a trajectory of increasing acceleration in media technologies, reaching back to the telegraph and forwards through computer-mediated convergences, particularly those linking mobile phones with the Internet. If we add to these technological developments innovations in media institutions themselves – for instance 24-hour television, online news services, media convergences made possible via domestic broadband provision – there emerges the sense of a broad communicational principle which we could call 'immediacy'. This principle of 'instant access' is, moreover, easily extended to grasp broader consumption practices (for instance, television or online shopping), entertainment (the downloading, storage and retrieval of music via devices like the now almost culturally iconic iPod), or simply to each other (mobile phone conversation or texting as a defining feature of contemporary youth culture). Assemble all these elements together and we may begin to see contemporary culture as dominated by a technology-driven obsession with speed, ubiquitous availability and (though this is to slip towards the judgemental) instant gratification.

However, a more subtle analysis may be called for. It may be that we are witnessing, in the emergence of 'immediacy', a cultural sensibility that is quite new, not easily accommodated to traditional understandings of the speed of events and processes, and thus not yielding to interpretation and critique in terms of values derived from these traditions. For example, 'speed' seems to connote some of the informing values of industrial modernity, in particular, functional rationality, regulation and the 'heroic' nature of technique, machine power and human labour – particularly of concerted effort – in the overcoming of distance. 'Immediacy', by contrast, grasps a much more insouciant stance towards technology, something of the lightness and effortlessness of what Zygmunt Bauman (2000) elegantly calls 'liquid modernity'. The technologies of communication with and through which we now routinely interact create the *impression* of a general effortlessness and ubiquity of contact which seems to be quite distinct from the purposiveness of mechanically accomplished speed. In the era of immediacy, it is as if the gap between departure and arrival, here and elsewhere, now and later, indeed, a certain order of desire and its fulfilment, has been closed by a sort of technological *legerdemain*. As Paul Virilio observes, the transport revolution of the nineteenth century – the unimaginable speed of rail travel – reduced the significance of a journey to two points: departure and arrival. By contrast, the coming of new communications technologies means that 'departure now gets wiped out and "arrival" gets promoted, the *generalized arrival of data*' (Virilio, 1997, p. 56). If we think of the condition of immediacy as involving 'the generalized arrival of data', it becomes clear that we cannot grasp its entailments merely in terms of a critique of the shallowness of popular cultural practices, laments over diminishing attention spans, the 'three-minute culture' and so forth. Our interaction with new communication technologies brings, along with the assumption of ubiquity (and associated suspicions of indolence), all sorts of new demands and obligations. To take just one example: the increasing tacit assumption – structured into both the work process and wider social etiquette – that we have a social *obligation* both to be skilled users of the technology and, more importantly, to be almost constantly available to and for communication – that it is a mark of neglect, of irresponsibility, to be off-line, off-message, incommunicado.

A sociology of deterritorialization, then, should include, at its core, analysis of the tele-mediatization of culture, of which the sensibility of immediacy comprises a central feature. Such an analysis might reveal something beyond the idea of a broad acceleration in interactions, or the closing of physical distance rather inadequately grasped in the idea of 'virtuality'. It might, for example, interpret the eclipse of certain older cultural values like patience or forbearance, while uncovering new values – perhaps the capacity to form trust relations and senses of moral obligation beyond the confines of physical locale. And, most generally, it might illuminate the profound penetration of mediated experience into everyday life, such that an experienced intimacy with distant others, under certain conditions of orchestration, becomes a commonplace.

3 Identity and Cosmopolitanism: The Cultural Politics of Globalization

I want to turn now to questions that connect cultural practice and experience with the institutional aspects of global modernity and with political questions, broadly conceived. In doing this I shall focus on the issues of the fate of cultural identity on the one hand, and the possibility (and desirability) of the emergence of cosmopolitan cultural and political outlooks and sensibilities on the other. For, as I hope will emerge, the two issues are rather closely related.

'Globalatinization'

One, admittedly slightly oblique, way into these issues is to be found in Jacques Derrida's essay 'On Forgiveness' (Derrida, 2001). Derrida poses the question of how a cluster of quasi-religious concepts – forgiveness, repentance, confession, apology – belonging, he says, to the 'Abrahamic' tradition, find a certain universal application in acts of public institutionalized, 'theatrical' contrition. He asks:

> If . . . such a language combines and accumulates powerful traditions within it ('Abrahamic' culture and that of a philosophical humanism, and more precisely a cosmopolitanism born from a graft of stoicism with Pauline Christianity), why does it impose itself on cultures which do not have European or 'biblical' origins? I am thinking of those scenes where a Japanese Prime Minister 'asked forgiveness' of the Koreans and the Chinese for past violence. (Derrida, 2001, p. 31)

Part of his answer to this invokes the (rather awkward) neologism 'Globalatinization', as Derrida says, 'to take into account the effect of Roman Christianity which today overdetermines all language of law [and] of politics' (2001, p. 32).

For Derrida, the juridical apparatuses of national and international tribunals – he cites, particularly the Truth and Reconciliation Commission in South Africa – embody a universalizing 'cosmopolitan' discourse in concepts like 'crimes against humanity' and 'universal human rights'. But, like pretty well all universal claims, the ethic that informs this discourse is a particular one – in which the universal status of 'humanity' derives from its 'sacredness' within the Judeo-Christian tradition. Derrida insists on the significance of this religious discourse (as against the secular rationalism of the Enlightenment tradition): 'No alleged disenchantment comes to interrupt it. On the contrary' (2001, p. 23).

What Derrida invites us to consider, then, is a sort of discursive fault line linking Christian theology with contemporary cosmopolitan humanism. According to Derrida the sort of universalism we can see enshrined in the discourses of international law, or in many proposals on global governance – despite their entirely secular context and even despite scrupulous attempts to exclude culturally disputed values – somehow remains the property of the Western cultural tradition. Humanism derives from the Christian ethic that – albeit via the European Enlightenment – pervades Western cultural-political thought. The universalizing of this ethic is what Derrida understands as 'Globalatinization'. Derrida's insistence on, as it were, the particular particularism of Christian theology is a view independently endorsed by Slavoj Žižek:

> In other 'particularistic' religions (and even in Islam, in spite of its global expansionism), there is at least a place for others, they are tolerated, even if they are condescendingly looked upon. The Christian motto, 'all men are brothers', however, means also that, 'Those who are not my brothers are not men'. . . . Christian universalism tendentially excludes non-believers from the very universality of mankind. (Žižek, 2001, p. 144)

Well, it is probably true to say that the Christian cultural tradition has tended to be more presumptuous in this respect than many others. We should be careful, however, not to overstate the culpability of any one cultural tradition in this respect. As Terry Eagleton reminds us, many other cultures, historically, have denied the status of 'human beings' to strangers and therefore, 'One should not be ethnocentric about ethnocentricity' (Eagleton, 2000, p. 57).

Despite these criticisms, Derrida has a point when it comes to the geo-cultural provenance of contemporary discourses of cosmopolitanism and the particular character of the universalism which they embody. Clearly there is *something* with its sources in the Western cultural experience that has been peculiarly successful in distributing itself globally throughout the discursive apparatuses of moral-political-juridical practice. But, to grasp the key to this success, perhaps we have to look for something beyond the set of actual values, beliefs and understandings which together make up the (anyway, rather loose) category of 'Western culture'.

Modernity and the institutionalization of identities

I want, then, to suggest a rather different approach to these issues by considering, not the contents or entailments of any particular cultural tradition, but rather the *formal* nature of global modernity. That is, its essential character in the *institutionalization and regulation* of social and cultural life.

This interpretation hangs on understanding modernity not merely as a certain determinant set of social institutions – capitalism, industrialism, urbanism, the nation-state system, the military-scientific complex and so on – but, at a somewhat deeper social-ontological level, as the very *tendency to form institutions* and to generate regulators of social-economic-cultural behaviour. The most frequently remarked examples of such institutionalization are, indeed, the organization and policing of social territory (most obviously in the nation-state system, but also in the urban–rural divide), or of production and consumption practices (the processes of industrialization, the capitalist economy). But modernity also institutionalizes and regulates *cultural* practices, including those by which we imagine our existential condition, our personal relations, and our attachment and belonging to a place or a community.

The *mode* of such imagination which it promotes is captured in the notion of 'cultural identity'. The *essentially modern*, 'organizational' category of cultural identity, then, consists in self and communal definitions based around specific, usually politically inflected, differentiations: gender, sexuality, class, religion, race and ethnicity, nationality. Some of these differentiations of course existed before the coming of modernity; some – like nationality – are more or less modern imaginings. However, as I have suggested, modernity has its impact not so much in the nature and substance of these differentiations, as in *the very fact of their institutionalization and regulation*. Modern societies organize and orchestrate existential experience according to well-policed categories and boundaries. We 'live' our gender, our sexuality, our nationality and so forth within public institutional regimes of discursively organized belongings. What could be much more amorphous, contingent, particular and tacit senses of belonging become structured into an array – one might say a portfolio – of identities, each with implications for our material and psychological well-being, each, thus, with a 'politics'.

Thus, as globalization distributes the institutional features of modernity across all cultures, it produces 'identity' in this modern sense, where none existed – where before there were perhaps more particular, more inchoate, less publicly represented and symbolized, less socially policed belongings.

One rather interesting interpretation of the impact of globalization to flow from this is that, far from destroying it, as many suppose, globalization has been perhaps the most significant force in *creating and proliferating* cultural identity (Tomlinson, 2003). Those who regard globalization as a *threat* to cultural identity tend to imagine identity quite differently. Rather than noticing its institutional features, they tend to see identity as something like an existential possession, an inheritance, a benefit of traditional long dwelling, of continuity with the past. Identity, according to this common view, is more than just a description of the experience of cultural belonging, it is a sort of collective treasure of local communities. Moreover, while long ensuring the culturally sustaining connections between geographical place and human experience, identity, according to this view, is suddenly discovered to be fragile, in need of protection and preservation, a treasure that can be lost. This is the story which implicates deterritorialization in the destruction of local identities.

There are, as I have already suggested, significant problems with the rather static, reified view of cultural processes which grounds this view of identity and the critique of globalization that proceeds from it (Tomlinson, 1991, 1997, 2003). There are therefore good reasons to doubt the most pessimistic predictions of a depletion in the variety of global cultural experience. Not the least of these is that they tend to radically underestimate both the adaptive and, indeed, the resistive resources of local culture.

This is a feature of globalization perhaps most comprehensively analysed by Manuel Castells, who devotes the second volume of his trilogy *The Information Age* to an analysis of *The Power of Identity*. For Castells, the primary *opposition* to the power of global capital lies in 'the widespread surge of powerful expressions of collective identity that challenge globalization . . . on behalf of cultural singularity and people's control over their lives and environment' (Castells, 1997, p. 2). Far from being the fragile flower that globalization tramples, identity is seen here as the upsurging dynamic of local culture that offers *resistance* to the centripetal force of capitalist globalization.

This more robust view of the 'power of identity' is one to which anyone surveying the dramatic rise of social movements based around identity positions (gender, sexuality, religion, ethnicity, nationality) might feel inclined to subscribe. But what is important to

grasp here is that these phenomena are intrinsic features of the modern institutionalization of identity. This is something which Castells himself seems not entirely to appreci-
ate: in casting identity as a sort of spontaneous cultural dynamic, welling up from the
grass roots of human life as an oppositional force to globalization, Castells fails to see the
rather compelling *inner logic* between the globalization process and the institutionalized
construction of identities. In the significant case of *national identity*, what is at stake is
quite clearly a deliberate cultural construction via both the regulatory and the socializing
institutions of the state: in particular, the law, the education system and the media. The
deterritorializing force of globalization thus meets a structured opposition in the form of
what Michael Billig (1995) has called 'banal nationalism' – the everyday minute reinforcement; the continuous routinized 'flagging' of national belonging, particularly
through media discourse – sponsored by developed nation-states. But even in cases
that appear more spontaneous and unruly – let us say, to be controversial, in such
starkly different cases as the anti-globalization movement itself or fundamentalist religio-
cultural movements such as al-Queda – the exertion of cultural power or resistance is
quite firmly located within the context of modern institutionalized – politicized – identities. In both these cases, identity is the category which organizes existential needs into collective political demands.

Identity and universalism

One issue that has lurked behind the discussion of identity so far is the common assumption that identity-formation is a *universal* feature of human experience. This notion is
evident in the 'protectionist' understanding of cultural identity in relation to globalization
that we have discussed, but even a sophisticated theorist like Castells seems implicitly to
take this view when he writes that 'Identity is people's source of meaning and experience'
(1997, p. 6). But it is vital to be precise here. All historical cultures, to be sure, have
constructed meaning via localized practices of collective symbolization: this is as near to
a universal feature of human societies as we can probably get. But not all historical cultures
'construct identity' in the institutionally regulated forms that are now dominant within
global modernity. There is, then, the danger of a sort of ethnocentric projection here and
this been criticized by both anthropologists and media and cultural critics. For example,
David Morley, commenting on Roger Rouse's study of Mexican labour migrants to the
United States, points out that these people 'moved from a world in which . . . *identity was
not a central concern*, to one in which they were pressed . . . to adopt a particular form of
personhood (as bearers of individual identities) and of identity as a member of a collective or "community" . . . which *was quite at odds with their own understanding of their
situation and their needs*' (Morley, 2000, p. 43; emphasis added).

This tells us something more general about the universalizing impetus of globalization.
Those who most distrust universalizing doctrines tend to see them as the passing off of
particular, local beliefs and values as universal ones. A good example is the philosopher
John Gray, who considers universalism to be 'one of the least useful and indeed most dangerous aspects of the western intellectual tradition . . . the metaphysical faith that local
western values are authoritative for all cultures and peoples' (Gray, 1997, p. 158). But if

we consider the issue of identity, it is clear that something more subtle is at stake. For what is being universalized here is not any particular set of values, not, indeed, any substantive cultural 'content', but rather an *institutionalized mode of social being*. If universalism is indeed dangerous (which, short of some contextual qualification, must remain a rather contentious claim), it is so probably more in respect of institutional changes than of the dominance of values.

Cosmopolitanism as an identity position

We are now in a position to connect these thoughts about the institutionalization of identity with the issue of cosmopolitanism. Cosmopolitanism is, of course, a much disputed terrain of discourse, both in terms of its viability as a political project in relation to global governance, and its desirability as a cultural goal (Cheah and Robbins, 1998; Featherstone et al., 2002; Vertovek and Cohen, 2002). I will not enter these debates here (see Tomlinson 1999, 2001, 2002) but restrict myself, again, to observing the *institutionalization* of cosmopolitan discourses. For one answer to Derrida's question about why cosmopolitan humanism 'overdetermines all language of law [and] of politics' today is to say that the discursive position of the cosmopolitan has, indeed, become a modern, globally distributed identity position.

Whatever the composition, or the provenance, of the discourse of modern humanism, its deeply impressive international distribution – *encompassing* for the most part, rather than contesting other universalisms – owes most to its institutional form. 'Humanity' – in its juridical form of an owner of rights or a victim of persecution or exploitation – is, in effect, a specific modern identity position which is universal by definition, but which remains compatible with a huge range of cultural variation, by dint of its precise contexts of invocation. 'Humanity' is an identity that can be invoked formally – for instance, in the International Court of Justice – to press the case of justice and equality across different cultural regimes. But it is also a sufficiently flexible category to allow the rhetorical association of *local* cultural struggles with the cause of humanity itself.

A prime example of this strategy is found on the cover illustration of Castells's book *The Power of Identity*. This consists of a reproduction of a poster advertising the international '*encuentro*' – the extraordinary cultural 'encounter' organized by the Zapatista rebels in the jungle of Chiapas in 1996 and attended by activists from across the world. What is significant in this – and, arguably, in the Zapatistas' sophisticated discursive strategy as a whole – is the way it manages to link the particular struggle of the Chiapas peasants – essentially issues of the disastrous effects of economic deregulation by the Mexican government on the local agricultural economy – with the fate of humanity itself. Among symbolic images of maize superimposed on the colours of the Mexican flag, the poster proclaims the *encuentro* 'Por la humanidad, y contra el Neoliberalismo'.

This is, of course, a matter of rhetoric. But the fact that local struggles can be so easily referred up to the level of the human universal is in itself worthy of attention. To be, without contradiction, 'human' in its rich pluralist acceptation of preserving cultural difference, and at the same time 'human' in universalist politico-juridical terms, is a trick brought off precisely by the institutionalized framing of *repertoires* of identity typical of

modernity. In the midst of the proliferation of localisms and sharpened identity discrim-
inations, globalization also – formally, adroitly and without any recourse to dominant
cultural traditions – globalizes universality. If, despite all the discouraging indications of
international relations in the early twenty-first century, cosmopolitanism as a political
project continues to look viable, this is in no small measure due to this modern shift in the
deep structure – in, as it were, the 'grammar' – of cultural-political discourse.

4 Conclusion: Global Culture between the Universal and the Particular

In this chapter I have tried to sketch out something of an agenda for the interpretation of
globalization, as seen from the perspective of cultural analysis. In doing this the main
points of principle I have stressed are the following:

Firstly, that cultural analysis, though by no means a more privileged standpoint than
any other in understanding the totality of globalization, has a specificity which cannot be
subsumed within that of any other approach. Moreover, the particular theoretical inflec-
tion that cultural analysis lends to the debate has a bearing on how discussions in the
political and the economic spheres are conducted. Culture, I have argued, has its *raison
d'être* in the constitution of meaning, but this does not prevent it from having (global)
consequences, among which we must include economic and political ones. Secondly, I
have suggested that globalization reveals the possibility of – indeed makes possible – the
relative independence of culture from place, and that this, rather than any idea of the
dominance of one geographically defined culture, is its most significant effect. Thirdly, in
probing this quality of 'deterritorialization', I have implied that the globalization process
demands analysis at the level, not just of macro-social phenomena, but of everyday 'lived
experience', reaching down ultimately into transformations in the very constitution of
that experience, particularly in respect of telemediatization. It is not inappropriate, then,
to speak of a 'phenomenology of globalization'. But, fourthly, in broaching the issue of
cultural identity, I have resisted the widespread interpretation of this category as a direct
expression of subjectivity, arguing, instead, that it should be regarded as one of the key
institutional entailments of global modernity. Finally, I have suggested, albeit only briefly,
that the cultural-political discourse around cosmopolitanism might usefully be interpreted by paying attention not just to issues of political values, but to the institutionalization of the identity position of 'humanity'.

Of course this agenda leaves many issues unaddressed and the critical reader will not
need my assistance in identifying these. But to conclude I will very briefly address two
stools between which this account might, reasonably, be said to fall. These are, on the one
hand, giving insufficient attention to at least one 'universal' and, on the other, to the larger
political significance of issues of cultural difference.

The universal I have in mind here is not a philosophical issue, but the claim that the
de facto common denominator of both the process and the experience of globalization is
the global capitalist economic system. Those who view globalization in this way may be
unhappy with my account for a number of reasons. But the issue that deserves most attention, in the light of my emphasis on lived experience, is that of the increasing general

commodification of culture. Critics of global capitalism may very plausibly claim that by far the most significant determinant of culture distributed by globalization is precisely that so many cultural practices and experiences in modernity have become transformed into commodities: into things which are bought and sold. Indeed the activity of shopping itself is now undoubtedly one of the most popular cultural practices in Western societies. The 'shopping element' is present – structured into – almost any contemporary leisure activity, and the fear is that this consumption principle will overwhelm all cultural practice.

While the drift of my argument has been sceptical of claims that extrapolate from this towards dystopian scenarios of a globally homogeneous consumer culture, I do, nonetheless, believe that anxieties over the commodification now so deeply structured into modern cultural life in the developed world deserve to be taken very seriously. For, left unchecked, the power of the capitalist market undeniably threatens a distinct narrowing of cultural experience: a marshalling of 'what we do with our lives' into one particular *form* of doing it. The threat here is not so much to cultural variety in itself, as to the capacity of cultural practices, institutionalized around economic principles, to answer to 'existential needs' – to sustain the ongoing life narratives according to which we, chronically, interpret our existence.

The cultural-political issue here, I suppose, comes down to the question of regulation: of what checks can and should be made on the cultural impact of the capitalist market in the context of globalization. A shortcoming of the account given here is that it implies no original answers to these questions, and space does not allow me to develop them.

However, there are strong reasons to believe that checks on the dominance of commodified culture may arise outside of deliberate regimes of regulation (whether considered as a function of the state or imagined as part of the remit of global governance). The most obvious example of this is the competition offered to capitalism as a universal organizer of cultural experience by traditional religions. Most notable among these, particularly in the focusing context of '9/11', must be counted those militant versions of Islam finding their adherents among the 'globalization losers' of the world. But this is not, of course, the exclusive context. More generally, religious and ethnic differences brought into juxtaposition through the connectivity of globalization mean that the world at the dawn of the third millennium can be seen as much less one of uniform capitalist ascendancy than of 'pressed-together dissimilarities variously arranged' (Geertz, 2000, p. 226). And this brings me to the other issue on which this account of globalized culture may be open to criticism.

This is that, in stressing the day-to-day experiences of deterritorialization, some rather stark issues of cultural conflict, indeed violence, have been ignored. As with the question of cultural regulation, neglect of this agenda can partly be excused by the constraints of space.[9] Nevertheless, there remains the issue of priority. In defending the level of analysis prioritized here, I would end by suggesting that attention to the dynamics of culture as enacted and experienced in the day-to-day context may ultimately offer the most valuable insights into the sources and possible remedies of conflict and political violence. Understanding cultural experience and its intrinsic relationship with economic and political advantage or disadvantage at this quotidian level must at any rate be a more promising approach than an analysis based on the assumption that there somehow exist in the world invariant and intractable tendencies to exclusive cultural difference.

Notes

1 See in this connection Bauman's astute observation of the lineage of inert conceptualizations of culture from structural-functionalism and modernization theory through to contemporary discourses of 'multiculturalism' (Bauman and Tester, 2001, p. 32).

2 Many theorists use the term 'deterritorialization' in relation to globalizing processes, *inter alia*, Appadurai, 1990; Featherstone, 1995; Garcia Canclini, 1995; Held et al., 1999; Latouche, 1996; Lull, 2000; Mattelart, 1994; Morley and Robins, 1995; Scholte, 2000; Urry, 2000, and the idea is implicit, or slightly differently named, in several more (Giddens, 1990; Thompson, 1995; Beck, 2000). Though there are different inflections involved, the general sense that globalization needs to be conceptualized in socio-spatial terms as much as in institutional or political-economic ones is common. The specifically cultural account developed here derives from my more extended discussion in Tomlinson, 1999, ch. 4.

3 Due to constraints of space, I will take it for granted here that the cultural homogenization scenario can be pretty confidently discounted (for critiques see e.g. Hannerz, 1990; Tomlinson, 1991; Scholte, 2000). Having said this, there remain separate, significant questions about the degree to which powerful currents in Western-modern culture – commodification under the sway of capitalism; the reach of institutions into existential experience – are coming to shape the contours of culture. I return to these issues, albeit briefly, in the conclusion.

4 There is an interesting parallel to this dualism in the debate about cosmopolitan versus localist cultural dispositions: see Hannerz, 1990, and Tomlinson, 1999, ch. 6.

5 Urry draws support for his claims by interpreting Heidegger, against the grain, as an analyst of mobility (see also Thrift, 1996, p. 286). Despite this, Heidegger still clearly associates sedentary dwelling with a certain sort of authenticity to which globalizing technologies are inimical.

6 See Giddens, 1990; Tomlinson, 1999, ch. 5. In terms of media technologies, the etymological clue is of course evident in, for example, the *tele* stem of television, telephone, and also in the German, *Fernsehen*.

7 Among the most suggestive approaches, see Thompson, 1995; Turkle, 1995; Durham Peters, 1999; Dreyfus, 2001; Crowley and Mitchell, 1994; Derrida and Stiegler, 2002; Virilio, 1997.

8 For a more extended discussion of these issues see Tomlinson, 2003.

9 I discuss the cultural politics of both regulation/deregulation and the question of universalism and difference in relation to cosmopolitan projects in greater detail elsewhere: Tomlinson, 2001 and 2002.

References

Appadurai, A. (1990). 'Disjuncture and Difference in the Global Cultural Economy', in M. Featherstone, ed., *Global Culture: Nationalism, Globalization and Modernity*. London: Sage, pp. 295–310.

Augé, M. (1995). *Non-Places : Introduction to the Anthropology of Supermodernity*. London: Verso.

Bauman, Z. (1998). *Globalization: The Human Consequences*. Cambridge: Polity.

Bauman, Z. (2000). *Liquid Modernity*. Cambridge: Polity.

Bauman, Z. and K. Tester (2001). *Conversations with Zygmunt Bauman*. Cambridge: Polity.

Beck, U. (2000). *What is Globalization?* Cambridge: Polity.

Beck, U. (2002). 'The Cosmopolitan Society and its Enemies', in M. Featherstone, H. Patomäki, J. Tomlinson and C. Venn, eds, *Theory, Culture and Society: Special Issue on Cosmopolis*, 19(1–2) (Feb.–April).

Billig, M. (1995). *Banal Nationalism*. London: Sage.

Castells, M. (1997). *The Power of Identity. The Information Age: Economy, Society and Culture* Vol. 2. Oxford: Blackwell Publishers.

Cheah, P. and B. Robbins, eds (1998). *Cosmopolitics: Thinking and Feeling beyond the Nation*. Minneapolis: University of Minnesota Press.

Clifford, J. (1992). 'Travelling Cultures', in I. Grossberg, C. Nelson and P. Treichler, eds, *Cultural Studies*. London: Routledge, pp. 96–116.

Clifford, J. (1997). *Routes: Travel and Translation in the Late Twentieth Century*. Cambridge, Mass: Harvard University Press.

Crowley, D. and D. Mitchell, eds (1994). *Communication Theory Today*. Cambridge: Polity.

Derrida, J. (2001). *On Cosmopolitanism and Forgiveness*. London: Routledge.

Derrida, J. and B. Stiegler (2002). *Echographies of Television*. Cambridge: Polity.

Dreyfus, H. (2001). *On the Internet*. London: Routledge.

Durham Peters, J. (1999). *Speaking into the Air: A History of the Idea of Communication*. Chicago: University of Chicago Press.

Eagleton, T. (2000). *The Idea of Culture*. Oxford: Blackwell Publishers.

Featherstone, M. (1995). *Undoing Culture*. London: Sage.

Featherstone, M., H. Patomäki, J. Tomlinson and C. Venn, eds (2002). *Theory, Culture and Society: Special Issue of Cosmopolis*, 19(1–2), (Feb.–April).

Garcia Canclini, N. (1995). *Hybrid Cultures: Strategies for Entering and Leaving Modernity*. Minneapolis: University of Minnesota Press.

Geertz. C. (1973). *The Interpretation of Cultures*. New York: Basic Books.

Geertz, C. (2000). *Available Light: Anthropological Reflections on Philosophical Topics*. Princeton: Princeton University Press.

Giddens, A. (1990). *The Consequences of Modernity*. Cambridge: Polity.

Gray, J. (1997). *Endgames: Questions in Late Modern Political Thought*. Cambridge: Polity.

Hannerz, U. (1990). 'Cosmopolitans and Locals in World Culture', in M. Featherstone, ed., *Global Culture*. London: Sage, pp. 237–51.

Heidegger, M. (1971). 'Building, Dwelling, Thinking', in *Poetry, Language,Thought*. New York: Harper and Row, pp. 143–62.

Held, D., A. McGrew, D. Goldblatt and J. Perraton, eds (1999). *Global Transformations*. Cambridge: Polity.

Latouche, S. (1996). *The Westernization of the World*. Cambridge: Polity.

Lull, J. (2000). *Media, Communication, Culture: A Global Approach*, 2nd edn. Cambridge: Polity.

Mann, M. (1986). *The Sources of Social Power*, vol. 1. Cambridge: Cambridge University Press.

Mattelart, A. (1994). *Mapping World Communication*. Minneapolis: Minnesota University Press.

Moores, S. (1993). *Interpreting Audiences: The Ethnography of Media Consumption*. London: Sage.

Morley, D. (1992). *Television Audiences and Cultural Studies*. London: Routledge.

Morley, D. (2000). *Home Territories: Media, Mobility and Identity*. London: Routledge.

Morley, D. and K. Robins (1995). *Spaces of Identity: Global Media, Electronic Landscapes and Cultural Boundaries*. London: Routledge.

Scholte, J. A. (2000). *Globalization: A Critical Introduction*. London: Macmillan.

Stalker, P. (2002). *The No-Nonsense Guide to International Migration*. London: Verso.

Thompson, J. B. (1995). *The Media and Modernity*. Cambridge: Polity.

Thrift, N. (1996). *Spatial Formations*. London: Sage.

Tomlinson, J. (1991). *Cultural Imperialism: A Critical Introduction*. London: Cassell.

Tomlinson, J. (1997). 'Internationalism, Globalization and Cultural Imperialism', in K. Thompson, ed., *Media and Cultural Regulation*. London: Sage/Open University, pp. 117–62.

Tomlinson, J. (1999). *Globalization and Culture*. Cambridge: Polity.

Tomlinson, J. (2001). 'Proximity Politics', in F. Webster, ed., *Culture and Politics in the Information Age*. London: Routledge.

Tomlinson, J. (2002). 'Interests and Identities in Cosmopolitan Politics', in S. Vertovek and R. Cohen, eds, *Conceiving Cosmopolitanism*. Oxford: Oxford University Press, pp. 240–53.

Tomlinson, J. (2003). 'Globalization and Cultural Identity', in D. Held et al., eds, *The Global Transformations Reader*, 2nd edn. Cambridge: Polity, pp. 269–78.

Turkle, S. (1995). *Life on the Screen: Identity in the Age of the Internet*. New York: Simon and Schuster.

Urry, J. (2000). *Sociology beyond Societies: Mobilities for the Twenty-first Century*. London: Routledge.

Urry, J. (2003). *Global Complexity*. Cambridge: Polity.

Vertovek, S. and R. Cohen, eds (2002). *Conceiving Cosmopolitanism*. Oxford: Oxford University Press.

Virilio, P. (1997). *Open Sky*. London: Verso.

Žižek, S. (2001). *On Belief*. London: Routledge.

Part II

The Remaking of Globalization

8

Reimagining International Society and Global Community

Chris Brown

Introduction

Contemporary realist accounts of international relations describe an international system which is dominated by egocentric states, each pursuing their own, self-defined interests under conditions of anarchy. In this 'self-help' system there are no effective international norms, and international law exists solely for the convenience of powerful states; periods of peace in the international system are temporary and unstable, and international cooperation, where it exists, is equally fragile (Waltz, 1979; Keohane, 1986). Such is the worldview of realists – although very few of the modern scholars who claim that title would subscribe to the whole of this depressing picture – and throughout the history of the so-called Westphalian system there have been diplomatists, lawyers and historians who have based their thinking on international relations around this perspective (Murray, 1996; Rosenthal, 1991; Smith, 1986).[1] There is, however, another worldview with an equally long history, which rejects key elements of this picture, while accepting the basic premise that international relations concerns the relations of states under conditions of anarchy. On this alternative account, the relations of states are norm-governed; rather than an international *system*, we have an international *society*, which sustains, and is sustained by, common practices, especially the practices of diplomacy and international law.[2]

Adherents of this alternative worldview share with realism a commitment to state-centricity, the view that the state is the key actor and driving force in international relations. It is, of course, precisely this state-centricity that is considered to be under attack by theorists of globalization; if the global socio-economic forces identified by those theorists have the impact that is claimed for them, then it is clearly not simply realists who will have to reimagine their key categories. This will be an equally important task for theorists of international society whose normative as well as analytical positions will be challenged by these developments. In any event, this chapter is devoted to examining the relationship between the notion of an international society and the (putative) reality of globalization. Can an international society survive in a globalized world? Does there exist the normative basis for an emergent global community in such a world, and, if so, how would this community relate to the existing society of states? And, finally, to what extent has 9/11 and the subsequent 'war on terror' changed the answers to these questions? This agenda defines the content of this chapter, but the first task is to elaborate the international society perspective, and distinguish it from both realist and cosmopolitan theories of international relations.

International Society

It is not clear who actually coined the term 'international society'; it is probably of nineteenth-century origin, but C. A. W. Manning, who taught a course under that title at the London School of Economics in the 1930s, was certainly the first British scholar to use the term extensively and with its modern meaning.[3] It was also the key term for the group of scholars who met regularly under the aegis of the Rockefeller-funded 'British Committee on the Theory of International Politics' in the 1950s and 1960s. These scholars, along with Manning, were later to be known as the 'English School', a term coined by one of their enemies.[4] In terms of the academic discipline of International Relations (IR), the English School were a rather marginal, indeed marginalized, group, on the edge of a discourse which was increasingly dominated by North American scholars applying the techniques of economics or the behavioural sciences to IR and uninterested in the tradition that the School represented. However, when a movement arose in resistance to the dominance of rational choice thinking and 'positivism' in IR theory in the 1980s and 1990s – a movement represented by both the turn to post-structuralism/late modern theory on the one hand and 'constructivism' on the other – the English School's rather mannered anti-modernism came to look prescient.[5] Add to this the high-quality work on the new post-Cold War normative agenda by English School writers such as Tim Dunne and Nicholas Wheeler and it is easy to see why the School is currently experiencing a revival.[6]

After appropriate homage to the English School, it needs to be made clear that while they may have coined (or at least popularized) the term 'international society', they can claim no ownership of the concept that lies behind this coinage. The idea that relations between states take place within a commonly agreed normative framework has a history going back to the founders of international law in the sixteenth and seventeenth centuries, a history that includes political thinkers such as Burke and Hegel, statesmen such as Metternich, Gladstone and Churchill, and, in the twentieth century, political theorists such as Terry Nardin.[7] The content of this normative framework consists of a series of practices shared by the members of the society of states, the most important of which are the practices of diplomacy and international law. Both of these practices in turn rest upon the idea that, although states are to be understood as sovereign – that is, legally autonomous – and thus entitled to pursue their own interests, they will do so in a manner which, even if it involves conflict, will not preclude future cooperation and, even if self-interested, will not be completely blind to the interests of the wider international community. Diplomacy was central to this idea, and A. J. P. Taylor catches perfectly the mind-set it requires of diplomats in the Preface to his survey of nineteenth-century international relations:

> [the] world of diplomacy was much like the world of business, in which respect for the sanctity of contract does not prevent the most startling reversals of fortune. Many diplomatists were ambitious, some vain or stupid, but they had something like a common aim – to preserve the peace of Europe without endangering the interests or security of their country. (Taylor, 1954, p. xxiii)

Along with diplomacy stands international law. The core principles of Westphalian international law are the sovereign equality of states and the norm of non-intervention.[8] As it developed from its medieval origins in the notion of natural law, international law came to be seen as both a constraint on and supporter of state sovereignty, simultaneously endorsing the idea that states are entitled to be autonomous, while attempting to limit their actions, thereby giving a measure of protection to the weaker members of international society. On this account, law is not necessarily incompatible with war, which is the prerogative of states, but ought to be conducted in accordance with commonly agreed rules, and which, in principle, does not involve civil society, although the emergence of nationalism as a force in international relations, and the destructive capacity of industrial society, have clearly made this constraint more difficult to achieve. Partly as a result, a norm of non-aggression is a twentieth-century addition to these core principles.[9]

Central to the Westphalian order is commitment to an ethic of coexistence; justice as between states is a matter of procedures rather than substance. Terry Nardin has argued persuasively that the society of states is analogous to an Oakeshottian association of citizens (*cives*) as opposed to an 'enterprise association'; that is, an association devoted to the pursuit of some substantive common goal.[10] Oakeshott, of course, argues that the state itself should not be an enterprise association, and is deeply suspicious of progressivist politics in general, but it is interesting to note that John Rawls – whose theory of justice as applied to national societies is the polar opposite of Oakeshottian – endorses the general proposition that as between societies notions of social justice are inappropriate (Rawls, 1999).[11] There is, incidentally, an important general point here; normative thinking about international relations rarely maps neatly into domestic distinctions between 'right' and 'left' which were developed in another context altogether.

The notion of an international society has constantly come under fire from two very different directions. Realist theorists, philosophers and statesmen have always expressed contempt for the idea that interstate relations can be governed by even a very loose-fitting normative code. Bismarck's maxims that the great questions of the day would be decided by 'blood and iron' and that 'Europe is a geographical expression' (as opposed to shorthand for a set of interstate norms) convey this contempt very nicely, and the fact that he was quite capable of using the notion of the 'Concert of Europe' when it served his purposes makes the point that such collective diplomatic initiatives were to him and his fellow realists no more than tools, to be used when convenient and otherwise ignored.[12] Equally contemptuous have been cosmopolitan critics, and for much the same reasons. Like the realists they believe the social side of international society to be pure fiction. Kant's description of the great founders of the law of nations as 'sorry comforters' whose work has done nothing to stem military aggression can be seen as a cosmopolitan counterpart to Bismarck's hostility (Kant, 1970). Both writers see the restraints on state conduct imposed by international law and diplomacy as, to all intents and purposes, non-existent.

It is quite difficult to argue against this joint position because it is clear that, even when fully operational, international society was indeed usually unable to provide a very effective restraint on the use of power by those who had it in abundance. Although compliance with conventional international law was actually quite good, this was only because so much of state conduct lay outside of the legal norms of the system. Still, even if the practices of international society only marginally affected the conduct of international relations, this margin may have been of some significance – and certainly, for much of its history, the practitioners of Westphalian diplomacy assumed that it was. It is perhaps worth noting that no previous 'international system' – the city-states of Greece or Renaissance Italy or the period of 'warring states' in China, for example – developed the idea of international law or the practice of permanent and protected diplomatic missions; and it is equally noteworthy that all previous international systems collapsed quite rapidly into chaos or empire. Clearly there are other reasons why the European states-system expanded and has become global rather than sharing this fate, but the point is still worth making that, even if 'the traditions of Europe' only deflected the European states marginally from the 'law of the jungle', this margin may have been worth something (Wight, 1978). However, the adequacy of international society as an appropriate normative framework for international relations faced a new challenge in the second half of the twentieth century, and it is this challenge that now needs to be investigated, because it prefigures the later challenge of globalization which is the ultimate subject of this chapter.

Europe and the World: Pluralism Before, During and After Imperialism

As will be apparent from this account there are two salient features of international society; it is a European phenomenon, and it promotes pluralism and difference – that is, by underpinning the notion of sovereignty it simultaneously underpins the ability of particular societies to pursue their own projects in the world. It is clear that, prior to *circa* 1945, the first of these characteristics severely limited the second. Pluralism meant, in effect, support for the various different ways of being European. Initially, the majority of significant members of international society were monarchies, and mutual respect for sovereignty meant mutual respect for one's fellow sovereigns.[13] Later, genuine republics were accepted as full members, but the central point is that all the European states shared a great deal culturally and in terms of political thought – most obviously the Graeco-Roman heritage and the Christian religion. Even Russia, the ideological outrider of the system, whose autocracy was based on a Byzantine rather than a strictly Roman model, shared much of this common background. At a time when politics, and especially international politics, were largely the preserve of the aristocracy, the cosmopolitanism of the European ruling class was quite striking – they intermarried, mixed socially, communicated with one another in a common language (both metaphorically and actually, speaking French as a matter of course) and saw nothing strange in the idea that a national of one country might be a diplomat for another.[14] Arguably, the fact that the practices of international society worked as well as they did is partly to be attributed to this unity-within-diversity. Thus, the reluctance of a gentleman to tell a direct lie to another gentleman certainly provided a better platform for a relatively honest diplomacy than could any convention or treaty not backed in this way by class-solidarity.

When European diplomacy came face to face with a genuine Other, it was a different story. In the Americas the result of such an encounter was tyranny, oppression and genocide-by-disease. In North Africa and much of Asia, the disparities of power that were so evident in Mexico and Peru did not exist until the nineteenth century, and relations were on a far more equal basis – indeed, the European powers quite often had to face local rulers from a position of inferiority – but the kind of cultural similarity that existed in Europe was absent here, with clear consequences for the style and conduct of international relations.[15] The mix of obsequiousness and brutality with which European and non-European powers conducted these relations is a useful indicator of the significance of the practices of international society; the mistreatment of envoys and murder of civilians and prisoners of war (by both sides) was commonplace, and, it should be noted, such atrocities also took place when Europeans met and fought each other 'beyond the line'.[16] There was a spatial as well as a cultural specificity to the practices of European international society; they applied to Europeans in Europe and not necessarily elsewhere.[17]

With the coming of industrial society, the politico-strategic balance of the world moved in favour of the Europeans, and political entities outside of Europe were subjected to direct or indirect imperialism; but, at the same time, the idea that international society was confined to Europeans was replaced by the idea that it was restricted to the 'civilized' – although the major European powers continued to determine what was meant by that term, and therefore to vet potential members of their club. The Ottoman Empire was allowed in, rather reluctantly, after the Crimean War in 1856, but the more interesting moves concerned the major Asian formations, China, Japan and Siam/Thailand. Here, the so-called 'standards of civilization' were applied, and 'regimes of capitulation' established (Gong, 1984; Bull and Watson, 1984). Effectively, the legal systems of these countries were placed on probation, with Europeans refusing to allow their own nationals to be tried in local courts or civil disputes involving Europeans to be settled there, until proper standards were established and the rule of law was in place, at which point the countries in question would be able to claim their sovereign rights including membership of international society. Understandably, these regimes were bitterly resented and removing them became important national goals (Japan succeeded in the 1890s, China not until the 1930s), but their true significance lies in the removal of the spatial dimension to international society, which was now no longer a club of Europeans, but a club of the 'civilized'.

The significance of this move was underlined in the twentieth century, when the European empires came under threat from local nationalisms and the emergence of global anti-imperialist ideologies – most obviously, Marxism–Leninism, but also liberal internationalism in its American, Wilsonian, version. In the British Empire, the idea that the colonies were held in trust for their inhabitants and that the role of imperial rule was to prepare the latter for self-government came to be held by a significant part of the political class – although the timespan required for this task was measured in centuries in the case of the African colonies (Jackson, 1990).[18] Those optimistic about the future of international society could anticipate its gradual expansion as former colonial territories achieved independence and met the conditions of membership. Pessimists, on the other hand, pointed to the undermining of the practices of international society in Europe itself. Even in those countries which remained committed to the rule of law and civilized values, the process of democratization did considerable harm to the culture of diplomacy. The Wilsonian demand for 'open covenants, openly arrived at' symbolized the difficulties this culture faced even in the liberal democracies. In communist and fascist Europe things were, of course, much worse; the old conventions of personal behaviour meant nothing to the Ribbentrops and Vyshinskyes of this new world, and the goal of preserving the peace of Europe, identified as crucial by Taylor, was equally meaningless.

In the event, when all these trends worked themselves out, the result was somewhere between the worst fears of the pessimists and the best hopes of the optimists. The threat of fascism was comprehensively defeated in the Second World War, and communism, although apparently victorious in that conflict, itself succumbed forty years later. In the intervening period the overwhelming majority of imperial territories achieved independence and entered international society – but the international society they entered was in crucial respects different from that which existed even in the 1930s, let alone the previous 300 years. Between 1945 and the formation of the United Nations, and 1948 and the Universal Declaration of Human Rights by the UN General Assembly, the normative basis of international society was redefined in ways which prefigured the later challenge to international society of globalization.

In the first place, the United Nations Charter actually strengthened the norms of sovereignty, non-aggression and non-intervention; the process of turning international society into a universal as opposed to a European club was completed – from now on all independent countries would be entitled to the protection of these norms.[19] Moreover, under the influence of both the United States and the Soviet Union, the old colonial empires were placed under considerable pressure to decolonize and the requirement that the former colonies be prepared for self-government was, in effect, dropped. As a consequence, in the next three decades UN membership trebled with the arrival of a large number of 'quasi-states', that is states that were recognized as sovereign members of international society but which lacked the actual capacity for self-government, indeed, in many cases relied upon external aid for the performance of the most basic functions of government.[20] International society moved from being a smallish club of European powers to being a larger association of representatives of all the continents, cultures and religions of the world.

Such a move on its own might have pushed the pluralism of international society and its ability to cope with difference to breaking point, but the situation was greatly complicated by the second development in this period, the emergence of an international human rights regime based on and elaborating the Universal Declaration of Human Rights of 1948. As Edward Keene helpfully comments, the human rights regime applied the 'standards of civilization' to Europe at the very same time as European standards of sovereignty and national independence were extended to the world (Keene, 2002). From now on there would be one normative order for the world rather than one for Europe and one for the rest of the world – the problem was (and is) that this normative order is characterized by a glaring contradiction between its central norms. On the one hand, states are deemed independent and entitled to develop their own projects and forms of political life; external interference in such matters is barred by the 'domestic jurisdiction' clause in the UN Charter, Article 2(7), unless such projects constitute a threat to international peace and security. On the other hand, the international human rights regime sets down a quite extensive template that (in principle, at least) severely restricts the actual scope for developing such projects or for political experimentation, and this is particularly true since the elaboration of the Universal Declaration by the two Covenants on Civil and Political, and Economic, Social and Cultural, Rights of 1966. There are now very few areas of human life which are not subject to international standard-setting via the human rights regime, and it is difficult to imagine how any political system other than a fully developed liberal democracy could come close to meeting all of its requirements. It is equally difficult to see how, in such circumstances, the pluralism that international society is supposed to protect could exist.

Of course, all this is predicated on the international standards being effectively applied, which, for the most part, they are not. Only in Europe is there compliance via an effective enforcement mechanism. The European Convention for the Protection of Human Rights and Fundamental Freedoms of 1950 has been written into the domestic legal codes of many European states, and is enforced ultimately by a European Court that has the capacity to make binding rulings. The reason for this European exceptionalism is clear enough – all the signatories are liberal democracies, sharing a common political and cultural heritage; and although the differences that remain (for example, between common law and Roman legal systems) produce the occasional complications, the extent to which the different member states actually represent different political principles is minimal, much less, in fact, than in the heyday of the old European political order which had to cope with constitutional and unlimited monarchies, autocracies and republics. In much of the rest of the world, outside of North America, Australasia and India, the human rights regime is, at best, aspirational – and in some important countries, most particularly the People's Republic of China, not even that.

Still, this does not undermine the basic point that there exists an underlying contradiction between norms supportive of national sovereignty and self-rule and norms supportive of universal standards. Moreover, the challenge to conventional notions of sovereignty has become more sharply defined in recent decades, for two reasons. First, the international human rights regime has become more and more detailed in its requirements, and has moved away from the civil and political agenda that dominated in 1948 to a far greater concern with economic and social issues, becoming in the process ever more intolerant of difference.[21] Second, the sovereignty norms have increasingly come under direct, as opposed to implicit, attack; whereas in early human rights treaties a rather implausible clause was always included to the effect that nothing in this legislation compromises national sovereignty, a number of recent developments have circumvented this courtesy. Universal jurisdiction and the International Criminal Court are part of the story here, but equally important is the notion that domestic oppression and denial of human rights could, in certain circumstances, constitute a threat to international peace and security such that 'humanitarian intervention' is justified. The challenge here to international society needs to be examined in greater depth. A key issue is whether there are readings of international society, such as the 'solidarism' supported by Tim Dunne and Nicholas Wheeler, that can incorporate such a challenge or whether there is a genuine incompatibility here (Wheeler, 2000, 1992; Dunne and Wheeler, 1996).[22] The answer to this question will be crucial to understanding the role, if any, for international society if the processes of globalization continue.

International Society: Beyond Pluralism?

The potential tension between sovereignty norms and human rights norms that has existed since 1945 did not become actual until the 1990s, for two reasons. First, although the human rights regime inherently contradicted the notion of state sovereignty, the fact that it was states that created and were expected to enforce this regime muted that contradiction; in effect, states were only obliged to take their human rights obligations seriously if they made a conscious decision so to do, and only the (West) Europeans took that decision – and although the human rights regime was initially founded largely because of atrocities committed by European states, in the post-1945 world these states were unlikely to be major offenders, which, of course, was why they agreed to allow themselves to be subject to mutual supervision in this area. The second reason why the potential tension was unrealized until the 1990s was, in short, the Cold War. Human rights were, between 1948 and 1989, weapons in this ideological conflict, but, equally, they were ignored when it did not suit the interests of the two blocs to bring them to prominence: when, for example, it was one's strategic allies who were in breach of the Universal Declaration.

The end of the Cold War in 1989 removed this second obstacle to the effective working of the human rights regime, and the way the Cold War ended, with the ideological defeat of Soviet communism, did a great deal to undermine the first as well. The apparent triumph of liberalism put heart into supporters of human rights and led to a multi-pronged campaign to extend the scope and range of the existing human rights regime, to promote democracy and to legitimize humanitarian intervention – a campaign that, at various times, involved cosmopolitan democrats, neo-conservatives and, sometimes and usually quite briefly, some Western governments.[23] Although this campaign generated considerable resistance – see, for example, the opposition of many Asian governments encapsulated by the 'Asian values' debate, and, at a more intellectual level, Samuel Huntington's warning of a 'clash of civilizations' – it also registered many successes (Huntington, 1993).[24] The gradual and partial acceptance by the UN Security Council that internal oppression might, in some circumstances, constitute the kind of 'threat to international peace and security' that could justify humanitarian interventions was one such (Wheeler, 2000). Another was the constitution of an International Criminal Court (ICC) based on the Rome Statute of 1998, which, unlike the International Court of Justice (ICJ) held individuals, as opposed to states, responsible for crimes carried out under the aegis of state sovereignty, and which, in theory, could hold individuals criminally responsible even if the state of which they were citizens had not ratified or even signed the Rome Statute.[25] The ICC has no retrospective jurisdiction, but former President Pinochet was also threatened by the operation of legal notions of universal jurisdiction when he lost his appeal in the British House of Lords against extradition to Spain on charges of having authorized the torture of Spanish citizens while head of state in Chile, and Slobodan Milosevic was on trial in The Hague for acts carried out while he held office as head of government in Serbia during the wars that accompanied the breakup of former Yugoslavia.[26] Add all these elements together and something like a new paradigm of international relations could be seen to be emerging in the 1990s, a paradigm in which state sovereignty was to be considered a valid norm of international society only when applied to essentially democratic governments that respect human rights (Franck, 1992).

From the perspective of traditional conceptions of international society, these developments can only be regarded with deep suspicion. As emphasized above, international society has generally been associated with pluralism, coexistence and respect for difference, even if, for much of its history, its European nature has imposed limits to this broad-mindedness. Still, there are minor themes in the international society literature which imply stricter limits to this pluralism and it is these themes that have been developed by Wheeler and Dunne in their account of a 'solidarist' reading of international society. A starting point here might be the proposition that although non-intervention has always been a key norm of international society, it has also been accepted that there are certain circumstances where this norm might be overridden (Krasner, 1999).[27] Martin Wight refers to 'gross violations of human dignity' as potentially justifying intervention (Wight, 1966), while Michael Walzer, a modern, non-English School theorist of international society talks of 'slavery and massacre' as being the kind of events that generate a right of intervention (Walzer, 1977). Beyond the issue of humanitarian intervention, other modern theorists of international society have also made some room for universalist as opposed to pluralist concerns; Hedley Bull generally favoured order over justice, but in one of his last writings referred to states as 'local agents of a common good', a phrase with clear universalist overtones (Bull, 1984), while R. J. Vincent's work on human rights pointed even more strongly in the same direction (Vincent, 1986).

What all of these writers can be read as saying is that although a multiplicity of political authorities – an international society – constitutes a rational political order for humanity taken as a whole (because problems of scale make global government impossible, laws lose their effectiveness at a distance, and tyranny is less likely if political society occurs on a human scale), the ultimate referent object of international society ought to be individual human beings rather than states as such. The *telos* of international society, to change modes of discourse, is not, in the last resort, simply to preserve a multiplicity of separate states, but ultimately to promote human flourishing; thus, although theorists of international society from Grotius, Pufendorf and Burke through to Bull, Walzer and Nardin have argued that this goal is best achieved via a society of legally autonomous, sovereign states, sovereign rights cannot be employed to justify conduct that clearly prevents human flourishing, such as large-scale human rights violations. As natural lawyers have generally argued, in any legal system there is a need for an accessible final point of decision and this is provided by the idea of state sovereignty, but, again, this cannot mean that everything done by state authorities is, by definition, legitimate.[28] The judges in the British House of Lords who held that authorizing torture was not the kind of legitimate exercise of sovereignty that ought to be protected by sovereign immunity did so on the basis of positive law – the International Convention against Torture of 1984, adopted into English law by the Criminal Justice Act of 1988 – but might equally have come to the same conclusion by returning to first principles and asking what sovereignty was *for*.

It should be noted that this solidarist version of international society cannot drift too far away from the pluralism more normally associated with the idea of a society of states without losing contact with the tradition as a whole. Gross violations of human rights may be regarded as a modern version of 'gross violations of human dignity', justifying external intervention on the part of anyone who can prevent them, but this is a long way away from the cosmopolitan notion that universal standards in all areas of human life should supplant the local. In essence, human rights are about intolerance, and international society is about tolerance; adherents to the idea of a society of states may agree that there are some things that ought not to be tolerated, but they are coming at matters from a different angle from human rights activists, and alliances between these two groups will always be uneasy and unstable. The solidarist account of international society amounts to a *reimagining* of what is involved in a society of states, an amendment to pluralist accounts not an alternative to them – and solidarism certainly does not amount to a case for replacing that society with the notion of a global community.

From International Society to Global Community?

Such a case can, of course, be made. A barely suppressed premise of the discussion so far has been that an international society supportive of pluralism is intrinsically valuable, to be reimagined perhaps, but not replaced by some notion of a global community. Why, and why not? Clearly many thinkers – cosmopolitan liberals, human rights activists – would react, and have reacted, rather differently to the developments described in the penultimate section of this chapter. They welcome the idea that the international human rights regime should be strengthened by notions of universal jurisdiction and the establishment of an International Criminal Court; rather than regarding these developments with suspicion, they regret only that the ICC does not have wider jurisdiction and that the full human rights package cannot usually be enforced. They welcome also at least the *idea* of humanitarian intervention even if they generally condemn those humanitarian interventions that have actually taken place as exercises in great power politics.[29]

This group of scholars, whose work is very well represented in this collection, believe that it is already possible to discern the outlines of a global civil society in our current situation, and in many cases advocate the development of institutions of global governance that will undermine the practice of state sovereignty.[30] Moreover, they believe that such developments are backed by, indeed immanent in, the processes of global social and economic change summarized by the term globalization (Held et al., 1999). Since the mid- to late nineteenth century industrial society has required increasing coordination among states and, it is argued, in the twenty-first century this process will need to be taken to the point at which the notion of national sovereignty will become meaningless.[31] Andrew Linklater adds to this package of ideas the notion that a wider sense of community beyond the nation-state is developing, representing a kind of moral growth (Linklater, 1998, 1999).

This is a powerful set of arguments and to them should be added, perhaps rather incongruously, the neoconservative take on foreign policy which has developed in the last decade especially in the United States.[32] The 'neocons' are, of course, bitterly hostile to the institutional developments strongly supported by cosmopolitan liberals, especially to the ICC, which they regard as a wholly improper organization designed to limit US power, but in many respects the values they wish to see promoted in the world are liberal and cosmopolitan, and they share the general cosmopolitan suspicion of the pluralism of international society.[33] The neoconservatives are, in fact, quite close to a version of Wilsonian idealism. Like Wilson, they believe that the characteristic American values – individualism, the rule of law, a free economy, representative and responsible government – apply universally and are universally desired, and that it would be morally irresponsible for the United States to fail to do what it can, consistent with its own interests, to promote these values in the world. For Wilson, in the first quarter of the last century, the way to promote these values was via international organizations and cooperation with others, but the neo-conservatives see the rise of the United States to supremacy as permitting it to act directly, cooperating only with like-minded allies. In an insightful article Max Boot has argued that neoconservatives adopt a 'Hard Wilsonianism' as opposed to the 'Soft Wilsonianism' of multilateralist liberal internationalists such as Joseph Nye and to the cosmopolitanism of writers such as Held and Linklater (Boot, 2002; Nye, 2002). Because of their willingness to use force to promote American values, the fact that those values are very close to those supported by cosmopolitan liberals and human rights activists is often missed – and it is worth making the point that the 'neocons' may actually be right in assuming that United States power is needed to promote these values in the world; liberals who believe in both human rights and multilateral institutions are, in certain respects, in denial, since it is clear that genuinely effective action to promote human rights is unlikely to be undertaken if the approval of multilateral institutions such as the UN is required. This is, of course, a controversial point – but the wider point that the neoconservatives are as hostile to international pluralism as cosmopolitan liberals, and for much the same reasons, holds.

There is, therefore, a powerful set of arguments in favour of some kind of global community as a replacement for the society of states, in favour, perhaps, of extending and deepening the solidarist account of international society to the point at which a global community will emerge – what, then, is the case for the defence of a pluralist conception of international society? There are, I think, two positions here, one pragmatic and the other principled – these positions are separable and rest on different bases, but they do not contradict each other; it is possible to be convinced by the pragmatic case while rejecting the principled and vice versa.

The pragmatic case in favour of a pluralist (or 'minimal solidarist') version of international society rests upon the political realities of twenty-first-century international relations. Cosmopolitan liberals acknowledge these realities, but offer only a partial description thereof, and thereby miss some of the most important features of the modern world. Such liberals correctly identify the power of the United States, and to a lesser extent of the EU and Japan, as a major stumbling block in the way of cosmopolitan institutional reform. The unwillingness of the rich and powerful to allow their conduct to be subjected to impartial scrutiny, or to pool their national sovereignties in effective multilateral institutions which could be directed towards the alleviation of world poverty or to arresting the processes of global environmental degradation is indeed a feature of the current world order.[34] But this is not the whole story. The poor and the weak also defend the principle of national sovereignty, regarding it as an essential, albeit inadequate, defence against the power of the new global forces; equally, they generally oppose cosmopolitan notions such as 'humanitarian intervention' because they have good reason to think that they are unlikely to be the interveners, quite likely to be intervened against. In the same vein, much has been made of the failure of the United States to join the ICC, but less often noted is the fact that no major Asian state has ratified the Rome Statute, and most have not signed it, indicating an unwillingness to accept even the very limited derogation of sovereignty involved in acceptance of the jurisdiction of the ICC. Nor is this latter reluctance simply a matter of undemocratic elites desiring to protect themselves from international scrutiny; this hardly applies to Asian democracies such as India and Japan, or even to generally law-abiding if quasi-authoritarian regimes such as that of Singapore.

The point is that these states have a rather more realistic understanding of the politics of globalization than a great many well-intentioned Northern liberals; they understand that the institutions of global governance are unlikely to work to their advantage, that too many of the forces working to create global governance actually serve the interests of the rich and powerful, including, it should be said, many components of the 'anti-global capitalism' movement that has developed in recent years – third-world nationalism is of little political significance by comparison with the nationalism of European farmers and American steelworkers, while the high environmental and labour standards favoured by human rights groups will undermine most of the advantages many developing countries possess. The point is that, perhaps paradoxically, economic globalization may just about work in favour of the interests of the global poor, but there is good reason to believe that cosmopolitan global government is unlikely to do so.[35]

To put the matter differently, the emergence of a global community served by effective institutions of global governance could only avoid being a tyranny that served the interests of only some parts of the world – most likely, those already rich and powerful – if it were based on a genuine sense of 'we-feeling' that was truly global. Within a functioning, democratic, national community, decisions can be taken without excessive coercion because the winners and losers consider themselves to be part of the same group; the losers trust the winners not to push their victory too far, and the winners are aware that they could be losers next time. None of this applies at the global level. Of course, cosmopolitan democrats are aware that this is so, and see global community as a ongoing project – the act of building the institutions of global government will, it is hoped, gradually create the community that will make them work. The practical danger here is clear; the temptation is to give the process a nudge – the neoconservatives with their programme of democracy-promotion, if necessary by force present the kind of crusading image that most cosmopolitans are keen to avoid, but they also have a realistic appreciation of the task faced by anyone who wishes to build a global community. The 'hard Wilsonian' option goes against many of the values in which cosmopolitan liberals place their faith, but at least faces up to the scale of transformation that would be required if a global community is to be brought into existence.

These positions offer good pragmatic reasons why a pluralist account of international society, modified to take on board some solidarist elements, would be preferable to the replacement of this model of world order by the notion of global community – but there are good non-pragmatic reasons for resisting this move as well. A pluralist international society provides the best mechanism for the preservation of cultural diversity, and this preservation is intrinsically valuable. Modern cosmopolitan liberals claim not to be against cultural diversity, but culture (and religion) are regarded by such liberals as matters for the private sphere, value-choices made by freethinking individuals that ought not to affect politics and the social order.[36] This is, indeed, how many post-Enlightenment secular intellectuals see culture and religion, but it hardly needs to be emphasized that, on a global scale, this is a minority point of view. Most people (and that includes most 'Westerners') do not define themselves as individuals set apart from their communities and cultural contexts, and they do not regard their religious beliefs as a purely private matter, the product of spiritual consumer choices; rather, they understand themselves to be constituted and formed by their cultural, communal and religious commitments.

Moreover, this self-understanding becomes more relevant, not less, when people feel, rightly, that it is under siege by globalizing socio-economic forces and the 'soft power' of liberal individualism.

Liberal secular intellectuals tend to regard these commitments with hostility as leading to 'fundamentalism' and irrationalism, but this blanket dismissal of forms of life which are not shaped by liberal individualism is patronizing and wrong-headed. The existence of different ways of living human lives enriches us all. Certainly those who attempt to impose their way of life on others by violence are to be condemned, but there is nothing irrational *per se* in the belief that the consumerist approach to culture and religion undermines the possibility of constructing a meaningful life. More, this critique of liberal cosmopolitanism can be situated firmly within the thought of the West. At the beginning of the Western tradition of political theory it was Aristotle who declared that 'man' is a political animal, designed to be a citizen of a *Polis*, a self-governing city. Cosmopolitanism was, initially, a cry of despair, a reaction by Greek thinkers to the destruction of the independent cities of Hellas by the Macedonian and later the Roman Empires – to be a 'citizen of the world' was a kind of spiritual, apolitical, compensation for the loss of real citizenship. Certainly to be a citizen of the world did not involve taking part in its government; the great Stoic, cosmopolitan thinker and Roman Emperor Marcus Aurelius would have had little truck with such a notion.[37] Later, again within the Western canon, it was Hegel who gave the strongest defence of the idea that a fulfilled life required citizenship of a sovereign state – it is only through a positive relationship with our fellow citizens that we are able to overcome the alienating individualism of the modern economy. Like cosmopolitan advocates of a global community, Hegel firmly believed in human equality, but, unlike them, he resisted the idea that this ought to be crystallized as a cosmopolitanism that set itself in opposition to the concrete life of the state (Hegel, 1991).

A pluralist conception of international society allows for the coexistence of different conceptions of the Good, and, in an age when global political and social forces are increasingly narrowing the options available to humanity, this must be seen as strong argument in its favour. Of course, as solidarist writers have suggested, there are limits here that need to be acknowledged – not all conceptions of the Good are worthy of respect, and in some cases may be incompatible with any reasonable account of human flourishing. A pluralist account of international society does not commit one to tolerating genocide or enslavement – but it does suggest a presumption in favour of the preservation of different forms of life whenever possible.

Conclusion: 9/11, the War on Terror and International Society

Nothing so far in this chapter could not have been written prior to the attacks on New York City and Washington on 11 September 2001, and the subsequent 'war on terror' declared by the US government. Since the events of 9/11 are often seen as ushering in a new era, the real start to the twenty-first century, this might be considered surprising, but what, actually, changed on that awful day? Certainly there have been some surprising developments in the last few years – an isolationist right-wing Republican government in the US adopting a programme of democracy promotion and nation-building, cosmopolitan liberals demonstrating in the streets in a vain attempt to preserve one of the most vile regimes in the world – but do such policy shifts or vignettes require a wholesale rethink of our categories? Certainly some of the rhetoric of globalization – a 'borderless world', for example – looks even more silly today than it did originally; the world has never been borderless for those flying economy class, and the security checks and controls that are being introduced today for all travellers simply extend to the privileged the sur-veillance and harassment that were previously reserved for the proles. Similarly, the undervaluing of the importance of brute military force that was characteristic of the 1990s, at least in Europe, looks the reverse of prescient; West Europeans may have reason to be proud of the way in which military power is no longer a factor in their international relations, but in the rest of the world, indeed in Eastern Europe, the possibility of war has clearly not disappeared (Kagan, 2003). Indeed, what is actually new is the fact that of the major industrial countries, only the United States has developed and maintained the kind of military machine that was common in the past, leading to a kind of American hege-mony – but in industrializing and non-industrial countries such as China and India no one shares the European illusion that military force is no longer an important factor in world politics. Still, as well as factors undermining the claims of, at least the more extreme, theorists of globalization, the post-9/11 world has also seen features that keep the notion of a global community on the international agenda, albeit somewhat on the back-burner; the US commitment to democracy promotion, although patchy and inconsistent, deserves mention here, along with the widespread belief that to deal with the roots of ter-rorism steps will have to be taken in the direction of a more just world.

Where does all this leave the notion of a reimagined international society? The first thing that needs to be said is that although such an international society is generally tol-erant of difference, it cannot be tolerant of those who would destroy it. Campaigns designed to impose liberal democracy on an unwilling world are certainly to be avoided, but the threats posed by the Islamic version of fascism espoused by al-Qaeda, and the more conventional fascism of Saddam Hussein are real and need to be dealt with (Brown, 2002; Berman, 2003). Al-Qaeda is not the kind of nationalist, terrorist movement where a combination of sticks and carrots might be expected to diffuse the threat, as has hap-pened to some extent in Northern Ireland – rather, there are no carrots that can be offered to al-Qaeda that would have the slightest impact on their campaign; their desire to impose a rigid theocracy on the Arabian peninsula, and then the entire world of Islam, past and present, destroying Israel and subverting Western governments in the process, simply is not negotiable on either side (Brown, 2004).

Second, and by the same token, although international society rests crucially upon respect for international law and for the institutions states have created to ease their rela-tions one with another, it is essential that these institutions and this law reflect current realities. A full-blown right to wage preventive war in response to any perceived threat, which, it is sometimes asserted – wrongly, I think – is claimed by the United States, is clearly impossible to reconcile with any conception of an international legal order, but at the same time some adjustment to the law on pre-emption does need to be made to respond to the fact that threats from abroad no longer take the form of the easily observ-able massing of troops on the border, or even of incoming bombers or intercontinental ballistic missiles.[38] Weapons of mass destruction present a real problem for all states, and if states allow terrorist groups to use their territory to train in the use of these weapons they cannot complain if potential targets take action against them.

Still, these two points taken together do not suggest that there is anything fundamentally at fault with an essentially pluralist account of international society, suitably reimagined via an input of moderate solidarism. The practices of such a society have to adapt to current circumstances, and dealing with religious fanaticism and outright fascism, especially when these enemies are capable of laying hands on appalling weapons, may require some quite serious adaptations, but the original notion can be preserved intact. International society is about coexistence and the preservation of alternative conceptions of the Good, but it has always been the case that there are some conceptions of the Good that cannot be incorporated within international society. At the moment this is true of al-Qaeda and similar movements, as it was once true of National Socialism. It is important that the steps that are taken to protect the world from this menace do not undermine the essential values upon which international society is based, but there is no reason for despair at the long-term prospects for the continuing existence of a reimagined society of states.

Notes

I am grateful to Tim Dunne, Nick Wheeler and Peter Wilson for comments on an earlier draft; the usual disclaimers for remaining errors of fact or interpretation apply. This chapter was completed in 2005.

1 Although classical realists such as Hans J. Morgenthau had a rather more nuanced view of the role of power and interest in international relations; for good commentaries see Murray, 1996; Rosenthal, 1991; and Smith, 1986.

2 This position is commonly identified by IR theorists as that of the 'English School', although it will be suggested that this is too limited a description of the approach in question. For the English School see Bull, 1977/1995; Dunne, 1998; and, most recently and relevantly for this chapter, Buzan, 2004.

3 The course, 'The Structure of International Society', still exists – I convened it between 2000 and 2002 – but, of course, with a somewhat different syllabus.

4 See Dunne (1998) for this history. The critic was Jones, 1981. The English School scholars were 'English' not by nationality, but by virtue of being based in England (cf. the Frankfurt School).

5 One of the leading American post-structuralists, James Der Derian, was a D.Phil. student of Bull at Oxford in the early 1980s, and has since written eloquently on his influence; see Der Derian, 1996; and, esp. Der Derian, 2003. The affinities between constructivism and the English School are emphasized by Dunne, 1995; and are apparent in Wendt, 1999.

6 See e.g. Wheeler, 2000; and Buzan, 2004 for a more general case for the English School's relevance.

7 For the historical origins of the notion see parts 5 and 6 of Brown, Nardin and Rengger, 2002. The introductions to these texts were written by Nardin, whose 1983 book is a modern account of international society at least the equal of any English School text.

8 'Westphalian' because the Peace of Westphalia of 1648 is conventionally taken as a convenient point after which European international society can unambiguously be said to be in existence.

9 I owe this point to Peter Wilson.

10 Nardin (1983) building on Oakeshott (1975).

11 Rawls's society of peoples is not the same as international society, but the notion of a common normative framework governing the relations of discrete entities (societies, states, peoples)

transfers between his work and the tradition quite well – although on his account the pluralism of a society of peoples is more limited in scope than in the original idea.

12 Taylor (1954) gives an extended and magisterial account of Bismarck's diplomacy.

13 The United Provinces and the Venetian Republic would be obvious exceptions (along with quite a large number of petty German city-states), but the Prince of Orange as Stadtholder and the Venetian Doge were at least semi-monarchical figures, as was England's Protector during the Commonwealth of the 1650s.

14 For example, the most famous of Austrian Chancellors was the non-Austrian Prince Metternich. The diplomatic corps of republican states such as France were particularly aristo-cratic, because of the difficulty that *soi-disant* aristocrats experienced in pursing a domestic political career. For similar reasons, the pre-1914 British diplomatic corps was heavily popu-lated by aristocratic Roman Catholics.

15 Linda Colley's fascinating *Captives* (2003) is a useful corrective to the idea that the Europeans were militarily and politically superior to non-Europeans prior to the nineteenth century.

16 The 'Amboyna Massacre' of 1623 is perhaps the most famous illustration of this point. The Dutch and English East India Companies were then competing for the spice trade of the East Indies; neither was satisfied with the division of the spoils set out in a trade treaty between the United Provinces and England of 1619, and in retaliation for an English attack on the Dutch 'Factory' on Jakarta, the Dutch at Amboyna on the Molucca Islands turned on the English Factory there – the ten English factors (i.e. traders) who survived the initial attack, and their nine Japanese assistants, were subsequently tortured to death.

17 Schmitt (2004) makes this spatial dimension the key to what he calls the Public Law of Europe.

18 Jackson (1990) provides a good account of British imperial thinking in the 1930s.

19 Always assuming they were 'peace-loving', which in practice meant that former enemy nations would need the permission of the Security Council before they could rejoin the comity of nations.

20 Jackson (1990) argues that these states possessed negative sovereignty (the right to non-intervention) but lacked positive sovereignty (the ability actually to govern themselves). It should be noted that this ability is not necessarily related to power as that term is usually employed in IR; Ireland, for example, has very little military capacity, but clearly possesses pos-itive as well as negative sovereignty.

21 A concern with economic rights (if such there be) is usually taken to focus on the obligations of the rich to transfer wealth or income to the poor, but must, if taken seriously, involve the economic and social policies of both rich and poor countries being subjected to international supervision and regulation; for economic rights see Shue, 1983 and Pogge, 2002.

22 The most impressive recent extended defence of a pluralist conception of international society is Jackson (2000); although Nardin does not use the term, his *Law, Morality and the Relations of States* (1983) can also be used to this effect.

23 Cosmopolitan democrats and neoconservatives are usually in denial about the extent to which they share the same goals. On democracy promotion as foreign policy under the Clinton Administration see Cox, Ikenberry and Inoguchi, 2000.

24 For the Asian values debate see Bauer and Bell, 1999 and Bell, 2000.

25 This could happen if the allegedly criminal acts took place on the territory of a member state. It is this provision that has caused most angst in the most prominent non-signatory state, the United States.

26 Pinochet was returned to Chile on health grounds, but the point was made. Milosevic faced trial before a Tribunal established by the UN Security Council so this was not strictly speaking a case of universal jurisdiction – but it certainly pushed the envelope as far as conventional inter-national law is concerned.

27 Krasner documents the many cases where interventions have occurred from the very beginning of the Westphalian system.

28 For a strong statement of the modern natural law position see Finnis, 1980.

29 But see the *Report of the Independent International Commission on Kosovo*, 2000, in which a group consisting largely of human rights activists and cosmopolitan liberals declared the intervention of 1999 to be illegal but legitimate.

30 The best source on global civil society is what has become the annual handbook *Global Civil Society*, edited (to date) by Anheier, Glasius and Kaldor, 2001, 2002, 2003. On cosmopolitan democracy see Archibugi and Held, 1995; and Archibugi, Held and Kohler, 1998.

31 Murphy (1994) has traced the early stages of this process. Hirst and Thompson (1999) argue that the global economy is internationalized rather than globalized.

32 The hostility of the American academy to neoconservatism makes it difficult to find programmatic statements in the academic literature; best is probably Kristol and Kagan, 2000; see also, for a brief but brilliant overview, Kagan, 2003.

33 For the neoconservative take on international legal developments see Rivkin and Casey, 2000/1.

34 The West Europeans have signed up to the ICC unlike the USA or Japan, but only because they are convinced, almost certainly correctly, that they will never be subjected to its operation.

35 For neoliberal and Marxist defences of economic globalization respectively, see Baghwati, 2004 and Desai, 2002.

36 For an extreme statement of this position see Barry, 2000.

37 Cosmopolitan liberals such as Held and Archibugi show little interest in pre-Kantian cosmopolitan thought, but there is a history here that cannot simply be swept under the table, as Martha Nussbaum recognizes; see e.g. Nussbaum, 1997.

38 For different perspectives on this issue see *Ethics and International Affairs*, 2003.

References

Anheier, H., M. Glasius and M. Kaldor, eds (2001, 2002, 2003). *Global Civil Society*. Oxford: Oxford University Press.

Archibugi, D. and D. Held, eds (1995). *Cosmopolitan Democracy: An Agenda for a New World Order*. Cambridge: Polity.

Archibugi, D., D. Held and M. Kohler, eds (1998). *Reimagining Political Community: Studies in Cosmopolitan Democracy*. Cambridge: Polity.

Baghwati, J. (2004). *In Defence of Globalization*. Oxford: Oxford University Press.

Barry, B. (2000). *Culture and Equality*. Cambridge: Polity.

Bauer, J. and D. Bell, eds (1999). *The East Asian Challenge to Human Rights*. Cambridge: Cambridge University Press.

Bell, D. (2000). *East Meets West: Human Rights and Democracy in East Asia*. Princeton: Princeton University Press.

Berman, Paul (2003). *Terror and Liberalism*. New York: Norton.

Boot, M. (2002). 'What the Heck is a "Neo-Con"? Neoconservatives Believe in Using American Might to Promote American Values Abroad', *Wall Street Journal* online, 30 December.

Brown, C. (2002). 'Narratives of Religion, Modernity and Civilisation', in K. Booth and T. Dunne, eds, *Worlds in Collision*. London: Palgrave.

Brown, C. (2004). 'Reflections on the War on Terror: Two Years On', *International Politics*, 41(1): pp. 51–64.

Brown, C., T. Nardin and N. J. Rengger, eds (2002). *International Relations in Political Thought*. Cambridge: Cambridge University Press.

Bull, H. (1977/1995). *The Anarchical Society*. London: Macmillan.

Bull, H. (1984). *Justice in International Relations: The Hagey Lectures.* Waterloo, Ontario: University of Waterloo.

Bull, H. and A. Watson, eds (1984). *The Expansion of International Society*. Oxford: Clarendon Press.

Buzan, Barry (2004). *From International to World Society?* Cambridge: Cambridge University Press.

Colley, Linda (2003). *Captives.* London: Pimlico.

Cox, M., J. Ikenberry and T. Inoguchi, eds (2000). *American Democracy Promotion: Impulses, Strategies and Impacts.* New York: Oxford University Press.

Der Derian, J. (1996). 'Hedley Bull and the Idea of Diplomatic Culture', in R. Fawn and J. Larkins, eds, *International Society after the Cold War*. London: Palgrave/Macmillan.

Der Derian, J. (2003). 'Hedley Bull and the Case for a Post-Classical Approach', in H. Bauer and E. Brighi, eds, *International Relations at LSE: A History of 75 Years*. London: Millennium Publication Group.

Desai, M. (2002). *Marx's Revenge*. London: Verso.

Dunne, T. (1995). 'The Social Construction of International Society', *European Journal of International Relations*, 1: pp. 367–89.

Dunne, T. (1998). *Inventing International Society*. London: Macmillan.

Dunne T. and N. J. Wheeler (1996). 'Hedley Bull's Pluralism of the Intellect and Solidarism of the Will', *International Affairs*, 72: pp. 91–107.

Ethics and International Affairs (2003). 'Roundtable: Evaluating the Pre-emptive Use of Force', 17(1).

Finnis, J. (1980). *Natural Law and Natural Rights*. Oxford: Clarendon Press.

Franck, Thomas (1992). 'The Emerging Right to Democratic Governance', *American Journal of International Law*, 86(1): pp. 46–91.

Gong, G. C. (1984). *The Standard of 'Civilization' in International Society*. Oxford: Oxford University Press.

Hegel, G. W. F. (1991). *Elements of the Philosophy of Right*, ed. Allen Wood. Cambridge: Cambridge University Press, section 209.

Held, D. et al., eds (1999). *Global Transformations*. Cambridge: Polity.

Hirst, P. and G. Thompson (1999). *Globalization in Question*. Cambridge: Polity.

Huntington, S. (1993). 'The Clash of Civilizations', *Foreign Affairs*, 72: pp. 22–49.

Independent International Commission on Kosovo (2000). *Report of the Independent International Commission on Kosovo*. Oxford: Oxford University Press.

Jackson, R. (1990). *Quasi-States: Sovereignty, International Relations and the Third World*. Cambridge: Cambridge University Press.

Jackson, R. (2000). *The Global Covenant.* Oxford: Oxford University Press.

Jones, R. (1981). 'The English School of International Relations: A Case for Closure', *Review of International Studies*, 7(1): pp. 1–14.

Kagan, R. (2003). *Of Paradise and Power*. New York: Alfred A. Knopf.

Kant, Immanuel (1970). *Perpetual Peace* in H. J. Reiss, ed., *Kant's Political Writings*. Cambridge: Cambridge University Press.

Keene, E. (2002). *Beyond the Anarchical Society*. Cambridge: Cambridge University Press.

Keohane, R. O., ed. (1986). *Neorealism and its Critics.* New York: Columbia University Press.

Krasner, Stephen (1999). *Sovereignty: Organized Hypocrisy*. Princeton: Princeton University Press.

Kristol, W. and R. Kagan, eds (2000). *Present Dangers: Crisis and Opportunity in American Foreign and Defense Policy*. New York: Encounter Books.

Linklater, A. (1998). *The Transformation of Political Community*. Cambridge: Polity.

Linklater, A. (1999). 'The Evolving Spheres of International Justice', *International Affairs*, 75: pp. 473–82.

Murphy, C. (1994). *International Organization and Industrial Change: Global Governance since 1850.* Cambridge: Polity.

Murray, A. (1996). *Reconstructing Realism.* Edinburgh: Keele University Press.

Nardin, T. (1983). *Law, Morality and the Relations of States.* Princeton: Princeton University Press.

Nussbaum, M. (1997). 'Kant and Cosmopolitanism', in J. Bohnman and M. Lutz-Bachmann, eds, *Perpetual Peace: Essays on Kant's Cosmopolitan Ideal.* Cambridge, Mass.: MIT Press.

Nye, J. (2002). *The Paradox of American Power.* Oxford: Oxford University Press.

Oakeshott, M. (1975). *On Human Conduct.* Oxford: Clarendon Press.

Pogge, T. (2002). *World Poverty and Human Rights.* Cambridge: Polity.

Rawls, J. (1999). *The Law of Peoples.* Cambridge, Mass.: Harvard University Press.

Rivkin, D. B. and L. Casey (2000/01). 'The Rocky Shoals of International Law', *The National Interest*, 62: pp. 35–46.

Rosenthal, J. (1991). *Righteous Realists.* Baton Rouge: University of Louisiana Press.

Schmitt, C. (2004). *The Nomos of the Earth.* New York: Telos.

Shue, H. (1983). *Basic Rights.* Princeton: Princeton University Press.

Smith, M. J. (1986). *Realist Thought from Weber to Kissinger.* Baton Rouge: University of Louisiana Press.

Taylor, A. J. P. (1954). *The Struggle for Mastery in Europe.* Oxford: Clarendon Press.

Vincent, R. J. (1986). *Human Rights and International Relations.* Cambridge: Cambridge University Press.

Waltz, Kenneth (1979). *Theory of International Politics.* Reading, Mass.: Addison-Wesley.

Walzer, Michael (1977). *Just and Unjust Wars.* New York: Basic Books.

Wendt, Alexander (1999). *Social Theory of International Politics.* Cambridge: Cambridge University Press.

Wheeler, N. J. (1992). 'Pluralist and Solidarist Conceptions of International Society: Bull and Vincent on Humanitarian Intervention', *Millennium: Journal of International Studies*, 21: pp. 463–87.

Wheeler, N. (2000). *Saving Strangers.* Oxford: Oxford University Press.

Wight, M. (1966). 'Western Values in International Relations', in H. Butterfield and M. Wight, eds, *Diplomatic Investigations.* London: George Allen and Unwin.

Wight, Martin (1978). *Power Politics.* Leicester: Leicester University Press.

9

The Liberal Peace, Democratic Accountability, and the Challenge of Globalization

Michael W. Doyle

In recent years global democratization rose to the international agenda as the three peak global economic associations all came under attack. In Seattle, at the meeting of the new World Trade Organization (WTO), and in Washington at the meetings of the World Bank and the International Monetary Fund (IMF), a diverse collection of labour unions and environmentalists from the industrial North and trade and finance ministers from the developing countries of the South each launched sharply critical barbs. The critics successfully disrupted the WTO meeting that had been designed to launch (and celebrate) a 'Millennium Round' of further reductions of barriers to global trade. The aims of the critics were very different, but together they derailed the entire proceedings and exposed important differences in priority among the developed states, and particularly the United States and Europe. Charlene Barshefsky, the US Trade Representative and the meeting's chair, later conceded, 'We needed a process which had a greater degree of internal transparency and inclusion to accommodate a larger and more diverse membership' (Khor, 1999). This highly regarded trade-o-crat had come to recognize that the eminently oligarchic WTO needed some democratization (as yet undefined).

Joseph Stiglitz, formerly the chief economist of the World Bank, offered a still broader criticism of the Bank's sister institution, the International Monetary Fund. The IMF was designed to rescue countries in temporary balance-of-payments difficulties. It actually operates, Stiglitz charges, more like a bureaucratic cabal than an international rescue team:

> The IMF likes to go about its business without outsiders asking too many questions. In theory, the fund supports democratic institutions in the nations it assists. In practice, it undermines the democratic process by imposing policies. Officially, of course, the IMF doesn't 'impose' anything. It 'negotiates' the conditions for receiving aid. But all the power in the negotiations is on one side – the IMF's – and the fund rarely allows sufficient time for broad consensus-building or even widespread consultations with either parliaments or civil society. Sometimes the IMF dispenses with the pretense of openness altogether and negotiates secret covenants. (Stiglitz, 2000)

Two themes resonate through the denunciations: global governance and global (or international) democratization. The key question is how they relate to each other. Three issues connect them. The first is the broad ethical question of how could and should the world be organized politically.[1] I present the claims for the leading organizational political framework today, one designed to promote world order while recognizing the reality of sovereign independence. This is the Kantian idea of a pacific union of free republics, or the liberal democratic peace. More controversially, I then argue that, however good the Kantian peace has been and could be, it has significant limitations that have been exposed by increasing globalization. Globalization both sustains elements of the Kantian peace and also undermines it, making it less sustainable and indeed vitiating some of the democracy on which it is founded. And third, I discuss a range of possible responses to the challenges that globalization poses for the existing international order. I conclude with a comment on why global democratic sovereignty is not yet viable although global norms – more democratically derived – seem needed to promote more perfect a union of order and democracy.

Global Political Theory

How could and should the world be politically organized? That is, how should one assess various forms of political organization of world politics with respect to their ability to fulfil a set of human values that would be very widely shared – even if not exactly in the same way – around the world? Take, for example, these values: peace; prosperity; national independence, cultural identity or pluralism (so that people can express their identities in some public form); and individual human rights (including democracy, participation, equality and self-determination).

How well do various schemes of international order fulfil these basic human values at the global scale? Political philosophers have told us that the international system is a mix of hard choices among values. The political theorist Michael Walzer has reformulated those choices well in an essay that explores the range of values from little to much international governance, that is from national autonomy (and international anarchy) to a global, hierarchical, centralized government over all individuals (Walzer, 2000). There is no single arrangement that obtains everything – one that procures international peace, domestic peace, liberty, democracy, prosperity, and pluralistic identity. Instead, while the virtues of the nation-state are domestic peace and perhaps national identity and national democracy, those same virtues are the foundations of international anarchy, geopolitical insecurity and international economic rivalry. Global government can be a foundation for global peace and a single efficient world market, and maybe even a global democratic polity, but it could also be the institution that represses national particularity, the global 'soul-less despotism' against which the eighteenth-century German philosopher Immanuel Kant eloquently warned the liberals of his day. In between global authority and national independence, one can imagine confederal arrangements that allow room for a diversity of civil societies, but again only at the cost of both national autonomy and international insecurity. The message of Michael Walzer's spectrum of global governance is hard choices: there is no comprehensive ideal solution.

Although there is no perfect solution to the problem of implementing human values on a global scale, the Kantian liberal peace lays claim to being the optimal combination, the one that gets us the most peace and global prosperity at the least cost in liberty, independence, and the least trampling on national identities.

Immanuel Kant's essay *Perpetual Peace*, published in 1795, was a direct response and alternative to both the autarkic nation-state and a sovereign world government. The key to the liberal argument is the claim that by establishing domestic liberty, political participation, and market exchange one can have the international payoff of peace as well.[2] Kant described a decentralized, self-enforcing peace achieved without the world government that the global governance claim posits as necessary. This is a claim that has resonated in the modern literature on the 'democratic peace'. It draws on the ideas of American presidents as diverse as Woodrow Wilson, Ronald Reagan and Bill Clinton and British prime ministers from Gladstone to Blair. Promoting freedom and 'enlarging' the zone of democratic rule were the doctrinal centrepieces of their foreign policies. Advocates of the 'democratic peace' have claimed that over time, country by democratizing country, a peace would spread to cover the entire world, building one world order – democratic, free, prosperous and peaceful.

Kant's argument was much more complicated, presented in three necessary conditions, each an 'article' in a hypothetical peace 'treaty' he asks sovereigns to sign. First, states should adopt a liberal constitutional, representative, republican form of government which would constrain the state such that the sovereign would, on average, usually follow the interest of most of the people, or the majority. Second, the citizens of this liberal, constitutional, representative republic should affirm a commitment to human rights, one holding that all human beings are morally equal. Then states that represent liberal democratic majorities in their own countries will regard with respect other states that also represent free and equal citizens. Tolerance for various national cultures and trust emerges among fellow liberal republics, as does non-aggression and peace. Third, given this trust, states will lower the barriers that have been raised to protect the state from invasion or exploitation in the competition of the balance of power. Trade, tourism and other forms of transnational contact grow, leading to prosperity, reinforcing mutual understanding, increasing opportunities for profitable exchange and producing contacts that offset in their multiplicity the occasional sources of conflict.

For many, this seems the optimal equilibrium, given both the world as it is and a commitment to the values of peace, liberty, prosperity, national identity and democratic participation. Does this mean that there are no tradeoffs? Far from it; for, again, there is no such thing as a perfect political equilibrium.

There are two major limitations. One is that this peace is limited only to other liberal republics. Outside the liberal peace, realpolitik and, at best, rational balance-of-power rule. International respect is only extended to other, similarly republican liberal states. The very same principle of trust that operates among liberal republics tends to corrode attempts at cooperation between liberal republics and autocratic states, whether modern dictatorships or traditional monarchies. The liberal warns: 'If the autocrat is so ruthless that he is unwilling to trust his own citizens to participate in the polity and control his behaviour, just think what he will do to us.' Liberals then raise trade and other barriers, ensuring that conflicts are not dampened. The prejudice may be true. Many dictators – think of Napoleon or Hitler – have been aggressive. Many dictators, however, are also quite shy and cautious. They like the benefits of being absolute ruler and may fear jeopardizing the quiescence of their subjects with costly foreign adventures. The distrust and hostility are probably thus a joint product. The autocrats do like to gain the profits and glory of expansion and their subjects – cannon fodder and taxpayers – have no constitutional right to stop them. At the same time, the liberals are prejudiced against the autocratic regime and do not extend to those regimes the normal trust in international exchanges or negotiations and may, indeed, launch 'freedom fighters' against them. Although the record of wars between liberals and non-liberals and the long history of nineteenth- and twentieth-century liberal imperialism testify to the depth of this tension, it can be overcome by autocratic prudence and liberal statesmanship.[3]

The second limitation is associated with the assumption of minimal interdependence. In order for liberal republics to remain effectively sovereign and self-determining, allowing free citizens to govern themselves, material ties to other liberal republics would need to be limited. Kant assumed that those ties were limited to non-aggression, collective security and hospitality (free trade and mutual transit privileges). This is 'light' interdependence[4] – some mutual sensitivity, some limited vulnerability, but not enough to challenge the liberal republic's ability to govern itself in the face of social and economic forces outside itself. Kantianism presumes marginal trade, marginal investment, marginal tourism; not extensive interdependence. This second limitation is increasingly unrealistic today. Does modern interdependence challenge the Kantian liberal peace? Can the liberal peace sustain extensive, 'heavy' interdependence? That is the question to which I turn next.

Challenges of Globalization

Global interdependence is the first challenge to the sustainability of the liberal peace. Can Kantian peace operate in a much more intensive environment of social and economic exchange? Globalization's second challenge is to the legitimacy of the liberal democratic system. Can the people truly govern themselves when much of their social and economic interaction is with other societies outside their borders and outside the reach of their representative government?

Globalization I

The first challenge to the sustainability of liberal peace was articulated in one of the great books of the twentieth century, Karl Polanyi's *The Great Transformation*.[5] His book is a profound study of the effects of the market economy both domestically and internationally. Polanyi's argument, in short, holds that marketization makes peace unsustainable. Kantian liberals hoped that over time, with some ups and downs, international markets would tend to liberalize non-liberal societies, leading to more and more liberal republics, which would eventually cover the whole world and thus create global peace. Polanyi says it cannot work that way: there are built-in sources of corrosion produced by economic interdependence that make liberal politics and the liberal peace unsustainable.

Polanyi acknowledges that, indeed, the combination of the domestic market economy, political representation, the gold standard and the international balance of power did create a sustaining circle of mutually reinforcing economic contacts that helped produce the peace of the nineteenth century – the Long Peace of 1815 to 1914. But, he warns us, contrary to Immanuel Kant, trade is not just an exchange of commodities at arm's length or at the border. Trade is a revolutionary form of exchange. Exchanging commodities changes the value in relative and absolute terms of the factors that go into producing the commodities that are exchanged. As was later elaborated in a set of theorems concerning 'factor price equalization', trade in commodities has potentially revolutionary effects in changing the returns to various factors – land, labour and capital – that go into the production of these commodities. Countries tend to export commodities that intensively use the factors with which they are most endowed and import commodities that embody scarce domestic factors. Trade thus increases demand, price, and eventually factor returns for relatively abundant factors as it shrinks price and return for scarce domestic factors. Together, this leads toward global factor price equalization (in theory, with many assumptions, and thus real-world qualifications).[6]

In 1795, however, Kant seemed to assume that trade simply was arm's-length commodity exchange. He neglected the potential effects of commodity trade on the factors that go into the production of the commodities exchanged (land, labour and capital). Why is this important? Trade, whether national or international, destabilizes the social relations among land, labour and capital, disrupting relations that had become embedded in social hierarchies and in political power. Treating land, labour and capital as commodities dislocates established communities, village life, regional life, the relations among classes, industries and sectors and eventually changes the international balance of power. Trade therefore produces a reaction. Farmers do not like to have the prices of their farm products drop to the prices set by more competitive rivals. Consumers might prefer the lower prices, but the usually better organized producers resist. Labourers and manufacturers do not want to compete with labour that makes one-tenth of their income or with firms that have costs a fraction of their own, whether in a newly integrated national or international market.

When people's livelihoods are marginalized, they tend to react. Polanyi recounts that, at the end of the nineteenth century, the reaction to the market took the form of either social democracy on the left or fascism on the right. National economies attempted to protect themselves from the swings of the global economy by raising tariffs in order to protect national consumption or by launching imperial conquests to expand national resources. The resulting rivalry produced, Polanyi continues, the First World War, the Great Depression and its competitive devaluations, and eventually the Second World War. Liberal peace, prosperity, democracy collapsed under the weight of heavy interdependence.

Globalization II

Following the Second World War, the allied leaders successfully rebuilt liberal interdependence, constructing a new way to mix together democracy and social stability. They developed a series of safety nets that would make people less vulnerable to the vagaries of the market both domestically and internationally. Rather than adjusting to an autarkic world of intense national competition (as in the 1930s) or letting trade and finance flow freely in response to market incentives (the nineteenth century), the capitalist democracies in the postwar period constructed the IMF, the GATT and the World Bank to help regulate and politically manage the shape of the world market economy. Trade was opened on a regulated basis. Currencies were made convertible when economies could sustain the convertibility and cushioned with financing to help maintain parities. Long-term financing, a form of global Keynesianism, was provided first to Europe and then (in lesser amounts) to the developing countries in order to spread opportunity and reduce the conflicts between the 'haves' and 'have nots' that had wracked the interwar period. All this helped promote stability, cooperation, and solidarity in the Cold War struggle against the Soviet Union. Thus, with a set of political-economic policies that have been called 'embedded liberalism', the postwar leaders of the West found a way to manage the tensions that Polanyi had described, the dangers of marketization (Ruggie, 1982).

It was good while it lasted, but by the 1980s frustration with over-regulation, falling productivity and the oil shock, together with a demand for ever more profit and cheap goods, produced a move back to marketization, the Thatcher–Reagan 'magic of the marketplace'. Reacting to the welfare state's restrictions on consumption and profit (and seeking a more dynamic spur to industrial reallocation and profits), many of the protections embedded in the postwar political economy were relaxed. Increasing trade, floating exchange rates, more open financial markets and privatization became the 'Washington Consensus', the watchword of international economic orthodoxy and the standard prescription of the IMF for countries experiencing balance-of-payment difficulties.

As the barriers to global marketization fell, the forces that propelled ever closer interdependence accelerated. One force accelerating the effects of global marketization was advances in communication and transportation technology. The costs of transportation and communication began to fall radically in the postwar period. In 1930 the cost of a telephone call between New York and London was (in 1990 dollars) $245 for three minutes. By 1998, the same call cost 35 cents – a vast reduction in the cost of communications. That and the related explosion of the Internet are what makes much of global banking – and all of global academia – possible. If we were still paying $245 for three minutes across the Atlantic, there would be less that we could afford to say.

The second force was trade. There has been a near revolution in the amount of trade tying the countries of the world together. Even the United States, which because of its continental scale is one of the less interdependent economies, has experienced a large change in the impact of trade. In 1910 (that is, during Globalization I) 11 per cent of US gross domestic product (GDP) was in trade (exports and imports). By 1950 this fell to 9 per cent. That is what the Globalization I crisis – the Great Depression and the two world wars – was all about. But by 1995 trade had risen to 24 per cent. This is more than double the extent of trade interdependence in the previous era of globalization. In the Germany of 1910, 38 per cent of its GDP was in exports and imports. By 1950 this fell to 27 per cent; by 1995 up to 46 per cent. The UK, the leader of the first wave of globalization and the most globalized economy at the time, in 1910 had 44 per cent of its GDP in trade. In 1950 this dropped to 30 per cent. By 1995 57 per cent was again in exchangeables. Among the highly developed industrial economies, only Japan is less dependent upon trade and investment income than it was in 1910. It is the only major industrialized economy that is less globalized now than it was in 1910.

And lest you think that trade alone is globalizing the world, you should examine foreign direct investment (FDI) and portfolio flows of finance. Between 1980 and 1994 trade doubled; but in that same period foreign direct investment grew six times, and portfolio flows of finance grew by nine times.

As in the earlier age of globalization, these flows of trade and finance are beginning to change the operation of the world's political economy – altering what is profitable, what is politically sustainable, and what is not. Perhaps most strikingly from an economic point of view, the world now increasingly appears as one large market, a single division of labour. From the standpoint of the multinational company, production strategies are genuinely global, as parts of the production process are allocated to subsidiaries and contractors in countries or regions around the world where they are most cost-effective. This has formed a global process of production and marketing that is a highly interdependent whole at the global level. In the old global interdependence, cars and shoes were traded among many countries or even made in many countries by one company; now one company makes cars or shoes globally with component factories spread around the world.[7]

Challenges to Liberal Democratic Peace

The new globalization poses three challenges to the liberal scheme of global democratic peace. In addition to the widely noted effects of transboundary 'collective bads', such as ozone depletion and cross-border pollution that tie national fates together, the three challenges have emerged: commodification, inequality and insecurity.

Commodification

The World Trade Organization meeting and demonstrations in Seattle against it demonstrate the first challenge, a tradeoff between globally regulated market prosperity and democracy. The tradeoff is becoming more politically costly as interdependence increases. Politically, the democratic challenge was well expressed recently by Edward Mortimer (then *Financial Times* foreign editor) when he said that too much democracy kills the market (that's Polanyi's account of national and social democracy in reaction to Globalization I) and, on the other hand, too much market kills democracy (this is the threat some see is posed by Globalization II). Commodities seem to rule citizens.

US environmentalists struggled for years in order to lobby for a US Endangered Species Act that protects turtles inadvertently caught in the course of the fishing for shrimp. It requires that shrimp nets be designed in a way that permits turtles to escape (the Turtle Excluder Device). The environmentalists struggled long and hard in order to pass the Bill, but they forgot that a new arena of interdependence had engendered a new arena of regulation. When the US government attempted to reduce the impact of the bill on favoured Caribbean Basin allies, the WTO not surprisingly declared the effort discriminatory and, therefore, illegal under international trade law. When the US government revised its guidelines to remove discrimination, environmentalists charged that it weakened the protection for turtles, creating loopholes that were soon exploited by Australia and Brazil (WTO, 1999).

In the European Union, many of its consumer advocates struggled for a campaign to protect European consumers from genetically engineered food – so-called 'Frankenfood'. The WTO has yet to rule on this issue that pits American corporations against European food activists. Signs of more sympathy toward health regulation are recently in evidence in WTO decisions. But the WTO earlier ruled that bans against hormone-treated food were a form of trade discrimination and illegal under international trade law (Meunier, 2000).

In a wider challenge, the developing countries have insisted upon the right not to be bound by the standards of labour safety, child labour prohibitions, and the minimum wages that hold within the industrialized world. They believe that it is only by taking advantage of their large supplies of talented, hard-working and inexpensive labour that they will be able to develop their countries. But the United States, responding to pressure from labour unions and human rights advocates, argued at Seattle that the US-level standards on labour rights and environmental protection should be applied to all traded goods. The developing countries saw this as a denial of their ability to choose their own development path. At the WTO in Seattle, moreover, the developing countries were outraged by the prevalence of so-called 'green room' procedures under which the wealthy industrial countries caucus and decide how to manage the WTO. The developing-country majority of the membership want much broader participation in order to avoid having rules imposed upon them that favour the industrialized market economies. National policymakers in the developing world thank the World Bank and IMF for the doors to development they open and for not as yet succumbing to the demands for increased global regulation made by the environmentalist protesters at Seattle and Washington (Aguirre-Sacassa, 2000).

In each of these cases, commodification through globally regulated norms of non-discrimination – however efficient and fair from a global point of view – erode democratic, or at least national democratic, accountability.

Inequality

The second challenge to democratization concerns both intra-national and international equality. Globalization allows for those who are most efficient to earn the most. That is what markets usually do. And as the barriers to global sales, production and investment fall, inequality – at least in the short to middle run – tends to rise.

Globalization does not appear to exacerbate poverty and may indeed contribute toward its reduction. Instances can be found in which global pressures, such as those to resolve the East Asian financial crisis of 1997, hurt the poor in a variety of countries, most notably Indonesia. But, worldwide, the proportion of those in extreme poverty ($1 a day) is falling, although this is largely a product of growth in China and India, while elsewhere in Africa, Eastern Europe and Central Asia the proportions of those in poverty are increasing. Moreover, the absolute number of those in poverty does not appear to be increasing – and may be falling – from the 1.2 billion of 1990 (Panagariya, 2003).[8]

Inequality appears to be the problem. Domestically in the United States, beginning about 1975, the economic fates of the top 5 per cent and bottom 20 per cent of the US population substantially diverged. By 1995, the real family income of the top 5 per cent stood at 130 per cent of the 1973 level, but over the same period, the real family income of the bottom 20 per cent stayed at the 1973 level. Internationally, we see what appear to be similar trends in a comparison of the OECD (the rich industrial economies) to the rest of the world between the 1970s and 1995. In 1970, the OECD countries enjoyed 66 per cent of global GDP. By 1978, their share was up to 68 per cent; in 1989, to 71 per cent; and in 1995, to 78 per cent. The rest of the entire world lived on the complement to that: their figures go from 34 per cent in 1970, sinking to 22 per cent in 1995 (Gilpin, 2000, p. 307).[9] In per capita terms, while the real per capita GDP of the developing countries increased from $936 to $1,417 from 1980 to 2000, in the developed countries it soared from $20,397 to $30,557 (UNCTAD, 2004, p. 18). The difficulty lies in explaining unequal growth. Some note the progress of India and China in recent years and differences in growth rates between open economies (3.5 per cent) and closed economies (less than 1 per cent) and therefore see trade interdependence leading to increasing global equality. Others noting various barriers to the trade of developing countries read the evidence very differently.[10]

Whatever the deep sources and potential cures, the most productive are winning, accumulating wealth in their own hands. The consequences of globalization appear to be favouring some over others – the rising tide is not lifting all the boats at the same rate. Not surprisingly, demands for accountability rise.

Insecurity

The third challenge is insecurity. Kantian liberalism produces security and peace (at least among the liberal republics). But globalization challenges the stability of liberal geopolitics in two ways. First, what Americans call globalization is what many others call Americanization. That is, the US leading role within the world economy which to Americans appears as an economic issue of dollars and cents is to other countries a power issue, one fraught with control and guns. Second, global rules for trade and investment have allowed China to benefit from its high savings rate and labour productivity, becoming one of the fastest-growing economies in the world. If you add rapid growth to a large population (and if China continues to grow at recent past rates), then soon after the year 2020 China will have a GDP that is not only larger than that of the United States or Europe, but as big as the two combined. From an economic point of view, the prospect of many more Chinese consumers and producers should make everyone content. But from a geopolitical point of view, China's growth entails a massive shift of world political power Eastward. That makes the statespeople of the United States and Europe nervous, especially if, referring again to the Kantian liberal argument, China does not democratize.

Responses

There have been a variety of responses of widely varying purpose and consequence to these three challenges. States are being tempted to reduce interdependence to fit national jurisdiction, expand effective national jurisdiction to internalize interdependence, and, in better measures, explore new forms of international cooperation. Nonetheless, the key question we face today is whether and how the liberal equilibrium can be reinvigorated, reincorporating a combined prospect of peace, prosperity and self-government.

Protectionism

Polanyi called this the 'Crustacean' strategy – one that reinforced the hard shell of the nation-state. It focuses on each nation protecting itself from globalization. This is familiar to us. In the United States, Ross Perot and Pat Buchanan made these kind of arguments; in France, Jose Bove (the anti-McDonald's impresario); and in Austria, Jorg Haider. Their themes are simple: 'globalization is a threat to the cultural integrity and prosperity of many of us who are vulnerable, it is a threat to democracy, to our way of life. Let us build a thick shell.'

In a much more sophisticated version, this is the heart of claims made by the organizers at Seattle. Lori Wallach, the chief organizer of the wide coalition that disrupted the WTO meeting, described her alternative to current globalization in this way: 'There would be a global regime of rules that more than anything create the political space for the kinds of value decisions that mechanisms like the WTO now make, at a level where people living with the results can hold decision makers accountable' (*Foreign Policy*, 2000). Interdependence would then be made subject to the reach of democratic accountability at the local level. This could lead to effective global rules for interdependence, but it is more likely to build national 'shells'. Apart from national non-discrimination (national treatment) provisions, each country would make its own rules for environmental standards, intellectual property, child labour, wages, and have a right to bar any import that it determined did not reflect those standards.

These movements may create democratic control and they may be good for national solidarity, but they could be very bad for overall national prosperity, as nation retaliates against nation for each restriction it finds unjustifiable. A recent study by a group of economists who are associated with the European Union estimates the possible benefits from the next Millennium Round of the WTO at $400 billion per year.[11] For many, whether rich or poor, that is too much extra world income to forgo. If this study is correct, there is a great deal to be lost if global trade suddenly starts closing down, or global investments start being drawn back.

National champions

If protectionism is a 'crustacean' strategy, we can extend Polanyi's aquatic metaphor, bringing into view the 'sea slug' strategy. The sea slug, a voracious and non-discriminating eater, consumes anything that is smaller than itself. This is the strategy of national champions. The nation-state supports its own firms in order to compete to win more global sales and seeks to lure foreign firms, increasing shares of inward FDI for the national economy. The Clinton administration was very successful in persuading Saudi Arabia to buy just American aircraft, built by McDonnell/Boeing, then headquartered in Seattle. The large sale included both F-15s and passenger airliners and was very popular in the American Northwest. The sale was not so popular in France (which also engages in the same practice) where Airbus was seen to be just as good a plane. Why did the Europeans not get the sale to Saudi Arabia? Many speculate that the US security relationship with the Gulf, and particularly the protection offered against the ambitions of

Saddam Hussein, had much to do with the business deal. But that does not make the French or other Europeans happy. Nor were Americans pleased when Qaddafi gave the contract to build the Mediterranean pipeline from Libya solely to a European consortium.

To the extent that states try to foster national champions or subsidize inward FDI to attract capital and jobs, they produce similar behaviour by other countries. This may benefit international consumers. It may also lead to a 'race to the bottom' with fewer and fewer environmental and labour standards, or increased international conflicts, as short-term prosperity is again pitted against long-run democratic autonomy.

Democratic solidarity

Let us turn to a third strategy, 'democratic solidarity'. Here statespeople seek to extend the liberal political peace into an economic arrangement: forget about the rest of the world, let us build a stronger WTO for the democracies, a democratic WTO. (Bill Antholis, recently of National Security Council's economic staff, is writing a fascinating book on this topic.) Why not have a democratic WTO where we will solve our problems more easily than we would in a global WTO? If you look at the US trade bill extending 'most favoured nation' status to China and exempting it from annual reviews, one of the things that made it more difficult for the administration to mobilize a Congressional majority is that China is regularly vulnerable to charges that it is threatening Taiwan with invasion and abusing its own nationals' human rights. If democracies limited their most extensive trade privileges to the area of fellow democracies, they would find progress toward further integration easier, or at least free from the baggage of political strife over human rights and security concerns.

The problem, of course, is that such a 'democratic WTO' leaves China and other rapidly developing countries out. Excluding the potentially biggest, fastest-growing economy in the world is not good for global prosperity or for global cooperation on other issues. If you will pardon me for quoting President Lyndon Johnson's apt reference to the higher logic of cooperating with an opponent, recall his words: 'Do you want him inside the tent pissing out, or outside the tent pissing in?' That is the China problem. If China is not part of the WTO, it is very likely to cause an immense amount of strife in the world political economy and be absent from important efforts to curb pollution or stabilize East Asian security.

Disaggregated cooperation

The fourth response – disaggregated cooperation – is the most pragmatic. It is 'disaggregated'. Proponents urge us to break down and multilateralize the problem. For them, the issue is not that national jurisdiction cannot manage an extra-national issue; it is that we need to establish international jurisdiction to manage an international problem. No one nation has a legitimate democratic claim to complete control; many nations, including those subject to non-democratic states, are affected and thus have a legitimate claim to a voice in its resolution.

Advocates of this strategy would allow the multinational corporations (MNCs) to deal with other MNCs, and markets to solve as many problems as they can. State bureaucracies will scramble to keep up, doing less than may be ideal but enough to avoid catastrophe. Genetically engineered food may be sold with less controversy if the United States labels organic food and then lets consumers buy it or not as they wish. US organic food exports, having been certified, could be sold in Europe. Consumers, not governments, will decide; thereby depoliticizing the issue (hopefully). Or, international institutions will allow beleaguered states and their bureaucrats to establish multilateral jurisdiction over fugitive transnational actors. States will find a 'new sovereignty' instantiated through their participation in international institutions (Chayes and Chayes, 1995). Courts, moreover, will deal with courts, bureaucrats with bureaucrats, experts with experts, thus taking problems out of 'politics' and solving the problems pragmatically (Reinicke, 1998; Slaughter, 1997). Indeed, international institutions dedicated to free trade may better represent the true interests of democratic national majorities than actual national legislatures with their well-known susceptibility to special-interest legislation (Petersmann, 1995).[12]

Unfortunately, there are some problems that are just not pragmatic. For the environmental organization that worked so hard to reform the Endangered Species Act in order to protect turtles, a turtle was not a technical question that they were willing to see negotiated away. It became a part of their own sense of identity, their own sense of moral worth, and their sense of responsibility to the globe – not something that they would let the bureaucrats decide. Feeling less than fully enfranchised in Washington, they had no reason to think that their views would receive a better hearing in Geneva, whose accountable connection to them was even more remote. And second, when things get tougher – that is, when the world economy moves into the next recession – it will be even more difficult to delegate to careful bureaucrats and their allegedly objective global criteria.

Global democratization

Responding to the concerns noted above, some have begun to wonder, 'Don't we need some increased accountability and increased legitimacy to contain and govern the practical negotiations among the experts? Don't we need to have norms that are more broadly shared, or even decisions that are legitimate because people across borders have participated in outlining their direction?'[13] We want expert pilots to fly the planes we ride in, but do we want them to choose our destinations (Dahl, 1989, ch. 5)? We are thus concerned about the dangers of increasingly expert, non-democratic control of key financial decisions (Berman and McNamara, 1999). For some it is now time for a global parliament or civic assembly, structured on the model of the European parliament in Strasbourg (Heinrich, n.d.; Falk and Strauss, 2000). That pillar of the burgeoning EU represents voters across Europe and operates through cross-national parties, not national delegations. Others hoped that the recent Millennium Assembly of the United Nations which provided a forum for non-governmental organizations from around the world, would take a first step in this direction.

Realistically, however, no strong version of global democracy is viable at the present time.[14] We will not soon see global legislation deciding new regulatory standards for the global economy. Why not? Because global democracy is not about being willing to win democratically, it is about being willing to *lose* democratically. None of the popular advocates of increased democratization, whether in Seattle or Strasbourg or New Delhi, is willing to lose an issue and accept it because it went through a democratic process. The world is simply too unequal and too diverse. To give an example, the top one-fifth of the countries have 74 times the income of the bottom one-fifth of the countries, and it is getting worse. That is more than double the greatest degree of inequality within the most unequal domestic economy, the Brazilian economy, where the ratio between the top fifth and the bottom fifth is 32 to 1; more than double the Brazilian ratio, and yet Brazil itself has found its democratic processes repeatedly subject to extra-constitutional pressures.

With respect to culture, moreover, the globe falls far short of the preconditions of ordinary democracy. India, the largest and one of the most linguistically diverse democracies, has 81 per cent of its population describing itself as Hindu and an elite all of whom are fluent in English. That is a huge core of common identity that helps sustain the Indian democracy despite all of its diversity and internal dissention. There is no such core identity in the globe today. There is no single such identity (other than the thin identity of basic human dignity) to which 81 per cent of the world will subscribe.

Our primitive political global condition is reflected in disputes about the very meaning of global democracy. Is the world more democratic when the majority of nations decide, when the most populous nations decide, when only democratic nations participate, or when the majority of the world's people decide? Unfortunately, there is as yet no agreed meaning of 'global democratization'.

Therefore, I suggest that while there is a need for democratic legitimation, we must be more moderate in our democratizing ambitions. For instance, international institutions will benefit from better mechanisms to improve transparency and accountability to those directly affected, such as by the establishment of ombudsmen and other fora suited to the redress of grievances (Keohane, 2003; Bradlow, 1994). The Security Council and other consequential organs of international authorization will benefit from an even more diverse representation of national interests and an inclusion of demographically under-represented nations and regions (Annan, 2002).

But none of those valuable reforms will directly provide a greater voice for the peoples of the world in setting goals. The role of global democratization should be limited to helping to develop global norms. Not legislation, but deliberation over norms will make the process of cooperation among the bureaucrats easier, more readily achievable, more legitimate, less contested. We must be very modest because norms do not usually do that much work. What they do, however, is make it easier for national politicians and international bureaucrats to cut pragmatic deals. Therefore, global democratization should be limited to endorsing measures such as those advocated in the Carlsson–Ramphal Commission, the Global Neighborhood report (Carlsson and Ramphal, 1995).

In addition to sending diplomats to the annual meetings of the United Nations General Assembly, we should also send legislators. Every country can put five members in the General Assembly. At least two of them should be elected from the legislatures of their home countries. Bringing in the other branches of government, those somewhat more tied to the people, may help to begin to create a transmission belt between home and globe, fostering a more legitimate articulation of global standards at the international level. The hope is that these elected legislators will take the role seriously and participate actively in the annual general debate in the fall of each year and interject a sense of democratic legitimacy and accountability.

Only a few countries, such as the United States, bother to appoint legislators or public delegates to the General Assembly. Washington's proximity and the foreign affairs responsibilities of the Congress, rather than any unusual internationalism, presumably account for this anomaly. But all countries have the prerogative of doing so. When they hopefully do, it will be important to avoid trampling on the formal rules of sovereignty and state responsibility. Only the diplomatic representatives of the national government should have the right to express sovereign will in UN voting. Elected legislators could, however, play a vital role in biennial Assembly debates concerning the monitoring of major international commitments, such as the Millennium Goals, which set forth an agenda in peace and security, human rights and democratization, development and the alleviation of extreme poverty and a range of other global commitments.

The second way to enhance global normative articulation and transparent accountability is to engage civil society. In 1955 there were fewer than 2,000 international non-governmental organizations (NGOs); today there are more than 20,000 (Annan, 2000, p. 70). None of them is genuinely democratic; their virtue is that they are voluntary and broad-based. But it is worth establishing an annual global forum that brings together representatives of global civil society.[15] Meeting the week before the General Assembly meets each year, the current Department of Public Information Annual NGO Forum does not quite serve this purpose; it serves more as an information and trade fair for NGOs. A stronger role would see NGOs invited from all over the world to present reports, discuss and issue recommendations (by majority vote) about global standards for the environment, humanitarian intervention, international economic assistance and reforms of international institutions such as the IMF, the World Bank, or the United Nations itself.

Conclusion

These recommendations are far from a cure-all. Electing legislators from non-democratic legislatures to the UN General Assembly does not enhance global democracy strikingly. Others will ask who elected the NGOs, for whom there is no internal process of democratic accountability to their members or to those whom their policies affect. But, on the other hand, merely that act of debating in a global forum about global problems and who is there legitimately and who is not – all in the same room, talking about global problems – will itself be a process which helps build global norms and gives more voice to those who bear the consequences of globalization. This is far short of democratic legitimation. In terms of democratic evolution, this represents much less than a modern equivalent of the meeting of the English barons at Runnymede in 1215 – a cautious consultation far short of accountability. There will be mounting tension between prosperity, stability and accountability. Global interdependence will subject the liberal peace to increasing stress. But it can be the preliminary to increasingly responsible deliberation. And that may well be the best we can do in the world as it is today.

Notes

I thank Daniel Noble and Huda Shashaa for research assistance. The chapter revises and updates an article published in the *Review of International Studies*, 26 (2000): pp. 81–94. Copyright © British International Studies Association.

1 A similar debate engages the European Union. See, e.g., Sandholtz and Stone, 1998; Hayward, 1995; and Keohane and Hoffmann, 1991.
2 I contributed a two-part essay to the elaboration of Kant's proposition; see Doyle, 1983. The extensive debate is well presented in Brown et al., 1996. I found 68 such liberal republics as of 1990 in Doyle, 1997, table 8.1, including countries from all major religions, levels of economic development and areas. As of 2002, there were 103 such countries, using the same coding rules.
3 For an interesting discussion of the effects of liberalism on a general disposition to abide by international law see Slaughter, 1992, 1995; Alvarez, 2001.
4 For a discussion of the features of interdependence see Keohane and Nye, 1977.
5 Polanyi, 1980. Originally published in 1944.
6 Theoretically, any trade, even at arm's length, should equalize factor prices, but tariff, transportation and other barriers mute trade's effects. Movements of factors – labour, capital or technology – multiply the effects of trade in commodities. The key theoretical contributions were made by Heckscher et al. For a non-technical survey, see Williamson, 1983, ch. 3. For a contemporary study of the collapse of what I call 'Globalization I', see James, 2001.
7 Drucker (1997) calls this 'transnational strategy'. Whitman (1999) explores how American companies that were once stable, lumbering, globe-striding giants with paternalistic ties to their home communities have become lean, mean and footloose.
8 Also, see the UN annual Millennium Goals Report.
9 For global GDP comparisons, see Beg, 2000, table 2; and Birdsall, 2001.
10 See, e.g., Dollar and Kraay, 2002, and a critical response by Galbraith and Wells-Dang, 2002. Contrary to both, Rodrik (2001) has argued that domestic institutional innovations make much more difference than trade in promoting growth.
11 http://www.europa.eu.int/comm/trade/2000_round/ecowtomr.htm
12 Also, see the valuable discussion of this and related issues in Rustiala, 2000.
13 A good introduction to this issue is in Archibugi and Held, 1995. For further discussion of cosmopolitan individual rights and democratic governance, see Pogge, 1997 and Thompson, 1999.
14 For one prominent critic of the idea, see Dahl, 1999. Dahl focuses on the extent of delegation international organizations currently embody. My criticism is different below.
15 For a valuable discussion of how civil society organizations have developed a role in global governance, see Charnowitz, 2003.

References

Aguirre-Sacassa, Francisco (2000). 'A Debt of Thanks to the World Bank', *Financial Times*, 4 May.
Alvarez, Jose (2001). 'Do Liberal States Behave Better?', *European Journal of International Law*, 12.
Annan, Kofi (2000). *We the Peoples: The Role of the United Nations in the 21st Century*. New York: UN.
Annan, Kofi (2002). 'Democracy as an International Issue', *Global Governance*, 8: pp. 135–40.
Archibugi, D. and D. Held, eds (1995). *Cosmopolitan Democracy*. Cambridge: Polity.
Beg, Tahir (2000). 'Globalization, Development and Debt-Management', *The Balance* (Spring), available at http://balanceddevelopment.org/articles/globalization.html.

Berman, Sheri and Kate McNamara (1999). 'Bank on Democracy', *Foreign Affairs*, 78(2): pp. 2–8.

Birdsall, Nancy (2001). 'Why Inequality Matters', *Ethics and International Affairs*, 15(2): pp. 3–28.

Bradlow, Daniel (1994). 'International Organizations and Private Complaints: The World Bank Inspection Panel', *Virginia International Law*, 34: p. 553.

Brown, M. E. et al., eds (1996). *Debating the Democratic Peace*. Cambridge, Mass.: MIT Press.

Carlsson, Ingvar and Shridath Ramphal (1995). *Our Global Neighborhood: The Report of the Commission on Global Governance* (Geneva: Commission on Global Governance, 1995), available at http://www.cgg.ch/contents.htm.

Charnowitz, Steve (2003). 'The Emergence of Democratic Participation in Global Governance (Paris, 1919)', *Indiana Journal of Global Legal Studies*, 10(1): pp. 45–77.

Chayes, Abram and Antonia Handler Chayes (1995). *The New Sovereignty: Compliance with International Regulatory Agreements*. Cambridge, Mass.: Harvard University Press.

Dahl, Robert (1989). *Democracy and its Critics*. New Haven: Yale University Press.

Dahl, Robert (1999). 'Can International Institutions be Democratic? A Skeptic's View', in Ian Shapiro and Casiano Hacker-Cordon, eds, *Democracy's Edges*. Cambridge: Cambridge University Press, pp. 19–36.

Dollar, David and Aart Kraay (2002). 'Spreading the Wealth', *Foreign Affairs*, 81(1).

Doyle, Michael W. (1983). 'Kant, Liberal Legacies and Foreign Affairs', Parts 1 and 2, *Philosophy and Public Affairs*, 12(3–4).

Doyle, Michael W. (1997). *Ways of War and Peace*. New York: Norton.

Doyle, Michael W. (2000). 'A More Perfect Union? The Liberal Peace and the Challenge of Globalization', *Review of International Studies*, 26, pp. 81–94.

Drucker, Peter (1997). 'The Global Economy and the Nation State', *Foreign Affairs* (September/October): p. 168.

Falk, Richard and Andrew Strauss (2000). 'On the Creation of a People's Assembly: Legitimacy and the Power of Popular Sovereignty', *Stanford Journal of International Law*, 36: p. 191.

Foreign Policy (2000), Interview, 'Lori's War', 118 (Spring): p. 34.

Galbraith, James and Andrew Wells-Dang (2002). 'Is Inequality Decreasing?', *Foreign Affairs*, 81(4).

Gilpin, Robert (2000). *The Challenge of Global Capitalism*. Princeton: Princeton University Press.

Hayward, Jack, ed. (1995). *The Crisis of Representation in Europe*. Ilford: Frank Cass.

Heinrich, Dieter (n.d.). 'The Case for a United Nations Parliamentary Assembly', World Federalist Movement.

James, Harold (2001). *The End of Globalization: Lessons from the Great Depression*. Cambridge, Mass.: Harvard University Press.

Keohane, Robert (2003). 'The Concept of Accountability in World Politics and the Use of Force', *Michigan Journal of International Law*, 24(4): pp. 1121–41.

Keohane, Robert and Stanley Hoffmann, eds (1991). *The New European Community*. Boulder, Colo.: Westview.

Keohane, Robert and Joseph Nye (1977). *Power and Interdependence*. Boston: Little, Brown.

Khor, Martin (1999). 'Take Care, the WTO Majority is Tired of Being Manipulated', *International Herald Tribune*, 21 December.

Meunier, Sophie (2000). 'Globalization and the French Exception', *Foreign Affairs*, 79(4).

Panagariya, Arvind (2003). 'International Trade', *Foreign Policy* (November/ December): pp. 20–8.

Petersmann, Ernst-Ulrich (1995). 'The Transformation of the World Trading System', *European Journal of International Law*, 6.

Pogge, Thomas (1997). 'Creating Supra-National Institutions Democratically', *Journal of Political Philosophy*, 5(2): pp. 163–82.

Polanyi, Karl (1980). *The Great Transformation: The Political and Economic Origins of our Time*. New York: Beacon Press.

Reinicke, Wolfgang (1998). *Global Public Policy: Governing without Government*. Washington, DC: Brookings Institution.

Rodrik, Dani (2001). 'The Global Governance of Trade as if Development Really Mattered', Report to the UNDP. New York: UNDP, July.

Ruggie, John (1982). 'International Regimes, Transactions and Change: Embedded Liberalism in the Postwar Economic Order', *International Organization*, 36 (spring): pp. 379–415.

Rustiala, Kal (2000). 'Sovereignty and Multilateralism', *Chicago European Journal of International Law*, 1.

Sandholtz, Wayne and Alec Stone, eds (1998). *European Integration and Supranational Governance*. Oxford: Oxford University Press.

Slaughter, Anne-Marie (1992). 'Law among Liberal States: Liberal Internationalism and the Act of State Doctrine', *Columbia Law Review*, 92.

Slaughter, Anne-Marie (1995). 'International Law in a World of Liberal States', *European Journal of International Law*, 6.

Slaughter, Anne-Marie (1997). 'The Real New World Order', *Foreign Affairs*, 76(5): pp. 183–97.

Stiglitz, Joseph (2000). 'What I Learned at the World Economic Crisis', *New Republic*, 17 April.

Thompson, Dennis (1999). 'Democratic Theory and Global Society', *Journal of Political Philosophy*, 7(2): pp. 1–15.

UN (United Nations) (2005). Annual Millennium Goals Report, available at http://www.un.org/millenniumgoals/MDG-Page 1.pdf.

UNCTAD (2004). *Development and Globalization: Facts and Figures*. Geneva: UNCTAD.

Walzer, Michael (2000). 'Governing the Globe', *Dissent* (fall).

Williamson, John (1983). *The Open Economy and the World Economy*. New York: Basic Books.

Whitman, Marina (1999). *New World, New Rules: The Changing Role of the American Corporation*. Cambridge, Mass.: Harvard Business School.

WTO (World Trade Organization) (1999). 'WTO Case: The Shrimp Turtle Case', *Seattle Post-Intelligencer*, 23 November, available at http://seattlepi.nwsource.com/business/case1.shtml.

10

Reframing Economic Security and Justice

Thomas Pogge

Everyone has the right to a standard of living adequate for the health and well-being of himself and of his family, including food, clothing, housing and medical care.

Everyone is entitled to a social and international order in which the rights and freedoms set forth in this Declaration can be fully realized.

Universal Declaration of Human Rights, Articles 25 and 28

1 Some Cautions about our Moral Judgments

During the last 220 years, moral norms protecting the weak and vulnerable have become increasingly restrictive and increasingly effective. Forms of conduct and social organization that were accepted and practiced in the eighteenth and nineteenth centuries and for millennia before – domestic violence, slavery, autocracy, colonialism, genocide – are now proscribed, outlawed, and displayed as paradigms of injustice. On the face of it, at least, there has been tremendous moral progress.

Yet how well are the weak and vulnerable faring today? Some 2,735 million or 45 percent of humankind are reported to be living below the World Bank's $2/day poverty line – precisely: in households whose consumption expenditure per person per day has less purchasing power than $2.15 had in the United States in 1993 (Chen and Ravallion, 2004, p. 153).[1] The global poor living below this line fall 42 percent below it on average (2004, pp. 152, 158).[2] Some 1,089 million of them or 18 percent of humankind are said to be living on less than half, below the World Bank's better known $1/day poverty line (2004, p. 153).[3] People so incredibly poor are extremely vulnerable to even minor changes in natural and social conditions as well as to many forms of exploitation and abuse. Each year, some 18 million of them die prematurely from poverty-related causes (WHO, 2004, pp. 120–5).[4] This is one-third of all human deaths – 50,000 every day, including 29,000 children under age five (UNICEF, 2005, inside front cover).

Such severe and extensive poverty persists while there is great and rising affluence elsewhere. The average income of the citizens of the affluent countries is about 50 times greater in purchasing power and about 200 times greater in terms of market exchange rates than that of the global poor. The latter 2,735 million people together have about 1.2 percent of aggregate global income, while the 955 million people of the "high-income countries" together have 81 percent (World Bank, 2003, p. 235). Shifting merely 1 percent of the global product – $315 billion annually[5] – from the first group to the second would eradicate severe poverty worldwide.

In reality, however, the shift in global income goes the other way. The gap between rich and poor continues to mount decade after decade as the affluent get richer and the poor remain at or below the subsistence minimum. With World Bank software (iresearch. worldbank.org/PovcalNet/jsp/index.jsp), it is possible to derive their estimate of how various percentiles of world population have fared over the 1990s. Here are some examples of changes in real (inflation-adjusted) consumption expenditure over the 1990–2001 period (labeling percentiles from the bottom up):

the 1st percentile lost	7.3%
the 2nd percentile gained	1.0%
the 5th percentile gained	10.4%
the 10th percentile gained	12.9%
the 20th percentile gained	15.9%
the 30th percentile gained	18.7%
the 40th percentile gained	21.1%
the 50th percentile gained	20.4%
high-income country population gained	52.7%[6]

This juxtaposition of great progress in our moral norms and conduct with a rather catastrophic moral situation on the ground raises two questions:

1 How can severe poverty of half of humankind continue despite enormous economic and technological progress and despite the enlightened moral norms and values of our heavily dominant Western civilization?
2 Why do we citizens of the affluent Western states not find it morally troubling, at least, that a world heavily dominated by us and our values gives so very deficient and inferior starting positions and opportunities to so many people?[7]

We can begin to answer these questions by appreciating how our moralities and social realities interact. Moral norms, designed to protect the livelihood and dignity of the vulnerable, place burdens on the strong. If such norms are compelling enough, the strong make an effort to comply. But they also, consciously or unconsciously, try to get around the norms by arranging their social world so as to minimize their burdens of compliance. Insofar as agents succeed in such norm avoidance, they can comply and still enjoy the advantages of their dominance. Such success, however, generally reduces not merely the costs and opportunity costs of moral norms for the strong, but also the protection these norms afford the weak.

This phenomenon is familiar from more formal, legal rules such as those of the tax code. Clever accountants for wealthy individuals and corporations are endlessly searching for loopholes and other methods of tax avoidance which keep their clients in compliance with the law and yet thwart legislative efforts at reducing inequality. Moral norms elicit similar strategic responses: corporations, concerned about harsh working conditions in a foreign plant, sell it and then buy its products from its new local owner. The so-called developing world has been similarly transformed from colonies into independent states. Many people there are still desperately poor and oppressed, and we still get the natural resources we need. But we now pay native rulers and "elites" for such imports and therefore are – or at least feel – morally disconnected from the misery of the locals.

There are grounds for suspecting, then, that the celebrated historic transformation of our moral norms has mostly produced cosmetic rearrangements. Imagine some visionary European statesman, in 1830 say, posing the question how the advanced states of Europe and North America can preserve and, if possible, expand their economic and political dominance over the rest of the world even while bringing themselves into compliance with the core norms of the Enlightenment morality. Find the best solution to this task you can think of and then compare it to the world today. Could the West have done any better?

The actual transformation was not, of course, the result of such a deliberate plan or grand conspiracy. It would probably have been far less successful for us if it had been pursued according to a plan. It came about through the uncoordinated activities of many influential players – each seeking its own advantage, learning from its errors, processing new data, and strategically adjusting itself to compelling moral norms by seeking to find and to exploit moral loopholes and other methods of morality avoidance. An invisible hand, rather less benign than the one acclaimed by Adam Smith, ensures that the world, driven by these self-seeking efforts, equilibrates toward a mode of organization that gives the strong as much as possible while still allowing them to be broadly in compliance with their moral norms. Such a process gravitates toward the worst of all possible worlds to which the strong can morally reconcile themselves.

The affluent Western states are no longer practicing slavery, colonialism, or genocide. But they still enjoy crushing economic, political, and military dominance over the rest of the world. And – huge economic gains notwithstanding – half of humankind still cannot securely meet their basic needs. The extent and severity of the deprivations they suffer, contrasted with our vastly higher standard of living, suggest caution against thoughtless approval of our conduct, policies, and global institutions. Given what is at stake, we cannot approve them thoughtlessly.

2 Five Easy Reasons to Ignore World Poverty

What reasons do people in the developed West have for being unconcerned with the persistence of severe poverty abroad? The inquiry into this question faces a difficulty: those who judge an issue not worthy of moral attention cannot have an elaborate defense for this judgment because such a defense presupposes the very attention they fail to summon. And yet, there must be something in their moral outlook that explains why the basic data about poverty, which are known, do not seem morally salient to them. If something of this magnitude does not strike people as worth serious inquiry and reflection, one would expect them to have at least a superficial reason. What superficial reasons do they have for not deeming massive global poverty and a vast and growing income gap important, and how well do these reasons stand up to critical reflection?

One easy assumption is that preventing poverty deaths is counterproductive because it will lead to overpopulation and hence to more poverty deaths in the future.[8] This assumption does not square with the facts. In the last few decades, the rise in the human population has been overwhelmed by enormous efficiency gains in food production, reflected in a 35 percent drop in real prices of basic foodstuffs over the 1980–2002 period.[9] More importantly, there is now abundant evidence that birth rates tend to fall dramatically wherever poverty is alleviated and women gain better economic opportunities, more control within their households, and better access to reproductive information and technologies. Accelerated progress against poverty and the subordination of women may actually be the best strategy *against* overpopulation and toward an early leveling-off of the human population below 10 billion (see e.g. Sen, 1994). In any case, the available evidence does not support the conclusion that efforts to reduce severe poverty must multiply human suffering and deaths over time.

A second easy assumption is that world poverty is so gigantic a problem that it simply cannot be eradicated in a few years, at least not at a cost that would be bearable for the rich societies. This assumption is widespread. Richard Rorty, for instance, doubts that we are able to help the global poor by appealing to the claim that

> the rich parts of the world may be in the position of somebody proposing to share her one loaf of bread with a hundred starving people. Even if she does share, everybody, including herself, will starve anyway. . . . A politically feasible project of egalitarian redistribution of wealth requires there to be enough money around to insure that, after the redistribution, the rich will still be able to recognize themselves – will still think their lives worth living. (Rorty, 1996, pp. 10, 14–15)

What Rorty presumes seems obvious: ending the poverty of 2,735 million human beings would sap our arts and culture and our capacity to achieve social justice at home. It would greatly damage our lives and communities and thus is clearly politically unfeasible.

Yet this presumption ignores the enormous extent of the global income gap. The aggregate shortfall of all poor people from the $2/day poverty line amounts to some $300 billion annually or just 1.1 percent of the aggregate annual gross national incomes of the high-income countries. On any credible account of Rorty's recognitional capacities, and ours, he and the rest of us could still recognize ourselves quite easily after accepting reforms that entail a 1.1 percent reduction in our incomes for the sake of eradicating severe poverty worldwide. Indeed, in a sense of the word Rorty would not allow, we might recognize ourselves for the very first time.

Moreover, the second easy assumption, even if it were true, cannot justify neglect of poverty. World poverty appears as one overwhelming – Herculean or rather Sisyphean – task to which we, as individuals, cannot meaningfully contribute. One makes a disaster-relief contribution after a tsunami and finds that, two years later, the damaged areas have been largely rebuilt, with our help. One makes a contribution to poverty relief and finds that, two years later, the number of people living and dying in extreme poverty is still unimaginably large. The former contribution seems meaningful because we think of the task as limited to one disaster – rather than including the effects of all natural disasters, say. The latter contribution appears pointless. But such appearances arise from our conventional sorting categories. Seeing the global poor as one vast homogeneous mass, we overlook that saving ten children from a painful death by hunger does make a real difference, *all* the difference for these children and their families, and that this difference is quite significant even when many other children remain desperately hungry.

A third easy assumption is that, as the history of failed attempts at development assistance illustrates, world poverty cannot be eradicated by "throwing money at the problem." Now it may be true that official development assistance (ODA) has done little for development. But this is not evidence for the prized conclusion because most such aid is not aimed at promoting development. Rather, our politicians allocate it to benefit those who are able and willing to reciprocate: export firms in the donor countries and political-economic elites of strategically important developing states. This diagnosis is confirmed by the donors themselves,[10] and supported by a detailed study of their aid allocations (Alesina and Dollar, 2000). It is also supported by the fact that ODA was sharply reduced after the end of the Cold War,[11] when our need for political support from developing states declined (whereas the needs of the global poor and our capacity to help did not). The diagnosis is further supported by how little of ODA is targeted toward meeting basic needs.[12] The unimpressive results of ODA fail to show, then, that money cannot be used effectively for poverty reduction. In fact, the appropriately targeted fraction of ODA has done a lot of good.

To be sure, good intentions do not always lead to success. Even the most dedicated anti-poverty organizations sometimes waste money and effort. But, if anything, this is a reason to think harder about world poverty and ways of attacking it, rather than less. Where corruption is an obstacle, we can try to reduce it, circumvent it, or focus our efforts elsewhere. If foreign donations of food depress demand, prices, and hence incentives for production in the target country, we can instead enhance the income of the poor. Where direct transfers to poor households create dependency, we can, targeting children especially, fund vaccination programs, basic schooling, school lunches, safe water and sewage systems, housing, power plants and networks, banks and microlending, road, rail, and communication links. Such projects augment the poor's capacity to fend for themselves and their access to markets while also stimulating local production. Such projects, publicly funded, played an important role in the eradication of poverty in the (now) developed world. And in the poor countries, too, such projects have been successfully realized by UN agencies, NGOs, and individual donor states.

Moreover, our financial contribution to overcoming world poverty need not take the form of spending and transfers. We could agree to restructure the global order to make it more hospitable to democratic government, economic justice, and growth in the poorer countries, and we could drive less hard a bargain against these countries in negotiations about international trade, intellectual property rights, investment, and taxation. Making such concessions, we would, for the sake of reducing world poverty, bear opportunity costs by not using our superior bargaining power to insist on onerous terms more favorable to ourselves. Such options further undermine the easy assumption that the Western states simply cannot influence the global income distribution so as to reduce world poverty.

A fourth easy assumption is that we citizens need not worry about world poverty because our politicians are already involved in a concerted and relentless effort to solve this problem. This assumption is nourished by the steady stream of summits, declarations, high-level working groups, and the rest. At the 1996 World Food Summit in Rome, for example, the 186 participating governments agreed to "pledge our political will and our common and national commitment to achieving food security for all and to an on-going effort to eradicate hunger in all countries, with an immediate view to reducing the number of undernourished people to half their present level no later than 2015" (www.fao.org/wfs).

Reflect on the word "immediate" here. The governments' plan envisaged that, even 19 years later, there would still be 420 million undernourished human beings and, assuming rough proportionality, 9 million annual poverty deaths. Are these levels we can condone? With a linear decline, implying a 474,000 annual reduction in the number of poverty deaths, the plan envisaged 250 million deaths from poverty-related causes over the 19-year plan period. Is so huge a death toll acceptable because these deaths would be occurring at a declining rate?

To help answer this question, imagine Western politicians getting together in 1943 to discuss joint action to stop the Nazi murder of Jews, gypsies, and other non-Aryans. And imagine these politicians grandly pledging their political will to end the Nazi murders and committing themselves to the "immediate" goal of lowering the killing rate to half its current level by 1962. Or imagine Western politicians getting together in 1994, while some 10,000 people were being hacked to death each day in Rwanda, and setting the "immediate" goal of reducing the slaughter to 5,000 per day no later than 2013.

You may think that eradicating poverty is such a huge undertaking that doing half the job in 19 years is pretty good. In fact, however, defeating Nazi Germany (and Japan!) in the 1940s was vastly more costly in blood and treasure than eradicating poverty today, which could be achieved at a (rapidly diminishing) cost of initially just 1 percent of the aggregate gross national incomes of the high-income countries.

Distinctly unambitious from the start, the promise of Rome has been further diluted since. The United States immediately disowned responsibility, publishing an "Interpretive Statement" to the effect that "the attainment of any 'right to adequate food' or 'fundamental right to be free from hunger' is a goal or aspiration to be realized progressively that does not give rise to any international obligations."[13] And the United Nations have, in 2000, adopted a superseding "millennium development goal," which cleverly retains but reinterprets the language of halving extreme poverty by 2015, thereby raising the number of extremely poor people deemed acceptable for 2015 from 548 million (Rome World Food Summit) to 884 million and thus substituting a 19 percent reduction in the number of extremely poor people for the earlier promised 50 percent reduction (see Pogge, 2004 for full details).

A fifth easy assumption is that, thanks to the benefits of globalization and free markets, poverty is in decline. This assumption, as well, is sustained by propaganda and creative accounting more than by reality. Chen and Ravallion (2004, p. 153) of the World Bank report a reduction in $1/day poverty from 1,171.2 million in 1987 to 1,089.0 million in 2001, a decline that is entirely due to China. But they also report that $2/day poverty has risen from 2,477.5 million in 1987 to 2,735.4 million in 2001 – an increase of 10.4 percent (22.6 percent if China is excluded). This reflects the fact that, according to their research (already documented above), increasing global inequality deprives the poorer segments of humanity of a proportional share in global economic growth. Moreover, deep methodological flaws in the Bank's poverty measurement methodology suggest that its figures may be quite inaccurate and that both the incidence and the trend may be worse than reported (Reddy and Pogge, 2007). This suggestion is supported by other indicators of extreme poverty: the number of human beings reported to be chronically malnourished, for example, is reported to have increased from 800 million (UNDP, 1990, p. 17) to 850 million (UNDP, 2005, p. 24) over the last 15 years. This suggests that a more plausible poverty measurement methodology would indicate an increase even in extreme poverty (now defined relative to the Bank's $1/day international poverty line).

The five easy assumptions I have briefly discussed provide superficial reasons that incline many in the affluent countries to disregard world poverty. None of these reasons can survive even a little reflection. They survive by discouraging such reflection. The survival of such flimsy reasons confirms the cautions of section 1: we cannot take for granted that our unreflective moral judgments regarding world poverty are well founded or reliable.

3 Is Our New Global Economic Order Harming the Poor?

The preceding discussion may elicit the concession that we are doing far too little about world poverty. But the truth may be even worse than that. We may not merely do too little to help the poor, but also, and more importantly, too much to harm them. Here a prime suspect is the new (WTO) global economic order, which is often praised for fostering open markets and free trade that benefit everyone and the global poor in particular.

We have already seen that the very poor have not participated proportionately in the global economic growth of recent years. What are we to make of the claim that WTO globalization has nonetheless been beneficial to them?

Harm and benefit are comparative notions suggesting that WTO globalization makes the poor, respectively, worse or better off. But worse or better off than what? One might invoke some earlier time as a baseline. In this vein it is often suggested that the global order must be benefiting the poor because poverty is in decline. Even granting the asserted decline, this argument is invalid. That the winds are benefiting you in your journey is not shown by your getting closer to your destination – your progress may be slowed badly by strong headwinds. Similarly, our global order may be exacerbating poverty even while, thanks to other causal factors, world poverty is in decline. And even if the global institutional order did contribute to improving living standards among the poor, it might still be harming them. To see this, consider a slave-owning society that gradually adopts legal constraints against the most brutal forms of mistreatment and abuse of slaves. Such a legal order would nonetheless be harming the slaves by authorizing their subjection to the will of their owners. By becoming less harmful, such a legal order is not benefiting the poor any more than a violent husband is benefiting his wife by beating her less frequently.

These thoughts reveal that one needs here not a diachronic comparison, but a subjunctive one that appeals to some morally plausible baseline. The current structure of the world economy is harming the global poor insofar as they are worse off than they would be if this order were just. But how should one judge whether some institutional order is just or unjust? Standards of social justice are controversial to some extent. To make my argument widely acceptable, I invoke a minimal standard that merely requires that any institutional order imposed on human beings must be designed so that human rights are fulfilled under it insofar as this is reasonably possible. Nearly everyone believes that justice requires more, that an institutional order can be unjust even if it meets this minimal standard; and there is disagreement about what else justice requires. But I can bypass these issues so long as we can agree that an institutional order *cannot* be just if it *fails* to meet the minimal human rights standard. Insofar as the present global institutional order falls short of even this minimal standard, and dramatically so, it can be shown to be unjust without invoking any more demanding and less widely acceptable standard.

I need to show, then, that the global order as presently structured causes foreseeable human rights deficits that are reasonably avoidable in the sense that there is a plausible alternative design that would not produce comparable human rights deficits or other ills of comparable magnitude.[14] This is easy to show by example. Let us begin with the protectionist permissions that were grandfathered into the WTO Treaty. Their role is well documented even in such publications as *The Economist* which, laboring to outdo all other news media in its defense of the WTO and in its vilification of protesters against it as enemies of the poor,[15] can certainly not be accused of anti-WTO bias:

> Rich countries cut their tariffs by less in the Uruguay Round than poor ones did. Since then, they have found new ways to close their markets, notably by imposing anti-dumping duties on imports they deem "unfairly cheap". Rich countries are particularly protectionist in many of the sectors where developing countries are best able to compete, such as agriculture, textiles, and clothing. As a result, according to a new study by Thomas Hertel, of Purdue University, and Will Martin, of the World Bank, rich countries' average tariffs on manufacturing imports from poor countries are four times higher than those on imports from other rich countries. This imposes a big burden on poor countries. The United Nations Conference on Trade and Development (UNCTAD) estimates that they could export $700 billion more a year by 2005 if rich countries did more to open their markets. Poor countries are also hobbled by a lack of know-how. Many had little understanding of what they signed up to in the Uruguay Round. That ignorance is now costing them dear. Michael Finger of the World Bank and Philip Schuler of the University of Maryland estimate that implementing commitments to improve trade procedures and establish technical and intellectual-property standards can cost more than a year's development budget for the poorest countries. Moreover, in those areas where poor countries could benefit from world trade rules, they are often unable to do so. . . . Of the WTO's 134 members, 29 do not even have missions at its headquarters in Geneva. Many more can barely afford to bring cases to the WTO.[16]

This report makes clear that some of the agreements reached in the Uruguay Round are very costly for the poorer countries and their people. Foreseeably, these agreements exacerbate poverty and bring about additional deaths from poverty-related causes. The governments of rich countries did not have to press for these agreements. They could have accepted that tariffs on manufacturing imports faced by poor countries should be no higher than those faced by rich countries, rather than four times as high. They could have agreed to open their markets to agricultural, textile, and footwear imports from the poor countries. They could have agreed to forgo their farm subsidies which climbed above $300 billion in 2002.[17] Our governments' successful insistence on the protectionist exemptions had a huge impact on employment, incomes, economic growth, and tax revenues in the poorer countries where many live on the brink of starvation. The magnitude of this impact is suggested by the $700 billion annual loss in export revenues estimated by UNCTAD. This figure is over 100 times what all affluent countries together spend on ODA for basic social services (see n. 12).

Many critics of the WTO regime are, and many more are dismissed as, opponents of open markets, free trade, or globalization. It is worth stressing then that my critique involves no such opposition. My complaint against the WTO regime is not that it opens markets too much, but that it opens *our* markets *too little* and thereby gains for us the benefits of free trade while withholding them from the global poor. I see the appalling trajectory of world poverty and of the global income gap since the end of the Cold War as a shocking indictment of one particular, especially brutal path of economic globalization which our governments have chosen to impose. But this is no reason to oppose any and all possible designs of an integrated global market economy under unified rules of universal scope. Indeed, I advocate not an alternative of greater mutual isolation, but a different path of globalization, involving political as well as economic integration, which would fulfill human rights worldwide and afford persons everywhere an opportunity to share the benefits of global economic growth (see Pogge, 2002, chs. 6–8).

There is a straightforward two-part explanation for why our new global economic order is so harsh on the poor. The details of this order are fixed in international negotiations in which our governments enjoy a crushing advantage in bargaining power and expertise. And our representatives in international negotiations do not consider the interests of the global poor as part of their mandate. They are exclusively devoted to shaping each such agreement in the best interest of the people and corporations of their own country. To get a vivid sense of the zeal with which our politicians and negotiators pursue this task, you need only recall to what incredible length the US government has gone to shift some of its share of the UN general budget onto other countries.[18] This hard-fought victory saves the US $35 million annually, 12 cents per US citizen each *year* – or 58 cents when one adds the similarly reduced US share of the cost of UN peacekeeping operations (www.pro-un.org/year 2000.htm). This is one example, chosen only because it is so well known. There are plenty of cases illustrating similar zeal by the representatives of other affluent states. Our new global economic order is so harsh on the global poor, then, because it is shaped in negotiations where our representatives ruthlessly exploit their vastly superior bargaining power and expertise, as well as any weakness, ignorance, or corruptibility they may find in their counterpart negotiators, to shape each agreement for our greatest benefit. In such negotiations, the affluent states will make reciprocal concessions to one another, but rarely to the weak. The cumulative result of many such negotiations and agreements is a grossly skewed global economic order under which the lion's share of the benefits of global economic growth flows to those already better off.

Inspired by John Locke, some would object that it is permissible for the more powerful to impose an institutional order that foreseeably produces avoidable human rights deficits on a massive scale so long as this order constitutes an improvement over the state of nature. I find this objection unclear, morally implausible, and inconclusive. It is unclear insofar as "the" state of nature can be imagined in many diverse ways none of which affords a salient benchmark. It is morally implausible in that it would permit outrageous practices, such as slavery, if only the oppressed are kept just above the chosen state-of nature baseline. And it is inconclusive insofar as no sustainable state of nature has yet been described that could match our globalized civilization's stunning record of 18 million annual deaths from poverty-related causes.

Inspired by Robert Nozick, some would object that an institutional order is just, and its imposition therefore permissible, if this order arose on a historical path – involving universal consent, for example – that did not violate persons' property rights in themselves and anything they justly acquired. According to this view, even the most brutal slavery would be morally acceptable so long as the slaves had once consented to their enslavement. This view is morally quite dubious, of course, but even if we accept it for the sake of argument, it cannot support a justification of the present global order. This order arose on a historical path that was pervaded by massive crimes such as violent enslavement, colonialism, and genocide – crimes still reflected in the present distribution of land, natural resources, wealth, and bargaining power. Moreover, as Nozick would agree, many of those who consented to the WTO agreement – Sani Abacha, Mobuto Sese Seko, Suharto, and Myanmar's SLORC junta among them – lacked moral standing validly to consent on behalf of those they managed violently to subject to their rule.

I conclude, then, that the present global institutional order is unjust by any plausible standard and its coercive imposition therefore a great harm done to the billions who suffer and all too often die prematurely from causes linked to the severe poverty that this order foreseeably and avoidably inflicts upon them.

4 Responsibilities and Reforms

In many cases our negotiators must know that the better they succeed, the more people will die of poverty. Our foreign and trade ministers and our presidents and prime ministers know this and so do many journalists and academics as well as the experts at the World Bank, which bills itself as the official champion of the global poor even while its management and decision-making are heavily dominated by the affluent states. After the terrorist attacks of September 11, 2001, the President of the World Bank publicized his estimate "that tens of thousands more children will die worldwide and some 10 million people are likely to be living below the poverty line of $1 a day . . . because the attacks will delay the rich countries' recovery into 2002." Where do we find similar estimates about our tariffs, anti-dumping duties, quotas, agricultural subsidies, and enforcement of property rights in seeds and drugs? Or at least a reasoned denial that we are causing grievous harms or that these harms are unjustifiable?

When some 800,000 Tutsis and moderate Hutus were slaughtered in Rwanda in early 1994, the world took notice. The massacres were widely discussed in academia and the media, with many discussants expressing dismay at the decisions by Western governments to avoid both the word "genocide" and a peacekeeping operation (see Pogge, 2006). They believe that we should have stopped the massacres, even if this would have meant risking the lives of our soldiers and spending a few hundred million dollars or more. We all felt a bit responsible, but bearably so. The deaths, after all, were brought about by clearly identifiable villains, and we were clearly not among them and also did not benefit from the killings in any way. Deaths caused by global economic arrangements designed and imposed by our governments are a different matter: These governments are elected by us, responsive to our interests and preferences, acting in our name and in ways that benefit us. This buck stops with us.

One lesson from the comparison with the Rwandan genocide is that we might feel more comfortable about the topic of world poverty if we could connect it to some foreign villains. There are indeed such villains, and I apologize for denying them the early and prominent stage appearance they have come to expect in Western treatments of world poverty. Let me try to make up.

As sketched thus far, my position on world poverty can be charged with leaving out the most important factor: the incompetence, corruption, and tyranny entrenched in the governments, social institutions, and cultures of many poor countries. This factor – much stressed by Rawls and other explanatory nationalists [19] – may seem to undercut much of my argument: if the vital interests of the global poor are neglected in international negotiations, it is because their own governments do not vigorously represent these interests. And even if our governments had nonetheless agreed to reduce protectionist barriers against exports from the poorer countries, this would have done far more toward enriching their corrupt elites than toward improving conditions for the poor. The main responsibility for the persistence of world poverty lies, then, with the leaders and elites of the poorer countries rather than with our governments and ourselves.

This objection is right about the responsibilities of local rulers and elites. Many governments of the poorer countries are autocratic, corrupt, brutal, and unresponsive to the interests of the poor majority. They are greatly at fault for not representing the interests of the poor in international negotiations and for consenting to treaties that benefit themselves and foreigners at the expense of their impoverished populations. But can we plausibly tell the poor that, insofar as the global economic order is unfair to them, they only have their own leaders to blame for this? They can surely point out in response that they did not authorize the clique that rules them in anything resembling free and fair elections and that their interests can be sold out by this clique only because *we* treat it as entitled to consent on behalf of the people it manages to subjugate. This response can be extended to show that we share responsibility not only for the damage authoritarian rulers can do to the interests of "their" people in international negotiations, but also for authoritarianism and corruption being so widespread in the "developing" world. In this vein it is often mentioned that our governments have instigated the violent installation of many oppressive rulers, are selling juntas and autocrats the weapons they need to stay in power,[20] and have fostered a culture of corruption by permitting our firms to bribe foreign officials and by blessing such bribes with tax deductibility.[21]

Still more significant are the international resource and borrowing privileges that our global order confers upon those who manage to bring a country under their control. Such rulers are internationally recognized as entitled to sell natural resources and to borrow money in the name of the country and its people. These international privileges facilitate oppressive rule and greatly encourage coup attempts and civil wars (Pogge, 2002, ch. 6).

The national social factors we most like to blame for the persistence of severe poverty – bad governments and corruption in the poorer countries – are not, then, wholly native ingredients of a lesser culture, but sustained by core features of our present global order. A reliable market supply of natural resources is important to the affluent consumer societies, and we therefore benefit from a rule that allows buyers to acquire legally valid ownership rights in such resources from anyone who happens to control them. But this rule fosters bad government in the resource-rich developing countries by giving repressive rulers a source of revenues and by providing incentives to try to seize political power by force.

A further insight follows directly. The international privileges benefit us and local elites and autocrats at the expense of the poor populations of resource-rich developing countries. This shows how thinking about global justice must not be confined to international relations. When we ask whether we are treating poor *countries* unfairly when we buy their resources at going world market prices, we will answer in the negative. In doing so, we are liable to overlook the far more important question of whether we are treating the poor *people* in these countries unfairly when we purchase their natural resources from their oppressors. The question is not what are we doing to the poor countries? The crucial question is what are we and the rulers and elites of the poorer countries *together* doing to their impoverished populations?

A third insight is that we must stop thinking about world poverty in terms of helping the poor. The poor do need help, of course. But they need help only because of the terrible injustices they are being subjected to. We should not, then, think of our individual donations and of possible institutionalized poverty eradication initiatives – like a Tobin Tax (a proposed tax on currency markets), or a global resources dividend – as helping the poor, but as protecting them from the effects of global rules whose injustice benefits us and is our responsibility. And we should not only think about such remedial measures, but also about how the injustice of the global order might be diminished through institutional reforms that would end the need for such remedial measures.[22]

Some critics of our complacency about world poverty argue that the existing global distribution of income and wealth is fundamentally unjust. Others criticize our individual consumption choices as sustaining exploitation and dispossession. I see what they point to as mere symptoms of a deeper injustice: the imposition, by our governments in our name, of a coercive global order that perpetuates severe poverty for many who cannot resist this imposition. On behalf of the global poor, I criticize not that they are worse off than they might be, but that we and our governments participate in depriving them of the objects of their most basic rights. This critique is Lockean in spirit: "Men being . . . by Nature, all free, equal and independent, no one can be put out of his Estate, and subjected to the Political Power of another, without his own Consent" (Locke, 1960: § 95). This principle forbids the affluent countries' substantial contribution to subjecting the global poor, without their consent, to their local rulers and to the rules of the world economy and to reducing the global poor, without their consent, below a proportional share of natural resources or its equivalent. This principle also challenges the benefits we derive from their subjection and deprivation, in particular through the cheap appropriation of global natural resources.

Mine is not, then, a leftist critique. The political right, too, condemns poverty caused by an unjust coercive institutional order – for instance, the severe poverty and dependence engendered by feudal regimes or by the collectivized agriculture imposed by Stalin in 1928. They agree that such poverty is unjust and that those causing it are responsible for it and also have a responsibility to eradicate it. Their moral and political outlook is thus quite consistent with my claim that we have a duty to help eradicate existing severe poverty. If they deny this claim, it is because they – along with most Westerners anywhere on the political spectrum – assume too easily that we, and the global order we impose, do not substantially contribute to severe poverty abroad.

Seeing how much depends on this assumption, it is disheartening to find how easily people in the West accept it – carried along by powerful personal motives and massive propaganda that ought to make them more vigilant rather than less. To be sure, it is rarely denied that many are born into desperate poverty that leads to their early death or else to permanently diminished physical and mental functioning and sparse opportunities for escaping poverty. Nor is there much doubt that unjust social rules coercively imposed upon the poor through no fault of their own substantially contribute to their poverty. But people do not see, and do not want to see, that we and the governments acting in our name are substantially involved in supporting such unjust rules and their coercive imposition.

So what are we responsible for? Am I seriously accusing those who represent us in WTO negotiations and at the International Monetary Fund (IMF), and also governments and corporations that sustain corrupt and oppressive elites with aid, loans, arms sales, and resource purchases, of being hunger's willing executioners? Would I describe us all as accomplices in a monumental crime against humanity? Questions like these are often posed as a *reductio ad absurdum* – not to continue the dialogue, but to break it off. Such interlocutors recognize that individuals and small groups, sociopaths and pedophiles, can be horribly mistaken in their moral judgments. But they find it inconceivable that we all, the civilized people of the developed West, could be so fundamentally wrong.

Why do they find this inconceivable, totally out of the question? There are surely enough poverty deaths for a full-sized crime against humanity: as many every seven months as perished in the Nazi death camps. So how can they be so absolutely certain that they have no responsibility for these deaths and thus no need for further dialogue and reflection?

Some trust the collective wisdom of our culture. They trust that others among us must have thought long and hard about world poverty and must have concluded that our conduct and policies are basically alright. They trust that any good reasons to doubt this conclusion would be seriously and prominently debated by politicians, academics, and journalists. Sections 1 and 2 have given preliminary reasons for thinking that such trust may be misplaced.

Others feel that there is no need to think long and hard about our shared moral world view because there are no objective moral truths it might misrepresent. Our moral judgments are the data that any moral conception must explain and reaffirm, the "fixed points" that count as more certain than any complex philosophical arguments to the contrary. This convenient thought can be used to shut oneself off from arguments aiming to show that there is, other things equal, little moral difference between failing to rescue people and killing them. But my arguments do not challenge the morality prevalent in the West. On the contrary, I invoke a central element of this morality: that it is wrong severely to harm innocent people for minor gains. What I challenge is the common view that we are not harming the poor, that the developed countries and the global economic order they sustain are not substantial contributors to life-threatening poverty suffered by billions. However attached one may be to one's moral convictions, one can hardly appeal to them in support of one's beliefs about world poverty and the causes of its persistence.

Is there any chance that we or our governments will decide to end world poverty? One might hope that one of the more powerful countries will produce a moral leader who will make us realize our responsibilities and represent them forcefully along with our interests.

But it seems less unlikely that the impetus for reform will come from us citizens. This scenario presupposes that some of us recognize the harms we are involved in producing or the benefits we derive from these harms, find the case for ending poverty morally compelling, and act on this moral judgment. As things are, this moral stance is rarely considered, very rarely attained, and hard to maintain.

Our world is arranged to keep us far away from massive and severe poverty and surrounds us with affluent, civilized people for whom the poor abroad are a remote good cause alongside the spotted owl. In such a world, the thought that we are involved in a monumental crime against these people, that we must fight to stop their dying and suffering, will appear so cold, so strained, and so ridiculous that we cannot find it in our heart to reflect on it any farther. That we are naturally myopic and conformist enough to be easily reconciled to the hunger abroad may be fortunate for us, who can "recognize ourselves", can lead worthwhile and fulfilling lives without much thought about the origins of our affluence. But it is quite unfortunate for the global poor, whose best hope may be our moral reflection.

Notes

This chapter adapts and updates materials from the introduction to Thomas Pogge's *World Poverty and Human Rights* (Cambridge: Polity, 2002). It is reproduced here with permission of the publisher.

1 Chen and Ravallion have managed the World Bank's income poverty assessments for well over a decade. Their data are for the year 2001. The $-sign stands for the US currency throughout. International poverty lines are stated in $PPP (purchasing power parity), inflating the incomes of the poor to reflect the greater purchasing power of money in their countries. In typical poor countries, the commonly used $1/day and $2/day poverty lines correspond to about $120 and $240 per person per year at market exchange rates.

2 Dividing the poverty gap index by the headcount index.

3 These people are reported to be living 28.4 percent below the $1/day line on average (Chen and Ravallion, 2004, pp. 152 and 158, dividing the poverty gap index by the headcount index). These extremely poor people were thus living on about $86 per person per year at market exchange rates.

4 In 2002 there were about 57 million human deaths. The main causes highly correlated with poverty were (with death tolls in thousands): diarrhea (1,798) and malnutrition (485), perinatal (2,462) and maternal conditions (510), childhood diseases (1,124 – mainly measles), tuberculosis (1,566), malaria (1,272), meningitis (173), hepatitis (157), tropical diseases (129), respiratory infections (3,963 – mainly pneumonia), HIV/AIDS (2,777), and sexually transmitted diseases (180) (WHO, 2004, pp. 120–5).

5 Based on a 2001 global product of 31,500 billion (World Bank, 2003, p. 235). I use the word "billion" in the American sense as signifying 1,000 million.

6 The last figure reports real growth in GNI per capita, PPP (current international $s) from World Development Indicators Online (World Bank, available only to subscribers). These findings confirm and extend earlier conclusions by Branko Milanović about 1988–93. He found that real growth in global average per capita income over this period was 5.7 percent. The top quintile (fifth) of the world's population got all of the gain – and then some: real incomes declined in all other income segments. "The bottom 5 percent of the world grew poorer, as their real

incomes decreased between 1988 and 1993 by 1/4 [!] while the richest quintile grew richer. It gained 12 percent in real terms, that is it grew more than twice as much as mean world income (5.7 percent)" (Milanovic, 2002, p. 88).

7 In this chapter I am using "we," "us," "our" to refer to adult citizens of the USA, EU, Canada, Australia, New Zealand – at least those who share the economic security and basic Western values of these countries. By focusing on our responsibilities with regard to world poverty, I am not suggesting that the responsibilities of the Japanese are importantly different, and certainly not that the "elites" in the poorer countries have no such responsibilities.

8 This thought goes back at least to Malthus (1982) and gained renewed popularity through Hardin (1974, 1993).

9 The World Bank Food Index fell from 139.3 in 1980 to 100 in 1990 and then to 90.1 in 2002. These statistics are published by the World Bank's Development Prospects Group. See www.worldbank.org/prospects/gep 2004/appendix2.pdf, p. 277.

10 This oft-quoted statement was recently removed from the USAID's main website: "The principal beneficiary of America's foreign assistance programs has always been the United States. Close to 80 percent of the U.S. Agency for International Development's (USAID's) contracts and grants go directly to American firms. Foreign assistance programs have helped create major markets for agricultural goods, created new markets for American industrial exports and meant hundreds of thousands of jobs for Americans."

11 From 0.33% of GNP in 1990 to 0.22% in 2000 (UNDP, 2002, p. 202). The United States led the decline by reducing its ODA from 0.21% to 0.10% of GNP in a time of great prosperity culminating in enormous budget surpluses (UNDP, 2002). After the invasions of Afghanistan and Iraq, ODA has recently been growing, in part through disbursements to these and neighboring states (Pakistan is now the largest ODA recipient). For 2003, ODA is reported at 0.15% for the United States and at 0.25% for the affluent countries collectively (UNDP, 2005, p. 278).

12 Last available numbers for 2003, putting ODA at $69 billion (UNDP, 2005, p. 278) and ODA spending for basic social services at $5.7 billion, versus an aggregate poverty gap of ca. $300 billion relative to the $2/day poverty line.
(millenniumindicators.un.org/unsd/mdg/seriesDetail.aspx?srid=592&crid=)

13 Annex II to the *Final Report of the World Food Summit* (www.fao.org/documents/show_cdr.asp?url_file=/docrep/003/w3548e/w3548e00.htm). The United States also argued that the FAO was greatly exaggerating the contribution needed from the developed countries (USDA 1999, appendix A).

14 I require that existing massive human rights deficits must be *reasonably* avoidable through modification in the global institutional order in order to preempt objections that declare such deficits morally acceptable when avoiding them would be extremely costly in terms of culture, say, or the natural environment.

15 For some typical examples of *Economist* editorializing, see its cover of December 11, 1999, showing an Indian child in rags with the heading "The real losers of Seattle." See also its editorial in the same issue (p. 15), its flimsy "The case for globalisation," (*The Economist*, September 23, 2000, pp. 19–20 and 85–7), and its remarkable lead editorial "A question of justice?" (*The Economist*, March 11, 2004).

16 *The Economist*, September 25, 1999, p. 89. The three cited studies – Hertel and Martin, UNCTAD, Finger and Schuler – are in the references list below.

17 A classic example of protectionist grandfathering is the so-called Peace Clause, Article 13 in the WTO Agricultural Agreement, added to protect the agricultural subsidies of the affluent countries; see www.tradeobservatory.org/headlines.cfm?RefID=18901. The resulting protectionist measures are deplored even by pillars of the establishment such as the former World Bank chief

economist Nick Stern. In a speech, "Cutting Agricultural Subsidies" (globalenvision.org/ library/ 6/309), Stern pointed out that cows receive annual subsidies of about $2,700 in Japan and $900 in Europe – far above the annual income of most human beings. He also cited protectionist anti-dumping actions, bureaucratic applications of safety and sanitation standards, and textile tariffs and quotas as barriers to poor-country exports: "Every textile job in an industrialized country saved by these barriers costs about 35 jobs in these industries in low-income countries." Stern was especially critical of escalating tariffs – duties that are lowest on unprocessed raw materials and rise sharply with each step of processing and value added – for undermining manufacturing and employment in poor countries, thus helping to confine Ghana and Côte d'Ivoire to the export of unprocessed cocoa beans, Uganda and Kenya to the export of raw coffee beans, and Mali and Burkina Faso to the export of raw cotton. He estimated that full elimination of agricultural protection and production subsidies in the rich countries would raise agricultural and food exports from low- and middle-income countries by 24 percent and total annual rural income in these countries by about $60 billion (about three quarters of the global poor live in such rural areas).

18 After years of heavy pressure and 10-digit arrears, the United States finally (Christmas 2000) won a reduction from 25 to 22 percent – even while its share of aggregate global income was 31 percent (World Bank, 2002, p. 233). While pressing mightily for the reduction, the US government was also debating what to do with its $100 billion plus annual budget surpluses that were then expected for the foreseeable future.

19 Rawls attributes the human rights deficits in the typical poor country only to local factors: "the problem is commonly the nature of the public political culture and the religious and philosophical traditions that underlie its institutions. The great social evils in poorer societies are likely to be oppressive government and corrupt elites" (Rawls, 1999, p. 77).

20 Arms sales facilitate repression, fuel civil wars, and divert funds from meeting basic needs. In 2003 the rich countries spent $5.7 billion on development assistance for meeting basic needs abroad (n. 12) while also selling the poorer countries over $20 billion in conventional weapons (CSR, 2005, p. 52). The main sellers of arms into the poorer countries are the United States, with 37 percent, followed by the UK, France, and Russia (2005, p. 53).

21 The post-Watergate Congress of the United States pioneered reform with its 1977 *Foreign Corrupt Practices Act* after the Lockheed Corporation was found to have paid – not a modest sum to some minor third-world official, but rather – a $2 million bribe to Prime Minister Kakuei Tanaka of powerful and democratic Japan. It took another 20 years for the other rich countries, pressured by the United States and Transparency International, to follow suit with the OECD Convention on Combating Bribery of Foreign Officials in International Business Transactions which requires signatory states to criminalize the bribery of foreign officials. This convention took effect in February 1999 and as of January 2005 has been ratified by 36 states (www.oecd.org/home). So, the reform proposed in the text is achieved: most rich states now have laws that forbid corporations to bribe foreign officials. "But big multinationals continue to sidestep them with ease" (*The Economist*, March 2, 2002, pp. 63–5).

22 Pogge, 2002, ch. 8 proposes and defends a global resources dividend; ch. 7 discusses a more comprehensive global institutional reform; and ch. 6 contains a detailed proposal concerning the reform of the international resource and borrowing privileges in particular.

References

Alesina, Alberto and David Dollar (2000). "Who Gives Foreign Aid to Whom and Why?" *Journal of Economic Growth*, 5: pp. 33–64 (http://papers.nber.org/papers/w6612).

Chen, Shaohua and Martin Ravallion (2004). "How Have the World's Poorest Fared since the Early 1980s?" *World Bank Research Observer*, 19: pp. 141–69. Also at wbro.oupjournals.org/cgi/content/abstract/19/2/141.

CSR (Congressional Research Service) (2005). *Conventional Arms Transfers to Developing Nations, 1997–2004*. Washington, DC: Library of Congress (http://fpc.state.gov/documents/organization/52179.pdf).

Finger, J. Michael and Philip Schuler (1999). "Implementation of Uruguay Round Commitments: The Development Challenge." World Bank Research Working Paper 2215, http://papers.ssrn.com/so13/papers.cfm?abstract_id=623972.

Hardin, Garrett (1974). "Lifeboat Ethics: The Case against Helping the Poor." *Psychology Today*, 8: pp. 38–43 and 123–6.

Hardin, Garrett (1993). *Living within Limits*. Oxford: Oxford University Press.

Hertel, Thomas W. and Will Martin (1999). "Would Developing Countries Gain from Inclusion of Manufactures in the WTO Negotiations?" www.gtap.agecon.purdue.edu/resources/download/42.pdf.

Locke, John (1960). *An Essay Concerning the True Original, Extent, and End of Civil Government* [1689]. In *John Locke: Two Treatises of Government*, ed. Peter Laslett. Cambridge: Cambridge University Press.

Malthus, Thomas Robert (1982). *An Essay on the Principle of Population* [1798]. Harmondsworth: Penguin.

Milanović, Branko (2002). "True World Income Distribution, 1988 and 1993: First Calculation Based on Household Surveys Alone." *Economic Journal*, 112(1): pp. 51–92.

Pogge, Thomas (2002). *World Poverty and Human Rights: Cosmopolitan Responsibilities and Reforms*. Cambridge: Polity.

Pogge, Thomas (2004). "The First UN Millennium Development Goal: A Cause for Celebration?" *Journal of Human Development*, 5(3): pp. 377–97.

Pogge, Thomas (2006). "Moralizing Humanitarian Intervention: Why Jurying Fails and How Law Can Work." In Terry Nardin and Melissa Williams, eds, *Humanitarian Intervention*, NOMOS vol. 47. New York: New York University Press.

Rawls, John (1999). *The Law of Peoples: With "The Idea of Public Reason Revisited."* Cambridge, Mass.: Harvard University Press.

Reddy, Sanjay and Thomar Pogge (2007). "How Not to Count the Poor." In Sudhir Anand and Joseph Stiglitz, eds, *Measuring Global Poverty*, Oxford: Oxford University Press.

Rorty, Richard (1996). "Who are We? Moral Universalism and Economic Triage." *Diogenes*, 173: pp. 5–15.

Sen, Amartya K. (1994). "Population: Delusion and Reality." *New York Review*, September 22: pp. 62–71.

Universal Declaration of Human Rights, approved and proclaimed by the General Assembly of the United Nations on December 10, 1948, as resolution 217 A (III).

UNCTAD (United Nations Conference on Trade and Development) (1999). *Trade and Development Report 1999*. New York: UN Publications.

UNDP (United Nations Development Programme) (1990). *Human Development Report 1990*. New York: Oxford University Press.

UNDP (2002). *Human Development Report 2002*. New York: Oxford University Press. Also at hdr.undp.org/reports/global/2002/en.

UNDP (2005). *Human Development Report 2005*. New York: UNDP. Also at hdr.undp.org/reports/global/2005.

UNICEF (United Nations Children's Fund) (2005). *The State of the World's Children 2005*. New York: UNICEF. Also at www.unicef.org.

USDA (United States Department of Agriculture) (1999). *U.S. Action Plan on Food Security* (www.fas.usda.gov/icd/summit/pressdoc.html).

WHO (World Health Organisation) (2004). *The World Health Report 2004*. Geneva: WHO Publications. Also at www.who.int/whr/2004.

World Bank (2002). *World Development Report 2002*. New York: Oxford University Press, also at http://econ.worldbank.org/wdr/structured_doc.php?sp=2391&st=&sd=2394.

World Bank (2003). *World Development Report 2003*. New York: Oxford University Press.

World Bank (2005). *World Development Report 2005*. New York: Oxford University Press.

11

Reconstructing Global Governance: Eight Innovations

Andrew Kuper

Prologue: How Did We Get Here?

States are failing us, especially the poorest among us. The problem is not primarily personal, though of course there are many corrupt and bellicose leaders, but rather structural. The state system is simply not designed to meet some of the major challenges that now confront our world and its vulnerable people. Globalization – particularly the massive growth in the extent, intensity, velocity, and scope of cross-border interactions (Held et al., 1999) – has not been met by a corresponding increase in our capacity to exercise political control over this enmeshed world. We have gaping holes where governance should be.

How did we get here? The short answer is that, in the face of dramatic de facto changes in economic and political power, there has been a combined failure to reconstruct political theory and to transform our political institutions – to the dramatic extent commensurate with this new reality. We are stuck with an ineffectual multilateral state system when what we need is a twenty-first-century, effective and democratic system of global governance. In two recent books, I have argued with, exhorted and cajoled both theorists and practitioners to recognize the nature of this historic problem and, when it comes to developing tentative solutions, to think bigger.

Democracy Beyond Borders (Kuper, 2004) pointed out that liberalism and democracy are now the most widely accepted forms of official justification for political rule, yet both doctrines were developed largely in and for nation-states. In the face of globalization, neither the multilateral, multipolar, nor unipolar models (sometimes caricatured as the UN, the French, and the American models) are up to the job. This is because all three models place states, and only states, at the centre of things. And states can no longer serve as the central organizing institutions around which other levels and kinds of political authority are constructed as mere supplements and band-aids. Where economy, society and politics are intrinsically global and multilayered, so too must be the forms and mechanisms that regulate and enable those spheres.[1]

Global Responsibilities: Who Must Deliver on Human Rights? (Kuper, 2005a) put this challenge more positively: where transnational actors, from multinational corporations (MNCs) to global citizen sector organizations (CSOs), exercise immense power, that power should be internalized and harnessed to deepen liberal democracy rather than escape or subvert responsiveness to citizens' interests and control. We must enable and restrain non-state actors in many more areas of life, and we must hold them responsible and accountable for the exercise of their power.

Thus the central challenge for our theory and practice becomes: how can we extend the principles and practices of liberal justice and representative democracy beyond the state contexts for which they were devised? I tried to offer a new and fundamentally non-statist theory of how to organize and institutionalize governance. I also articulated an inter-locking set of authoritative structures, and authorized actors, that could facilitate a change in the configurations of power (de jure and de facto).

I cannot recapitulate all these arguments here. Instead, I have been asked to offer a manifesto, collecting and linking eight of my proposals as to how we might move forward politically in the face of globalization. As such, I ask the reader to be forgiving if, in the effort to be succinct and synthetic, I sometimes speed over issues I have addressed rigor-ously elsewhere. The eight proposals are labelled as follows:

1 Securing Rights by Defining Obligations
2 Bringing Non-state Actors into Governance
3 Redistributing Responsibilities
4 Enabling Neo-electoral Democracy
5 Instituting a Plurality of Powers
6 Extending Accountability Agencies
7 Enshrining a Charter of Obligations
8 Restructuring Corporate and Citizen Sectors

Each innovation would constitute a substantial step towards realizing rights and deep-ening democracy. My hope is that these future-oriented reflections and provocations help define the focus of the next generation (my generation, the global generation) of political thinkers about governance.

1 Securing Rights by Defining Obligations

Human rights are now the dominant normative language of international affairs and human development. The number and types of claims made in the name of human rights have proliferated far beyond the expectations of the drafters of the Universal Declaration of Human Rights – notably, into once-remote areas of social, economic and cultural rights. But these facts stand awkwardly alongside the fact that billions of people's rights are violated or unrealized every day and, most of the time, no one does anything about it.

When people witness these widespread instances of 'all talk and little action', they may suspect that the discourse of human rights is mostly vacuous rhetoric. Worse, the deploy-ment of such rhetoric may be offensive and damaging, acting as a sop to the righteous anger of those who are poor and needy, while serving as a salve to the consciences of the rich and powerful.

What makes 'human rights' more than empty words? The answer is that this notion marks out a particular set of human claims as peculiarly urgent, such that they should have priority in public reasoning and political action.[2] Rights will be meaningful if they are practical entitlements that make a difference to the people that hold them, by making justifiable claims on other agents to take ameliorative action.

Yet, if we think about it this way, we may quickly recognize an appalling vagueness that besets our attempts to identify and realize rights. Most of the time, with the best intentions in the world, people are simply pointing to terrible situations and saying – in effect – 'somebody must do something'. That generic reaction will make a limited difference at best. We need to be far more specific and ask, consistently and systematically: *who* must do *what* for *whom*?[3] We need to identify the particular agents (whether states or non-state actors or individuals) who are able and obliged to deliver on the rights of poor and needy individuals and groups.

Why is this the central question we should be asking? The simple answer is: responsibility. If a definite agent or set of agents has obligations to a person or group – and is failing to live up to those obligations – then there is someone at fault and someone who should remedy the fault. There is someone against whom that person or group or their representatives could lay a complaint – whether in the court of public opinion or preferably in more formal fora. There even may be an effective procedure through which to ensure that their rights are enforced or violations of their rights properly remedied. Once we identify relevant actors, there is the prospect of substantive action. We can then move beyond desperate and dispiriting hand-wringing, as well as infelicitous use of language.

2 Bringing Non-state Actors into Governance

The central reason that rights discourse has been largely blind to problems of responsibility, historically, is an excessive focus on *states* as the agents who would supposedly deliver on human rights. In attributing responsibility for rights, for instance, the Preamble to the Universal Declaration of Human Rights slips seamlessly from 'the conscience of mankind' to 'peoples' to 'Member States'. If it was grievously optimistic in 1948 to believe that states could meet all human rights claims, it is evidently entirely implausible today, for two main reasons.

First, even as the number and types of human rights claims have proliferated, states have retreated from numerous areas of policy and practice that are central to realizing those rights. The causal story here is a complex one – involving the rise of certain economic worldviews and trade regimes, resistance to 'big government', state failure, and more.

Second, this retreat of the state – and ever larger lacunae in governance – has bolstered, and been bolstered by, the rise and flexing of muscles of non-state actors: 191 states now share the global stage with over 60,000 multinational corporations (MNCs) and over 44,000 international non-governmental organizations or citizen sector organizations (UNDP, 2000, 2002, p. 19), along with millions of more local CSOs; many of them are performing tasks traditionally seen as the preserve of state governments. Of the 100 most powerful economic entities in the world, only 49 are states; the majority, 51, are corporations (Anderson and Cavanagh, 2000). These numerous and newly powerful actors ensure that the era of complete state monopolies on governance is over.

It is, quite simply, empirically inaccurate and politically defeatist to presume that non-state actors are invariably malevolent or indifferent to human rights. Some MNCs are rogues while some are at the forefront of innovative human development efforts (there is Enron but then there are also the Cisco Networking Academies). Some CSOs are pernicious fronts for special interests while some are saving lives and livelihoods exactly as they proclaim (there is the National Rifle Association but then there is also Médecins sans Frontières). A reactive posture, that rejects one kind of agent outright as a threat to justice, is simplistic and irresponsible. Above all, such knee-jerk reactions make us overlook significant opportunities.

If we are to adapt to globalization and to the rapid rise of non-state actors, our main aim must be to structure our global political order such that we weed out and diminish malevolent or indifferent agents, while harnessing and helping potential agents of justice and development. This will require two connected changes:

Redistributing responsibilities   Establishing and entrenching principles for fairly and felicitously assigning obligations to deliver on human rights and other valuable ends; and

Reconfiguring representation   Introducing mechanisms that facilitate the use of power (by state and non-state actors) to realize the views and interests of the public, as well as mechanisms that constrain the abuse of that power.

We must find a fair and accurate way to identify responsible agents, we must empower them to use their power wisely and well, and we must position them so that they minimally abuse their power. I now discuss these essential changes in turn.

3 Redistributing Responsibilities

The first step in assigning obligations to states as well as non-state actors (such that we can rightly call them agents of justice and development) is to establish the principled bases for attributing such political responsibilities. We can pick out the responsible agent or agents on at least seven principled grounds:

1 The agent caused the deprivation
2 The agent contributed to the deprivation
3 The agent is morally responsible for the deprivation
4 The agent is a beneficiary as a result of the person's deprivation
5 The agent has the greatest capacity to remedy the deprivation
6 The agent is closely connected to the deprived person by ties of community
7 The agent was best positioned to bear a risk that the person would become deprived[4]

The second step is to apply and adjudicate between these principles in grave cases of deprivation where it is essential that someone do something. David Miller has rightly argued that no one principle is likely to be satisfactory and superordinate in every instance. Instead, we must adopt a theory that is more openly pluralist, using the principles to elicit our intuitions and clarify our convictions as to the *strength of connection* between potential actors and deprived persons in each context (Miller, 2005). No final ranking of principles is possible, but the principles are still profoundly useful in deciding fairly and felicitously who can be expected to deliver on human rights.

The third and final step is to convince the relevant agents to act on their obligations. This is a deeply political and contextual exercise. Nonetheless, the ways we structure our systems of governance (and the public normative arguments we use to justify these systems) make a dramatic difference to the incentives and disincentives that drive powerful agents.

4 Enabling Neo-electoral Democracy

The most significant factor in structuring our political order is how we reconceptualize and reinvigorate democracy in the face of globalization. At a minimum, democracy has the great virtue of being a non-violent and regularized way to mediate conflicts between factions and between potential rulers. While democracies have typically experienced more strikes and public protests than dictatorships, democracies suffer war only every 21 years, on average, compared with every 12 years for dictatorships (UNDP, 2002). Moreover, no famine has ever occurred in a democracy, since rulers have the information and incentives (mostly deriving from the risk of being cast out of office) to prevent many thousands of their citizens from suffering avoidable death (as covered in graphic detail by free media) (Sen, 1983, 1999/2001).

However, democracy is not synonymous with elections, and it is crucial to understand what elections can and cannot do. Certainly, elections are the most effective mechanism we have devised to select and remove government representatives, to encourage them to pay attention to the interests and views of the public, and to discourage them from abusing their power. But, on their own, they are nowhere near sufficient to ensure adequate democratic representation. There is the age-old problem of the tyranny of the majority. There is the all-too-prevalent problem of permanent minorities. There is the notorious problem of wealthy special interests that, unchecked, exercise undue influence over candidates and processes of election, as well as distorting policies and priorities between elections.

These problems, and a legion of others, have been examined and elaborated since Socrates' time; but our globalized world presents a new problem: elections typically appoint, empower and constrain officers of or within *states*; yet if the state is only one powerful actor among many, and not always the dominant actor, then electoral mechanisms will fail to regulate the use and abuse of vast swathes of de facto (and sometimes de jure) political power.

So we face a choice: *either* we must find ways to elect the leaders of multilateral bodies, multinational corporations, international CSOs, and so forth, *or* we must find non-electoral mechanisms that operate synergistically with state-based electoral mechanisms to ensure adequate representation of our views and interests. The first of these options is, to my mind, a mixture of nonsense and fantasy. While it is conceivable (though deeply unlikely) that 6 billion people in this world could directly elect a 'People's Assembly' in the UN – as Richard Falk and Andrew Strauss (Falk and Strauss, 2000) have suggested – it is ridiculous to suppose that 6 billion of us could, for instance, elect the leaders or boards of 80,000 MNCs and 44,000 international CSOs. Nor could we elect them indirectly through our chosen state representatives; after all, our dilemma originates precisely in the fact that state rulers do not have the power to impose their will in this way (and, for a host of reasons to do with safeguarding freedoms, probably should not).

We are left with one hope: that we might, with effort and imagination, develop non-electoral mechanisms that act as powerful complements to electoral mechanisms, rescuing democracy from increasing marginalization in the face of reconfigured global power relations. And here we can take our cue from the mechanisms that have been devised *within* states to mitigate the many problems of electoral democracy.

5 Instituting a Plurality of Powers

Primary among non-electoral mechanisms for helping secure democracy is the separation of powers. As the framers of the Constitution of the United States put it,

> A dependence on the people is, no doubt, the primary control on the government; but experience has taught mankind the necessity of auxiliary precautions. This policy of supplying, by opposite and rival interests, the defect of better motives . . . [is] particularly displayed in all the subordinate distributions of power, where the constant aim is to divide and arrange the several offices in such a manner as that each may be a check on the other. (Madison et al., 1788)

Separation of powers can address asymmetries of both power and information between citizens and rulers by inducing institutions (i.e. office holders in institutions) to – in the now immortal phrase – check and balance one another. The basic idea is to assign authorities well-defined powers over distinct and potentially conflicting governmental functions, and yet make all those authorities dependent upon one another if they are to fulfil their respective functions. They are then faced with strong reasons to agree to a common set of laws and policies, and this need for consensus or compromise has at least two effects. Where their preferred ends or means for fulfilling their functions come into conflict, authorities tend to attempt to harness the capacities of citizens and other authorities as resources of power against one another. Authorities also attempt to monitor and constrain one another in their daily operation so as to ensure that no authority or subset of authorities comes to dominate.

This much is widely accepted in the literature. But in any context there is a need to consider how many and what kinds of separate authorities are best. A distinctive question I have asked in my work is: can the idea of a separation of powers, developed to deal with potential problems internal to states, be adopted and adapted to address challenges to democratic representation beyond the state? The answer to this question is more familiar and promising than one might think.

We commonly talk not only about representative *agents* but also about a *system* of representative government. The latter locution emphasizes the way in which political institutions function so as consistently to produce outcomes that take into account the interests and views of the public. This means that we have to go beyond assessing our control over individual agents of justice (or injustice). For the purposes of an overall judgement of the extent to which the public are democratically represented by their political order, we must also consider the complex division of labour between citizens and representatives and between representatives themselves. We are required, in short, not merely to tally up the quantity and quality of various representatives but in addition to examine the cumulative effects over time of institutionalized interactions.

Such a system-centric analysis can pull us in a different direction from agent-centric analyses. For instance, adopting an agent-centric view, we may regard the inclusion of certain actors (for example, an international CSO such as Transparency International) in formal structures of governance as unwarranted, because citizens do not appoint such actors. But, adopting a system-centric view, we may discover that the inclusion of these actors increases the responsiveness of other representatives and of the political system overall to the views and best interests of the public. Moreover, other (elected and unelected) representatives may in turn constrain the unelected actors in important ways, reducing the scope of those actors themselves for unresponsiveness. In such cases, we may have good reasons to give priority to system-centric representation: we may care more about overall citizen control over governance and its outcomes than about whether any particular agent is elected or not.

None of this is to say that global representation can dispense with elections or states. Rather, it is to stress that the mechanisms for securing democratic representation go beyond both vibrant civil society and elections to state offices. The Montesquieuian separation of powers advances democracy not despite but *because of* the fact that it introduces unelected elements into the framework of government – mechanisms that ultimately give citizens greater control over their individual and collective lives. The analogy is not exact, but the principle is the same. Our hope lies in the direction of developing a similar working framework at the global level – a framework that balances the power of states against that of corporations and that of citizen sector organizations, such that each checks the other, and they collectively improve the responsiveness of the current global order.[5]

In *Democracy Beyond Borders* (Kuper, 2004), I termed this framework 'a plurality of powers' and articulated it at length. In the next two sections, I want to briefly elucidate the two most important ways that it could be instantiated in global institutions. Clearly, our present world stands at a great remove from any such institutional order. But the enduring relative decline of the state leaves us with no other justifiable route.

6 Extending Accountability Agencies

Within most states, there exist a variety of ombudsmen, commissions, auditors-general and other mechanisms of accountability. In practice, these bodies cross traditional divides, since they are institutional hybrids that (in principle or in practice) have judicial, legislative, and executive elements to them. That is precisely what makes them interesting and, often, extremely useful as disciplines on governance. From the Human Rights and Gender Commissions in South Africa, to the Corruption Commission in India, to the Scottish Legal Ombudsman, to Special Prosecutors in the United States, these entities have a history that is at once promising and vexed.

Institutions of this kind that are effective share certain features, in that they (a) use those powers to demonstrate the credible threat of exposure and sanction for malfeasance or neglect by authorities; (b) strongly resist being co-opted or overridden by any arm of governance; (c) are so constituted that they do not become a law unto themselves (e.g. 'rogue prosecutors'); and (d) complement or compensate for the limits of civil society (e.g. the lack of statutory powers and/or developed advocacy capacities in certain areas) by being sensitive to its concerns. Properly constituted, such accountability agencies enjoy entrenched powers, secure resources, and a depth of expertise and experience that enables them to access information, provide analyses and make arguments on citizens' behalf.

Global governance is in its relative infancy, and so we lack many such accountability agencies that look and operate beyond individual states. (Of course, there are ad hoc commissions, such as the UN Commission that examined the Iraq oil-for-food scandal, yet few standing entities.) But it is precisely the limits of civil society and governmental institutions that give rise to an intense need for accountability agencies at the regional and global levels too.

Consider the alternatives. Even more so than within states, internationally we cannot necessarily rely on courts to elicit and confront the most pressing issues of the day. Courts – domestic and international – respond to cases, and many cases never get their day in court, sometimes because they lack a champion and sometimes for more unsavoury or realpolitik reasons. Even more so than in states, we cannot rely on professional politicians or diplomats to hold each other to account, not least because most are loath to challenge the orthodoxies and advantages of their profession. We are all too familiar with the intense resistance by incumbents to campaign finance reform, across party lines within states, and the shared desire of ambassadors to avoid international embarrassment, across country lines. Even more so than in states, we cannot rely on media outlets to obtain and sustain coverage of global issues of great concern to vulnerable people, who are thought to have limited purchasing power or simply to be too far away to be of continuing intense interest. Courts, interstate diplomacy, and the media are vital for democracy and development, but they are far from sufficient disciplines on the exercise of power.

How should we think about and constitute these accountability agencies at the global level? Strong, standing, and semi-independent certainly. With non-trivial powers to investigate circumscribed domains, propose reforms and monitor the implementation of changes. But the most difficult set of questions concerns how to guard these guardians in such ways that they are insulated from direct political meddling while ultimately remaining under democratic control.

The answers involve detailed institutional design, but note that similar questions have been posed and answered rather effectively for the idea and practice of an independent judiciary. The range of solutions includes: a professional code of ethics, long-term appointments, a multi-stakeholder commission of appointment, agreement by a majority of legislators on both sides, review by higher courts, and so forth. None of these measures removes the possibility of 'rogue' judges but they do make a world with a largely independent judiciary better than a world without it. In the case of accountability agencies, we may be even more optimistic, since the judiciary now exists that may be able to oversee and perhaps appoint some office-holders, and could act as a firewall against such situations as malevolent budget cuts by politicians who aim to avoid scrutiny.

In short, the strength and independence, and yet social sensitivity, of accountability agencies will be a challenge to maintain. But it is an immensely worthwhile challenge – to which we should direct greater imagination if we aim to secure democratic responsiveness beyond borders.

7 Enshrining a Charter of Obligations

I have argued that we should extend the separation and balancing of powers beyond the state in two senses – to different *types* of actors (corporations, CSOs, accountability agencies, etc.) and different *levels* of actors involved in governance (from international CSOs and MNCs to local government). This systemic approach has distinct advantages. Yet it runs counter to a strong Hobbesian strand of political thought and practice: the view that there must be an overall sovereign authority in the last instance. In my view, the history of constitutionalism is a historic progression away from this idea: the Hobbesian sovereign was soon deprived of his formal absolutism, and soon parcelled up into several kinds of authority with distinct personalities. Our conceptions of governance have moved instead towards the idea of a framing document that structures an effective division of power, in a system that ultimately secures responsiveness of rulers to the citizenry.

But how will this complex system work globally, and not become mired in bureaucracy? Here, the burden of proof actually falls upon the Hobbesian statist: it is the challenges of practice, even more than the evolution of principle, that have shown such a balancing of powers to be effective. The complexity of more institutions or authorities can be and has been offset by the better coordination and distribution of responsibilities that such plurality allows. In both the United States and India, for example, with hundreds of millions of citizens, highly federalist and largely decentralized government is taken to be an essential cause of relative stability and prosperity.

I am not here suggesting a world constitution or world federalism – in fact, I take both these ideals to be neither desirable nor feasible. But I do recommend a framing document, to complement the Universal Declaration of Human Rights, which clarifies the duties of diverse actors and authorities, and their relationships to one another.[6] It might be called the Universal Declaration of Human Responsibilities. Three underlying principles should infuse such a document:

The principle of distributive subsidiarity   Formal powers are to be allocated according to the functional capacities at each locus of governance, with the most local level preferred, except where combining functions into clusters will result in substantial improvements in delivery (realizing rights and capabilities).

The principle of cumulative democracy   New authorities are to be introduced, and new powers conferred, only if it can be shown that they are reasonably likely to increase the overall responsiveness of representative structures. Accountability agencies, for instance, are to be introduced only where current authorities are inadequate or substantially suboptimal mechanisms of empowerment and constraint.

The principle of communicative competence   Authorities are to have well-defined and interlocking requirements and capacities to communicate, such that there are clear lines of responsibility for knowledge-sharing and coordination – and not merely for command and control. Bureaucratic inertia and misinformation are reduced by avoiding vague injunctions to 'consult' or 'take into account', and instead creating compelling institutional disincentives to obstructionist office-holders who are not communicating or cooperating.

I have discussed these principles and their application elsewhere (though this is the first time I have formalized them all) and shown how they are based on the same underlying theory of knowledge and action.[7] But note: there is no unique institutional configuration or 'final moment' that instantiates these three principles. Instead, they provide an evaluative standpoint for reform of institutional arrangements and for political action. It is this room for continuity and flexibility that lies at the heart of great enduring pluralist democratic political arrangements, and that would make the Universal Declaration of Human Responsibilities a living document.

8 Restructuring Corporate and Citizen Sectors

It is one thing to envision this system and its principles, and quite another to encourage and enable powerful individual actors in the global arena to pursue it in such a way that democratic innovations are diffused across the globe, and become the new norm in both attitudes and institutions. To put it in a language popularized by Malcolm Gladwell but pioneered by Nobel Laureate Robert Schelling: Who are the 'tipping point' actors? What actions should they take to catalyse such global transformations? What incentives will work to involve them consistently and correctly in this long-term project?

Given the numbers and power of multinational corporations and global citizen sector organizations described above, the mobilization of these actors will be critical (and I have explored these mobilization and motivation questions in various writings). But especially transformative could be those actors who combine the best of both sectors: *social enterprises*. I shall therefore leave aside the discussion of conventional actors here and focus on these hybrid organizations, and the actions and incentives that matter most for them. I do so because, quite simply, they embody the possibility of the structural transformation of the corporate and citizen sectors, and thence of some of the underlying conditions and forms of governance.

The rise of these newly prominent actors can be charted in brief as follows.[8] For several centuries, the for-profit and non-profit sectors have been kept separate and often at loggerheads. Businesses have aimed to satisfy demand, not need, to be efficient and competitive, not fair and inclusive, and to care about the growth of wealth, not the extent of its distribution. Citizen organizations have tended to disparage this kind of thinking and, in contrast, viewed their social justice missions as compensating for and anathema to 'bottom line' thinking. This binary has become increasingly untenable in practice.

Numerous corporations are finding that, in order to succeed on a sustainable basis, they require a mission beyond profit and a structure that involves ethical engagement with various stakeholder communities. Companies that fail to adjust are stuck in an industrial age model of business, and can be outcompeted by companies which utilize social capital, networks and diversity to achieve sustainable competitive advantage in a global informational economy. Leaders in the citizen sector, meanwhile, are finding that for-profit activities and a host of business strategies are often essential to sustainability and 'scaling-up' so as to multiply their social impact.

Evidently, the attitudes of many people in these two sectors are behind the curve, but icons of both sectors have merged social and financial goals. Muhammad Yunus, who has enabled tens of millions of people to lift themselves out of poverty through microcredit and related financial mechanisms, did so by creating Grameen Bank and the Grameen Family of Companies. His Grameen Phone, for instance, loans phones to low-income rural women who rent out telephone time in their villages, and – partly through this model of empowering micro-entrepreneurs – fast became the second largest cellular phone network in South Asia. Sticking with Bangladesh, Fazle Abed founded BRAC, the world's largest citizen organization, which has pioneered innovations in education, health and social finance. It has over 30,000 direct employees, over 4 million borrowers, has created programmes and companies with a further 100,000 full- or part-time employees, and serves tens of millions of needy citizens, 'organizing the poor for power'. (BRAC is working well in places where governments and MNCs and CSOs have often failed to change things, such as Afghanistan and Sri Lanka, and is expanding fast in various countries in Africa.) Such models of achieving social justice from the grass roots up, on an unprecedented scale, make conventional labelling such as 'non-profit' positively obsolete.

In the domain ordinarily labelled 'for profit', meanwhile, Larry Page and Sergey Brin, founders of Google, have created their highly valued company by erecting a company infrastructure (from the physical campus to the mission statement) around social values that sometimes fly in the face of ordinary profit-maximizing mantras. They also recently launched Google.org, which they intend will eventually eclipse Google.com. Similarly, Pierre Omidyar, founder of eBay, envisioned the central purpose of his company as engendering 'global economic democracy', with notable effects on societies and cultures. By creating an infrastructure for trust, self-reporting and mutual policing as a community, eBay has enabled strangers to engage in trust-dependent transactions, and thereby produced the largest market in the world, with over a hundred million registered users.[9]

The implications of hybrid organizational forms for governance are profound.[10] First, they present an opportunity to move beyond some stale debates about mandatory regulation of companies (by states) versus voluntary self-regulation (through corporate social responsibility), neither of which seems particularly plausible on its own. That is, companies can move beyond a self-restraint in their operations for fear of bad publicity to an approach that incorporates social aims into the very modus operandi of the company in order to achieve sustainable competitive advantage. (The new languages of 'base of the pyramid', 'hybrid value chains', and 'ethics – the leadership edge' are manifestations of this underlying shift.) States can move beyond pure disincentive-focused regulation by developing enabling regulatory environments for hybrid ventures – for example, legal structures that do not force organizations to pigeon-hole themselves as for- or non-profit. I am not suggesting that state- or self-regulation are not important, but these defensive and knave-centred approaches have limited motivational force, and should be supplemented and in some cases supplanted by opportunity-centric approaches.

Second, hybrid ventures should mute a number of the objections that have been raised against my view that corporations can play a representative role in governance, alongside states and citizen organizations. The image of representatives of Enron and Philip Morris sitting with leaders of states and citizen organizations and making political decisions on our behalf is a rightly perturbing one. But we would feel rather differently – and rightly so – about a corporate presence represented by people with the proven social commitment and impact of Yunus, Abed, Page and Brin, or Omidyar. Put more systematically, the criteria for entry into a shared governance role might be sufficiently stringent that only companies that cross a certain social threshold would be entitled to collectively appoint representatives to the table of governance. This threshold is difficult to establish but could be assessed by (increasingly sophisticated) evaluation metrics covering the organization's mission, structure, impact, and accountability.[11]

A threshold approach to inclusion of non-state actors in governance has several advantages. It generates incentives for companies that do not yet make the grade to become more socially oriented. It rewards and recognizes those who have made the determined effort to meet the criteria. It ensures that corporate representatives are of a kind that understand the nature and support the purposes of development organizations and states. And it increases the likelihood that corporate representatives would exercise good judgement (never perfect, never entirely impartial) in pursuit of the best interests of the public.[12]

Cultivating, cumulating and connecting social enterprises promises to alter the daily impact of citizen organizations and companies fundamentally. In so doing, we may also transform the daily experiences and attitudes of people in every sector of society. Without such changes in our major cultural and socio-economic organizations there can be no lasting reconstruction of global governance.

Conclusion: Where Do We Go from Here? Toward Responsive Democracy

A multilateral system based predominantly on states is not working. If we stop pretending that it could *ever* work on its own, an unprecedented opportunity becomes apparent. It is the opportunity to resolve two challenges simultaneously: in our time, the pressing challenges are not only *what* liberal democracy is and ought to be (content) but also *where* liberal democracy is and ought to be (scope). By addressing both, this generation of thinkers and actors can help liberal democracy to break out of the doctrinal shackles of nation-statism that hold its global potential at bay.

The aim is to harness non-state actors and reframe the division of political labour, introducing new forms of power, responsibility, and mutual accountability. In so doing, we answer the liberal constitutionalist preoccupation with checking the wrongful use of power against individuals; but we *also* answer to the democratic preoccupation with producing political decisions that show rich and inclusive concern for a wide range of citizens' interests and their actions to control the use of power. It is for this reason that I have called the ideal institutional configuration advanced in these practical reflections Responsive Democracy.[13]

I do not pretend that the eight aspects of the transition toward Responsive Democracy, articulated above, will be easy or immediately achieved. Quite the contrary: the ambitious scope of these innovations is intended to constitute an enabling framework for ongoing institutional reform and collective action. It is a pivotal purpose of long-termist political imagination to defeat the sense of despair that occasionally besets anyone who faces honestly the immense problems of this difficult world, and to help us to discern and inspire the kinds of change that make hope meaningful in politics.

Notes

1   In response to a few misguided critics, who are not prone to close reading, let me say explicitly: I rejected the absurd view that we can dispense with states and state-building. But I *also* rejected the spurious view that the state system could be adequate to meet our needs entirely and realize basic human rights in this world.

2   The following formulations draw on *Global Responsibilities* (Kuper, 2005a), particularly the definitional parsings by O'Neill, James, and Miller.

3   This is Onora O'Neill's pioneering and precise formulation of the question.

4   These principles are examined by various contributors to *Global Responsibilities* (2005). However, it was Miller (2005) who originally elucidated four of the principles (1, 3, 5 and 6), while Barry (2005) suggested three further principles (2, 4 and 7) in response to Miller (2005).

5   In *Democracy Beyond Borders* (Kuper, 2004), I illustrate how the inclusion of non-state actors in formal structures and proceedings of three major institutions – the United Nations, International Court of Justice and International Criminal Court – would result in more and better utilization of these political organs, enhancing global justice and democracy. Take, for example, the International Court of Justice (ICJ): currently, only states may be parties in cases before the ICJ and states have to agree to submit their dispute to the Court. (The only exception to this restriction is that UN organs and agencies may petition the Court for non-binding 'advisory opinions'.) In practice, this means that the Court is drastically under-utilized and is not a significant presence in international affairs. While the European Court of Human Rights decides about 60 cases a year, and the US Supreme Court decides about 100, the ICJ renders judgments annually on a grand total of four cases. A careful study shows one factor to be the dominant cause: states and state bureaucrats want 'neither to lose political and administrative control of disputes nor to embarrass other states and organizations' (Janis, 1997, pp. 208–12). Meanwhile, *all* the cases before the European Court, bar one, were brought by individuals (supported by NGOs and others) and not by states (1997, pp. 211–12). As long as only one *kind* of actor is present, the situation of the ICJ is unlikely to be rectified. If, however, other actors – perhaps certain NGOs and chambers of commerce – are given standing before the international court (*locus standi in judicio*), then more cases and more kinds of cases will be brought to the ICJ, and it may attain some of the reach and credibility of other major courts. We should be thinking about these kinds of institutional reforms, reforms that break the logic of statism, for other political organs of global society too.

6   The (Valencia) Declaration of Duties was a first attempt at such a complementary document, and was ably chaired by constitution-writer and Constitutional Court judge Richard Goldstone. But, for a host of reasons, it is a pale shadow of what is needed (see Kuper, 2005a, pp. 116–17). Notably, it is unspecific and non-binding, and fails to recognize that most duties are requirements, not aspirations, so it loses the model and motivational structure that lends force to an approach based on duties. (For other critiques, see Pogge, 2005). British Prime Minister Tony Blair proposed a (statist) 'charter of competences' for the European Union in his 'A Superpower, but Not a Superstate' speech, reprinted in *The Guardian*, 7 October 2000.

7 These principles are elaborated at most length in Kuper, 2004, pp. 33n., 113–17, 167–8, 197. They are based on a distinctive approach to political knowledge and action that can be put fairly simply: we should not falsely assume or seek to attain any political perspective that locates the totality of authoritative political knowledge or action. Instead, we should recognize that different authorities with different purposes and logics focus on different aspects of issues, and develop special capacities to make high-quality judgements (of needs or rights, and how to meet or realize them) in their areas of competence and responsibility.

8 I am indebted to Bill Drayton, CEO of Ashoka, and Laurance Kuper, Managing Director of Competitive Strategy (my father), for valuable conversations and insights on this story. See Drayton, 2007, and Kuper, 2006; also Bornstein, 2004.

9 The narrative of social missions unlocking new markets for businesses is not confined to technology companies in the 'new economy', but extends to large companies with such concrete core products as drip irrigation equipment (e.g. Amanco, part of Group Nueva) and cement (e.g. Cemex).

10 It should be noted that none of these ventures is without its significant flaws, or invariably beneficial, but that should hardly surprise us – after all, they are built around mechanisms for human interaction, and we are a polymorphously flawed species.

11 I discuss these metrics, in relation to a range of exemplary approaches such as the Global Accountability Project, in Kuper, 2005b.

12 On judgement, partiality, and the best interests of the public, see Kuper, 2004, pp. 113–17, 167–8, and the Conclusion.

13 For a summary of Responsive Democracy as compared to two major alternatives, Rawls's liberal statism and Habermas's deliberative democracy, see the Conclusion in Kuper, 2004.

References

Anderson, S. and J. Cavanagh (2000). 'Top 200: The Rise of Corporate Global Power', Institute for Policy Studies, December.

Barry, Christian (2005). 'Applying the Contribution Principle', in A. Kuper, ed., *Global Responsibilities: Who Must Deliver on Human Rights?* London: Routledge.

Blair, Tony (2000). 'A Superpower, but Not a Superstate', speech to the European Union, reprinted in *The Guardian*, 7 October.

Bornstein, David (2004). *How to Change the World.* Oxford: Oxford University Press.

Drayton, Bill (2007). 'The Citizen Sector Transformed', in A. Nichols et al., *Social Entrepreneurship.* Oxford: Oxford University Press.

Falk, Richard and Andrew Strauss (2000). 'On the Creation of a People's Assembly: Legitimacy and the Power of Popular Sovereignty', *Stanford Journal of International Law*, 36: p. 191.

Held, D. et al., eds (1999). *Global Transformations,* Cambridge: Polity.

Janis, Mark W. (1997). 'Individuals and the International Court', in A. S. Muller, D. Raic and J. Thuramzky, eds, *The International Court of Justice: Its Future Role after Fifty Years.* The Hague: Martinus Nijhoff.

Kuper, Andrew (2004). *Democracy Beyond Borders: Justice and Representation in Global Institutions.* Oxford: Oxford University Press.

Kuper, Andrew (2005a). *Global Responsibilities: Who Must Deliver on Human Rights?* London: Routledge.

Kuper, Andrew (2005b). 'Redistributing Responsibilities: The UN Global Compact with Corporations', in A. Follesdal and T. Pogge, eds, *Real World Justice: Grounds, Principles, Human Rights and Social Institutions.* New York: Springer.

Kuper, Laurance (2006). *Ethics – The Leadership Edge*. Johannesburg: Zebra.

Madison, James et al. (1788), *Federalist*, 51.

Miller, David (2005), 'Distributing Responsibilities', in A. Kuper, ed, *Global Responsibilities: Who Must Deliver on Human Rights?* London: Routledge.

Pogge, Thomas (2005). 'Human Rights and Human Responsibilities', in A. Kuper, ed., *Global Responsibilities: Who Must Deliver on Human Rights?* London: Routledge.

Sen, Amartya (1983). *Poverty and Famines: An Essay on Entitlement and Deprivation*. Oxford: Oxford University Press.

Sen, Amartya (1999/2001), *Development as Freedom*. Oxford: Oxford University Press.

UNDP (2000, 2002). *Human Development Report* 2000, 2002. Oxford/New York: Oxford University Press.

12

Reframing Global Governance: Apocalypse Soon or Reform!

David Held

The Paradox of our Times

The paradox of our times can be stated simply: the collective issues we must grapple with are of growing extensiveness and intensity and, yet, the means for addressing these are weak and incomplete. Three pressing global issues highlight the urgency of finding a way forward.

First, little, if any, progress has been made in creating a sustainable framework for the management of global warming. The concentration of carbon dioxide in the global atmosphere is now almost 35 per cent higher than in pre-industrial times (Byers, 2005). The British government chief scientist, Sir David King, has recently warned that 'climate change is the most serious problem we are facing today, more serious than the threat of terrorism' (King, 2004, p. 177). Irrespective of whether one agrees with this statement, global warming has the capacity to wreak havoc on the world's diverse species, biosystems and socio-economic fabric. Violent storms will become more frequent, water access will be a battleground, rising sea levels will displace millions, the mass movement of desperate people will become more common, and deaths from serious diseases in the world's poorest countries will rise rapidly (largely because bacteria will spread more quickly, causing greater contamination of food and water). The overwhelming body of scientific opinion now maintains that global warming constitutes a serious threat not in the long term, but in the here and now. The failure of the international community to generate a sound framework for managing global warming is one of the most serious indications of the problems facing the multilateral order.

Second, little progress has been made towards achieving the millennium goals – the agreed human development targets of the international community, or, one could say, its moral consciousness. The millennium goals set down minimum standards to be achieved in relation to poverty reduction, health, educational provision, the combating of HIV/AIDS, malaria and other diseases, environmental sustainability and so on. Progress towards these targets has been lamentably slow, and there is evidence that they will be missed by a very wide margin. In fact, there is evidence that there may have been no point in setting these targets at all, so far are we from attaining them in many parts of the world. Underlying this human crisis is, of course, the material vulnerability of half of the world's population: 45 per cent of humankind live below the World Bank's $2/day poverty line; 18 per cent (or some 1,089 million people) live below the $1/day poverty line. As Thomas Pogge has appropriately put it, 'people so incredibly poor are extremely vulnerable to even minor shifts in natural and social conditions. . . . Each year, some 18 million of them die prematurely from poverty-related causes. This is one third of all human deaths – 50,000 every day, including 29,000 children under age five' (Pogge, 2006; cf. UNDP, 2005). And, yet, the gap between rich and poor countries continues to rise, and there is evidence that the bottom 10 per cent of the world's population has become even poorer since the beginning of the 1990s (Milanović, 2002).[1]

Third, the threat of nuclear catastrophe may seem to have diminished, but it is only in abeyance, as Martin Rees has recently argued (Rees, 2003, pp. 8, 27, 32–3, 43–4). Huge nuclear stockpiles remain, nuclear proliferation among states is continuing (for example, in India, Pakistan and perhaps Iran), nuclear weapons and materials, due to poor accounting records, may have been purloined (after the demise of the Soviet Union), new generations of tactical nuclear weapons are being built, and 'dirty bomb' technology (the coating of plutonium on the surface of a conventional bomb) makes nuclear terrorism a serious threat. Other dangers exist including terrorist attacks on nuclear power stations, many of which may be in countries with little protective capacity. Adding to these considerations, the disquieting risks stemming from microbiology and genetics (engineered viruses), Rees concludes that 'the odds are no better that fifty–fifty that our present civilisation on Earth will survive to the end of the present century without a serious setback' (2003, p. 8). Certainly, huge questions are raised about accountability, regulation and enforcement.

These global challenges are indicative of three core sets of problems we face – those concerned with sharing our planet (global warming, biodiversity and ecosystem losses, water deficits), sustaining our humanity (poverty, conflict prevention, global infectious diseases) and our rulebook (nuclear proliferation, toxic waste disposal, intellectual property rights, genetic research rules, and trade, finance and tax rules) (Rischard, 2002, p. 66). In our increasingly interconnected world, these global problems cannot be solved by any one nation-state acting alone. They call for collective and collaborative action – something that the nations of the world have not been good at, and which they need to be better at if these pressing issues are to be adequately tackled. Yet the evidence is wanting that we are getting better at building appropriate governance capacity.

Why be Concerned with Global Challenges?

Why do these global issues matter? The answer to this may seem intuitively obvious, but four separate reasons are worth stressing: solidarity, social justice, democracy and policy effectiveness. It is important to clarify each of these because they provide a map of the dimensions we need to keep in mind for thinking about the nature and adequacy of governance at the global level. By solidarity I mean not just empathetic recognition of another's plight, but the willingness to stand side-by-side with others in the creation of solutions to pressing collective problems. Without solidarity between rich and poor, developed and developing countries, the Millennium Development Goals will not be met,[2] and, as Kofi Annan simply put it, 'millions of people will die, prematurely and unnecessarily' (Annan, 2005: 139). These deaths are all the more poignant because solutions are within our grasp. Insofar as challenges like global warming and nuclear proliferation are concerned, we need to add to the definition of solidarity a focus on our own sustainability, never mind that of citizens of the future. Contemporary global challenges require recognition of, and active participation in, the forces that shape our overlapping communities of fate.

A second reason to focus on global challenges is social justice. Standards of social justice are, of course, controversial. To make my argument as accessible as possible, I will, following Pogge, take social justice to mean the fulfilment of human rights in an institutional order to the extent that it is reasonably possible (Pogge, 2007). Of course, most argue that social justice requires more, and so it can be claimed with some confidence that an institutional order that fails to meet these standards cannot be just. Accordingly, it can be reasoned that insofar as our existing socio-economic arrangements fail to meet the Millennium Goals, and the broader challenges of global warming and the risks of nuclear proliferation, they are unjust, or, simply, beyond justice.

The third reason is democracy. Democracy presupposes a noncoercive political process in and through which people can pursue and negotiate the terms of their interconnectedness, interdependence and difference. In democratic thinking, 'consent' constitutes the basis of collective agreement and governance; for people to be free and equal there must be mechanisms in place through which consent can be registered in the determination of the government of public life (Held, 2006). Yet, when millions die unnecessarily, and billions are threatened unnecessarily, it can clearly be held that serious harm can be inflicted on people without their consent and against their will (Barry, 1998). The recognition of this reveals fundamental deficits in our governance arrangements which go to the heart of both justice and democracy.

Finally, the failure to act sooner rather than later on pressing global issues generally escalates the costs of dealing with them. In fact, the costs of inaction are high and often vastly higher than the costs of action. For instance, it has been estimated that the costs of inaction in dealing with communicable diseases in Africa are about one hundred times greater than the costs of corrective action (Conceição, 2003). Similar calculations have also been undertaken in areas of international financial stability, the multilateral trade regime, and peace and security, all of which show that the costs of deficient global public goods provision are extremely large and outweigh by significant margins the costs of corrective policies (Kaul et al., 2003). And yet, we too often stand paralysed in the face of urgent collective challenges, or actively engage in the reproduction of political and social arrangements that fail to meet the minimum standards that solidarity, justice and democracy require.

Deep Drivers and Governance Challenges

The post-war multilateral order is threatened by the intersection and combination of humanitarian, economic and environmental crises. There are, moreover, forces pushing them from bad to worse; I call these the emergent system of structural global vulnerability, the Washington policy packages and the constellation of contemporary geopolitics. The first factor – structural global vulnerability – is a feature of our contemporary global age, and in all likelihood is here to stay. The other two factors are the outcome of clear political choices, and they can be modified. Their force is willed, even though it often presents itself in the form of inevitability. Or, to put the point another way, the current form of globalization is open to transformation, even if the Doomsday clock (the 'logo' on the Bulletin of Atomic Scientists) is rather too close to midnight.

The world we are in is highly interconnected. The interconnectedness of countries – or the process of 'globalization' as it is often called – can readily be measured by mapping the ways in which trade, finance, communication, pollutants, violence, among many other factors, flow across borders and lock the well-being of countries into common patterns (Held et al., 1999). The deep drivers of this process will be operative for the foreseeable future, irrespective of the exact political form globalization takes. Among these drivers are:

- the changing infrastructure of global communications linked to the IT revolution;
- the development of global markets in goods and services, connected to the new world-wide distribution of information;
- the pressure of migration and the movement of peoples, linked to shifts in patterns of economic demand, in demography and in environmental degradation;
- the end of the Cold War and the diffusion of democratic and consumer values across many of the world's regions, alongside some marked reactions to this;
- the emergence of a new type and form of global civil society, with the crystallization of elements of a global public opinion.

Despite the fractures and conflicts of our age, societies are becoming more interconnected and interdependent. As a result, developments at the local level – whether economic, political or social – can acquire almost instantaneous global consequences and vice versa (Held, 2004, pp. 73–116; Giddens, 1990, pp. 55–78). Link to this the advances in science across many fields, often now instantly diffused through global communication networks, and the global arena becomes both an extraordinary potential space for human development as well as for disruption and destruction by individuals, groups or states (all of whom can, in principle, learn the lessons of nuclear energy, genetics, bacteriology and computer networking) (Rees, 2003, pp. 62, 65).

The second set of driving forces can be summed up in two phrases: the Washington economic consensus and the Washington security agenda. I take a detailed look at these in *Global Covenant* (Held, 2004), and *Debating Globalization* (Barnett et al., 2005). Any assessment of them must be grounded on the issues each seeks to address. But they are now also connected drivers of the specific form globalization takes. Together, they promulgate the view that a positive role for government is to be fundamentally distrusted in core areas of socio-economic life – from market regulation to disaster planning – and that the sustained application of internationally adjudicated policy and regulation threatens freedom, limits growth, impedes development and restrains the good. Of course, neither exhaustively explains the current structures of globalization, but they form a core part of its political circumstances.

The thrust of the Washington Consensus is to enhance economic liberalization and to adapt the public domain – local, national and global – to market leading institutions and processes. It thus bears a heavy burden of responsibility for the common political resistance or unwillingness to address significant areas of market failure, including:

- the problem of externalities, for example the environmental degradation exacerbated by current forms of economic growth;
- the inadequate development of *non*-market social factors, which alone can provide an effective balance between 'competition' and 'cooperation', and thus ensure an adequate supply of essential 'public goods' such as education, effective transportation and sound health; and
- the underemployment or unemployment of productive resources in the context of the demonstrable existence of urgent and unmet need.

Leaving markets alone to resolve problems of resource generation and allocation misses the deep roots of many economic and political difficulties; for instance, the vast asymmetries of life chances within and between nation-states; the erosion of the economic fortune of some countries in the sectors like agriculture and textiles while these sectors enjoy protection and assistance in others; the emergence of global financial flows which can rapidly destabilize national economies; and the development of serious transnational problems involving the global commons. Moreover, to the extent that pushing back the boundaries of state action or weakening governing capacities means increasing the scope of market forces, and cutting back on services which have offered protection to the vulnerable, the difficulties faced by the poorest and the least powerful – north, south, east and west – are exacerbated.

The Washington Consensus has, in sum, weakened the ability to govern – locally, nationally and globally – and it has eroded the capacity to provide urgent public goods. Economic freedom is championed at the expense of social justice and environmental sustainability, with long-term damage to both. And it has confused economic freedom and economic effectiveness. Moreover, the systematic political weaknesses of the Washington Consensus have been compounded by the new Washington security doctrines.

The rush to war against Iraq in 2003 gave priority to a narrow security agenda which is at the heart of the new American security doctrine of unilateral and pre-emptive war. This agenda contradicts most of the core tenets of international politics and international agreements since 1945 (Ikenberry, 2002). It throws aside respect for open political negotiations among states, as it does the core doctrine of deterrence and stable relations among major powers (the balance of power). We have to come to terms not only with the reality that a single country enjoys military supremacy to an unprecedented extent in world history, but also with the fact that it can use that supremacy to respond unilaterally to perceived threats (which may be neither actual nor imminent), and that it will brook no rival.

The new doctrine has many serious implications (Hoffmann, 2003). Among these are a return to an old realist understanding of international relations as, in the last analysis, a 'war of all against all', in which states rightly pursue their national interests unencumbered by attempts to establish internationally recognized limits (self-defence, collective security) on their ambitions. But if this 'freedom' is (dangerously) granted to the United States, why not to Russia, China, India, Pakistan, North Korea, Iran and so on? It cannot be consistently argued that all states bar one should accept limits on their self-defined goals. The flaws of international law and multilateralism can either be addressed, or taken as an excuse for further weakening international institutions and legal arrangements.

It would be wrong to link current threats to the multilateral order just to these policy packages, and specifically to policy shifts introduced by the Bush administrations. First, elements of the Washington Consensus clearly pre-date Bush. Second, the end of the Cold War and the huge geopolitical shifts that have come in its wake may also form a key geopolitical factor. John Ikenberry has formulated the argument thus: 'the rise of America's unipolar power position during the 1990s has complicated the old post-war logic of cooperation among allied democratic states. America's power advantages make it easier for it to say no to other countries or to go it alone' (Ikenberry, 2005). Connected to the decline in incentives for the United States to multilateral cooperation are the divisions within Europe which make it less effective in promulgating an alternative model of global governance. The current state of the leading organizations and institutions of the multilateral order needs unfolding.

Global Governance: Contemporary Surface Trends

In a survey of the current state of key global and regional governance arrangements – the UN, EU and NATO prominent among them – Ikenberry has suggested that they have all weakened. To quote him again: 'today the machinery of the post-war era is in disrepair. No leader, international body or group of states speaks with authority or vision on global challenges' (2005, p. 30). This is my judgement as well. The value of the UN system has been called into question, the legitimacy of the Security Council has been challenged, as have the working practices of many multilateral bodies. While the UN still plays a vital and effective role in peacekeeping, natural disaster mitigation, protecting refugees, among other tasks, the war in Iraq dramatized the weakness of the UN system as a vehicle for global security cooperation and collective decision-making on the use of force. The management of the UN system is also under suspicion, with the oil-for-food programme in Iraq becoming a scandal and UN-helmeted troops in Africa being implicated in sexual violence and the abuse of children. In September 2005 the UN members came together to try to establish new rules and institute bold reforms. But member states were unable to agree on a new grand vision and the summit failed in many key respects. (I return to these issues later.) As a result, the deeply embedded difficulties of the UN system remain unresolved – the marginalization or susceptibility of the UN to the agendas of the most powerful states, the weaknesses of many of its enforcement operations (or lack of them altogether), the underfunding of its organization, the inadequacies of the policing of many environmental regimes (regional and global) and so on.

The future direction of the EU is also highly uncertain. There is a deep sense of unease in Brussels about what the next few years will bring. Anxious about the increasing success of low-cost economies, notably China, India and Brazil, and about whether the European social model can survive in its current form, voters are increasingly expressing scepticism about both European integration and expansion. The French 'no' to the proposed European constitution partly reflects this, as does the Dutch 'no' – although the latter was also fuelled by a perception that the Dutch 'host culture' was under threat from historical waves of immigration. The capacity of Europe to project its 'soft power' alternative to US 'hard power' looks frail, as does its capacity to play a more active global leadership role.

In the absence of the negative unity provided by the Cold War, old foreign policy rival-ries and differences among the big states are reasserting themselves (Ikenberry, 2005, p. 30), and the existing generation of leaders appears as much part of the growing impasse as its solution (i.e. Tony Blair's authority sapped by his alliance with George W. Bush; the French President, Jacques Chirac, a nationalist in European clothing; Gerhard Schroeder out and the new German Chancellor Angela Merkel hamstrung by coalitional con-straints; José Luis Rodriguez Zapatero too junior; etc.). Add to this the limited impact of the Lisbon process,[3] the mixed results at best of the Growth and Stability Pact, and it is clear that the European model, for all its extraordinary innovation and progress, is suffering something of an identity crisis (Held, 2006, ch.12).

While the economic multilaterals are still functioning (although the WTO faces a crit-ical test over whether the Doha round can be brought to a successful conclusion), many of the multilaterals that coordinate the activities of the United States, EU and other leading states all look weaker now: NATO, the G8, treaty-based arms control, among others. Since 9/11 the future of NATO has become clouded. The global redeployment of US forces, and divisions in Europe about the conditions for the use of NATO troops, have rendered the role of NATO increasingly unclear. The G8 has always been more of a 'talking shop' than a vehicle for collective action, but today its meetings appear to have minimal, if any, lasting impact. Tony Blair succeeded in using the 2005 G8 meeting to focus on Africa, but how much will follow from this of a durable kind is an open ques-tion. Arms agreements like the non-proliferation treaty are in crisis. The United States has ignored its NPT obligations, and its announcement that it would create a new generation of tactical 'bunker-busting' missiles has introduced new levels of uncertainty about nuclear risks. In addition, the United States has ignored protocol III on the use of incen-diary weapons of the 1980 Geneva Convention on unconventional weapons (and, arguably, the 1993 Chemical Weapons Convention) by deploying white phosphorus in Falluja, an area of concentrated civilian population.

Against these mounting challenges to the post-war multilateral system, one might place the global outpouring of support for the campaign for tsunami relief. But six months after the tsunami, many countries had not fully paid their pledged support (the United States had paid 43 per cent, Canada 37 per cent, Australia 20 per cent, for example) and UN pleas for assistance in the Niger (where 2.5 million people face starvation) and Malawi (where 5 million are facing starvation) have been largely ignored (Byers, 2005).

The post-war multilateral order is in trouble. With the resurgence of nationalism and unilateralism in US foreign policy, EU disarray and the growing confidence of China, India and Brazil in world economic fora, the political teutonic plates appear to be shift-ing. Clear, effective and accountable global decision-making is needed across a range of global challenges; and, yet, the collective capacity for addressing these matters is in serious doubt.

Problems and Dilemmas of Global Problem-Solving

The field of contemporary geopolitics is merely the chaff, significant though it is. Prior to it, beneath it, underlying it, restricting it are the limits of the post-war settlement itself and of the institutional nexus of the multilateral order. Four deep-rooted problems need highlighting.

In the first instance, there is no clear division of labour among the myriad of international governmental agencies; functions often overlap, mandates frequently conflict, and aims and objectives too often get blurred. There are a number of competing and overlapping organizations and institutions all of which have some stake in shaping different sectors of global public policy. This is true, for example, in the area of health and social policy where the World Bank, the IMF and the WHO often have different or competing priorities (Deacon et al., 2003, pp. 11–35); or, more specifically, in the area of AIDS/HIV treatment, where the WHO, Global Fund, UNAIDS, the G1 (i.e. the United States) and many other interests vie to shape reproductive healthcare and sexual practices.

Reflecting on the difficulties of interagency cooperation during his time as head of the WTO, Mike Moore wrote that 'greater coherence amongst the numerous agencies that receive billions of taxpayers' dollars would be a good start . . . this lack of coherence damages their collective credibility, frustrates their donors and owners and gives rise to public cynicism . . . the array of institutions is bewildering . . . our interdependent world has yet to find the mechanism to integrate its common needs' (Moore, 2003, pp. 220–3).

A second set of difficulties relates to the inertia found in the system of international agencies, or the inability of these agencies to mount collective problem-solving solutions faced with disagreement over means, objectives, costs and so on. This often leads to the situation where, as mentioned previously, the cost of inaction is greater than the cost of taking action. Bill Gates, Chairman of Microsoft, recently referred to the developed world's efforts in tackling malaria as 'a disgrace'; malaria causes an estimated 500 million bouts of illness a year, kills an African child every 30 seconds, and costs an estimated $12 billion a year in lost income, yet investment in insecticide-treated bed nets and other forms of protective treatment would be a fraction of this (Meikle, 2005). The failure to act decisively in the face of urgent global problems not only compounds the costs of dealing with these problems in the long run, but it can also reinforce a widespread perception that these agencies are not just ineffective but unaccountable and unjust.

A third set of problems emerges as a result of issues which span the distinction between the domestic and the foreign. A growing number of issues can be characterized as intermestic – that is, issues which cross the *inter*national and do*mestic* (Rosenau, 2002). These are often insufficiently understood, comprehended or acted upon. For there is a fundamental lack of ownership of global problems at the global level. It is far from clear which global public issues – such as global warming or the loss of biodiversity – are the responsibility of which international agencies, and which issues ought to be addressed by which particular agencies. The institutional fragmentation and competition leads not just to the problem of overlapping jurisdictions among agencies, but also to the problem of issues falling between agencies. This latter problem is also manifest between the global level and national governments.

The fourth set of difficulties relates to an accountability deficit, itself linked to two interrelated problems: the power imbalances among states as well as those between state and non-state actors in the shaping and making of global public policy. Multilateral bodies need to be fully representative of the states involved in them, and they are rarely so. In addition, there must be arrangements in place to engage in dialogue and consultation between state and non-state actors, and these conditions are only partially met in multi-lateral decision-making bodies. Investigating this problem, Inge Kaul and her associates at the UNDP have made the telling point that 'the imbalances among states as well as those between state and non-state actors are not always easy to detect, because in many cases the problem is not merely a quantitative issue – whether all parties have a seat at the negotiating table'. The main problem is often qualitative, 'how well various stakeholders are represented' (Kaul et al., 2003, p. 30). Having a seat at the negotiating table in a major intergovernmental organization (IGO) or at a major conference does not ensure effective representation. For even if there is parity of formal representation, it is often the case that developed countries have large delegations equipped with extensive negotiating and technical expertise, while poorer developing countries often depend on one-person delegations, or have even to rely on the sharing of a delegate. The difficulties that occur range from the significant under-representation of developing countries in agencies such as the IMF – where 24 industrial countries hold 10–11 seats on the executive board while 42 African countries hold only 2 – to problems that result from an inability to develop substantial enough negotiating and technical expertise even with one person/one country decision-making procedures (Buira, 2003; Chasek and Rajamani, 2003; Mendoza, 2003). Accordingly, many people are stakeholders in global political problems that affect them, but remain excluded from the political institutions and strategies needed to address these problems.

Underlying these institutional difficulties is the breakdown of symmetry and congruence between decision-makers and decision-takers (Held, 1995, pp. 141–218). The point has been well articulated recently by Kaul and her associates in their work on global public goods. They speak about the forgotten *equivalence* principle (Kaul et al., 2003, pp. 27–8). This principle suggests that the span of a good's benefits and costs should be matched with the span of the jurisdiction in which decisions are taken about that good. At its simplest, the principle suggests that those who are significantly affected by a global good or bad should have a say in its provision or regulation. Yet, all too often, there is a breakdown of 'equivalence' between decision-makers and decision-takers, between decision-makers and stakeholders, and between the inputs and outputs of the decision-making process. To take some topical examples: a decision to permit the 'harvesting' of rain forests (which releases carbon dioxide into the atmosphere) may contribute to ecological damage far beyond the borders which formally limit the responsibility of a given set of decision-makers. A decision to build nuclear plants near the frontiers of a neighbouring country is a decision likely to be taken without consulting those in the nearby country (or countries), despite the many risks for them.

As a result, we face the challenge of:

- *Matching circles of stakeholders and decision-makers*: to create opportunities for all to have a say about global public goods that affect their lives.
- *Systematizing the financing of global public goods*: to get incentives right and to secure adequate private and public resources for these goods.
- *Spanning borders, sectors, and groups of actors*: to foster institutional interaction and create space for policy entrepreneurship and strategic issue management (Kaul et al., 2003, pp. 5–6)

Failures or inadequacies in global political processes often result from the mismatch between the decision-making circles created in international arenas, and the range of spillovers associated with specific public goods or public bads. 'The challenge is to align the circles of those to be consulted (or to take part in the decision making) with the spill-over range of the good under negotiation' (2003, p. 28).

Strengthening Global Governance

To restore symmetry and congruence between decision-makers and decision-takers, and to entrench the principle of equivalence, requires a strengthening of global governance and a resolve to address those institutional challenges just discussed, and those underlying fault lines running through global governance provision, set out earlier (pp. 246–7). In the first instance, this agenda can be thought of as comprising three interrelated dimensions: promoting coordinated state action to tackle common problems, reinforcing those international institutions that can function effectively, and developing multilateral rules and procedures that lock in all powers, small and major, into a multilateral framework (Hirst and Thompson, 2002, pp. 252–3). But to do what exactly? It cannot be to pursue more of what we have had: the misleading and damaging policy packages of the Washington Consensus and the Washington security doctrines. Indeed, both need to be replaced by a policy framework that:

- encourages and sustains the enormous enhancement of productivity and wealth that the global market and contemporary technology make possible;
- addresses the extremes of poverty and ensures that the benefits are fairly shared;
- creates avenues of 'voice', deliberation and democratic decision-making in regional and global public domains;
- puts environmental sustainability at the centre of global governance;
- provides international security which engages with the causes as well as the crimes of terrorism, war and failed states.

I call the approach that sets itself this task social democratic globalization and a human security agenda.

The Washington Consensus needs to be replaced by a wider vision of institutions and policy approaches. Liberal market philosophy offers too narrow a view, and clues to an alternative vision can be found in an old rival – social democracy (Ruggie, 2003; Held, 2004). Traditionally, social democrats have sought to deploy the democratic institutions of individual countries on behalf of a particular project; they have accepted that markets are central to generating economic well-being, but recognized that in the absence of appropriate regulation they suffer serious flaws – especially the generation of unwanted risks for their citizens, and an unequal distribution of those risks.

Social democracy at the level of the nation-state means supporting free markets while insisting on a framework of shared values and common institutional practices. At the global level it means pursuing an economic agenda which calibrates the freeing of markets with poverty reduction programmes and the protection of the vulnerable. Moreover, this agenda must be pursued while ensuring, on the one hand, that different countries have the freedom they need to experiment with their own investment strategies and resources and, on the other, that domestic policy choices uphold basic universal standards (including human rights and environmental protection). The question is: how can self-determination, markets and core universal standards coexist?

To begin with, bridges have to be built between international economic law and human rights law, between commercial law and environmental law, and between state sovereignty and transnational law (Chinkin, 1998). What is required is not only the firm enactment of existing human rights and environmental agreements and the clear articulation of these with the ethical codes of particular industries (where they exist or can be developed), but also the introduction of new terms of reference into the ground rules or basic laws of the free market and trading system. Precedents exist, for instance, in the Social Chapter of the Maastricht Agreement or in the attempt to attach labour and environmental conditions to the North American Free Trade Agreement (NAFTA) regime, for the pursuit of this objective.

At stake, ultimately, are three interrelated transformations. The first would involve engaging companies in the promotion of core UN universal principles (as the UN's Global Compact does at present). To the extent that this led to the entrenchment of human rights and environmental standards in corporate practices, that would be a significant step forward. But if this is to be something other than a voluntary initiative, vulnerable to being sidestepped or ignored, then it needs to be elaborated in due course into a set of codified and mandatory rules. The second set of transformations would, thus, involve the entrenchment of revised codes, rules and procedures – on health, child labour, trade union activity, environmental protection, stakeholder consultation and corporate governance – in the articles of association and terms of reference of economic organizations and trading agencies. The key groups and associations of the economic domain would have to adopt, within their very *modus operandi*, a structure of rules, procedures and practices compatible with universal social requirements, if the latter are to prevail. This would require a new international treaty, laying down elements of universal jurisdiction and clear avenues of enforcement. (Of course, poorly designed regulatory structures can harm employment levels, but countries with strong social democratic traditions, above all the Scandinavian, show that it is possible to be both business-friendly and welfare-orientated.)

There are many possible objections to such a scheme. However, most of these are misplaced (Held, 2002a, pp. 72ff.). The framework of human rights and environmental values is sound, preoccupied as it is with the equal liberty and development possibilities of all human beings. But it cannot be implemented without a third set of transformations, focused on the most pressing cases of economic suffering and harm. Without this commitment, the advocacy of such standards can descend into *high-mindedness*, which fails to pursue the socio-economic changes that are a necessary part of such a commitment.

At a minimum, this means that development policies must be directed to promote the 'development space' necessary for national trade and industrial incentives (including infant industry protection), to build robust public sectors nurturing political and legal reform, to develop transparent, accountable political institutions, to ensure long-term investment in healthcare, human capital and physical infrastructure, to challenge the asymmetries of access to the global market, and to ensure the sequencing of global market integration into a framework of fair global rules for trade and finance. Moreover, it means eliminating unsustainable debt, seeking ways to reverse the outflow of net capital assets from the South to the North, and creating new finance facilities for development purposes. In addition, if such measures were combined with a (Tobin) tax on the turnover of financial markets, and/or a consumption tax on fossil fuels, and/or a shift of priorities from military expenditure (now running at $900 billion per annum globally) to the alleviation of severe need (direct aid amounts only to some $50 billion per annum globally), then the developmental context of Western and Northern nation-states could begin to be accommodated to those nations struggling for survival and minimum welfare.

The shift in the agenda of globalization I am arguing for – in short, a move from liberal to social democratic globalization – would have pay-offs for today's most pressing security concerns. At the centre of this argument is the need to connect the security and human rights agendas and to bring them into a coherent international framework. This is the second aspect of global policy: replacing the Washington security doctrines. If developed countries want swift movement in the establishment of global legal codes that will enhance security and ensure action against the threats of terrorism, then they need to be part of a wider process of reform that addresses the insecurity of life experienced in developing societies. Across the developing or majority world, issues of justice with respect to government and terrorism are not regarded as a priority on their own, and are unlikely to be perceived as legitimate concerns unless they are connected with fundamental humanitarian issues rooted in social and economic well-being, such as basic education, clean water and public hygiene. At issue is what I call a new 'global covenant' or, as the High Level Panel on UN reform recently put it, a new 'grand bargain' (Held, 2004; UN, 2004).

Specifically, what is needed is to link the security and human rights agenda in international law; reform the United Nations Security Council to improve the legitimacy of armed intervention, with credible threshold tests; amend the now outmoded 1945 geopolitical settlement as the basis of decision-making in the Security Council and extend representation to all regions on a fair and equal footing; expand the remit of the Security Council or create a parallel Social and Economic Security Council to examine and, when necessary, intervene in the full gamut of human crises – physical, social, biological, environmental – that can threaten human agency; and found a World Environmental Organization to promote the implementation of existing environmental agreements and treaties, and whose main mission would be to insure that the world trading and financial systems are compatible with the sustainable use of the world's resources. This would be a grand bargain indeed! (See the box at the end of the chapter for a summary of the policy shifts I am arguing for to replace the Washington Consensus and the Washington security doctrines.)

Of course, it has to be conceded that the moment to pursue this agenda has been missed, marked by the limits of the UN Summit in September 2005 and the 'no vote' on the European constitution. But some progress at the Summit was made on human rights (with an agreement in principle to create a Human Rights Council), on UN management (with a commitment to strengthen mechanisms of internal accountability), on peace building (with the establishment of a Peace Building Commission), and on the acceptance of the 'responsibility to protect' those facing grave harm irrespective of borders

(Feinstein, 2005). And there is some measure of agreement about what needs doing in the area of UN institutional reform, which can be evinced by comparing the UN High Level Panel on *A More Secure World* with the Newt Gingrich and George Mitchell report to Congress (UN, 2004; Gingrich and Mitchell, 2005).

But even if the moment has been missed, it has not been lost. The Washington Consensus and Washington security doctrines are failing – market fundamentalism and unilateralism have dug their own graves (Held, 2004; Barnett et al., 2005). The most successful countries in the world (China, India, Vietnam, Uganda, among them) are successful because they have not followed the Washington Consensus agenda (Rodrick, 2005), and the conflicts that have most successfully been diffused (the Balkans, Sierra Leone, Liberia, Sri Lanka, among others) are ones that have benefited from concentrated multilateral support and a human security agenda (Human Security Centre, 2005). Here are clear clues as to how to proceed, and to build alternatives to both the Washington Consensus and the Washington Security Doctrines.

Global Governance and the Democratic Question

The reflections developed so far are about taking steps toward solidarity, democracy, justice and policy effectiveness after the failures of current policy have come home to roost. Yet the problems of global governance today require a much longer time horizon as well. The problems of democracy and justice will only be institutionally secured if we grasp the structural limits of the present global political arrangements, limits which can be summed up as 'realism is dead' or, to put it more moderately, *raison d'état* must know its place.

Traditionally, the tension between the sphere of decision-makers and the sphere of decision-takers has been resolved by the idea of political community – the bounded, territorially delimited community in which decision-makers and decision-takers create processes and institutions to resolve the problem of accountability. During the period in which nation-states were being forged, the idea of a close mesh between geography, political power and democracy could be assumed. It seemed compelling that political power sovereignty, democracy and citizenship were simply and appropriately bounded by a delimited territorial space (Held, 1995). But this is no longer the case. Globalization, global governance and global challenges raise issues concerning the proper scope of democracy, and of a democracy's jurisdiction, given that the relation between decision-makers and decision-takers is not necessarily symmetrical or congruent with respect to territory.

The principle of all-inclusiveness is often regarded in democratic theory as the conceptual means to help clarify the fundamental criterion for drawing proper boundaries around those who should be involved in particular decision-making domains, those who should be accountable to a particular group of people, and why. At its simplest, it states that those significantly affected by public decisions, issues, or processes should have an equal opportunity, directly or indirectly through elected delegates or representatives, to influence and shape them. Those affected by public decisions ought to have a say in their making. But the question today is: how is the notion of 'significantly affected' to be understood when the relation between decision-makers and decision-takers is more spatially complex – when, that is, decisions affect people outside a circumscribed democratic entity, as is the case, for example, with agricultural subsidies, the rules governing stem cell research, and carbon omissions? In an age of global interconnectedness, who should key decision-makers be accountable to? The set of people they affect? The answer is not so straightforward. As Robert Keohane has noted, 'being affected cannot be sufficient to create a valid claim. If it were, virtually nothing could ever be done, since there would be so many requirements for consultation and even veto points' (Keohane, 2003, p. 141). This is a hard issue to think through. The matter becomes a little easier to address if the all-affected principle is connected directly to the idea of impact on people's needs or interests.

If we think of the impact of powerful forces on people's lives, then impact can be divided into three categories: strong, moderate and weak. By strong I mean that vital needs or interests are affected (from health to housing) with fundamental consequences for people's life expectancy. By moderate I mean that needs are affected in such a way that people's ability to participate in their community (in economic, cultural and political activities) is in question. At stake here is the quality of life chances. By weak I mean an effect which impacts upon particular lifestyles or the range of available consumption choices (from clothes to music). These categories are not watertight, but they provide some useful guidance:

- If people's urgent needs are unmet their lives will be in danger. In this context, people are at risk of serious harm.
- If people's secondary needs are unmet they will not be able to participate fully in their communities and their potential for involvement in public and private life will remain unfulfilled. Their choices will be restricted or depleted. In this context, people are at risk of harm to their life opportunities.
- If people's lifestyle needs are unmet their ability to develop their lives and express themselves through diverse media will be thwarted. In this context, unmet need can lead to anxiety and frustration.

In the light of these considerations, the principle of all-inclusiveness needs restating. I take it to mean that those whose life expectancy and life chances are significantly affected by social forces and processes ought to have a stake in the determination of the conditions and regulation of these, either directly or indirectly through political representatives. Democracy is best located when it is closest to and involves those whose life expectancy and life chances are determined by powerful entities, bringing the circles of stakeholders and decision-makers closer together. The argument for extending this consideration to decisions and processes which affect lifestyle needs is less compelling, since these are fundamentally questions of value and identity for communities to resolve for themselves. For example, whether McDonald's should be allowed access across China, or US media products given free range in Canada, are questions largely for those countries to resolve, although clearly serious cross-border issues concerning, for example, the clash of values and consumption choices can develop, posing questions about regional or global trade rules and regulations.

The principle of all-inclusiveness points to the necessity of both the decentralization *and* centralization of political power. If decision-making is decentralized as much as possible, it maximizes the opportunity of each person to influence the social conditions that shape his or her life. But if the decisions at issue are translocal, transnational, or transregional, then political institutions need not only be locally based but also to have a wider scope and framework of operation. In this context, the creation of diverse sites and levels of democratic fora may be unavoidable. It may be unavoidable, paradoxically, for the very same reasons as decentralization is desirable: it creates the possibility of including people who are significantly affected by a political issue in the public (in this case, transcommunity public) sphere.

To restore symmetry and congruence between decision-makers and decision-takers, and to entrench the principle of all-inclusiveness, requires a redevelopment of global governance and a resolve to address those challenges generated by cross-border processes and forces. This project must take as its starting point, in other words, a world of overlapping communities of fate. Recognizing the complex processes of an interconnected world, it ought to view certain issues – such as industrial and commercial strategy, housing and education – as appropriate for spatially delimited political spheres (the city, region or state), while seeing others – such as the environment, pandemics and global financial regulation – as requiring new, more extensive institutions to address them. Deliberative and decision-making centres beyond national territories are appropriately situated when the principle of all-inclusiveness can only be properly upheld in a transnational context; when those whose life expectancy and life chances are significantly affected by a public matter constitute a transnational grouping; and when 'lower' levels of decision-making cannot manage satisfactorily transnational or global policy questions. Of course, the boundaries demarcating different levels of governance will always be contested, as they are, for instance, in many local, subnational regional and national polities. Disputes about the appropriate jurisdiction for handling particular public issues will be complex and intensive; but better complex and intensive in a clear public framework than left simply to powerful geopolitical interests (dominant states) or market-based organizations to resolve them alone. In short, the possibility of a long-term institutional reform must be linked to an expanding framework of states and agencies bound by the rule of law, democratic principles and human rights. How should this be understood from an institutional point of view?

Multilevel Citizenship, Multilayered Democracy

In the long term, the realignment of global governance with solidarity, democracy and social justice must involve the development of both independent political authority and administrative capacity at regional and global levels. It does not call for the diminution *per se* of state power and capacity across the globe. Rather, it seeks to entrench and develop political institutions at regional and global levels as a necessary supplement to those at the level of the state. This conception of politics is based on the recognition of the continuing significance of nation-states, while arguing for layers of governance to address broader and more global questions. The aim is to forge an accountable and responsive politics at local and national levels alongside the establishment of representative and deliberative assemblies in the wider global order; that is, a political order of transparent and democratic cities and nations as well as of regions and global networks within an overarching framework of social justice.

The long-term institutional requirements include:

- multilayered governance and diffused authority;
- a network of democratic fora from the local to the global;
- strengthening the Human Rights Conventions and creating regional and global Human Rights courts;
- enhancing the transparency, accountability and effectiveness of leading functional IGOs; and building new bodies of this type where there is demonstrable need for greater public coordination and administrative capacity;
- improving the transparency, accountability and voice of non-state actors;
- use of diverse forms of mechanisms to access public preferences, test their coherence and inform public will formation;
- establishment of an effective, accountable, regional and global police/military force for the last-resort use of coercive power in defence of international humanitarian or cosmopolitan law.

I call this agenda, and the institutions to which it gives rise, cosmopolitan democracy (Held, 1995, 2004, 2006; Archibugi and Held, 1995). Since I have elaborated it elsewhere, I will restrict myself here to the change it entails in the meaning of citizenship.

At the heart of a cosmopolitan conception of citizenship is the idea that citizenship can be based not on exclusive membership of a territorial community, but on general rules and principles which can be entrenched and drawn upon in diverse settings. This conception relies on the availability and clarity of the principles of democracy and human rights. These principles create a framework for all persons to enjoy, in principle, equal moral status, equal freedom and equal participative opportunities. The meaning of citizenship shifts from membership in a community which bestows, for those who qualify, particular rights and duties to an alternative principle of world order in which all persons have equivalent rights and duties in the cross-cutting spheres of decision-making which affect their vital needs and interests. It posits the idea of a global political order in which people can enjoy an equality of status with respect to the fundamental processes and institutions which govern their life expectancy and life chances.

Within this context, the puzzling meaning of a cosmopolitan or global citizenship becomes a little clearer. Built on the fundamental rights and duties of all human beings, cosmopolitan citizenship underwrites the autonomy of each and every human being, and recognizes their capacity for self-governance at all levels of human affairs. Although this notion needs further clarification and unpacking, its leading features are within our grasp. Today, if people are to be free and equal in the determination of the conditions which shape their lives, there must be an array of fora, from the city to global associations, in which they can hold decision-makers to account. If many contemporary forms of power are to become accountable and if many of the complex issues that affect us all – locally, nationally, regionally and globally – are to be democratically regulated, people will have to have access to, and membership in, diverse political communities. As Jürgen Habermas has written, 'only a democratic citizenship that does not close itself off in a particularistic fashion can pave the way for a *world citizenship* . . . State citizenship and world citizenship form a continuum whose contours, at least, are already becoming visible' (Habermas, 1996, pp. 514–15). There is only a historically contingent connection between the principles underpinning citizenship and the national community; as this connection weakens in a world of overlapping communities of fate, the principles of citizenship must be rearticulated and re-entrenched. Moreover, in the light of this development, the connection between patriotism and nationalism becomes easier to call into question, and a case built to bind patriotism to the defence of core civic and political principles – not to the nation or country for their own sake (Heater, 2002). Only national identities open to diverse solidarities, and shaped by respect for general rules and principles, can accommodate themselves successfully to the challenges of a global age. Ultimately, diversity and difference can flourish only in a 'global legal community' (Brunkhorst, 2005; Held, 2002b).

There was once a time when the idea that the old states of Europe might share a set of economic, monetary and political institutions seemed improbable, to say the least. It also appeared improbable that the Cold War would be brought to an end by a peaceful revolution. The notion that Nelson Mandela would be released from jail alive, and that apartheid would be undone without substantial violence, was not anticipated by many. That China and India would be among the fastest-growing economies in the world once seemed unlikely. Let us hope that the task of reframing global governance is similarly possible, even though now it seems remote! Let us hope as well that this task is pursued with an increasing sense of urgency. For many, it is already 'apocalypse now'; for the rest of us it may well be 'apocalypse soon' unless our governance arrangements can meet the tests of solidarity, justice, democracy and effectiveness.

Policy shifts to replace the Washington Consensus and security doctrines

The Original Washington Consensus

- Fiscal discipline
- Reorientation of public expenditures
- Tax reform
- Financial liberalization
- Unified and competitive exchange rates
- Trade liberalization
- Openness to foreign direct investment (FDI)
- Privatization
- Deregulation
- Secure property rights

Washington Consensus (augmented)
The original list plus:

- Legal/political reform
- Regulatory institutions
- Anti-corruption
- Labour market flexibility
- WTO agreements
- Financial codes and standards
- "Prudent" capital-account opening
- Non-intermediate exchange rate regimes
- Social safety-nets
- Poverty reduction

The Social Democratic Agenda Local

- Sound macroeconomic policy
- Nurturing of political/legal reform
- Creation of robust public sector
- State-led economic and investment strategy, enjoying sufficient development space to experiment with different policies
- Sequencing of global market integration
- Priority investment in human and social capital
- Public capital expenditure on infrastructure
- Poverty reduction and social safety-nets
- Strengthening civil society

The Social Democratic Agenda Global

- Salvaging Doha
- Cancellation of unsustainable debt
- Reform of trade-related intellectual property rights (Trips)
- Creation of fair regime for transnational migration
- Expand negotiating capacity of developing countries at international finance institutions (IFIs)
- Increase developing country participation in the running of IFIs
- Establish new financial flows and facilities for investment in human capital and internal country integration
- Reform of UN system to enhance accountability and effectiveness of poverty reduction, welfare and environmental programmes.

The Washington Security Doctrine

1 Hegemonic
2 Order through dominance
3 'Flexible multilateralism' or unilateralism where necessary
4 Pre-emptive and preventive use of force

5 Security focus: geopolitical and, secondarily, geoeconomic

6 Collective organization where pragmatic (UN, NATO), otherwise reliance on US military and political power

7 Leadership: United States and its allies

8 Aims: making world safe for freedom and democracy; globalizing American rules and justice

The Human Security Doctrine

1 Multilateralism and common rules
2 Order through law and social justice
3 Enhance multilateral, collective security

4 Last-resort use of internationally sanctioned force to uphold international humanitarian law
5 Security focus: relinking security and human rights agendas; protecting all those facing threats to life, whether political, social, economic or environmental
6 Strengthen global governance: reform UN Security Council; create Economic and Social Security Council; democratize UN

7 Leadership: develop a worldwide dialogue to define new global covenant
8 Aims: making world safe for humanity; global justice and impartial rules

Notes

This chapter first appeared in *New Political Economy*, 11(2) (2006): pp. 157–76, © 2006 Taylor and Francis. It appears here with permission of the publishers.

1 More recently, see Milanović, 2005; see also Pogge, 2006.
2 The eight Millennium Development Goals, established by the UN and agreed upon by the UN General Assembly in September 2000, are to: eradicate extreme poverty and hunger; achieve universal primary education; promote gender equality and empower women; reduce child mortality; improve health; combat HIV/AIDS, malaria and other diseases; ensure environmental sustainability; and develop a global partnership for development – all by the target date of 2015. See UN, 2000.
3 The goal of the Lisbon process, agreed upon by European leaders in March 2000, is to make the European Union 'the most dynamic and competitive knowledge-based economy in the world' by 2010. This goal entails a series of policy recommendations to help move European economies in this direction. When referring to the limited impact of the Lisbon process, I refer to how modest has been the movement in this direction.

References

Annan, K. (2005). 'Three Crises and the Need for American Leadership', in A. Barnett, D. Held and C. Henderson, eds, *Debating Globalization*. Cambridge: Polity, pp. 134–40.

Archibugi, D. and D. Held, eds (1995). *Cosmopolitan Democracy: An Agenda for a New World Order*. Cambridge: Polity.

Barnett, A., D. Held and C. Henderson, eds. (2005). *Debating Globalization*. Cambridge: Polity.

Barry, B. (1998). 'International Society from a Cosmopolitan Perspective', in D. Mapel and T. Nardin, eds, *International Society: Diverse Ethical Perspectives*. Princeton: Princeton University Press, pp. 144–63.

Brunkhorst, H. (2005). *Solidarity: From Civic Friendship to Global Legal Community*. Cambridge, Mass.: MIT Press.

Buira, A. (2003). 'The Governance of the International Monetary Fund' in I. Kaul et al., *Providing Global Public Goods*, pp. 225–44.

Byers, M. (2005). 'Are You a Global Citizen?', *Views*, 5 October, available at: http://thetyee.ca/Views/2005/10/05/globalcitizen/, p. 4 (accessed 10 February 2006).

Chasek, P. and I. Rajamani (2003). 'Steps towards Enhanced Parity: Negotiating Capacity and Strategies of Developing Countries', in I. Kaul et al., *Providing Global Public Goods*, pp. 245–62.

Chinkin, C. (1998). 'International Law and Human Rights', in T. Evans, ed., *Human Rights Fifty Years On: A Reappraisal*. Manchester: Manchester University Press, pp. 105–28.

Conceição, P. (2003). 'Assessing the Provision Status of Global Public Goods', in I. Kaul et al., *Providing Global Public Goods*, pp. 152–84.

Deacon, B. et al., (2003). 'Global Social Governance Reform: From Institutions and Policies to Networks, Projects and Partnerships', in B. Deacon, E. Ollida, M. Koivusalo and P. Stubbs, eds, *Global Social Governance*. Helsinki: Hakapaino Oy.

Feinstein, L. (2005). 'An Insider's Guide to UN Reform', available at: http://www.american-broad.tpmcafe.com/story/2005/9/14/142349/085 (accessed 11 February 2006).

Giddens, A. (1990). *The Consequences of Modernity*. Cambridge: Polity.

Gingrich, N. and G. Mitchell (2005). *American Interests and UN Reform: Report of the Task Force on the United Nations,* June, available at: http://www.usip.org/un/report/usip_un_report.pdf (accessed 11 February 2006).

Habermas, J. (1996). *Between Facts and Norms: Contributions to a Discourse Theory of Law and Democracy*, trans. W. Rehg. Cambridge: Polity.

Heater, D. (2002). *World Citizenship*. London: Continuum.

Held, D. (1995). *Democracy and the Global Order: From the Modern State to Cosmopolitan Governance*. Cambridge: Polity.

Held, D. (2002a). 'Globalization, Corporate Practice and Cosmopolitan Social Standards', *Contemporary Political Theory*, 1(1): pp. 59–78.

Held, D. (2002b). 'Law of States, Law of Peoples: Three Models of Sovereignty', *Legal Theory*, 8(1): pp. 1–44.

Held, D. (2004). *Global Covenant*. Cambridge: Polity.

Held, D. (2006). *Models of Democracy*, 3rd edn. Cambridge: Polity.

Held, D., A. G. McGrew, D. Goldblatt, D. J. Perraton (1999). *Global Transformations: Politics, Economics and Culture*, Cambridge: Polity.

Hirst, P. and G. Thompson (2002). 'The Future of Globalization', *Cooperation and Conflict*, 37(3): pp. 252–3.

Hoffmann, S. (2003). 'America Goes Backward', *The New York Review of Books*, 50(10): pp. 74–80.

Human Security Centre (2005). *Human Security Report 2005: War and Peace in the 21st Century*, http://www.humansecurityreport.info (accessed 11 February 2006).

Ikenberry, J. (2002). 'America's Imperial Ambition', *Foreign Affairs*, 81(5): pp. 44–60.

Ikenberry, J. (2005). 'A Weaker World', *Prospect*, 116 (October): p. 32.

Kaul I., P. Conceição, K. Le Goulven, and R. V. Mendoza, eds (2003a). *Providing Global Public Goods*. Oxford: Oxford University Press.

Kaul, I., P. Conceição, K. Le Goulven and R. V. Mendoza (2003b). 'Why Do Global Public Goods Matter Today' in I. Kaul et al., *Providing Global Public Goods*, pp. 1–58.

Keohane, R. O. (2003). 'Global Governance and Democratic Accountability' in D. Held and M. Koenig-Archibugi, eds, *Taming Globalization*. Cambridge: Polity, pp. 130–59.

King, Sir David A. (2004). 'Climate Change Science: Adapt, Mitigate, or Ignore?' *Science*, 303 (January): pp. 176–7.

Meikle, J. (2005). 'Bill Gates Gives $258m to World Battle against Malaria', *The Guardian*, 31 October, p. 22.

Mendoza, R. V. (2003). 'The Multilateral Trade Regime', in I. Kaul et al., *Providing Global Public Goods*, pp. 455–83.

Milanović, B. (2002). 'True World Income Distribution, 1988 and 1993: First Calculation Based on Household Surveys Alone', *Economic Journal*, 112 (January): pp. 51–92.

Milanović, B. (2005). *Worlds Apart: Measuring International and Global Inequality*. Princeton: Princeton University Press.

Moore, M. (2003). *A World without Walls*. Cambridge: Cambridge University Press.

Pogge, T. (2007). 'Reframing Economic Security and Justice', in D. Held and A. G. McGrew, eds, *Globalization Theory*. Cambridge: Polity.

Rees, M. (2003). *Our Final Century*. London: Arrow Books.

Rischard, J. F. (2002). *High Noon: Twenty Global Problems, Twenty Years to Solve Them*. New York: Basic Books.

Rodrick, D. (2005). 'Making Globalization Work for Development', Ralph Miliband Public Lecture, London School of Economics, 18 November.

Rosenau, J. N. (2002). 'Governance in a New Global Order', in D. Held and A. G. McGrew, eds, *Governing Globalization*. Cambridge: Polity, pp. 70–86.

Ruggie, J. (2003). 'Taking Embedded Liberalism Global: The Corporate Connection', in D. Held and M. Koenig-Archibugi, eds, *Taming Globalization*. Cambridge: Polity, pp. 93–129.

UN (2000). 'Millennium Development Goals', available at: www.un.org/millenniumgoals/ (accessed 14 February 2006).

UN (2004). 'A More Secure World: Our Shared Responsibility', Report of the High-Level Panel on Threats, Challenges and Change, available at: www.un.org/secureworld/ (accessed 11 February, 2006).

UNDP (2005). *Human Development Report 2005*, Oxford/New York: Oxford University Press. Also available at: http://hdr.undp.org/reports/global/2005/.

Index